Open Access and the Future of Scholarly Communication

Creating the 21st-Century Academic Library

About the Series

Creating the 21st-Century Academic Library provides both conceptual information and practical guidance on the full spectrum of innovative changes now underway in academic libraries. Each volume in the series is carefully crafted to be a hallmark of professional practice and thus:

- Focuses on one narrowly defined aspect of academic librarianship.
- Features an introductory chapter, surveying the content to follow and highlighting lessons to be learned.
- Shares the experiences of librarians who have recently overseen significant changes in their library to better position it to provide 21st-century services to students, faculty, and researchers.

About the Series Editor

Bradford Lee Eden is one of librarianship's most experienced and knowledgeable editors. Dr. Eden is dean of library services at Valparaiso University. Previous positions include associate university librarian for technical services and scholarly communication at the University of California, Santa Barbara; head of web and digitization services and head of bibliographic and metadata services for the University of Nevada, Las Vegas Libraries. He is editor of *OCLC Systems & Services: International Digital Library Perspectives* and *The Bottom Line: Managing Library Finances*, and he is on the editorial boards of *Library Hi Tech* and the *Journal of Film Music*. He has recently been named associate editor/editor-designate of *Library Leadership & Management*, the journal of the Library Leadership & Management Association (LLAMA) within ALA.

Titles in the Series

Open Access and the Future of Scholarly Communication

Implementation

Edited by
Kevin L. Smith
Katherine A. Dickson

ROWMAN & LITTLEFIELD
Lanham • Boulder • New York • London

Published by Rowman & Littlefield
A wholly owned subsidiary of The Rowman & Littlefield Publishing Group, Inc.
4501 Forbes Boulevard, Suite 200, Lanham, Maryland 20706
www.rowman.com

Unit A, Whitacre Mews, 26-34 Stannary Street, London SE11 4AB

British Library Cataloguing in Publication Information Available

Library of Congress Cataloging-in-Publication Data

[CIP to come]

♾™ The paper used in this publication meets the minimum requirements of American
National Standard for Information Sciences Permanence of Paper for Printed Library
Materials, ANSI/NISO Z39.48-1992.

Printed in the United States of America

Contents

Preface

This book, our second of two in the series Creating the 21st-Century Academic Library that deals with the topic of open access in academic libraries, moves that discussion deeply into library practice. The discussion in volume 9 centers on policy and infrastructure for open access and considers such topics as advocacy, budgeting, and the library as publisher. This book continues that conversation with a focus on the implementation of open access in academic libraries.

The first three chapters address the legalities and practicalities of open access in academic libraries. In chapter 1, Anne T. Gilliland considers the effects of different types of copyright transfers and licenses on academic authors' retention of rights in their published works and examines the sometimes divergent interests of authors and publishers in the terms of such agreements. Next, Nancy Sims explores the rhetoric of "protection" that libraries use to discuss issues associated with copyright, licensing, and intellectual property. Chapter 3, by Micah Zeller and Emily Symonds Stenberg, discusses how libraries can provide support for courses that require open access distribution of student work, taking account of platform choice, licensing, student privacy, and the impact of such requirements on pedagogy.

The next three chapters take up the topic of library services in support of open access. Stephen M. Arougheti looks at the author fees some publishers charge for making an article openly available and the funds libraries are establishing to help defray those costs. Chapter 5 introduces open educational resources, with William Cross describing the library's role as an ally and driver of their adoption, and proposes that libraries take an active role in advocating for and supporting them. In chapter 6, Hui Zhang and Korey Jackson offer a case study of one university's use of an assessment survey to determine whether and how it would provide services around alternative metrics for its users.

Chapters 7 through 9 take a detailed look at open access in the context of undergraduate research. Chapter 7, by Stephanie Davis-Kahl, looks at how librarians can engage undergraduates in conversations about open access, shifting their perspectives on how they share their own work and contribute to scholarly conversations in their campus communities. Next, Genya O'Gara and Laura Drake Davis provide a case study that illustrates the successes and challenges one university encountered during the first year of a program to support open access publication of undergraduate research. Chapter 9 uses the Association of College and Research Libraries' Framework for Information Literacy for Higher Education to support Rachel Scott's discussion about how librarians can engage undergraduate students in the use, understanding, evaluation, and creation of OA resources.

The perennial issues about open access and graduate students are the subject of chapters 10 through 12. Hillary Corbett describes the development of electronic thesis and dissertation (ETD) programs and the library's role in balancing the need for greater access to graduate student work with concerns about the consequences of openness. Jill Cirasella and Polly Thistlethwaite examine those anxieties more deeply, touching on concerns about book contracts and sales, plagiarism, and changes in scholarly research and production. In chapter 12, Kyle K. Courtney and Emily Kilcer make recommendations for easing student concerns and helping them to make reasoned decisions about distribution of their dissertations and future work.

The final three chapters look at open data. In chapter 13, Tara Das deals with open government data and library services in critical data librarianship, including advocacy, preservation, and instruction. Laura Krier and Kathryn Stine then examine open access to library metadata and the products of bibliographic control. Finally, Stewart Varner details one university's approach to facilitating text mining by offering access to the data behind its own homegrown digital collections in formats that are easily processed by common text mining tools.

Chapter One

Copyright Assignment, Transfer, and Licensing

What Is Best for Scholarly Journal Authors?

Anne T. Gilliland

As academic authors have become more interested in open access publishing and rights retention, scholarly publishers have responded with what is often a bewildering array of choices. These choices differ from what many think of as the traditional model, where the author of an article signs over the copyright to the publisher as part of the publishing contract. They may include—among many other variations—options where the author transfers copyright to the publisher but retains a license to deposit a copy of the article online, where the author keeps the copyright but gives an exclusive license to the publisher, and where the author grants a nonexclusive license to the publisher for first publication and keeps the copyright.

In some cases, publishers present only one model for transferring and retaining rights. In other cases, an author must choose in a way that is very much like choosing from a menu, with various drawbacks and advantages and sometimes author fees that come with each choice. These options can be bewildering to the author, who is likely to be an expert in his or her field but not an expert at copyright or contract law. Information on the publisher's website explaining the options may be limited and, in some cases, biased or misleading. An editor or publisher's representative who assists the author may also have a limited knowledge of the rationale behind the choices offered or the legal implications of those choices.

Why is it important to understand publishing options for and the effect of different licenses on rights retention? Increasingly, the goals of academic authors and their publishers have diverged, though to some degree they continue to complement each other. The author intends to publish in the most appropriate and prestigious journal possible and achieve the widest readership possible. The publisher intends to attract the most appropriate and prestigious authors and also achieve the widest readership it can. The author and publisher typically make a deal to accomplish these converging goals in a bargain where no money changes hands. The author is paid indirectly by publication and eventually by prestige, promotion, and tenure.

After initial publication, the goals of author and publisher begin to diverge. Both academic authors and publishers see ongoing uses for the work. The academic author often seeks an audience beyond scholars at peer institutions that subscribe to a particular journal. This wider audience may include scholars and students at less wealthy institutions in the home country or abroad, independent scholars, clinicians or other practitioners in the field working outside of the academy, and interested members of the public. The academic publisher is also aware of this wider audience and often wishes to capture revenue from that market. On the other hand, the academic author often sees a pay wall as a limitation to wider readership and the continuing efforts to commercialize these transactions as a disadvantage.

In addition, both publishers and authors are aware of other ongoing uses for a scholarly article. These include reusing all or portions of the article in a new periodical or book, reproducing the article for teaching, and including the article in text or data mining and analysis. In many cases, the publisher looks on these uses as a source of additional revenue, while the author often sees them as natural extensions of the original act of authorship, regardless of what the publication agreement said. This inevitably leads to the academic author's desire for the publishing contract to reflect the bargain the author actually wants to make. The academic author often wants a work to be available in developing countries and easily accessed by practitioners in the field, to be able to use portions of the work in other works or for teaching, and colleagues to be able to do the same without payment to a rights holder.

RIGHTS

Most academic authors think of themselves as the owners of their works, even after they have signed a contract transferring their copyright. Regardless of who holds the copyright, their professional identity is caught up in the work they have done, and they are judged by its standard and impact. An individual article is often part of a larger, continuing body of research or analysis, and it is natural that scholars feel an ongoing proprietary interest as each part of the research is published and distributed.

In addition, some academics, especially those who began their careers before the 1976 Copyright Act took effect in the United States, may believe that copyrights in their articles only come into existence once the work is published or registered. In actuality, under the present law, a copyright is formed whenever "original works of authorship [are] fixed in any tangible medium of expression."[1] Finally, many academic authors do not read the publishing contracts they sign, read their contracts hurriedly, or do not completely understand them even if they do read them. Sometimes it is difficult or impossible to study the contract carefully if it is presented as a click-through agreement online.

What are the rights that the owner of the copyright possesses and that are at issue in these transactions? In U.S. law, there are six rights that are exclusive to the copyright holder: to reproduce the copyrighted work, to prepare derivative works (such as new editions, translations, sequels, etc.), to distribute copies, to perform the work publicly, to display the copyrighted work, and to perform through digital audio transmissions.[2] These rights are often called the bundle of rights because of the rights holder's ability either to exercise them as a whole or to separate them and work with them individually. For example, a copyright holder can transfer the right of reproduction to one person while excluding others from the right of reproduction and keeping the monopoly on all other rights. Similarly, at the rights holder's discretion, exercise of any or all of the rights by others can be limited by time, place, media, or other restrictions.

Ironically, the right of attribution, one of the rights most dear to academic authors, is not available for most copyrighted material under U.S. law. Moral rights are a category of rights that are standard in Western Europe and other countries but that the United States recognizes only for certain works of visual art.[3] The exact scope and list of these rights differ from country to country but may include the rights of attribution (to receive credit or not receive credit for the work) and integrity (to keep the work from being altered or from being presented in some way the author finds prejudicial). Other moral rights allow the creator to control the display of the work and to prevent the work from being destroyed, either on purpose or through negligence. The creator continues to hold these moral rights even if the copyright has been transferred to another.

Congress added moral rights to U.S. law with the Visual Artists Rights Act (VARA) of 1990 in part to comply with the Berne Convention international treaty. Visual art was seen as a category of creative work where additional rights would not overly burden commercial interests.[4] A more widespread adoption of moral rights, however, might disturb the fair use doctrine or copyright's balance with the First Amendment's free speech requirement. Even within the boundary of visual art, the VARA only applies to fine art that is unique or is produced in very limited quantities, such as limited edition prints. These are works where it is relatively easy to monitor their use and treatment.

While most academic authors receive their rewards from work indirectly in the form of prestige, promotion, and tenure, unless they are working in the visual arts, the right of attribution is not available to them. For example, consider a faculty member who contributes a chapter to a scholarly book. When she sees the newly printed book, she realizes that the publisher accidently attributed the chapter she wrote to a faculty member at another institution. The real author of the chapter was not paid for her contribution and had not expected to be. Because the publisher made the mistake about authorship, she lost the only thing of worth to her in the transaction—the opportunity to have her name associated with her writing. Fortunately, although the author has no legal right to attribution under U.S. law, the publisher recognized the ethical problem at hand and took steps to rectify the error.

When the parties in the Google Book Search class action litigation attempted to negotiate a settlement, a group of academic authors realized that their interests were quite different from those of authors whose work was part of the popular press. As they later expressed it when they founded the Authors Alliance, they were a group of authors who "write to be read."[5] As academic authors, they have a primary interest in being able to disseminate their work widely, even in the absence of monetary compensation. The Authors Alliance takes note of the importance of attribution for academic authors, even when a copyright transfer has occurred. They favor amendments in copyright law that would require attribution, both for the authors' sakes and for the good of readers inside and outside the academy who may wish to trace and explore how ideas have been adopted and communicated.[6]

UNIFORMITY AND ITS DISCONTENTS

In his 2009 law review article "One Size Does Not Fit All," Michael W. Carroll discusses the concept of uniformity cost and its application to public policy around intellectual property. One primary assumption of U.S. copyright law is that the best way to promote creativity and innovation is through the granting of intellectual property rights in a way that Carroll describes as "blunt policy instruments" instead of tailoring rights to the economic interests of different kind of creators and inventors.[7] This leads to classes of works and types of authors where the prevailing way of rewarding rights holders is not in line with their economic and professional priorities.

Carroll explicitly calls out the current way that copyright is conferred and apportioned as at odds with the needs and best interests of most academic authors and identifies how uniformity serves them poorly. He notes that "scholars and researchers do not receive royalties for their journal articles, and it is likely that they would continue to research and to write even without copyright in their articles because they receive direct compensation to do research and there are a variety of indirect benefits that flow from publication."[8] Economists have identified three areas where academic authors realize these indirect monetary benefits: from salary increases given to faculty members who publish; from promotions in rank and the resulting salary increases awarded to faculty members on the strength of their publication records; and from the salary increases that accompany esteemed faculty members' administrative appointments, outside paid employment, or moves to more prestigious institutions with higher rates of pay.[9] Copyright law does a poor job of addressing these indirect methods of compensation.

TRANSFER OF COPYRIGHT

A publication agreement between an author and a publisher is a contract and must contain requirements and rewards for both parties. Ideally, all the parties to the contract understand its terms and know what they are giving up and what they are getting. All too often, however, people on both sides of a publishing contract—the author and the publisher's staff—do not completely understand the language used and the full consequences of the agreement. Ideally, a contract should also be free of extrinsic terms and side agreements. Such verbal assurances as "We never actually do that" or "It's in the agreement, but we don't really mean it" are not desirable and may not be enforceable.

In many cases, the author and the publisher have different views of the most important benefits of the contract. The contract, usually written by the publisher, focuses on what the publisher can do and what others, often including the author, may not do. Such contracts may transfer the author's rights to the publisher and then grant some rights back to the author. Many times during that process, the publisher has a monetary interest at stake that is simply not at the forefront of the academic author's concerns. The rights granted back may work well for the publisher's purposes, but the author's interest in heightening distribution of the work may get short shrift.

In this situation, it is important to remember that copyright's "bundle of rights" is divisible. The copyright holder may allow another to exercise the bundle as a whole or to break up the bundle into individual rights for transfer. The U.S. Copyright Act recognizes the degree of complexity that is possible by defining a transfer of copyright ownership as an "assignment, mortgage, exclusive license, or any other conveyance, alienation, or hypothecation [a pledge of collateral to secure a loan] of a copyright or of any of the exclusive rights comprised in a copyright, whether or not it is limited in time or place of effect, but not including a nonexclusive license."[10]

LICENSES

Licenses in copyright work similarly to other licenses that we deal with in everyday life; they give a person or entity permission to do certain acts within certain limits. These limits are the scope of the license and define which acts are permissible. For example, a person may have a license to practice law in one state but not in another state, and that license to practice law does not also give the licensee a driver's license. When granting a copyright license, the scope of the license may also be bounded by time or by the type of licensee to whom it is granted. It may be restricted by the types of use the licensee may make of the work or by the parts of the bundle of rights granted.

The concept of dividing and licensing parts of the bundle of rights was not possible until the 1909 Copyright Act was comprehensively revised with the 1976 act and the concept of divisibility was introduced. Before then, a license transferred all parts of the bundle of rights or none. The change can be seen in 17 USC § 201. The first part of 17 USC § 201 states explicitly that the rights holder may transfer all of the copyright or only part of it: "The ownership of a copyright may be transferred in whole or in part by any means of conveyance or by operation of law, and may be bequeathed by will or pass as personal property by the applicable laws of intestate succession."[11] The second part of 17 USC § 201 addresses the divisibility of the bundle of rights: "Any of the exclusive rights comprised in a copyright, including any subdivision of any of the rights specified by section 106 [reproduction, derivative works, public distribution, public display, and performance through digital audience transmissions] may be transferred as provided by clause (1) and owned separately."[12]

A license to use a copyrighted work may also be limited by the degree to which it excludes other licensees. An exclusive license by definition does exclude others in some way even if it is narrow in scope in some of the ways previously enumerated. For example, a licensee might hold an exclusive license for the rights of reproduction and distribution but have no license for making derivative works. In contrast, a rights holder may give a nonexclusive license to many people or entities. None of the licenses will have the ability to exclude others who might hold the same license. A nonexclusive license has been defined as a "mere promise not to sue [the licensee] for conduct that would otherwise be infringing."[13]

Although the best practice is to grant nonexclusive licenses in writing, they may also be formed orally or by implication. A court often looks to the conduct of the parties to ascertain the existence of an implied license. For example, a court is likely to construe a nonexclusive license in circumstances like the following: A business hires an artist to create illustrations, but there is no written agreement, and the situation falls outside one where the illustrations would belong to the business as a work made for hire.[14] The artist would own the copyright in the illustrations, but the delivery of the artwork to the business owner would be evidence that the artist intended to grant a nonexclusive license. This situation illustrates the possibility for dispute over the scope of such "implied" licenses. Because of that potential doubt over the scope of the rights transferred, most academic publishing contracts are, and should be, in writing.

Creative Commons licensing is a scheme that allows an author to preemptively publicize license terms before a license is requested.[15] There are many types of Creative Commons licenses, ranging from a relatively open license requiring attribution only to licenses that permit noncommercial reuse only and limit the making of derivative works. All are nonexclusive licenses because the rights holder grants them to a wide variety of largely unknown users. Creative Commons licenses are sometimes inaccurately described as granting the copyright to the public, but while even the most liberal of these licenses grants considerable rights to all comers, the copyright still belongs with the author.

CHOOSING A LICENSE

When the question "Which license is best?" is asked in the context of a contract for publishing an article in an academic journal, the obvious rejoinder is "Best for whom?" All authors are concerned about the reach and impact of their work, but academic authors have a less direct interest in monetary compensation. Although academic authors are concerned for the prestige, reputation, and financial well-being of the journal in which he or she publishes, this concern is only one component in the author's concern for the indirect benefits publication confers.

A nonexclusive license to publish with a journal allows the author to continue to exercise the copyright and to contract with other entities in the future. The journal publisher becomes only one of what could be many licensees, with a limited exercise of the benefits of the rights holder. The rights holder is free to make other uses of the copyrighted work and to allow others to do the same through such activities as publishing and distributing through additional channels, reusing parts of the work, and making derivative works. In contrast, granting an exclusive license to a publisher leaves the author with the copyright in theory, but all ability to exercise those rights now belongs to the publisher, who is the licensee. The publisher now has the right to further publication, distribution, the making of derivative works, and so on, and it also has the ability to license the work to others. Also, an exclusive license gives the publisher another important right, that of standing to sue.

STANDING

Standing is a "party's right to make a legal claim or seek enforcement of a duty or right." To pursue a suit in federal court, which is where almost all copyright litigation is brought, the plaintiff must show that the defendant's conduct has caused him or her an actual injury and that the interest to be protected is within the purview of the interests that the statute or the constitution is meant to regulate.[16] This relatively simple sentence actually expands into a variety of stipulations and conditions that make up the issue of standing in federal court. In addition, one of the requirements for bringing a copyright lawsuit is that only the "legal or beneficial owner of an exclusive right under a copyright is entitled to . . . institute an action for any infringement of that particular right committed while he or she is the owner of it."[17] (Other requirements are those described in 17 USC § 411, where registration or preregistration of the copyrighted work must be a prelude to litigation.[18]) A legal owner is one who has acquired the copyright through the means described in the statute defining a copyright transfer: an assignee, mortgagee, exclusive licensee, and others, even if the transfer is for a limited time or place.[19] As William Patry puts it, under sections 201(d)(1) and 501(b), the "owner of any exclusive right, no matter how limited (e.g., the exclusive right to sell the *New York Daily News* at the southwest corner of Fifth Avenue and 42nd Street in Manhattan on Monday mornings from 6:30 a.m. to 9:30 a.m.) may sue anyone who infringes."[20]

A beneficial owner also has standing to bring a copyright lawsuit. A common form of beneficial ownership is an author who has written a book and transferred copyright to the publisher but still has an interest in the form of royalties to be received from book sales. In contrast, the Copyright Act definitely bars a nonexclusive license from the definition of a copyright transfer and so cuts off that license holder's right to sue.[21] Consequently, the desire to exclude other rights holders and to litigate if there is infringement will almost always mean that publishers will prefer an exclusive license.

These requirements around standing to litigate are related to the rules that govern ownership of a collective work. The Copyright Act defines a collective work as work "such as a periodical issue, anthology or encyclopedia, in which a number of contributions, constituting separate and independent works in themselves are assembled into a collective whole."[22] Without an unambiguous copyright transfer, the owner of the collective work's copyright has something less than full copyright ownership in the works that make up the collection: "In the absence of an express transfer of the copyright or of any rights under it, the owner of copyright in the collective work is presumed to have acquired only the *privilege* [emphasis added] of reproducing and distributing the contribution."[23]

CONCLUSION

Based on these requirements, many scholarly journal publishers require an exclusive license from the author before publication. For example, the American Chemical Society (ACS) uses this rationale for requiring a full transfer of copyright:

> Transfer of authors' copyright to ACS serves several useful ends. The ACS generally has more and better resources to defend and protect copyright than do most individual authors. The ACS provides a single, central contact for dealing with grants of copyright permissions, and allows consistent policies to be used to govern copying uses. The transfer Agreement itself grants back to the authors considerable rights for how they may use material they have created. As a scientific society, the ACS accepts the responsibility for promoting the scientific integrity of published work, and defense of copyright is an element in that process.[24]

These statements and conditions show the gap that is evolving between the publisher's position and interests and the author's. Academic authors do not condone piracy or egregious infringement, but attribution and wide distribution are often of greater concern to them than the unauthorized reproduction or distribution that concerns the publisher. A publisher may relieve authors of the responsibility of dealing with copyright permissions but impose fees or restrictions that the author would not. Similarly, a publisher may grant many rights back to authors, but the authors are unlikely to receive the ability to grant those rights further to research partners or colleagues. A publisher may consider defending copyright as part of maintaining scientific integrity; the publisher's control of the version of record, however, may impede other components of scientific integrity, such as the ability to replicate research, which the author would wish to foster.

Initially, an academic author's greatest concern is often the prestige and reach of the journal where the article makes its first appearance. In the long term, however, the need and desire to reproduce the material in other ways and places, to make derivative works, and to provide content to colleagues become more pressing. Many academic authors would benefit from a departure from common contract terms and licenses toward terms that maximize the benefits they want to realize in the long term.

NOTES

1. 17 USC § 102 (2015).
2. 17 USC § 106 (2015).
3. 17 USC §106(a) (2015).
4. U.S. Copyright Office, "Waiver of Moral Rights in Visual Artworks," 2003, http://www.copyright.gov/reports/exsum.html.

5. Authors Alliance, "About Us," 2015. http://www.authorsalliance.org/about.

6. Authors Alliance, "Principles and Proposals for Copyright Reform," n.d., http://author-salliance.org/wp-content/uploads/Documents/Au-thors%20Alliance%20%7C%20Principles%20and%20Proposals%20for%20Copyright%20Ref orm.pdf.

7. Michael W. Carroll, "One Size Does Not Fit All: A Framework for Tailoring Intellectual Property Rights," *Ohio State Law Journal* 70, no. 6 (2009): 1361.

8. Ibid., 1409.

9. P. Tuckman and Jack Leahy, "What Is an Article Worth?" *Journal of Political Economy* 83 (1975): 951–52.

10. 17 USC § 101 (2015).

11. 17 USC § 201(d)(1) (2015).

12. 17 USC § 201(d)(2) (2015).

13. Plaintiffs, paraphrasing *Jacobsen v. Katzer*, 2007 WL 2358628, at 6 (N.D. Cal. Aug. 17, 2007), in William F. Patry, "§ 21:15 Standing: Requirements for Standing," in *Patry on Copyright*.

14. 17 USC § 201(b) (2015).

15. Creative Commons, "About the Licenses," n.d., http://www.creativecommons.org/licenses.

16. Bryan Gardner, ed., *Black's Law Dictionary*, 2nd pocket ed. (2001), 661.

17. 17 USC § 501(b) (2015).

18. 17 USC § 411 (2015).

19. 17 USC § 101 (2015).

20. Patry, 3:19, chap. 21.

21. 17 USC § 101 (2015).

22. Ibid.

23. 17 USC § 201 (2015).

24. American Chemical Society, "Frequently Asked Questions about the ACS Journal Publishing Agreement," 2016, http://pubs.acs.org/page/copyright/journals/faqs.html.

Chapter Two

"Protecting" Our Works—From What?

Nancy Sims

Academic libraries increasingly dedicate significant resources to providing information and guidance to their campuses about copyright, other kinds of intellectual property, and related issues. It seems likely that this trend will continue over the next several decades. Library workers are well-suited for this effort due to their library skills and experience, and many have developed significant additional relevant technical expertise. But we can be even stronger partners with academic creators by developing fluency in the many different ways copyright, intellectual property, and credit are discussed both within and outside the academy. This chapter explores one focus of that rhetoric: protection.

WHY LIBRARIES?

There are numerous ways in which library staff members are well-suited for supporting academic creators' information needs around copyright and other legal issues related to their research and scholarship. Library workers are not necessarily *better* suited to this work than others with related expertise, but we do offer some unique strengths.

One of those unique strengths is the broad and deep knowledge library staff members have of the ecosystems of research and scholarship. This expertise arises in part from the focus of library and information science as its own academic discipline: We study the systems of knowledge and information production, dissemination, use, and development across and within human social structures. But the deep and broad understanding of scholarly information systems that librarians and other library staff members have to offer also comes from the practice and experience of library work. Many academics have deep knowledge of the systems of a few particular fields of study, but because academic library staff members are usually called upon to work across more disciplines than the average academic, we have more opportunities to develop knowledge and experience of the similarities and differences across disciplines and fields. [1]

Reference interview skills are another unique strength of library professionals that influence our information interactions. Many fields have developed valuable techniques for drawing information and perspectives out of an interviewee; journalism, documentary art, sociology, anthropology, psychology, medicine, law, and many other disciplines all have their own valuable tools and approaches to interviewing. Law is a particularly apt comparison for the topics at hand because creators with legal information needs often seek information from lawyers. Both legal interviewers and library staff members are likely to be aware that a client's initial inquiry may fail to fully communicate their actual information needs. A good legal interviewer will probably provide information and solutions that are at least as satisfactory to the client as those available through a library worker. But the practices tend to diverge around assumed knowledge outcomes. A legal interview may be predicated on the assumption that a satisfactory conclusion can involve unequal understanding. It is not uncommon for a legal interview to be aimed at extracting information from the interview*ee* so that the interview*er* can make expert decisions about how to proceed. Library interviews, by contrast, are often oriented to building a shared understanding of information needs and relevant systems or structures among participants and usually aim at providing the information and support needed for the interview*ee* to proceed independently. The library-style approach is particularly well-suited to helping academic creators with legal issues related to their works because academic creators may often need to proceed independently and also because this approach shares some of the learning-and-discovery values of academia in general.

For all the unique strengths of a background in academic library work, solid support for academic creators requires in-depth knowledge of specific legal and policy trends, issues, options, and opportunities with respect to academic creations. When library workers put together our professional backgrounds in libraries with specialist knowledge on legal issues related to scholarship, we can build an especially deep understanding of the systems involved. Our unique backgrounds and strengths can bring clarity and build connections among the various goals academic creators may have for their work; the various ways they may communicate about those goals; and the ways in which copyright law, other legal provisions, and legal and industry practices may or may not align with those goals.

DEVELOPING RHETORICAL COMPETENCE

One area that library workers can explore to improve support for academic creators is the rhetoric of copyright, which shapes the mental models we all possess of the legal and practical issues at hand. Awareness of the various ways people talk about copyright is key for developing a better understanding of practices and structures, both inside and outside academia, and for helping creators to make those connections. Library staff members who have built this awareness may be able to anticipate and address creators' preconceptions about how the law functions and provide creators with new mental models that better reflect both their own expectations and the legal landscape.

Developing a better understanding of existing rhetoric around copyright can also help with opening new channels for discussion. Open licensing provides some highly relevant solutions in problem areas where academic creators' expectations and the provisions of copyright law conflict. However, it can be difficult to create dialogue about "alternative" options for academic creators when the alternatives conflict with creators' existing understandings of legal systems. Understanding existing rhetoric can help us to deploy it to advocate for open or other alternative approaches where appropriate and to deconstruct it when that may improve communications with creators.

It is also important to recognize when the dominant rhetoric around copyright provides for useful communication with academic creators. Some academic creators may be working in situations very similar to those fields outside academia where copyright is relevant and may be more interested in controlling their work or receiving royalties. Even in fairly traditional academic contexts, open licensing is not a perfect solution to all existing problems related to copyright. In some situations, being aware of rhetorical influences and sometimes intentionally invoking them can create opportunities for smoother connection with authors.

Finally, there are some times when creators' expectations do not match *any* existing legal systems or tools. In such cases, the challenge for library staff may be to use their understanding of copyright rhetoric to help creators adjust their expectations to fit reality.

"PROTECTION" FOR CREATIVE WORKS

It is very common for discourse about copyright to make reference to "protecting" creative works. This kind of discourse is often about works with immediate commercial value that must be protected against unauthorized (and unrecompensed) use or copying. In addition to protecting *works*, this kind of discourse also often talks about protecting *creators* or their interests but frequently fails to acknowledge that creators of works with immediate commercial value often do not own or receive direct compensation for those works.[2] Sometimes, but not always, rhetoric about copyright as "protection" for works or creators is also associated with talk that characterizes unauthorized use as "theft" or "stealing."

Rhetoric about copyright as protection for works or their creators often appears in legislative or policy settings. The constitutional clause on which U.S. copyright law is based does not mention protection (U.S. Constitution, art. I, § 8, cl. 8), but the current U.S. statutory copyright law frequently does (17 U.S.C., inclusive). Legislative hearings on copyright issues often involve testimony from creators or industry organizations who celebrate the protections copyright provides to creators. For example, Metallica drummer Lars Ulrich provided testimony before Congress in 2000 of the importance of copyright to people at every level of the music industry. He said that the "backbone for the success of our intellectual property business is the protection that Congress has provided with the copyright statutes. No information-based industry can thrive without this protection" and later equated unauthorized music downloading with theft (Ulrich 2000). More recently, musician David Lowery urged the House Judiciary Committee against any potential expansion of fair use, testifying that "our current copyright laws protect creators based on the notion that permission, or consent, is the foundation of civilization" (Lowery 2014).

The mainstream and popular media often employs similar rhetoric. One notable set of examples includes advertising and public service announcement campaigns like "Home Taping Is Killing Music," as well as the "You Wouldn't Steal a [fill in the blank]" and "Piracy Is a Crime" videos (British Phonographic Industry 1980s; Motion Picture Association of America 2004). Amusingly, the sometimes over-the-top rhetoric of copyright as protection for beleaguered artists and rights holders has such widespread penetration in pop culture that parodies of this rhetoric are also widespread. The "Piracy Is a Crime" and "Home Taping" antipiracy PSAs are parodied in images and videos that rise high in search results for those phrases in a variety of online search engines. Both types of parodies have entries in the (not exactly authoritative but certainly reflective of public interest) online compendium *Know-YourMeme.com*. "Weird Al" Yankovic also parodied overblown appeals to protecting recording artists' interests in his song "Don't Download This Song." Lyrics include "Don't take away money from artists just like me / How else can I afford another solid gold Humvee?" (Yankovic 2006).

Copyright discourse that centers on the concept of protection also implies the presence of a threat or threats from which protection is needed. There are different ways of characterizing that threat: unauthorized copying or use, unpaid-for copying or use, a person making unauthorized copies, a "thief" stealing the work. But this inherent threat is one of the drawbacks of this form of copyright rhetoric: It implies a fairly negative view of the ecosystems of creativity and expression. It also lends itself to expansionism: It is not hard to step from the idea that some copying is a threat to the idea that most, if not all, copying is a threat. The extremist version of this rhetoric suggests that creators and rights holders should have the right to authorize (or withhold authorization for) any and all uses. But although protection rhetoric can be associated with extremism, it is not inherently incorrect or universally inappropriate. It is one valid framing for discussion of the benefits and drawbacks of past, current, and possible future formulations of copyright and other intellectual property law and policy.

PROTECTION RHETORIC IN ACADEMIA

Some academic creators may follow the larger policy debates about intellectual property issues, but other than creators whose academic specialties are in related fields (and perhaps a small number of copyright dilettantes), it seems likely that many academic creators have been exposed to protection rhetoric more in mainstream media sources than in the policy arena.

However, academics may have been exposed to and absorbed protection-oriented rhetoric from another source: Many academic publishers and distributors produce information that employs similar language. ProQuest, for example, offers to register the copyright in theses and dissertations, explaining, "For only $55, you can protect your dissertation or master's theses and become immediately eligible for statutory damages and attorney fees" (ProQuest 2015a). ProQuest also provides a more extensive explanation of the benefits of registration, covering the necessity of registering before filing a copyright lawsuit, the benefits of registration with respect to statutory damages and attorneys' fees, and the possibility that registration can help block importation of infringing copies of a work (ProQuest 2015b). ProQuest does not require dissertation authors to transfer the copyright to them or provide exclusive licenses, so registration may indeed be a direct benefit for dissertation authors. But these resources do not notify authors that self-service registration is available via the Copyright Office for thirty-five dollars for single works by single authors (United States Copyright Office 2014) or acknowledge that lawsuits and customs actions are highly unlikely to ever be relevant to the dissertations penned by most student authors. Aside from these minor omissions, the information provided is accurate and largely neutral.

All of the "big four" academic publishers use some variation on "protection" to talk about copyright in information they provide for journal authors. They also all, in different ways, wedge additional issues into their explanations of copyright. Most of these publishers require copyright transfer or an exclusive license before they will publish a journal article—sometimes even for open distribution options:

Elsevier: "Copyright aims to protect the specific way the article has been written to describe an experiment and the results. Elsevier is committed to its authors to protect and defend their work and their reputation and takes allegations of infringement, plagiarism, ethic disputes and fraud very seriously. If an author becomes aware of a possible plagiarism, fraud or infringement we recommend contacting their Elsevier publishing contact who can then liaise with our in-house legal department" (Elsevier 2015).

Springer: "Authors will be asked to transfer the copyright of their article to the publisher (or grant the publisher exclusive publication and dissemination rights). This will ensure the widest possible protection and dissemination of information under copyright laws" (Springer 2015).

Taylor & Francis: "Copyright allows you to protect your original material and stop others from using your work without your permission. It means others will generally need to credit you and your work properly, increasing its impact." "Asking you to assign copyright means we are showing our commitment to:

- Act as stewards of the scholarly record of your work.
- Defend your article against plagiarism and copyright infringement.
- Enable you to share your article (using your free eprints and green open access at Taylor & Francis).
- Assure attribution of your work, by making sure you are identified as the author." (Informa UK Limited 2015)

Wiley-Blackwell: Explains to journal authors that their policy of requiring copyright transfer or an exclusive license "facilitates international protection against infringement, libel or plagiarism; enables the most efficient processing of publishing licensing and permissions in order that the contribution be made available to the fullest extent both directly and through intermediaries, and in both print and electronic form" (John Wiley & Sons 2013).

Several of these publishers explain quite plainly that copyright transfers and exclusive licenses facilitate the publisher's distribution of the works—which is a true statement. But to varying degrees, most of these explanations also elide the fact that much of the "protection" that copyright provides for works will, after a transfer or exclusive license, no longer accrue to the authors. Some even hide the ball on the "Protection for whom?" question by raising a smokescreen of other issues like attribution/plagiarism (which are discussed in more detail later in this chapter), fraud, unethical behavior, and libel.

Closely associating these concepts with copyright may suggest to some authors that copyright law has applicability to those issues, when it usually does not. It is true that in Europe and the United Kingdom, where some of these publishers are based, attribution may have a direct legal connection to copyright, and there may be some legal protections for plagiarism that do not exist in the United States. Conversely, protections for authors against claims for libel and defamation may be weaker in those jurisdictions than they are in the United States. In any case, it will be a rare occasion when a publisher chooses to protect one of its authors on any of these points of concern, copyright related or not, unless the author's interests are directly and completely aligned with those of the publishing company.

ALTERNATIVE AND COMPLEMENTARY
COPYRIGHT RHETORIC

Given the prevalence of rhetoric that frames copyright as protecting works or creators, it is useful to highlight copyright rhetoric that focuses on the law's benefits to creators without talking about protection. The intellectual property clause in the U.S. Constitution speaks only of giving creators "exclusive rights" for "limited times" (U.S. Constitution, art. I, § 8, cl. 8). A focus on positive rights can be a bit less pessimistic than a focus on "protection." Rights *may* be violated, but there is not usually an assumption that they will be; protection, by contrast, usually implies an inherent threat. Much copyright theory is framed in terms of the incentives (usually economic) and benefits that copyright provides to creators via their exclusive rights.

It is also worth noting that quite a bit of copyright discourse considers that the primary beneficiaries of the system of intellectual property law are neither creators nor rights holders but the public. The Constitution frames Congress's power to give time-limited, exclusive rights to creators as having the public-interest goal of "promot[ing] the progress of science and useful arts." In this framing, owner/creator rights are secondary, a means by which the primary public benefit is realized.

None of these forms of copyright rhetoric inherently exclude one another unless they are very far to an extreme. But each has interesting effects on conversations around copyright. The rhetoric that frames copyright as providing protections for creators, while prevalent, is often quite out of step with the goals, practices, and expectations of academic creators. Sometimes, introducing other types of copyright rhetoric or explicitly challenging the applicability of protection-oriented concepts may enable the most robust and productive interactions between academic creators and library staff members.

PUTTING RHETORICAL UNDERSTANDING INTO PRACTICE: COMMUNICATING ABOUT ACADEMIC COMMERCIAL INTERESTS

Legislative, pop-cultural, and publisher rhetoric about protection is often primarily concerned with the commercial exchanges that copyright facilitates. These commercial concerns are often not shared by academic creators. Many academic creators receive monetary compensation for their intellectual and creative work up front in the form of a salary and research grants. But regardless of salary or grant status, few academics receive significant monetary compensation in direct exchange for the monographs or textbooks they produce. Almost no academics receive any monetary compensation for papers or journal articles—in fact, they may well be paying fees to support the publication of these works. Usually publishers receive payment for subscriptions, individual purchases, or licensed reproduction of these works; they rarely send direct, use-based payments back to academic creators. Thus, although many academic works are of some commercial value to *someone*, that someone is rarely the creator of the work. Because the commercial value of authorized copies of the work does not accrue to its creators, much of the time those creators do not care on economic grounds about protection from unauthorized use or copying.

There are, however, situations in which academic creators do receive direct commercial benefit from their academic creations. While many textbooks do not make much profit, authors of very popular academic textbooks may receive significant monetary compensation for those works through upfront payment, royalties, or both. Similarly, although many academic monographs are not particularly profitable, some outliers produce significant monetary returns for both press and author. Increasingly, some academic creators are finding varying commercial success self-publishing works via a wide array of e-book and print-on-demand outlets. Academic creators may also find direct commercial opportunities for creations other than textbooks or literary works; assessment and measurement instruments can be lucrative, as can patentable inventions or processes and even sometimes curricula or other learning objects. Some academic creators on design and arts faculties create art as part of their academic work, and those works have as widely varied a likelihood of stand-alone commercial success as most other artworks.

Because patentable inventions are usually handled in a university technology transfer or "commercialization" office, it is less likely that academic creators will seek help about patent-related issues from their libraries.[3] But creators may seek help from libraries with other kinds of commercially valuable materials. In these situations, the rhetoric of protection so common outside of academia may be quite applicable, without any adjustments to mental models, to work produced inside of academia. Making use of this rhetoric when it is appropriate and relevant can be reassuring; evidence that libraries can and do provide information relevant to an individual's commercial interests can help build trust.

As an illustration, academic creators often request information about "protecting" forms, assessments, or measurement instruments. At first blush, it may not be clear that the motivating forces behind these inquiries can in some ways be quite different from those behind questions about books and journal articles. An open-ended, reference-style interaction can reveal that compensated, commercial use is a possibility creators are considering, which can explain why these creators are often more concerned than usual with wanting to know how to "own" their works. Sometimes these creators are familiar enough with copyright issues to bring up registration, but sometimes they operate from near-zero background knowledge; in these latter cases, creators often find it reassuring to hear that, if their work is copyrightable at all, the copyright came into existence as soon as the work did.[4] When their worries about protection are allayed, creators may be better able to consider the pros and cons of registering their work: While registration can be beneficial and is not difficult to undertake, it does cost money and is not a necessary step toward owning a copyright in a work.

Creators of specialized assessments or forms also often see a narrow, specific audience for their work; sometimes, after an extended interview, they independently conclude that commercial distribution does not seem like the most effective way of getting their work into the hands of their perceived audience. At such times, recognizing and acknowledging the creator's possible commercial interests has sometimes been the key factor allowing the interaction to extend to the potential of open distribution.

At other times, acknowledging potential commercial interests can help creators articulate that they have broader information and support needs related to business development—at which point they are often happy to hear a suggestion to pursue formal legal representation, talk to a business expert, or be referred to a technology transfer office. At least once, a creator I had referred to tech transfer subsequently returned with a different question about an academic creation and directly referenced his positive experience in previous interactions at the library as a reason for his return.

Recognizing and supporting creators' commercial interests in situations where they *are* relevant may foster increased respect for the knowledge and skills of library staff members and, as discussed later, encourage return inquiries for more traditional academic works. Supporting creators' commercial interests may also foster receptivity to considerations a library staff member may seek to present that diverge from, but complement or supplement, commercial models.

NONCOMMERCIAL THREATS FROM WHICH ACADEMIC CREATORS MAY SEEK PROTECTION

Outside academia, protection of works is often discussed in connection with commercial interests, but there are some alternate interests of academic creators for which protection may also be sought. While many of these interests are not well-protected by current legal systems, alternative systems may actually address some of these concerns in more robust ways.

Lack of Attribution

As we saw earlier in the information some academic publishers provide to their journal authors, it is not uncommon for copyright, plagiarism, and attribution or credit to be conflated rhetorically. This conflation is also common in the minds of academic creators across many different groups.[5] There are many fundamental concepts, such as authorship, creativity, and justice, that do span all of these issues, so the conflation is understandable.

It is also not uncommon for academic publishers in particular to suggest that copyright provides "protection" in all of these areas, as we saw previously. It is true that legal protections around plagiarism, attribution, and credit may be tied to copyright in some jurisdictions outside the United States, but such protections are much weaker in the United States, and where they do exist, they are not usually related to copyright. Other than provisions in the Visual Artists Rights Act (VARA; 17 U.S.C., § 106a (1990)), which do in fact create a right of attribution (and disattribution) for creators of certain very specific types of visual artworks, there is no explicit provision in U.S. copyright law for a right of attribution.[6] To the extent that attribution rights exist in U.S. law outside of VARA, they are considered to be addressed in trademark law, defamation law, or law around fraud and unfair competition.

Attribution and credit are some of the most deeply resonant forms of "compensation" academics receive for their work, so it is not at all surprising that publishers invoke those issues when discussing "protections" for authors. But taking basic practicalities into consideration, it remains a bit odd that so few academic authors realize that attribution has little connection to copyright ownership; academic authors frequently transfer legal ownership of their works to publishers, and yet in almost any form of academic citation, attribution is provided to the authors regardless of rights ownership. This practice alone should make it clear that copyright ownership and attribution, whether they are both addressed by statute or not, are separate issues.

Nevertheless, the association of copyright with attribution/credit persists, and persists strongly, for many academic creators. I learned more about this association in research I pursued with faculty members at the University of Minnesota a few years ago (Sims 2011). I knew from experience that academics care quite a lot about attribution and citation, so I drafted a survey question that asked whether authors had legal rights to attribution and control after transferring their copyright away. Eighty-nine percent of faculty respondents and 79 percent of library employee respondents believed that a legal right of attribution persists after copyright transfer. Academic norms around attribution are strong enough and carry such moral weight[7] that I was not surprised respondents failed to distinguish between a legal right and a moral imperative.

What did surprise me was that, in open-ended interviews, when faculty members were asked to identify legal considerations relevant to using material that belonged to someone else, they raised credit or attribution before *any other* considerations. Similarly, a separate survey included a series of questions intended to assess whether respondents could identify legal considerations relevant to use of third-party material, and even when attribution and credit were not among the prepopulated response options, respondents *wrote them in*. Notably, on one question with fifty-one total responses, ten of the eleven respondents who used the write-in field referenced citation or attribution.

There *are* some situations in which legal systems provide recourse for academic creators whose work is copied or referenced without credit. Such a situation may arise, for instance, if the lack of credit meets the legal definition of fraud. Usually, fraud requires intentional deceit, so while failure to provide credit due to accident, error, or sloppiness may well be academic misconduct, it is not fraud. Even if lack of credit is sufficiently deceitful to count as fraud, in the United States, legal redress for fraud is primarily oriented to restitution for financial harm, so *authors* will often have difficulty proving they suffered the kind of harm that a civil case for fraud could address. Their publishers may actually have better legal standing in cases like this.

Copying another's work without credit may also sometimes rise to the level of copyright infringement, regardless of the copier's intentions.[8] Because there are provisions in most legal systems allowing some unauthorized copying by scholars, researchers, and teachers, unethical academic copying will usually have to be fairly egregious before it can plausibly be argued to be infringing. But extensive unauthorized copying may indeed be copyright infringement. If an author has transferred copyright to a publisher, only the publisher will have the right to bring a complaint or to receive damages if infringement is found; an author who retains copyright ownership may sometimes find copyright an avenue of legal redress for uncredited copying of her work.

It can be quite challenging to convince academic creators that, in the United States at least, there is no stand-alone legal basis to require or control attribution or credit. Once convinced of this, some creators seem to equate the idea that there is no legal protection for attribution via copyright law with the idea that there is no protection for attribution at all. Many creators who are upset at this proposition also resist suggestions that the normative, extra-legal enforcement mechanisms of the academic community[9] seem to be doing a fairly good job of ensuring appropriate attribution. Nevertheless, many creators do seem to respond positively to the suggestion that the imposition of a legal system of enforcement of these norms might end up worse than the existing extralegal system. It can be particularly helpful to remind creators of the persnickety standards of legal citation (or outline the common practices, if they are not familiar) and then suggest that judges might impose the attribution standards with which they are most familiar.

One very legitimate point academic creators sometimes raise about the insufficiency of the existing extralegal systems enforcing attribution and academic ethical norms is that redress is not equally available to all members of the community. It is sadly true that junior scholars, less prestigious scholars, scholars in the developing world, and others may have more limited ability to seek redress through the systems of the academic community for unattributed uses of their work. However, most of the creators who raise this point already understand, or easily recognize when it is pointed out, that there is little likelihood that a legal system of enforcement, with court costs and attorneys' fees, could provide any *improved* availability of redress to disempowered participants.

Misuse

There is one threat from which academic creators articulate a need for protection that is not present in most of the mainstream "protection"-oriented copyright rhetoric, or even in the information academic publishers provide— the threat of use by individuals or for purposes that the creator would not want to authorize. Often, these concerns are expressed in terms of responsibility or ethics: Creators worry that their research subjects may have their privacy violated or be portrayed in disreputable ways or that their research may be cast in a harshly negative light or be put to harmful or destructive use. Very infrequently, creators express these concerns in terms of wanting to control any and all discussion of their work and to bar any negative or critical use.

In general, a scholar's ethical responsibility to protect research subjects must be dealt with prior to publication—information that may violate an obligation to research subjects if released is very hard to put back into a box postpublication. And although it is often painful to receive criticism or negative feedback, most academic creators are fairly committed to the free exchange of ideas and would consider a scholar's attempt to deploy legal mechanisms against valid criticisms of her work, however unkindly framed, incompatible with academic values. Nevertheless, some academic creators seek to deploy copyright as a protection against these kinds of concerns.

Whether the desire to protect against misuse arises from a sense of responsibility and ethics or from a wish to censor, the idea that copyright provides any sort of protection in this arena again reflects some major misconceptions. Use of a work in ways that cast negative light on its creator may possibly be addressable through defamation or libel law, but in the United States, that requires proving that the negative commentary was both factual (as opposed to an opinion) and untrue. Negative commentary within the bounds of normal scholarly exchange may be an unpleasant experience for an author, but it will rarely be actionable as defamation. And copyright is quite definitely not an alternate avenue to bar use of a work simply due to a distasteful user viewpoint. U.S. courts have frequently stated that copyright is not intended for purposes of censorship:[10] "[W]hen a lethal parody, like a scathing theater review, kills demand for the original, it does not produce a harm cognizable under the Copyright Act" (*Campbell v. Acuff-Rose Music* 1994); "copyright does not immunize a work from comment and criticism" (*Suntrust Bank v. Houghton Mifflin Co.* 2001). So this threat, along with several others of concern to many academic creators, is not particularly aligned with the protections offered by statutory law.

A THREAT ACADEMIC CREATORS MAY FAIL TO RECOGNIZE

There is nothing incorrect about rhetoric that speaks of copyright protecting works, creators, and rights holders against the threat of unauthorized uses. As discussed previously, however, academic creators' concerns often diverge from the economic concerns reflected in much protection-oriented rhetoric. These areas of divergence can mean that copyright itself *actually poses a threat* to academic creators. For many academic creators, one of their most important goals is that their work be widely disseminated and used. But because copyright applies automatically to all works, and because most potential users assume that copyright requires payment (or at least permission) for use, copyright actually creates barriers to achieving the widest possible dissemination of a work.

Recent research has demonstrated ways in which copyright is sometimes a threat to distribution and use of a work. In two related papers, Paul Heald explored commercial availability of out-of-print but in-copyright books. He found both that "[c]opyright correlates significantly with the disappearance of works rather than with their availability" (2013) and that there is quite likely demand for out-of-print, in-copyright books that is not being supplied in print or electronic form by the publishing industry (2014). Heald does suggest that some of the lack of availability of in-copyright books is simply due to short-sightedness on the part of the book-publishing industry; older popular music appears to be more available than older books. But Heald also suggests that divergent court opinions about translating existing works to new formats, as well as the higher cost of digitizing books, may explain the differences in availability (2014).

Academics are by no means the only creators who seek widespread dissemination of and access to their work, nor are they the only creators who sometimes value distribution over remuneration. Fred Rogers, the children's television personality (who notably was also the head of the production company for his shows), testified in the copyright case establishing the legality of VCRs that unauthorized home taping of his shows was a "real service to families" and not anything he would want to prohibit (Rogers, quoted in *Sony Corp. v. Universal City Studios* 1984.) But academic creators as a group may be more likely than other groups of creators to value distribution above remuneration and thus be receptive to communications that highlight and acknowledge this drawback inherent in "protection."

Thankfully, despite the threats posed by copyright to dissemination and use of creative works, there are legal tools that seek to ameliorate these problems. "Free" and "open" licensing have existed in the world of software development since at least the 1980s (Vaidhyanathan 2001, 155), and open licenses custom-crafted for creative works have existed since at least 2002 (Creative Commons n.d.).[11] Creative Commons licenses are probably the most widely used and robustly tested open content licenses available today. They work by offering a license that may be taken up by any member of the public and that preauthorizes certain types of uses. If a user wants to make a use that is not preauthorized by the Creative Commons license, they can still rely on any of the exceptions to copyright law (such as fair use) or ask the rights holder for permission. Creative Commons also offers a different legal tool, CC0, which allows rights holders to relinquish or waive as many rights as possible.[12]

In parallel with the development of open content licenses, many academic creators also explored free and open distribution of their publications. The arXiv, one of the oldest established venues for authors to provide free online distribution of their academic works, was founded in 1991 (Cornell University Library 2012). Some of the foundational definitions of "open" distribution of academic work require not just that the work be accessible at no charge online but also that reuse of the work be unrestricted. The Budapest Open Access Initiative wrote in 2002 that:

> By "open access" to this literature, we mean its free availability on the public internet, permitting any users to read, download, copy, distribute, print, search, or link to the full texts of these articles, crawl them for indexing, pass them as data to software, or use them for any other lawful purpose, without financial,

legal, or technical barriers other than those inseparable from gaining access to the internet itself.

To many academic creators, however, access is more important than reuse rights: Some consider research that is simply accessible online free of charge to meet the definition of *open access*. Today, many academic distribution venues that are wholly open access require the use of open licenses—usually Creative Commons—but many others do not require particular licenses, only that works be made freely available. PLoS takes the former approach: "Open Access (OA) stands for unrestricted access and unrestricted reuse" (2015). ArXiv takes the latter, stating in their operating principles, "Access to arXiv content via https://arXiv.org is free to individual end users," but omitting any mention of licensing or reuse (Cornell University Library 2012).

Open access for academic creations does seem to mitigate some of copyright's "threat" to widespread use; several studies have shown that open access publications have increased citations, although the presence and size of the effect seems to vary across academic fields (Swan 2010). Open access may not even necessarily reduce the commercial value of academic publications, and it does seem to increase their accessibility and use (Ferwerda, Snijder, and Adema 2013).

Open licenses are not a perfect solution to the threat copyright poses to widespread distribution and use; they may not be supported in all of the most desirable publishing venues, and not every member of the hoped-for audience may be familiar with what open licenses permit. Creative Commons licenses do address one of the threats academic creators perceive that is not necessarily well-addressed by existing law: They can create a binding *contractual* requirement of attribution, even in jurisdictions where *copyright* law does not much concern itself with the specifics of attribution and credit.

Many academic creators find the *idea* of open licenses appealing but have some qualms about their breadth. They may express concerns that open licenses will encourage misuse of their works or use by individuals they would prefer not to authorize (this category varies widely and may include commercial users, competing researchers, or a number of other kinds of users). When consulting with a creator who is certain that they want to make their work publicly available online but is not sure she wants to use an open license, I may remind her that, because the law already authorizes a number of uses without permission, she is already prevented from picking and choosing authorized users much of the time. Once the work is available online, the law will authorize some uses that the creator cannot control, and there will quite likely be some users who make unauthorized or illegal uses of their work.

While traditional approaches to copyright do not entirely preclude unwanted uses, open licenses may encourage *wanted* users; this idea can be quite exciting for some academic creators. In the absence of information to the contrary, some potential users whom the creator would like to authorize will assume that copyright prevents their use. For example, many academic creators would be very happy to have their work used in K–12 classrooms, but many K–12 teachers presume both that copyright prevents their use and that permission would require payment that they and their students cannot afford. When the work is licensed openly, these users can see that their use is not just permitted but also encouraged. Open licensing, when the creator has already determined that they *do* want to make their work available online, does no worse with respect to unauthorized or infringing users than no open licensing and does better with respect to encouraging the kinds of users that creators may most want to attract.

It is worth noting that academic creators' hopes that their works be widely used and influential may at times be in conflict with another common goal of academic creators: that their works be received and evaluated in ways that will forward their careers. An academic blogger recently spoke of this as a tension between "academics" (i.e., career building) and "science" (i.e., knowledge building) (Carter 2015). His discussion focuses specifically on disciplines most would label "science" (as opposed to "humanities," "social science," or "the arts"), but the distinctions apply across most academic fields. Many existing means of evaluating research output give higher value to works published in certain periodical outlets or with certain academic presses. Many of the publishers whose publications carry these higher values can compel creators to transfer their copyrights or grant exclusive licenses to those publishers. And the business models of many of those publishers depend on payment for access to the work, which necessarily requires some limitations on access. For many (but assuredly not all) high-value publishers, copyright's protections against unauthorized use are financially beneficial. But because academic creators' careers may depend on access to those high-value publishers, copyright's "protections" may threaten research goals even where they simultaneously forward career goals.

Some academic creators may also fail to recognize the full breadth of an open license. Academic authors may be surprised to find their open-licensed articles republished in compilation volumes whose editors never contacted the original authors. This type of use is entirely permitted by open licenses, assuming the conditions of specific license terms are met, but is fairly far outside the norms of academic publishing. Some of these republications may be legitimate academic uses—for example, a few disciplines are developing "overlay" journals, which collect and publish selected works that have already been made openly available online. Other republications may be attempts to scam academic libraries by selling "monographs" made up of content that is already freely available. It seems likely that the unethical versions of this practice will sort themselves out over time, but the surprise of seeing one's work reproduced without prior communication may be quite an un-pleasant shock for some academic creators. For creators surprised by such uses of their work, it may also come as a surprise that Creative Commons licenses are irrevocable. It is imperative that library staff members who provide information about open licensing to academic creators both acknowledge the realistic drawbacks of open licenses and seek to avoid and combat misunderstandings that may be true sources of conflict for academic creators.

Open licenses may also create an opportunity to stymie misuse of works. Creators who wish to restrict questionable commercial uses of their work may find some peace of mind in attaching a noncommercial clause to a Creative Commons license. More interestingly, in jurisdictions with legal rights of attribution, it is not uncommon to find a parallel right of *dis*attribution—a legal right for the creator *not* be publicly associated with her work. While this right is not very commonly invoked, it may be useful when works are altered in ways that are permitted by law but unacceptable to the creator. Although they remain irrevocable so that permission may not be withdrawn after an objected-to use is begun, the current versions of the Creative Commons licenses all allow rights holders to stipulate nonattribution for uses of their work. In jurisdictions where the law does not address attribution, Creative Commons licenses may create a contractual obligation not to name the creator, with the odd result of works that can be reused, but for which attribution information may not be shared. Such odd results do address academic creators' concerns about being associated with uses of their work that they find distasteful; they also could undercut profiteering from republication of openly licensed works. While few academic creators will be excited about removing their attribution information from a work, pointing out this counterintuitive option may help library staff to alleviate fears that open licenses will exacerbate potential misuse of their work.

CONCLUSION

Library staff have long been a trusted source of information for academic creators on a variety of issues. Copyright, licensing, and intellectual property issues are areas in which academic creators increasingly expect their libraries to be able to provide information and support. As we move into the twenty-first century, more library staff members will be developing knowledge and expertise on the particulars and technicalities of law and policy in these areas. It will be to our benefit, and to the benefit of other academic creators who seek our support, to also develop understanding and insight into how those issues are discussed, both within and outside academia. Technical knowledge and rhetorical insight are both essential to teasing apart the many potentially conflicting issues, goals, and expectations presented when a creator approaches us and asks, "How do I protect my work?"

NOTES

1. This is not to suggest that no one working in disciplines outside information and library science has such broad or deep systems knowledge, simply that on average a library staff member is somewhat more likely to possess the outlook and experience necessary to develop such a perspective.

2. Some creators who do not own their commercially valuable works are paid more when the work is used more (as in most royalty arrangements), but sometimes they are not (as when a work was created "for hire" or when it was purchased with a lump sum payment or without any direct compensation to the creator).

3. Academic creators who do seek information from their libraries may have some interests better served by a tech transfer or commercialization office. Partnership with such entities can be very profitable for providing a more comprehensive suite of support services to academic creators.

4. Creators may be less reassured to hear that forms and some instruments may not contain sufficient creative expression to give rise to a copyright. But even where this may be true, there can still be opportunities for commercial development if the creator is determined.

5. Elementary and secondary educators, as well as creators outside of academia, also often hold beliefs that conflate copyright infringement and plagiarism or that unrealistically simplify issues of credit and attribution, in my experience. In one particularly fruitful training, a large group of K–12 library and media staff were overjoyed to learn that they could teach about plagiarism without necessarily also invoking threatening legal concepts that were difficult and sometimes off-putting for their young students.

6. There is a provision in the Digital Millennium Copyright Act that addresses attribution-related information, making it illegal to provide false information or alter or remove existing information, but this provision is directed to "Copyright Management Information," which may or may not include information relevant to the attribution of performers or creators (17 U.S.C. § 1202).

7. Many people have learned about plagiarism in contexts where it is given such moral weight, that to suggest there are times when it is appropriate to *omit* attribution for a quoted or referenced work often provokes disdain from academics and nonacademics alike. It remains true, however, that, in many areas of intellectual and creative production, it is accepted practice not to give credit. For example, collage artworks rarely come with source citations, attorneys are overjoyed when their briefs are incorporated uncredited into a court opinion, and many forms of art celebrate subtle allusions that are only "credited" if readers/listeners/watchers are fully in the know.

8. Copyright is "strict liability" law. If copying occurred and was impermissible by law, then it may be found to be infringement. The copier's intent is irrelevant.

9. These mechanisms include but are not limited to: failing classes, being kicked out of programs of study, revocation of degrees, firings from jobs, retraction of publications, and loss of reputation.

10. Historically, copyright law—and its predecessors, like crown patents for printers—were employed for purposes of state censorship. Realistically speaking, copyright is often effective in achieving de facto censorship because many accused infringers do not have the resources or knowledge to contest a censorious accusation. See, for example, *ChillingEffects.org*.

11. Open and/or free software licenses have sometimes been applied to more artistic or literary works, and non–Creative Commons licenses aimed at art and literature (such as the GNU Free Documentation License) do exist.

12. In a number of jurisdictions, a variety of rights under copyright law are permanently lodged with the creator (and sometimes her heirs); these rights cannot be waived or transferred away by contracts or licenses.

REFERENCES

17 U.S.C., inclusive.

British Phonographic Industry. 1980s. "Home Taping Is Killing Music" advertising campaign.

"Budapest Open Access Initiative." 2002. *Budapest Open Access Initiative.* http://www. budapestopenaccessinitiative.org/read.

Campbell v. Acuff-Rose Music. 1994. 510 U.S. 569.

Carter, Gerald. 2015. "Goals of Science vs Goals of Scientists (& a Love Letter to PLOS One)." *SocialBat.org.* http://socialbat.org/2015/08/12/goals-of-science-vs-goals-of-scientists-a-love-letter-for-plos-one.

ChillingEffects.org.

Cornell University Library. 2012. "arXiv Operating Principles." https://confluence.cornell.edu/ download/attachments/127116484/arXivPrinciplesMarch12.pdf.

Creative Commons. n.d. "History." https://creativecommons.org/about/history.

Elsevier. 2015. "Copyright." https://www.elsevier.com/about/company-information/policies/ copyright.

Ferwerda, Eelco, Ronald Snijder, and Janneke Adema. 2013. *OAPEN-NL: A Project Exploring Open Access Monograph Publishing in the Netherlands, Final Report.* http://oapen.org/ download?type=export&export=oapen-nl-final-report.

Informa UK Limited. 2016. "Copyright and You." *Author Services: Supporting Taylor & Francis Authors.* http://authorservices.taylorandfrancis.com/copyright-and-you.

John Wiley & Sons. 2013. "Copyright and Permissions." Accessed October 8, 2015. http:// exchanges.wiley.com/authors/copyright-and-permissions_333.html..

KnowYourMeme.com. 2013. "Piracy, It's a Crime." Accessed October 6, 2015. http:// knowyourmeme.com/memes/piracy-its-a-crime.

———. 2014. "Home Taping Is Killing Music." Accessed October 6, 2015. http:// knowyourmeme.com/memes/home-taping-is-killing-music.

Lowery, David. 2014. Testimony before the Committee on the Judiciary on the Scope of Fair Use. https://judiciary.house.gov/wp-content/uploads/2016/02/012814-Testimony-Lowery.pdf.

Motion Picture Association of America. 2004. "Piracy, It's a Crime" advertising campaign.

ProQuest. 2015a. "Submitting Your Dissertation or Thesis to ProQuest." http://www.proquest. com/products-services/dissertations/submitting-dissertation-proquest.html.

———. 2015b. "Why Copyright?" http://media2.proquest.com/documents/whycopyright.pdf.

Sims, Nancy. 2011. "Lies, Damned Lies, and Copyright (Mis)Information: Empowering Faculty by Addressing Key Points of Confusion." ACRL 2011 Conference, Philadelphia, PA. http://www.ala.org/acrl/files/conferences/confsandpreconfs/national/2011/papers/lies_ damned_lies.pdf.

Sony Corp. v. Universal City Studios. 1984. 464 U.S. 417.

Springer. 2015. "Can You Give Me More Information about Copyright?" *Frequently Asked Questions.* https://www.springer.com/us/authors-editors/journal-author/frequently-asked-questions/3832.

Suntrust Bank v. Houghton Mifflin Co. 2001. 268 F.3d 1257 (11th Cir.).

Swan, Alma. 2010. "The Open Access Citation Advantage: Studies and Results to Date." *University of Southampton.* http://eprints.soton.ac.uk/id/eprint/268516.

Ulrich, Lars. 2000. Testimony before Senate Judiciary Committee on Music Downloading. http://transcripts.cnn.com/TRANSCRIPTS/0007/11/se.01.html as of 10/7/2015.

United States Copyright Office. 2014. "Copyright Office Circular 4: Copyright Office Fees." http://copyright.gov/circs/circ04.pdf.

U.S. Constitution.

Vaidhyanathan, Siva. 2001. *Copyrights and Copywrongs.* New York: New York University Press.

Yankovic, "Weird Al." 2006. "Don't Download This Song." *Straight Outta Lynwood.* Volcano Records.

Chapter Three

Faculty Require Online Distribution of Student Work

Enter the Librarian

Micah Zeller and Emily Symonds Stenberg

There is not anything especially futuristic about the scenario of academic librarians providing support to the university faculty who teach undergraduates by providing reference services, leading instruction sessions, or embedding within a specific course. What is changing is how the work produced in these classes is being submitted, shared, and published—and, by extension, the role academic librarians play in the creation and dissemination of this work. Academic libraries offer such open access platforms as institutional repositories and functional specialists with knowledge of intellectual property, the law, and scholarly communication issues; they are thus well positioned to facilitate such distribution. For the library and university of the future educating the students of the next millennium, this should be a perfect match.

Yet, even as the future arrives with incremental adjustments rather than immediate transformations, library professionals do not necessarily agree on how to respond to these changes. A 2015 discussion on the ACRL Scholarly Communication LISTSERV on the topic of student license agreements indicates how difficult it is to establish a clear answer or policy on handling student work and how easy it is to get lost in the quagmire of faculty, student, and librarian rights, roles, and responsibilities (2015).[1] Librarians, lawyers, and lawyer-librarians who regularly deal with such questions have difficulty agreeing on a single way to address the issues. Given the number and variety of higher educational institutions, there is no one-size-fits-all approach. Answers are often variations of "It depends," which underscores the importance of librarians being aware of both the relevant issues and the open access or student publishing environment at their specific institutions. "It depends" is a more knowledgeable and helpful answer than "I don't know" and leads to productive discussion of situation-specific facts and possible outcomes.

Guidance on open access and scholarly communications is now a common component of the services offered by libraries, including at authors' own institutions. On staff at Washington University Libraries are the authors—a digital publishing and digital preservation librarian and a copyright and digital access librarian with a JD and a law license—as well as a scholarly communications coordinator who is also a subject librarian. These positions collaborate with colleagues on providing services for content created by faculty, graduate students, and undergraduate students, the latter at an increasingly frequent rate.

In 2013, when the authors started in their respective positions, the university repository had only two collections containing undergraduate work: senior honors papers and research symposium posters. Two years later, there are four additional collections built on undergraduate student works completed for specific classes, as well as complete digital runs of two print publications produced through the university's undergraduate research office. These collections complement course projects on other platforms, such as Omeka, WordPress, and YouTube, and all were created with the direct involvement of a librarian or the university libraries. But here and elsewhere, undergraduates have been required to post to Facebook or Twitter, edit Wikipedia entries, contribute to GitHub, create or comment on a blog, and even engage in open access publishing—none of which necessarily involves libraries or librarians. Whether a librarian knows about individual assignments or facilitates their distribution, he or she often has experience and perspective related to building online collections, establishing access options, and supporting positive pedagogical outcomes.

This chapter is not the final word on how libraries will be involved in this area, nor is it an exhaustive discussion of the relevant issues. It begins by examining literature on scholarly communications, undergraduate students, and the role of libraries and then shares the authors' specific experience with a cross-section of courses: an engineering capstone where students are required to "publish" their final papers to the institutional repository, an archaeology course where students create and upload videos to YouTube, and an American culture studies seminar where students conduct oral history interviews that they must add to a Documenting Ferguson repository and to the University Archives. For each of these assignments, the instructor and a librarian were in communication about requirements and various policies. These courses demonstrate the issues academic libraries are now encountering as a result of the services they provide and illustrate how cultivating expertise in a range of fields promotes the ability to continue providing meaningful support. Here we address legal mechanisms, privacy rights, on-line identity, platform choice, and ethical questions related to mandating a digital presence.

If libraries do not become involved in these developments, then it does not mean the developments will not occur at all. Instead, it indicates that faculty are proceeding on their own and that the future exists without us.

LITERATURE REVIEW

Of the many roles held by academic librarians, one of growing importance is that of scholarly communications expert for faculty and students. Tensions over access to the results of taxpayer-funded research combined with an increasing awareness of the implications of digital distribution have made open access, privacy, copyright, and other intellectual property issues more important to both librarians and universities. As Kevin Smith (2015) wrote in his preface to volume 1 of this series, "[a]cademic libraries will have a vital role in supporting these [social and educational] processes and in helping our students adapt to the several different styles of study and communication with which they will need fluency" (x). Librarians are increasingly speaking this language of scholarly communication to graduate and undergraduate students in direct relation to their current schoolwork and academic careers, not just as possible issues for their future careers. Stern (2014) emphasizes the importance of copyright training when classwork is added to an institutional repository, or IR (7), but this training may be necessary for more than just classwork or IRs, and often librarians will be the ones to provide it. Hensley (2013) argues:

> Undergraduate research programs offer new opportunities for librarians to weave together their expertise in areas of student learning, information literacy, and scholarly communication. In fact, one could argue that the librarian's expertise is best positioned to lead support for the last phase of the research process—publication and dissemination of original undergraduate student work. (114)

Questions related to scholarly communication are incorporated throughout the Association of College and Research Libraries' "Framework for Information Literacy for Higher Education" (2015). Under the concept "Information Has Value," research practices include "[articulating] the purpose and distinguishing characteristics of copyright, fair use, open access, and the public domain" and "[making] informed choices regarding their online actions in full awareness of issues related to privacy and the commodification of personal information" (Association of College and Research Libraries 2015). Whether student work is published online in a repository or other platform or is not published at all, students need to understand these concepts as consumers and creators, and librarians are in a position to educate them throughout the entire process. As Davis-Kahl (2012) writes, "[a]sking students to consider if and how they want their own work to be shared and used by others shifts the nature of discussions from cautionary and reactive to reflective and proactive, and explicitly acknowledges that the students' work is valued enough to be shared if they choose" (213). One of the key purposes of this chapter is to look at that "if they choose" moment. Sometimes the sharing is not up to the student, but the method or process of sharing may involve the library. University instructors may require that students make the works or assignments they have created available to the public outside the classroom. Doing so may be a condition of course credit and indeed may be closely tied to a clearly articulable pedagogical purpose. In today's digital environment, this public presentation requirement may be more than an on-campus poster session or print publication with limited distribution across campus; it may also extend to online and other widely accessible platforms.

Beyond facilitating access to collections, the role of many librarians has expanded to include that of educating students on these issues. What are the pedagogical advantages, if any, of publishing undergraduate work? Does requiring or encouraging submission to a repository or other online platform in advance also encourage students to work harder to produce their best possible work? Undergraduates who participate in student research "face new decisions regarding copyright, data management, open access (OA), authors' rights, and the creation of metadata for preservation purposes" (Hensley 2013, 116).

Various academic libraries have presented and published on the methods they use to incorporate scholarly communication issues into the work of subject and repository librarians, among others. "Getting Superior Work in the IR: A Self-Supporting Loop," originally a presentation at the 2013 USETDA conference, discusses how librarians in the Claremont University Consortium embedded and integrated themselves into the student research process to meet the dual goals of (1) teaching information literacy concepts to undergraduate students and (2) improving the quality of the senior theses written in the Environmental Analysis capstone course and made publicly available in the repository (Lowe and Stone 2014). Librarians moved beyond one-shot instruction sessions to a more comprehensive model and incorporated a rubric to evaluate how students had learned and employed these concepts in their research papers. Following the implementation of this model, a rubric analysis project indicated an improvement in both the quality of the scholarship and what Lowe and Stone called students' "alacrity"—that is, the willingness and eagerness of students who submitted papers to the repository (2014).

A recent survey by Utah State University discusses the benefits of publishing undergraduate work in institutional repositories as perceived by undergraduate research directors and IR librarians. Posited benefits included the fact that "exposure showcases student work, provides examples to other students, and highlights the diversity of student research" (Rozum et al. 2015, 809). Additional benefits as perceived by librarians were increasing scholarly communication awareness (810) and "providing concrete examples of open access scholarship to students early in their academic career" (806), both of which indicate a role for librarians in undergraduate publishing. Davis-Kahl (2012) observes, "Teachable moments around copyright and CC [Creative Commons] result from discussions and decisions about disseminating student work" (215). These discussions can happen in the libraries, in the classroom, and across the university between librarians and faculty and between librarians and students. Buckland (2015) argues for viewing students as future researchers and involving them in the peer-review and publishing process: "Libraries have long helped students become better consumers by teaching them about authority and authenticity in publishing (be that online or in print) and are key to growing informed graduates. Currently, libraries are able to support a different role for students in this continuum—that of creator" (193). Buckland advocates incorporating scholarly publishing issues into education and offering students a "place at the table" (195).

We cannot only discuss what we are doing now and next semester, but we must also determine how we will act and respond in the months and years ahead. We must determine how we define the future with regard to both ideological goals and practical needs. Among the relevant considerations are the future of academic libraries and librarians, the role(s) they serve, and the future—particularly the preservation—of the work that is digitally collected and published by these libraries and librarians. Buckland (2015) advocates for the library as a partner "instead of simply a resource" (194). Smith (2015) argues that librarians will need to "take a leadership role" in developing preservation guidelines for faculty digital scholarship (xii). As he explains, "[m]ore and more of the scholarly works we will be dealing with in academic libraries will be born digital, locally created, and existing in a wide variety of formats" (xi). This trend will apply not only to digital works by faculty and not only to books and scholarly articles but also to student work, including graduate theses, dissertations, and even undergraduate coursework. An instructor may want a record of student work as an example for other students to model or as an example of the type of work produced under the instructor's teaching of a course; the university may want an example or record for accreditation or recruitment purposes. Access does not mean just current or short-term access. Incorporated into the role of digital publishing within libraries is developing and maintaining preservation plans for the original digital scholarship that is collected, curated, and published.

For authors, two possible, if lofty, definitions of *future* are suggested in articles from the July 2014 special issue of *portal: Libraries and the Academy*, "Imagining the Future of Academic Libraries." Menchaca (2014) envisions an academic library where funding is tied to student achievement. "In this version of tomorrow," he says, "libraries rediscover their core mission, not just as purchasers and stewards of material, but as providers of intellectual property that is differentiated, especially from what is freely available on the Web, in terms of its quality and specific bearing upon students' learning objectives" (354). Miller (2014), building on Johanna Drucker's article in the same issue, explores seven strategies for the "academic research library of *this* university to begin to transform itself into the academic research library of the *next* university" (331). Incorporating some of Miller's strategies, he describes the "future-present library" as one that is both innovative and focused on the mission of education (339), inviting the student "to contribute to building new collections and interpreting existing ones" (341) and both showcasing and celebrating learning by "expanding the audience for student research and creativity within library spaces, both physical and digital, by providing new opportunities to display, exhibit, perform, and share that work" (343).

AT THE LOCAL LEVEL

The authors are part of Washington University's Digital Library Services and Scholarly Publishing unit, which was created to "assist faculty, departments and students with developing digital projects" (Digital Gateway Blog n.d.). The university repository Open Scholarship is managed by the libraries and was created in response to a faculty senate open access resolution adopted in 2011. It states in part, "The Faculty of Washington University in St. Louis is committed to making its scholarship and creative works freely and easily available to the world community. Faculty members are encouraged to seek venues for their works that share this ideal." The resolution also encouraged the provost's office and the libraries "to establish digital repositories and provide author support services to aid the Faculty in providing greater access to their work" (Washington University 2011). While the resolution refers to faculty work and specifically to scholarly articles, student-created materials have increasingly become a focus; since 2009, most theses and dissertations have been submitted in electronic format only and are housed in and accessed through the repository.

A primary role of the digital publishing librarian is that of consultant. She works with subject librarians, who work more directly with faculty and students across the university. A major portion of her position description is to manage the repository, and so she gathers information from subject librarians and other people interested in creating or contributing to a collection and discusses options for administration of the collection, access possibilities for the submissions, potential areas of concern, metadata requirements, and time lines. Many of the materials added to the repository since 2014 have come from these relationships. As the coordinator for the repository, this position is able to recognize patterns across collections, not only in how content contributors want collections to display, but also in how broadly they want collections to be accessible. Many of these consultations end up involving the copyright librarian, who can provide a risk-benefit analysis of copyright questions and make collections open versus restricted.

The copyright librarian at Washington University has a JD and a law license. His primary responsibility is helping faculty, students, and staff address intellectual property issues that connect to research, teaching, and library services. This work includes drafting license language for Open Scholarship repository collections and customizing asset agreements for digital projects. Different collections, of course, raise different issues. The driving considerations when structuring agreements are to secure sufficient permission to distribute the work quickly and efficiently, optimize short- and long-term access to it, and make it available in a variety of formats with clear terms governing downstream use.

The projects the authors take on at the library come from multiple directions and are initiated both internally and externally. None of the projects need necessarily be hosted in a library's repository in order for librarians to be involved. Platforms abound for making student work publicly available, and indeed it is in these contexts that many of the thornier legal, technical, and pedagogical questions arise. In this context, library staff may play a valuable role as what Smith (2015) calls "consulting knowledge managers"—ready to provide service and expertise in fluid situations (xv).

YOUTUBE

In one example, a Washington University lecturer met with library instructional support staff to explore options for hosting student-created videos as part of an introduction to archaeology course she was teaching. After discussing logistics and selecting YouTube as the platform of choice, it was suggested she speak with the copyright librarian to "review rights"—in other words, to hash out any potential legal issues with requiring as a condition of course credit that she or the students upload videos they create using the instructor's account with a shared log-in. From the perspective of the reasonable observer, does the objective conduct of the students and the instructor indicate that there is agreement (a license) for the work to be shared on YouTube? And if such a license exists, can the student revoke her consent?

Does it authorize the instructor to grant the platform a sublicense and agree to its terms of use?

For better or worse, we have scant case law for guidance, at least that which is directly on point (the law on licenses is discussed in a later section). But no matter one's level of certainty, it is possible that a court may in short order adopt a contrary and unexpected position. It is useful, then, to remember that none of the conduct giving rise to permission occurs in a vacuum. Instead, the relevant focus should be on the totality of the circumstances. Librarians are accustomed to balancing different parties' interests, and when discussing how or whether to make student work publicly available, it is wise to consider first what the instructor's and students' reasonable expectations are.

DOCUMENTING FERGUSON

In another example, in August 2014 Washington University Libraries created a digital repository—Documenting Ferguson—that was meant to preserve and make accessible community-generated content that was created following the police killing of eighteen-year-old Michael Brown in Ferguson, Missouri. Part of the project's purpose was to use these collections to create opportunities for engagement and learning. One result was a partnership with a professor teaching a sophomore seminar called Slavery and Memory in American Popular Culture, part of which required students to interview residents of Ferguson and contribute their recorded work to both the Documenting Ferguson repository and the University Archives Oral History Collection. This library-initiated collection naturally involved librarians, especially the copyright librarian, in addressing IP rights and ethical concerns; sharing guidelines, principles, and best practices for conducting oral history interviews; providing technical expertise and equipment; and drafting release forms and other paperwork, all with the underlying intent to promote the seminar's pedagogical objectives.

Structuring the oral histories seminar raised the question of whether the students' proposed activities—that is, conducting interviews with local residents and making the recordings and associated materials available to the public online through the Documenting Ferguson repository and in perpetuity via University Archives—would be subject to IRB oversight.[2] In this and all other such projects, it is the investigator's responsibility to ask whether her and her students' research requires the examination and approval of protocols under the jurisdiction of an IRB. There are certainly resources, both local and more general, available to help instructors sort through the application policies and determine what must be done and when. But timetables can be inefficient and costly when trying to put a course together and have it approved in time for the next semester. Enter the librarian. Here is the value of having professional staff, a copyright librarian who is comfortable working through the regulatory definitions and contemplating whether certain activities fall within IRB purview, well-versed in the exemption and approval process (having facilitated submissions in the past), conversant with the issues on which IRB officers are most keen, and on the ball about unconsidered potentialities (e.g., Does anything change if a student wants to use an interview in a senior thesis?).[3]

THE UNIVERSITY REPOSITORY

In 2014, Washington University's engineering librarian, who had worked with faculty on Open Scholarship collections previously, suggested creating a collection in the repository as an option for the final projects produced in a senior-level mechanical engineering capstone course. Students in the course work in teams to develop a working prototype and are required to produce a "publication that will inform other interested parties of its [the prototype's] existence" (http://openscholarship.wustl.edu/mems411). This publishing component was already required before a repository collection was created, and earlier discussions between the librarian and faculty had focused on the possibility of developing an open-source database for students to publish to. In the meantime, students published to blogs, Facebook, or other personal websites with no concern for the longevity of the work or the stability of the site. Students would often remove their links or posts shortly after the end of the semester, fulfilling the publication requirement of the course but not perhaps the intent behind it—to share research with their peers. Instructors, however, were interested in developing a record of the work produced by the student groups.

The fall 2014 mechanical engineering class was the first one required to publish to Open Scholarship. Students were allowed to either restrict access to on-campus users only or allow wider access with an embargo of up to two years. Although restricted access and embargoes do come with the risk of developing collections that are not completely open access, they have become increasingly common as options in the university repository, particularly for undergraduate collections. Most discussions between the digital publishing and copyright librarians about new repository collections include a conversation about possible access options, sometimes because the collection includes materials from previous years without direct permission from the student/author and sometimes to give students autonomy over how much they share. The engineering librarian explained the access options to the class; however, in the spring, a few students were surprised when their projects or even just the citations were still online and contacted the librarian to ask, "Why is my paper still up?" Addressing these sorts of questions is also a perfect opportunity for subject liaisons or other librarians to discuss larger issues of open access, online identity, and even search engine optimization when appropriate.

The political science collection is a curated collection of papers from an upper-level undergraduate course for which the professor always requires students to complete a group research project comparing one aspect of governance among the same three local municipalities. The librarian proposed the idea of sharing past papers as a way to highlight exemplary student projects and allow groups to build on research completed in previous years. Working with the digital publishing librarian, she developed a repository collection for the course. The professor identified which papers she would like included, and the political science librarian added the material. While the work from previous years was restricted, going forward the professor will request permission from the students whose papers she would like to share. Students will be able to sign a release that will be developed in conjunction with the copyright librarian, and they will be asked to select restricted or unrestricted access; they will be able to refuse to participate if they choose.

The engineering technical writing collection developed in a similar manner as the political science collection and was created with a similar structure. In the case of technical writing, the department had been making examples of "successful student papers" available in binders in the department office. Not only was this method unwieldy and disorganized, but it was also not secure and raised potential Family Educational Rights and Privacy Act (FERPA) issues (also discussed in the next section). Faculty now encourage selected students to submit their papers to the repository instead of requesting permission and posting the papers on behalf of students or asking the library to post the papers. While this might give students more autonomy, however, it is also a barrier—while multiple students have been approached, only one has contacted the engineering librarian about submitting, and the collection is empty, even as a new semester starts.

FOCUS ON THE ISSUES

These examples raise a host of related issues. Before proceeding, though, it should be said that specific facts drive particular outcomes, and while it is possible to outline the general parameters of the relevant law, every situation involves circumstances with the potential to control results in unexpected ways. Rarely are librarians, even those with law degrees and state bar licenses, empowered to give legal advice in their capacity as librarians. The legal information provided in this chapter concerns copyright, contracts, privacy, and other regulations relevant to higher education, and the discussion is general.

Licenses

How does an instructor know whether she has legal justification to make student work available online? Copyright grants each student author the exclusive right to do (and authorize others to do) six things with her work: reproduce it; prepare derivative works based on it; distribute copies of it to the public; perform and display it publicly; and, if it is a sound recording, perform it publicly by means of a digital audio transmission (17 U.S.C. § 106).[4] Making her work publicly accessible, for example, by uploading it to a public channel on YouTube, thus involves one or more of the student's rights under copyright.[5]

Ideally, the instructor has each student's written authorization to make his or her work publicly available; in other words, a valid, binding contract in the form of a license agreement through which the student grants the instructor permission to use the student's (preexisting or prospective) original work of authorship for specific purposes in conjunction with the course. At base, a license is a privilege that protects its grantee from a claim of infringement by the copyright owner. The requisite license need not be broad: Creators may readily retain copyright in their work, with the terms drawn as narrowly as possible.

But it may be lawful—if not necessarily wise—for an instructor to make a student's work publicly available even absent such an express, written grant through the operation of a nonexclusive license. Such a license may be granted orally or implied from conduct (Nimmer and Nimmer 2014, §10.03(a)(7), hereinafter Nimmer 2014). So the individual circumstances of a given course may indeed give rise to the requisite permission to make the student's work publicly available.

Though licenses are often conveyed in contractual terms through written instruments that meet all requisite formalities, the existence of a license and its associated privileges or permission does not necessarily depend on the prior existence of an underlying contract. Instead, a court may imply after the fact the existence of enforceable obligations arising from an agreement (read: contract) between the parties. Different federal courts have different tests to determine whether such a license may be implied-in-fact. The primary focus is on the totality of the parties' conduct—language and behavior demonstrating assent to permit the use of the work in a certain way in exchange for reciprocal obligations by the other party (Nimmer and Dodd 2014, §10.12).

Some courts reduce the inquiry to enumerated criteria; for example, (1) the duration and nature of the parties' prior and existing relationship, (2) past use of written contracts providing that the materials could only be used with permission or the creator's involvement, and (3) whether the creator's conduct indicates that use of the material without consent was permissible (Nimmer and Nimmer 2014, §10.03(a)(7), citing first circuit and fourth circuit cases). Even when applied, these factors are nonexhaustive—though in all cases, the party claiming a license as defense bears the burden of proving its existence and scope.[6] Seeking to classify which principle courts will apply given the facts of a specific case is difficult because of the extent to which the underlying concepts and categories overlap. As the authors of one treatise put it, the "multiplicity of labels obscures the commonality of the issue" (Nimmer and Dodd 2014, §10.12).[7]

It is worth noting a slightly different way in which an implied license may be found to exist—not founded in contract principles but instead as an "incident of copyright" implied from the relationship of the parties and based on the legal doctrine of equitable estoppel.[8] This doctrine—colloquially understood as "fairness"—may be invoked where one party misrepresents material facts and intends that the other will act on the concealment to her detriment (Garner 2014).[9] Its principles are likely to apply only in extreme situations—if, for example, a student knew her instructor would upload a work she created as coursework to YouTube and acquiesced thereto but did so with the concealed intention of bringing an infringement suit against the university after the video was posted (all to bargain for a better grade).

As administrators of the platform and drafters of the governing agreements, librarians are well-positioned to explain why elements of the license are included; what informs their scope; and how the arrangement for distribution, preservation, and sharing of rights serves mutual interests in promoting widespread dissemination of scholarship while preserving control and flexible use by creators. And in providing information, answering questions, and supporting collaborative processes giving rise to the structure of collections, library staff fulfill an educational role that is becoming increasingly central to their identity within the academic enterprise.

Privacy

In addition to its implications for intellectual property, making student work publicly available also requires that those involved consider information privacy—which as used here concerns the "collection, use, and disclosure of personal information" and the "power of commercial and government entities over individual autonomy and decision making" (Solove and Schwartz 2009, 1–2). Librarians have experience with privacy norms in other contexts: protecting the confidentiality of library records, identifying and restricting access to sensitive content in archival materials and special collections, and watching for terms in subscription agreements with vendors that permit collection of user data.[10] Faculty, for their part, may be familiar with FERPA, though fluency varies across departments and disciplines. In most cases, though, it is with FERPA that conversations about privacy and the public web environment often begin (and occasionally end).

FERPA affords students general rights with respect to their education records. Full treatment of the law and its amendments and interpretation is beyond the scope of this chapter (and its authors' knowledge). For present purposes, our focus is on students' FERPA-granted rights to control disclosure of information that can identify them. FERPA protects as confidential any information that a student is required to produce in conjunction with attendance at an educational institution. Such "education records" are materials that—broadly defined and with certain exceptions—contain information directly related to an individual student and that are maintained by the institution or a party acting for it.[11] This definition encompasses a broad range of academic data, such as students' names, identification numbers, e-mail addresses, assignments, exams, photographs, and videos containing their likeness.

But there are instances in which schools can release personally identifiable information contained in a student's record without her prior written consent. One such circumstance involves "directory information," categories of information defined by FERPA whose release generally would not be considered harmful or an invasion of privacy (20 U.S.C. §1232g(a)(5)(A)–(B)). For the directory information exception to apply, an institution must give public notice of the categories it so designates, inform eligible students of their rights, and provide a reasonable period of time during which opt-out requests may be made.

In light of the law, it seems likely that in most cases an instructor would need to obtain written, signed, and dated consent in order to make a student's work publicly available. But FERPA is inapplicable where students themselves release information contained in their education records. That said, delineating what actions implicate FERPA and when a waiver is required is not always clear. Given these uncertainties, it is important to ask what the library's role, if any, should be in this process. FERPA is an explicit practice area of nearly every university general counsel's office. As the exclusive source of legal advice and services for most institutions, its attorneys are responsible for preparing consent forms, ensuring compliance with applicable regulations, and evaluating when waivers are required. But if a library has staff who are experienced in working with university counsel on related matters (e.g., reviewing licenses, collaborating on deposit agreements, establishing policies for course reserves, and evaluating digitization plans), then it is well-positioned to serve as an intermediary in addressing such issues as FERPA and publicly available student work.

It is also useful to consider what it is we are seeking to protect and why. FERPA is not a new law, nor is it intended to be comprehensive with regard to student privacy.[12] Libraries have long been involved in publishing student theses and dissertations without explicit waiver of FERPA rights.[13] Experienced practitioners like Steve McDonald (2014) have spoken of an "implied pedagogical exception" to FERPA's regulatory reach. At the same time, there are circumstances in which a student's privacy interests carry serious personal consequences and in which legal remedies are not well-suited for undoing damage after it has been done.[14]

Without question, there is mounting attention—evident in popular culture and from the increased focus of legislatures—on the responsibilities of educators and institutions with respect to the privacy interests of students.[15] Many universities now employ chief privacy officers. There may be an opportunity for libraries to play an educational role in this space, drawing on their experience with privacy and in related areas. What reasons, for example, are there to be wary of feeding university-generated data to private technology companies? Are there lessons to be learned from higher education's sometimes problematic relationship with the for-profit publishing industry? To what extent should (or can) an instructor control a student's autonomy and decision-making?

Online Identity

Students may be apprehensive about having their work made publicly available "in perpetuity." Sometimes assignments do not turn out well. When academics and librarians talk about building our online presence, do we talk about a presence that includes examples of a potentially flawed undergraduate group research report or engineering design? We warn about controversial tweets or embarrassing photos that can never be completely deleted from the Internet. Do we also need to warn that formal, structured course assignments might exist forever as a form of the new permanent record? Do we discourage experimentation while trying to encourage awareness of scholarly communication issues? Will these students be embarrassed in ten or twenty years by a senior paper, abstract, or group assignment, especially those who seek to become public figures?

In 1999, one of the authors of this chapter produced a project for an upper-level English class as an undergraduate under a different surname; reference to it shows up as a result on Google but only as a top result if one also knows the name of the university—otherwise, it is buried in the results. Is it embarrassing to know that reference to her contribution to English 414's "American Short Stories—A Re/Presentation" can be found online? Sixteen years later, memories of the details of the project and assignment are lost, but the title indicates, obviously, a familiarity with American literature and perhaps an early exploration of digital humanities in the late 1990s. For someone who was a writer and editor before becoming a librarian, this would not be professionally or personally embarrassing; neither would the fact that the project involved the entire class. As a digital publishing and preservation librarian, it is actually more embarrassing to know that it is a dead link: "404 Not Found." The project was on the professor's university website, and the professor is no longer affiliated with the university.[16] The parameters of the assignment and the student work are lost. For today's students and students of the future, a university repository or other university-affiliated website with course-specific collections can prevent that record from being erased following a change in institutional affiliation.

Within an appropriate context, such as that of a university repository, these records can serve as artifacts of a specific time rather than samples of students' potential future contributions as writers, researchers, engineers, and even librarians or lawyers. The institutional brand of the repository also serves as a time stamp for the course—what it was about, what it required, and what was produced in this specific course at this specific time. In these situations, the works assigned are frequently factual—Wikipedia entries, summaries of a course unit, research papers—and their validation requires public consumption. More personal creations—those reflecting beliefs, new ideas, or still-nascent thoughts—depend on a degree of protection from broader scrutiny. Rarely do instructors need to be reminded to keep such works more closely guarded. Students have not been asked to share highly personal work and have not been required to post papers or projects from early in their college careers. Nor have students posted creative work, which might have stricter definitions as to what counts as a previous publication. The examples discussed in this chapter are from upper-level courses for juniors and seniors who will soon apply for jobs or graduate school. Must we be defined by our thoughts and outcomes for a specific undergraduate course far into the future? Will students be more aware of the public eye and access and therefore less willing to experiment or take chances with an assignment, particularly students who aspire to highly visible careers?

Platform Choice

An additional concern beyond issues of copyright and FERPA is that students may be required to create an account on a third-party platform in order to submit an assignment online. This account may be on YouTube (although, in at least one instance at Washington University, students used the instructor's shared log-in credentials), but it could also be in the university's repository, Open Scholarship. Students and anyone else who contributes content to the repository must provide a full name, e-mail address, and optional institutional affiliation and create a password separate from their university credentials. Bepress's (2015) online privacy policy states that it "neither sells nor rents contact information to third parties" and goes into further detail about what information the company will collect or share and under what circumstances. One stated reason for sharing that information—"We transfer information about you if The Berkeley Electronic Press is acquired by or merged with another company"—illustrates the fact that, once individuals share their personal information, even for a specific purpose, they lose control over what happens to those details and where they might end up. Even when we ignore the very relevant and timely discussions of online security and vulnerability to hacking, there is still the question of requiring students to register with a third-party vendor, provide personal information, and create a username and password beyond the credentials used to access library services, all in order to complete a course assignment. Students may opt out of receiving notifications from bepress, including download counts of their work, but unless there is a designated administrator adding materials, students must create personal accounts to add their assignments. Creating an account in most circumstances is not difficult, but deleting one can be onerous.

IMPLICATIONS AND IMPACT

A great many educational activities are now mediated by technologies. Nearly all courses have an online presence. E-book platforms can capture rich reading trails, from the basics of who read what when to increasingly refined levels of granularity. An individual's progress and performance can be charted against a full dossier of directory information and education records—data drawn from applications before the student even sets foot on campus and compiled in alumni records long past his or her graduation. This information can be extraordinarily useful, both practically and pedagogically.[17] But most undergraduates understand and are influenced by very little of it. Should students be given the opportunity to opt out? How likely is the library to win favor by asking the administration whether it has (and follows) clear guidelines on what it will and will not do internally with student data?[18] For even the most perspicacious, it is difficult to grasp how issues converge and relate unless you have dealt with them before. The boundaries of privacy and control over created works and accumulated personal information remain unsettled. Putting expertise in an academic and research library—which, through its tentacles of services, platforms, resources, and physical proximity, confronts a variety of topics, problems, and circumstances—positions staff to recognize and address many of the corollary issues now arising in the higher education ecosystem. In other words, there is realizable value in getting out in front of issues that are coming sideways into the academic enterprise.

While the digital publishing and copyright librarians at Washington University have each met with faculty, offered internal training sessions within the libraries, and coordinated information sessions for students, neither position has worked directly with an undergraduate class to incorporate scholarly communication concepts. That is already beginning to change. The libraries hope to develop rotating pairs of librarians across units, including Scholarly Publishing, to educate specific undergraduate classes about issues related to copyright, intellectual property, and publishing. This effort is in direct response to concerns about the dissemination of unpublished research data contained in senior honors papers and research symposium posters; it also connects directly to the ACRL "Framework" and indicates that instruction is becoming more incorporated into all librarian roles in many academic libraries. The authors are developing lesson plans to address these topics before they become an issue. In order to approach digital publishing projects more methodically, the authors have also developed two checklists to document the process going forward (see the appendix at the end of this chapter). The first is a series of questions for an instructor developing an online assignment in conjunction with the libraries; it may be answered directly by the instructor or used by a librarian as a reference when gathering more information. The second is a checklist for a librarian to follow during the development of an online component of a course. At a minimum, each document helps bring order to a process that often involves multiple issues and parties with sometimes conflicting goals. While these checklists may be applicable to other librarians and other institutions, there are no best practices or universal processes. Libraries can and should be aware of the potential issues and benefits discussed earlier and recognize and build on their roles as educators on such issues as copyright, scholarly communications, and information and digital literacy; facilitators of access platforms; and curators of research.

The collections for undergraduate engineering courses at Washington University grew out of a working relationship between the engineering librarian and the digital publishing librarian on a large collection of faculty-authored computer science technical reports that had been added to the repository. This process gave the engineering librarian more information on the repository and more familiarity with developing collections in it. This familiarity allowed her to offer the repository as a solution for the question "Where do we publish the final mechanical engineering projects?" which then led to the technical writing collection. The copyright librarian was heavily involved in the development of the Documenting Ferguson repository and was well-positioned to facilitate publicly accessible student work built from that content. These are just two examples of collaborations between librarians and between librarians and faculty. The digital publishing and copyright librarians work within a larger digital library services unit involved in faculty-driven digital projects, and the experiences of those library staff have influenced later procedures. None of this work can be done by a single person. Some universities are more centralized than others, but in any scenario, it is important to develop collaborative relationships within the libraries and across the university. And an individual unit within the organization as a whole should have its own house in order before advocating notions of privacy and courses of conduct.

At many libraries, user trust has been hard won. How important is it to act with a purpose to preserve it? There is a compelling opportunity for libraries and universities to set standards in this area and make a transparent attempt to balance the interests of students, faculty, administrators, third-party vendors, and commercial content and service providers. There has probably never been a time when this was not true, but as libraries expand beyond a specific building on campus, it becomes even more important. It may be less "Enter the librarian"—one staff member called on to help with specific elements of a project—and more "Enter the libraries," a university department with specialized staff serving as a resource for undergraduate courses with an online component in addition to undergraduate publishing and scholarly communication discussions.

Students' work online is not an area in which libraries can choose to opt out. Instructors are assigning projects with an online component and will continue to do so whether librarians are involved or not. In some ways, the future brings more work to librarians, but it also brings more integrated work—digital incorporated with instruction, collections, preservation, copyright, and so on. Advances in technology and online publishing will not necessarily make the librarian's job easier, and they certainly will not spell the end of libraries. Instead, they will bring about more reasons for us to be aware of potential issues; know how to work with faculty in addressing these issues in the classroom; become experts in scholarly communications, copyright, and other rights; or at least know where and when to find more information. The work is more local—produced on our campuses by our faculty and students—but its reach is potentially worldwide.

APPENDIX: QUESTIONS FOR LIBRARIANS TO CONSIDER WHEN WORKING WITH UNDERGRADUATE ASSIGNMENTS WITH AN ONLINE PUBLISHING COMPONENT

Checklist 1: Questions to Ask about the Assignment

1. What is the assignment, and what is the online component?
2. Is this a required part of the course, and are the requirements specified in the syllabus? Does the instructor provide the opportunity for students to opt out?
3. Are these individual or group projects?
4. Who will add or upload the content to the distribution platform?

5. What options do the students have for selecting the user-access level, such as restricted to on campus or selecting an embargo?
6. What platform do you want to use? What is the trustworthiness and stability of that platform?
7. Do you have examples of other assignments or undergraduate collections, here or elsewhere, you'd like to model?
8. What do you want to happen with the assignments after the course? Do you want them to be available for future students or other users to access?
9. Can we (the library) talk to the class about copyright, intellectual property, and how this assignment might connect to other research questions?

Checklist 2: For Internal Planning in the Libraries

1. Gather more information about the assignment—from subject liaison, faculty member, and so on. Are there specific considerations based on the discipline or assignment?
2. Look for similar projects to see which policies they have used.
3. Are there policies specific to your university about student rights or publishing student work electronically?
4. Determine rights: copyright law, intellectual property, IRB, FERPA, university policy, specifics of the assignment.
5. Create or find a student license agreement: previously drafted document or model license you may tailor or adapt from the submission form from the institutional repository.
6. Check licensing terms of the platform, especially if it is not one hosted by the library or university.
7. Develop metadata requirements.
8. For a library platform, such as a repository, assign access options (restricted to university or embargo options).
9. Work with the subject librarian to develop the collection, talk with the instructor, try to arrange to talk to the class (or for the subject librarian to talk to class).
10. What are the preservation plans and goals?

These checklists are by no means comprehensive. A number of resources are available online, including the following:

HASTAC. 2012. "Guidelines for Public, Student Class Blogs: Ethics, Legalities, FERPA and More." https://www.hastac.org/blogs/superadmin/2012/11/30/guidelines-public-student-class-blogs-ethics-legalities-ferpa-and-more.

Indiana University, Center for Innovative Teaching and Learning. 2015. "Social Media: Legal and Privacy Concerns, Teaching." http://citl.indiana.edu/resources_files/teaching-resources1/social-media-legal-and-privacy-concerns.php.

McClurklin, Jeffrey W. n.d. "Public." https://github.com/curateteaching/digitalpedagogy/blob/master/keywords/public.md.

NOTES

1. The initial post was June 16, 2015, and responses continued until June 23 on this and related discussions.

2. Institutional Review Boards (IRBs) review and approve protocols for projects that involve use of human participants. For more information on their purpose, history, and areas of oversight, see http://www.hhs.gov/ohrp/assurances/irb.

3. Again, the librarian's entrée here comes with the caveat that he is not positioned or qualified to tell an investigator whether her research is subject to review or falls within an exception.

4. Though U.S. law does not contain explicit reference to "making available" or "communication to the public," such uses are within the exclusive rights provided in Title 17.

5. Student ownership of copyright in scholarly works created for course credit is generally unencumbered by institutional IP policies. But ownership can be more difficult to resolve for works created by an undergraduate in conjunction with sponsored research projects or developed using significant university resources.

6. Other circuits hold that an implied nonexclusive license applies when (1) a person requests the creation of a work, (2) the creator delivers the work to that person, and (3) the creator intends that the person who requested it will copy and distribute it (*Atkins v. Fischer*, 331 F.3d 988, 992 (D.C. Cir. 2003); *I.A.E., Inc. v. Shaver*, 74 F.3d 768, 776 (7th Cir. 1996); *HGI Associates, Inc. v. Wetmore Printing Co.*, 427 F.3d 867, 785 (11th Cir. 2005)). These copyright estoppel factors are most frequently applied in cases involving commissioned works. Some commentators argue that a license is less like a contractual obligation but instead better understood as a property interest. See generally Newman (2013). State law is relevant insofar as it provides applicable canons of contractual construction to resolve questions of formation and interpretation within a given purported contract. The more intrepid reader may further consider issues of state and federal comity, preemption, choice of law, the relevance of conditions precedent, illusory promises or other inadequacies of consideration, distinctions between covenants and conditions, and the type and availability of remedies.

7. See also Lipinski (2013), p. 378 ("The law of implied license in the courts is less than consistent").

8. *Foad Consulting Group, Inc. v. Azzalino*, 270 F.3d 821, 832 (9th Cir. 2001) (Kozinski, J., concurring).

9. *Black's Law Dictionary* defines *equitable estoppel* as "preventing one party from taking unfair advantage of another when, through false language or conduct, the person to be estopped has induced another person to act in a certain way, with the result that the other person has been injured in some way"; "The gravamen of estoppel . . . is misleading and consequent loss" (Garner 2014; *Petrella v. Metro-Goldwyn-Mayer, Inc.*, 134 S. Ct. 1962, 1977 (2014)). For discussion of its application in the context of implied licenses, see Newman (2013), pp. 522–23.

10. "We protect each library user's right to privacy and confidentiality with respect to information sought or received and resources consulted, borrowed, acquired or transmitted" (American Library Association 2008, no. III). See also International Federation of Library Associations (2015), which provides eight recommendations on practice and education. Libraries arguably have a poorer track record in protecting patron privacy when it comes to e-books.

11. FERPA does not define *maintained*. The Supreme Court has interpreted it under its ordinary meaning: "to keep in existence or continuance; preserve; retain." *Owasso Independent School District No. I-011 v. Falvo*, 534 U.S. 426, 432–33 (2002).

12. The act passed in 1974, and though subsequently amended, its substance is largely unchanged. See "Joint Statement" (1974) for discussion of its original purpose, and U.S. Department of Education (2004) for an overview of its amendments.

13. See Ramirez and McMillan (2010), quoting the then-director of the Department of Education's Family Policy Compliance Office from a 1993 statement that an "institution need not obtain a student's signed and dated specific written consent to disclose or publish a thesis in the library or elsewhere at the institution" because of the nature of such works as "research sources for the academic community."

14. Strictly speaking, FERPA provides for the withholding of federal funds to educational institutions that have policies or practices of permitting the release of educational records. Though it imposes burdens and prohibits certain behavior, the law does not create an express cause of action for a private remedy. For example, *DeFeo v. McAboy*, 260 F. Supp. 2d 790, 793 (E.D. Mo. 2003). A student can, however, file a complaint with the Department of Education concerning alleged failure by the institution to comply with the law's regulations. See Family Policy Compliance Office (n.d.).

15. The Student Digital Privacy and Parental Act of 2015 was introduced in the House of Representatives in April 2015. The law, if enacted, would significantly amend FERPA. Forty-six states introduced 182 bills addressing student data privacy in 2015, according to a legislation summary prepared by Data Quality Campaign (2015).

16. "American Short Stories—A Re/Presentation" was an exhibit in *Hypermedia Writing*, no. 2 (Fall 1999) of English Matters, George Mason University, http://englishmatters.gmu.edu/issue2/body_current.html. The link points to http://mason.gmu.edu/~hbergman/414mainpage.htm. The rest of the issue is still available (as of August 20, 2015) at http://englishmatters.gmu.edu.

17. If your university has reliable data on which majors and courses more often lead students to graduate satisfied and on time, should this information influence the curricular paths on which academic counselors advise? Who balances the interests of the various offices at your institution and would be keen to know and act on information furnished through increasingly sophisticated analytics?

18. Most universities have well-established policies on information technology security and its related topics. But it is difficult to find rules or restrictions on internal, institutional use of sophisticatedly mined student data by school officials with legitimate educational interests.

REFERENCES

ACRL Scholarly Communication LISTSERV. 2015. "Question—Student License Agreement." http://lists.ala.org/sympa/info/scholcomm.

American Library Association. 2008. "Code of Ethics of the American Library Association." January 22. http://www.ala.org/advocacy/proethics/codeofethics/codeethics.

Association of College and Research Libraries. 2015. "Framework for Information Literacy for Higher Education." http://www.ala.org/acrl/standards/ilframework.

Bepress. 2015. "Privacy Policy." http://www.bepress.com/privacy.html.

Buckland, Amy. 2015. "More than Consumers: Students as Content Creators." In *Getting the Word Out: Academic Libraries as Scholarly Publishers*, edited by M. Bonn & M. Furlough, 93–202. Chicago: Association of College and Research Libraries.

Data Quality Campaign. 2015. "Student Data Privacy Legislation: What Happened in 2015, and What Is Next?" September 24. http://2pido73em67o3eytaq1cp8au.wpengine.netdna-cdn.com/wp-content/uploads/2016/03/DQC-Student-Data-Laws-2015-Sept23.pdf.

Davis-Kahl, Stephanie. 2012. "Engaging Undergraduates in Scholarly Communication: Outreach Education, and Advocacy." *C&RL News* (April): 212–15, 222.

Digital Gateway Blog. n.d. *Washington University Digital Gateway*. http://digital.wustl.edu.

Drucker, Johanna. 2014. "The University as a Fully Integrated and Distributed Platform: A Vision." *portal: Libraries and the Academy* 14, no. 3: 325–28.

Family Policy Compliance Office. n.d. "Filing a Complaint under the Family Educational Rights and Privacy Act (FERPA)." http://familypolicy.ed.gov/complaint-form.

Garner, Bryan A., ed. 2014. *Black's Law Dictionary*. 10th ed. St. Paul, MN: Thomson Reuters.

Hensley, Merinda Kaye. 2013. "The Poster Session as a Vehicle for Teaching the Scholarly Communication Process." In *Common Ground at the Nexus of Information Literacy and Scholarly Communication*, edited by Stephanie Davis-Kahl and Merinda Kaye Hensley, 113–31. Chicago: Association of College and Research Libraries.

International Federation of Library Associations. 2015. "IFLA Statement on Privacy in the Library Environment." August 14. http://www.ifla.org/files/assets/hq/news/documents/ifla-statement-on-privacy-in-the-library-environment.pdf.

"Joint Statement in Explanation of Buckley/Pell Amendment." 1974. *Congressional Record: Proceedings and Debates of the U.S. Congress* 120, no. 30 (December 13): 39862–66.

Lipinski, Thomas A. 2013. *The Librarian's Legal Companion for Licensing Information Resources and Services*. Chicago: American Library Association.

Lowe, M. Sarah, and Sean M. Stone. 2014. "Getting Superior Work in the IR: A Self-Supporting Loop." Library Staff Publications and Research, Paper 19. http://scholarship.claremont.edu/library_staff/19.

McDonald, Steven J. 2014. "Heads in the Cloud: FERPA, Online Education, and Social Media." Webinar presentation. http://learn.uvm.edu/wordpress_3_4b/wp-content/uploads/Webinar-2014-06-12.pptx.

Menchaca, Frank. 2014. "Start a New Fire: Measuring the Value of Academic Libraries in Undergraduate Learning." *Libraries and the Academy* 14, no. 3: 353–67.

Miller, Kelly E. 2014. "Imagine! On the Future of Teaching and Learning and the Academic Research Library." *portal: Libraries and the Academy* 14, no. 3: 329–51.

Newman, Christopher M. 2013. "A License Is Not a 'Contract Not to Sue': Disentangling Property and Contract in the Law of Copyright Licenses." *Iowa Law Review* 98, no. 3: 1101–62.

Newman, Christopher M. 2014. "'What Exactly Are You Implying?' The Elusive Nature of the Implied Copyright License." *Cardozo Arts & Entertainment Law Journal* 32, no. 3: 501–59.

Nimmer, Melville, and David Nimmer. 2014. *Nimmer on Copyright*, rev. ed. Newark, NJ: Matthew Bender.

Nimmer, Raymond T., and Jeff C. Dodd. 2014. *Modern Licensing Law*. Eagan, MN: Thompson Reuters.

Ramirez, Marisa, and Gail McMillan. 2010. "FERPA and Student Work: Considerations for Electronic Theses and Dissertations." *D-Lib Magazine* 16, nos. 1–2. http://www.dlib.org/dlib/january10/ramirez/01ramirez.html.

Rozum, Betty, Becky Thoms, Scott Bates, and Danielle Barandiaran. 2015. "We Have Only Scratched the Surface: The Role of Student Research in Institutional Repositories." In *The Proceedings of the ACRL 2015 Conference*, 804–12. Portland, OR: Association of College and Research Libraries. http://www.ala.org/acrl/sites/ala.org.acrl/files/content/conferences/confsandpreconfs/2015/Rozum_Thoms_Bates_Barandiaran.pdf.

Smith, Kevin L. 2015. "Preface: The Value of Telling the Future." In *Leading the 21st-Century Academic Library: Successful Strategies for Envisioning and Realizing Preferred Futures*, edited by Bradford Lee Eden, vii–xx. Lanham, MD: Rowman & Littlefield.

Solove, Daniel J., and Paul Schwartz. 2009. *Information Privacy Law*, 3rd ed. New York: Aspen.

Stern, David. 2014. "Student Embargoes within Institutional Repositories: Faculty Early Transparency Concerns." *Journal of Librarianship and Scholarly Communication* 2, no. 2: eP1080.

U.S. Department of Education 2004. "Legislative History of Major FERPA Provisions." February 11. http://www2.ed.gov/policy/gen/guid/fpco/ferpa/leg-history.html.

Washington University. 2011. "Open Access Resolution." May 9. https://facultysenate.wustl.edu/files/2015/05/Open_Access_Resolution-5911-x3fzac.pdf.

———. 2014. "Introduction to Open Scholarship." Fall. Mechanical engineering course description. http://openscholarship.wustl.edu/mems411.

Chapter Four

Paying to Publish

Open Access Author Fees and Libraries' Initiative to Fund Publishing Costs

Stephen M. Arougheti

Free to read but not produce, some open access journals impose author fees to subsidize operational cost; as faculty indicate, these fees are the primary deterrent to publishing in open access journals. In response to popular demand and favorable returns, an increasing number of academic libraries in the United States are paying author fees on behalf of researchers affiliated with their universities, thus supporting the dissemination of scholarship and promoting the benefits of open access. With author funds gaining increasing prominence, librarians are deriving lessons for improving service, utilizing their financial resources, and expanding impact.

Serving as a microcosm of libraries' efforts to affect the role of open access within scholarly publishing, author funds establish an impactful tool for altering and incentivizing the long-term publishing habits of faculty. Beyond allocating funds to subsidize author fees, libraries' cost-minimizing responses to the "pay to publish" model include institutional membership subscriptions and consortium agreements. Libraries demonstrate a history of commitment to disseminating scholarship so that it reaches the greatest audience possible and optimizes research's potential for societal impact. Author funds are a viable strategy to advance the unfettered sharing of knowledge and fulfill a library's commitment to open access.

OPEN ACCESS AS A FUNDAMENTAL RIGHT AND ITS CHALLENGE TO THE TRADITIONAL MODEL OF PUBLISHING

Definitions of *open access* primarily draw on three authoritative documents: the "Bethesda Statement on Open Access Publishing," the "Berlin Declaration on Open Access to Knowledge in the Sciences and Humanities," and the "Budapest Open Access Initiative." Although generally well-understood, what qualifies as open access often contains nuance depending on the organization or individual defining the term. In brief, open access may be thought of as the "free, immediate, online availability of research articles, coupled with the rights to use these articles fully in the digital environment" (Scholarly Publishing and Academic Resources Coalition 2007).

Open access was born from the idea that information deserves to be free—with *free* defined not as absent cost but rather without barriers that prevent access to information and the knowledge it confers. Ideas are most powerful when shared, and too often it is artificial, societally created barriers that restrict the dissemination of information. Arguments supporting open access rely on a dual reasoning rooted first in a principled stance derived from moral standards and second from a functional recognition that shared knowledge inspires innovation.

The ethical argument contends that people deserve "to know what is known" (Willinsky and Alperin 2013, 25). This idea is inspired by an ethical conviction that inherent to research is the indispensable quality of knowledge, giving rise to the moral standard of equity. The functional argument considers the influence of knowledge in strengthening the disenfranchised and helping a society to achieve its potential. Increased access to knowledge "leads to opportunities for equitable economic and social development, and intercultural dialogue, and has the potential to spark innovation" (Swan 2012, 6).

Within the larger context of societal advancement are segments of the population (e.g., doctors, businesses, and scholars) that are implementing open access policies as a strategy for optimizing operations. The Human Genome Project, a monumental undertaking by the government and private sector to sequence three billion letters of the human DNA code, provided incomparable opportunities for geneticists to understand the correlation between genes and disease. Permitting decoded genetic sequences to be publicly available engendered advances in medicine to the benefit of society.

Throughout universities and across the world, open access is becoming ingrained within scholarly publishing. One is hard-pressed to identify a large American university that does not actively foster an open access culture and promote its benefits. As the premier institutions on university campuses for connecting researchers with information, libraries are ideally situated to promote open access throughout the academic community.

For 350 years, scholarly publishing and the peer review process served as a model for the dissemination of research and became the cornerstones of academia (Royal Society 2015). Developments within the scholarly publishing industry created an environment conducive to the growth of open access. An exponential rise in the yearly price of journal subscriptions—serial costs at ARL libraries rose 402 percent from 1986 to 2011—coupled with reduced library budgets necessitated a reevaluation within libraries of collection development methodologies (Association of Research Libraries 2012). Reacting to worsening financial challenges, libraries recognized that open access provided a counterbalance to rising costs.

Beyond the ethical and functional aspects of open access, libraries are struggling to resolve the practical implications of implementing open access. For many individuals, *open access* connotes *free* (i.e., without cost to create), but this assumption is based on false generalizations. When discussing open access, the term *free* relates instead to the individual being able to access content at no cost. As discussed in an FAQ related to the 2002 Budapest Open Access Initiative,

> "Free" is ambiguous. We mean free for readers, not free for producers. We know that open-access literature is not free (without cost) to produce. But that does not foreclose the possibility of making it free of charge (without price) for readers and users. The costs of producing open-access literature are much lower than the costs of producing print literature or toll-access online literature. (Budapest Open Access Initiative 2012a)

As open access is not completely free, it is valuable to understand the structure publishers use to finance their costs. According to the traditional publishing model, publishers financed their business operations by charging to access content; this cost was often assumed by academic libraries to ensure access for the universities' constituencies. Library budgets were strained, and access was denied to those without the financial wherewithal to pay these often-prohibitive charges.

To finance the costs associated with producing open access literature, publishers are imposing charges on authors when their manuscripts are accepted for publication. Charges ranging from hundreds to thousands of dollars often require authors to seek financial assistance from third-party partners. Although financial assistance for authors is available from a variety of sources, most notably from grants, there is a persistent void in monetary support for large portions of the research community. To compensate for this void, librarians are pursuing a variety of alternatives to ensure that authors who wish to make their work available through author fees based open access have the funding necessary to do so. For academic libraries seeking to promote open access throughout the universities, financially subsidizing author charges provides a fulcrum to assert influence within scholarly publishing.

Efforts by libraries to implement a sustainable open access policy model are not without challenges; an assortment of barriers inhibits the advancement of open access. Each barrier represents a real hurdle, whether it is artificial (e.g., permission barriers created by copyright restrictions), economic (e.g., funding the publication of articles in open access journals), or technological (e.g., creating discoverable content in an institutional repository). Modern and innovative approaches are required to surmount these barriers.

IMPEDIMENTS TO A SUSTAINABLE OPEN ACCESS MODEL: RECOGNIZING AND OVERCOMING PERMISSION AND PRICE BARRIERS

Peter Suber, a "champion for open access" and the recipient of the ALA's prestigious L. Ray Patterson Copyright Award for his seminal contribution to scholarly communications, identifies both permission and price barriers as inhibiting the free sharing of research (Suber 2012, 8; Terry 2011). Permission barriers involve the exclusive rights conferred on the copyright holder to restrict others' use of a copyrighted work. Designed to protect the intellectual and financial entitlements of the creator, copyright bestows on its owner a right to allow or restrict access. The permission barrier results in a price barrier when a copyright owner assesses a fee to access a protected work, denying access to those unable to afford the price. Both price barriers and permission barriers limit the utility of information and ideas.

Permission and price barriers not only disadvantage the greater segment of society that is unable to access content but also limit the author's ability to share the value and maximize the impact of their research. Permission barriers restrict others' ability to innovate by denying them the opportunity to reuse or repurpose information. Examples of price barriers' negative effects include unaffordable article processing charges, exorbitant prices for users to access information, and the straining of finite library budgets. Either independently or in confluence, each artificially designed barrier hampers access to content and limits the opportunity for research to achieve optimal potential and influence.

The permission barrier presents itself to many users when published research is not readily available in a library's collection. Universities operate as engines for innovation, but permission barriers limit researchers' ability to repurpose ideas for the development of knowledge. While permission barriers are at times readily evident, for many university constituents, the limitations imposed by price barriers are frequently inconspicuous.

Select scholars who choose to publish in open access journals may confront the obstacle of paying article processing charges. But many university constituents, although they may be aware of such limitations in the abstract, do not often confront such barriers as a regular occurrence when sharing research through the traditional publishing model. The article processing charges for scholars publishing in open access journals are a barrier deterring researchers who are unable to pay the price. Just as price barriers present themselves at the front end of the publishing process in the form of article processing charges, they are likewise recognizable at the back end, when the cost of purchase is unaffordable.

Universities pay a considerable financial price for permission to grant their users access to published research. Librarians are responsible for licensing content from publishers through paid subscriptions to scholarly journals. Due to declining library acquisitions budgets and a precipitous rise in subscription costs, librarians are required to decide which content will be readily available to university constituents and which content will remain hidden behind a paywall. Both article processing fees and library subscription costs present price barriers that impose recognizable limitations on the free sharing of information.

To a certain extent, the term *open access* is a misnomer; it leads people to think in terms of "no cost." On the contrary, while the cost may be concealed from some users, many publishers require authors to pay for the option of making their work openly accessible. Needing to cover costs associated with the peer review process and publishing the article, many publishers assess authors a fee for their work to be available through open access. For many authors, this price barrier dissuades them from offering their work openly. But for authors with a preference for circulating their research through open access, libraries are emerging as a suitable recourse.

The publisher Public Library of Science explains that to "provide Open Access, PLOS uses a business model to offset expenses—including those of peer review management, journal production and online hosting and archiving—by charging a publication fee to the authors, institutions or funders for each article published" (Public Library of Science 2015). A business model predicated on charging authors a prepublication fee rather than institutions a postpublication subscription rate evidences a not-so-subtle paradigm shift in the publication process. This fundamental shift occurs with both the payment structure and, more importantly, the accessibility of the article.

Although both models, to some extent, require libraries to continue financing access to articles, the costs are dramatically reduced as a result of the paradigm shift to library funding being offered prepublication rather than postpublication. Whereas the postpublication model requires libraries to subsidize access to journal content by paying annual subscription costs in perpetuity, the prepublication model requires a single payment to permit the deposit of the article on an open access platform. More importantly, research submitted through the prepublication model results in articles that are no longer restricted to subscribers but rather immediately and freely available to all.

The postpublication business model requires scholars to submit their research to a journal, which oversees the peer review process. Once the article is approved for publication, the author's involvement largely ceases. Authors often cede copyright control under this model, granting the publisher exclusive rights to control and disseminate the article. Granting exclusive rights often results in publishers selling access at a prohibitive price, requiring libraries to assume the costs in order to guarantee their constituents access to the content. Of the portion of academic libraries' budgets reserved for the acquisition of information resources, half is allocated for electronic current serial subscriptions (U.S. Department of Education 2014). Financially, the postpublication business model serves publishers well by generating lucrative profits. As reported in November 2012 by the International Association of Scientific, Technical, and Medical Publishers (a collection of 120 members in 21 countries who collectively publish 66 percent of global journal articles), the "annual revenues generated from English-language STM journal publishing are estimated at about $9.4 billion in 2011 (up from $8 billion in 2008), within a broader STM information publishing market worth some $23.5 billion" (Ware and Mabe 2012). This financial boon for publishers occurred at the expense of libraries, as exponentially rising costs depleted acquisition budgets.

Authors create artificial permission and price barriers when they relinquish their intellectual property rights and grant a publisher the exclusive right to control distribution of their work. In addition to such artificial barriers, other recurring access barriers are societal in nature.[1] Peter Suber identifies four societally infused barriers that inhibit universal access to information: censorship, language barriers (a work not translated beyond the published language), accessibility for the disabled, and technological hurdles (Suber 2012, 26–27). While considerable efforts by governments, businesses, and nonprofit organizations to overcome societal barriers are proving successful, librarians and the open access movement are primarily focused on the artificial barriers imposed by authors and publishers.

Understandably or not, publishing companies prioritize profit margins above altruistic concerns for authors and society. To improve public access to published research, academic librarians are actively pursuing strategies to persuade authors to preserve the intellectual property rights to their work. To transform the traditional publishing model to a sustainable open access business model, authors and librarians will need to provide the impetus for change. Librarians have been the primary vanguard for the transformation to open access. As champions for the egalitarian principles encapsulated in open access, librarians and global advocates across disciplines and national-ities continue to pursue sustainable publishing business models.

Under either publishing model, an economic framework that can sustain the costs associated with the peer review process is necessary. The 2011 "PEER Economics Report," which was devised to study, among other issues, publishers' cost structure, states,

> Reputation is a critical source of competitive advantage in scholarly publish-ing. Robustness of selection and the involvement of prestigious reviewers drives reputation. At the same time, peer review is a costly activity that can be standardized only marginally. Even if it is outsourced and rarely remunerated the publisher still has to bear the cost of managing peer review. Such costs correlate with the rejection rate of the journals, to the number of reviewers per manuscript and to the number of rounds of review. (Centro ASK, Università Bocconi 2011, 39)

Premier journals maintain a respected reputation because of their selective peer review process. In general, it is true that the more prestigious a journal's reputation, the higher its operational costs and the greater the need to assess higher rates to sustain operations.

Because open access journal publishers do not charge libraries and other purchasing institutions the subscription costs necessary to subsidize peer review expenses, they must pursue other channels—including imposing arti-cle processing charges on authors—to recoup their overhead. By doing so, they transfer remittance from the back end to the front end of the publication cycle—from libraries to authors. Total article processing charges, determined by competitive considerations, market conditions, journal impact factor, arti-cle type, journal function, editorial processes, and technical features, can range between five hundred and five thousand dollars. Because article pro-cessing charges can be expensive, third-party support is needed to subsidize their payment.

Many scholars receiving financial support for their research through grants are able to apply the awarded funding toward paying article processing charges. As the primary funder of research at American universities, the federal government requires that publicly funded research be freely available online; this mandate increases opportunities for researchers to receive the financial support necessary to publish in open access journals.[2] Nevertheless, not all researchers who desire to publish in open access journals are able to obtain financing to subsidize article processing charges. At times, the great-est obstacle to research being freely available is a lack of impetus from authors to take action. Realizing an avenue to advance open access, librarians are providing the necessary motivation by allocating portions of their budgets to pay the article processing charges for researchers affiliated with their universities. Library subsidization of article processing charges through author funds helps guarantee that researchers who want their work freely available have the means to do so.

For academic libraries, the "old model" of traditional publishing provided a reliable stream of quality information that was vetted through the peer review process. Despite these benefits, the exponentially rising cost of bundled journal subscriptions has become increasingly untenable. Michael Eisen notes, "Every year universities, governments and other organizations spend in excess of $10 billion dollars to buy back access to papers their researchers gave to journals for free, while most teachers, students, health care providers and members of the public are left out in the cold" (2013).

Beyond these practical implications, many librarians possess an ideological commitment to a philosophy of egalitarianism—as eloquently stated by the American Library Association motto adopted in 1892 and reinstated by the ALA Council in 1988, "The best reading, for the largest number, at the least cost" (American Library Association 1988). Along with the technological advances associated with the proliferation of digital publishing and the growing ubiquity of the Internet, the increasing resolve of researchers, universities, libraries, publishers, and nonprofits provides an opportunity to shift the publishing industry to a "new model." Relying on article processing charges, the new model enables research once restricted by paywalls to be freely available to the greater public.

During the nascent stages of open access, librarians anticipated a variety of benefits, including a solution to the exponentially rising cost of serials subscriptions. Although the potential persists for open access to reduce prices over the long term, libraries remain reliant on bundled subscription packages. A study of the availability and growth of open access (charting trends within a pair of publication ranges from 1998 to 2006 and 2005 to 2010) reveals that open access publications account for only 23.8 percent of the market, with 1 percent annual growth (Gargouri et al. 2012). Despite historical trends indicating limited growth of open access, many still predict that the predominance of open access journals is inevitable: "Gold OA could account for 50 percent of the scholarly journal articles sometime between 2017 and 2021" (Lewis 2012). The adoption by companies like Elsevier and Springer of financially stable open access policies sustained by article processing charges is indicative of the continued proliferation of open access journals in the marketplace. If open access journals are to reduce the impact of subscription costs on library budgets, then investing in such supportive strategies as author funds may be a sensible endeavor to effect change.

CONSTRUCTING AN OPEN ACCESS MODEL TO ACCOUNT FOR FACULTY'S MOTIVATING FACTORS

Academic libraries operate as an ancillary institution within universities and are increasingly redefining their role within an evolving university landscape. Library support for the university involves a core mission of facilitating faculty research efforts. To achieve this mission, librarians are optimizing the value of open access to help meet the needs of researchers. Influencing faculty publishing habits to support open access involves aligning library services and policy with their professional interests. Appreciating the factors that motivate the publishing habits of faculty involves recognizing, first, the expectations and requirements of faculty to publish their research and, second, how open access can best be positioned to serve their interests.

Librarians embed with faculty throughout the university to better appreciate their research and publishing motives. Rather than seeking involvement at the end of the process, when faculty are submitting their manuscripts to journals, librarians are becoming active participants early in the research process, for example, by assisting with grant writing and data curation. "Embedded librarianship is a distinctive innovation that moves the librarians out of libraries and creates a new model of library and information work. It emphasizes the importance of forming a strong working relationship between the librarian and a group or team of people who need the librarian's information expertise" (Shumaker 2012, 4). As a result, librarians are better positioned to appreciate the factors motivating faculty publishing and influence how research is disseminated.

Despite many researchers' positive opinion of open access and its benefits, it is not the primary factor most scholars consider when determining where to publish. Concerns pertaining to a journal's reputation, proficiency, openness of peer review process, indexing in disciplinary databases, and impact factor were most important in determining where to publish (Bird 2010). Librarian intentions to persuade faculty to publish in open access journals require consideration of these predominant concerns.

Although increased discoverability and an upsurge in an article's impact factor are among the more well-perceived benefits of open access for researchers, there is contention about the correlation between open access and impact factor. In an effort to ascertain the extent of this possible correlation, the Scholarly Publishing and Academic Research Coalition Europe identified seventy studies designed to evaluate the connection between open access and impact factor by evaluating citation metrics (Scholarly Publishing and Academic Research Coalition Europe 2015). Implementing different methodology and data, forty-six studies found a positive correlation, seventeen indicated no advantage related to increasing citation totals, and seven were deemed to be inconclusive or failed to establish a significant increase. Beyond these conclusions regarding their own impact factors, researchers should also consider additional advantages, including the personal benefit of gaining greater access to the data and experience of others. The opportunity to expand and build on the studies of others allows researchers to broaden their own research to achieve greater results.

Despite the benefits of open access, there remain significant deterrents that inhibit faculty willingness to publish in open access journals. The primary factor deterring researchers from publishing in open access journals is the cost of article processing (Dallmeier-Tiessen et al. 2011). A smaller percentage of researchers indicate a variety of other barriers, including accessibility, a perception of inferior quality, unawareness of open access journals relevant to their areas of study, or simply established habits.

Because authors emphasize journal impact factor when determining where to submit their research, publishers assess higher article processing charges for publication in more influential journals with higher ISI impact factor rankings (Solomon and Bjork 2012). These higher-ranked journals are frequently associated with well-funded disciplines of study whose authors are often recipients of grants that can be used to aid in payment of article processing charges (Solomon and Bjork 2012). For those in the research community able to obtain outside funding, the lack of a financial deterrent provides an open avenue to publication in open access journals.

Faculty in disciplines not receiving sufficient funding from outside sources, along with less-established researchers (e.g., adjuncts, postdocs, or graduate students), comprise a valuable portion of the university constituency that would be well served by receiving support in the form of funding from the library. Libraries offering author funds provide an effective and advantageous resource for researchers who would otherwise be unable to afford the cost of article processing.

SUPPORTING THE "PAY TO PUBLISH" MODEL: LIBRARIES AND THE CREATION OF AUTHOR FUNDS

With an agenda to promote and expand open access, academic libraries employ creative strategies to market their benefits and encourage researchers within the university to publish in open access journals. For a diversity of reasons, including an appreciation for the ethical and functional imperative and improving opportunities associated with career advancement, many researchers readily publish in open access journals. In an effort to better appreciate the motives and perceptions of researchers regarding open access, an international and multidisciplinary study solicited feedback from 53,890 individuals, 46,006 of whom identified as active researchers and 38,358 of whom "published at least one peer-reviewed research article in the last five years" (Dallmeier-Tiessen et al. 2011). The results of the study demonstrate substantial support for open access among respondents and highlight barriers (some resulting from a misperception of open access) that prevent their publishing in open access journals.

For those with a history of publishing in open access journals, there is, as expected, a high level of support for the intrinsic benefits of open access, with 89 percent of respondents believing open access directly benefits their field of study. For researchers without experience in open access publishing, 39 percent (the largest grouping) identify concerns with funding as the primary impediment to publishing in open access journals. Academic libraries overcome the deterrent of financial obstacles for many researchers by establishing author funds to subsidize the article processing charges involved with publishing in open access journals. Designed in part as a marketing tool to promote open access, author funds help libraries reach out to the universities' researchers and incentivize faculty to publish in open access journals.

For many researchers, grants and endowments provide financial support to pay article processing charges. The federal government's effort to promote open access by mandating that federally funded research and data be immediately and freely available improved the ability of researchers to receive financial assistance to publish their research in open access journals. Still, a void exists for many authors who are unable to afford these costs or receive subsidies through grant funding. Academic libraries have compensated for this void by establishing author funds in the hope that this would encourage faculty to publish in open access journals. Demonstrating the dramatic rise of open access journals and efforts by libraries to support them, the number of established author funds in universities rose from seventeen in 2011 to fifty-five in 2014 (Scholarly Publishing and Academic Resources Coalition 2011, 2014).

While the specifics of each author fund vary subtly by institution—with relevant factors including the total pool of money, the source of funding, reimbursement eligibility requirements, and cap levels on a per-article basis—the overall approach is largely similar. The university operates a total annual allotment of funds (often in the range of $25,000 to $50,000) and reimburses authors for the cost of publishing within the limits of a cap after a manuscript passes the peer review process. Article processing charges range from several hundred dollars to upward of five thousand dollars. Recognizing the limitations of finite resources, it is necessary to determine parameters for the author fund to optimize impact in accordance with the library's objective. Requiring an understanding of the fund's objective, be it to change faculty publishing habits or to increase the amount of scholarship that is freely available, knowing the issues that are important to the library is essential in devising a well-tailored policy.

A crucial component of establishing an author fund is evaluating whether the service is fulfilling its objective and receiving a return on investment. If the objective is marketing and incentivizing faculty to publish in open access journals, then success may be determined based on the number of faculty who are aided by the author fund. If the objective is to provide the public with access to meaningful research, then a library may need to be selective in deciding which articles receive funding, judging them on merit and anticipated value to scholarship in the field. Altmetrics can be used to analyze the impact of articles supported by an author fund and thus its overall success in funding worthwhile research, but doing so requires time for the significance of articles to be adequately determined.

Questioning the value of today's saturated cache of research, Barbara Fister (2015) contends that the "publish or perish" model within academia incentivizes faculty to publish frantically for the benefit of job security: "Why does everyone have to publish so much? Are we really advancing knowledge, or is this some weirdly inflated reputational currency that is running out of control? I'm not saying we should quit doing research, but maybe we should be a little more selective about what we feel needs to be part of the record." Historically, it was assumed that the peer review process and the expert critical analysis accorded to each article provided the necessary verification of the value of an author's research. At times, however, the publishing industry—an increasingly lucrative business—is undermining the integrity of the peer review process in an effort to improve profits. While it is perhaps impractical for librarians to assess the merit of research prior to funding, it behooves them to be discerning in evaluating which requests will be funded based on a quantitative analysis of the accepting journal's ranking and influence.

Increased demand from researchers for their publications to be readily and freely available has fostered an environment allowing for the proliferation of open access journals in the marketplace. By the law of supply and demand, publishers have responded by increasing the opportunities for authors to make their work available through open access. Seeking a sustainable business model for open access journals, many publishers adopted article processing charges to address the costs associated with the peer review process. Inevitably, the prospect of financial gain attracted parties willing to exploit individuals' eagerness to publish in open access journals. Termed predatory publishers, these "low quality, fly by night operations" behave contrary to the core mission of academic publishers to disseminate knowledge and "exist for the sole purpose of profit" (Berger and Cirasella 2015, 132). Predatory publishers increased 31 percent from 2014 to 2015, for a total of 693 predatory publishers (Beall 2015).

Article processing charges and the pursuit of profit are not themselves indicators of predatory publishing. Often the process for determining the merit of a journal and the legitimacy of a publisher's intentions is not well delineated. The Committee on Publication Ethics has identified a code of conduct for publishers enumerating criteria related to transparency, editorial independence, appreciation for the role of peer review, and clear communication of policy (Committee on Publication Ethics n.d.).

Predatory publishers are a single contributor to an evolving malaise within the publishing industry. The pursuit of financial gain, including "fast-tracking" the extensive and slow peer review process for parties who are willing to pay, runs contrary to the traditional objective of publishers to guarantee the integrity of research. John Bohannon, an editor for *Scientific Reports*, resigned in public protest over expedited peer review, arguing that "it sets up a two-tiered system and instead of the best science being published in a timely fashion it will further shift the balance to well-funded labs and groups" (Bohannon 2015). Expedited peer review is symptomatic of a trend by which profit is prioritized above advancing scholarship.

Criticism of diluted publishing standards extends beyond the well-exposed practices of predatory publishers and is not exclusive to open access journals. In his article *Does Peer Review Do More Harm than Good?* Luc Rinaldi (2015) quotes psychology professor Alex Holcombe of the University of Sydney on the controversial and hazardous practice of fast-tracking: "What appears in scientific journals is determined not by money, but rather the merit of the actual science. . . . [F]ast-tracking is a formula for taking shortcuts—such tight timelines may force reviewers and editors to make decisions without proper scrutiny." Researchers are too often willing to pay this cost in order to add an additional publication to their curriculum vitae.

Librarians are discovering that demand from faculty authors for financial support to publish in open access journals frequently exceeds the funds available. While this imbalance signifies the successful proliferation of the open access movement in academia, it also mandates that librarians judiciously assess the purposes and objectives of their author funds; consider which university constituents are eligible to receive funding; establish the source of funds and how much money each author is permitted to apply for; determine which publishers and journals are approved for reimbursement; and establish who within the library is responsible for promoting the service throughout the university. Sustainability of the author fund demands not only a careful analysis of the program's objectives and parameters prior to implementation but also the flexibility to reevaluate them on a continuing basis.

APPRAISING ALTERNATIVE STRATEGIES FOR FUNDING OPEN ACCESS: A METHODOLOGY FOR LOWERING THE COST STRUCTURE ASSOCIATED WITH THE "PAY TO PUBLISH" MODEL

Establishing the extent of author funding is essential for ensuring that the impact of investment in open access is maximized. Formulating a policy and refining current arrangements, while vital to the sustainability of an author fund, is only a single strategy designed to maximize potential. Many proponents of open access argue that, rather than conforming to the business model implemented by publishers and financing article processing charges, libraries should proactively partner with other institutions in order to reduce prices in the marketplace. Libraries have implemented a pair of notable strategies to diminish pay-to-publish costs: the development of consortia and using institutional membership subscriptions as leverage to negotiate discounted costs.

Strategies to reduce the costs of open access publishing, including institutional memberships with publishers and consortium discounts, endeavor to minimize article processing charges. Institutional memberships operate as agreements between a university and a publisher in which the institution pays a fixed annual cost, predetermined by the size of the institution and the anticipated number of submitted articles, and authors affiliated with the university receive a discounted rate on the article processing charge to make their work available through open access.

While this sort of arrangement presents immediate benefits to the publisher and the university by reducing administrative costs, there are concerns that providing selective preference to larger publishers at the expense of smaller companies could reduce competition in the marketplace over the long term. According to the Open Access Scholarly Publishers Association,

> membership schemes that are based on up-front commitments for a university to publish a particular volume of content with a given publisher can potentially reduce competition within the Open Access ecosystem, making it difficult for smaller publishers to compete on a level playing field with larger publishers, who are inherently better positioned to negotiate individual deals with universities. (Sutton 2013)

Consortium membership offers economic advantages by providing members increased leverage to negotiate terms. Promoting standardization and equal access to resources for a broad coalition of members reduces costs for authors. Strengthened bargaining power allows the consortium to advance user rights beyond the abilities of an individual library. Collective bargaining improves return on investment for each member of a consortium and equalizes access to resources for smaller partners. A collection of libraries in the University of Colorado system proved both the economic and qualitative benefits of a cooperative arrangement when they recorded a return on investment of 715 percent for Auraria (the consortium's smaller partner) and 56 percent for Boulder (Pan and Fong 2010, 191).

Using a model of collective bargaining and encompassing three thousand libraries from forty-two countries, SCOAP[3] centralizes the payment to publishers of article processing charges for the open access dissemination of particle physics research (Sponsoring Consortium for Open Access Publishing in Particle Physics 2015). SCOAP[3] notes its mission and benefits: "The SCOAP[3] vision for tomorrow is that funding bodies and libraries worldwide would federate in a consortium that will pay centrally for the peer-review and other editorial services, through a re-direction of funds currently used for journal subscriptions, and, as a consequence, articles will be free to read for everyone" (Gentil-Beccot, Mele, and Vigen 2010, 45). Although far from a panacea, institutional memberships and consortia provide libraries additional resources to support open access journals, lowering the costs of article processing charges and improving efficiency.

CONCLUSION

Although widely supported by proponents, open access journals are not without their detractors. Misgivings about open access journals focus in part on the unsustainability of the author-pay model. With a limited percentage of researchers supported by grant funding to publish in open access journals, questions as to where the necessary funding will originate are of concern, and libraries are challenged to address these financial demands with reduced budgets. Without a significant shift to a greater proportion of research being available open access, libraries are in the unenviable position of supporting access to research through reimbursement of article processing charges while continuing to pay exorbitant subscription prices. Libraries must consider that, although some open access journals require the payment of article processing charges, many others do not. According to the *Directory of Open Access Journals*, though "nearly two-thirds of OA journals . . . do not charge authors, a recent study indicates that 50% of OA articles have been published after the author paid a fee" (Fruin and Rascoe 2014, 240). Despite opportunities to publish in open access journals without cost, researchers continue to submit to journals that charge author fees for reasons related to prestige and impact factor.

Given the value of supporting open access journals by establishing author funds, institutions cannot view their actions as insulated from the decisions of other universities. Assessing the benefits of an author fund requires determining the rates of article processing charges and such charges are contingent on the state of the publishing marketplace. As the rates of article processing charges rise, the economic burdens increasingly exceed the benefits. When a university acts unilaterally, the cost of open access can outweigh the benefits; only once aggressive support for open access publishing in lieu of subscriptions is ubiquitous in the research community will the full benefits be realized. Uniform, worldwide adoption would represent significant savings for universities if the current average article processing charges remain consistent at an average of $906. However, "[u]niversities adopting an all 'gold' mode of publishing their research results when the rest of the research community retain the current model (a mix of open access and subscription publishing) would find costs outweighing benefits in all cases" (Swan and Houghton 2012, 13). For open access journals to supplant the subscription model, all libraries must make a concerted effort to shift the approach they take to supporting scholarly publishing.

NOTES

1. For example, the digital divide in the United States creates a dichotomy by which "35 percent of schools across the nation still lack access to fiber networks capable of delivering the advanced broadband required to support today's digital-learning tools" (Federal Communications Commission 2015). For those lacking the technological infrastructure necessary to utilize the Internet for access to information, a barrier is created that inhibits growth.
2. "Colleges and universities are the primary performers of basic research, with the federal government being the largest funding source. In FY2008, the federal government provided approximately 60% of an estimated $51.9 billion of research and development funds expended by academic institutions" (Matthews 2012).

REFERENCES

American Library Association. 1988. "Mission & Priorities." http://www.ala.org/aboutala/missionpriorities.
Arlitsch, Kenning, and Patrick S. O'Brien. 2012. "Invisible Institutional Repositories: Addressing the Low Indexing Ratios of IRs in Google Scholar." *Library Hi Tech* 30, no. 1: 60–81.
Association of Research Libraries. 2012. "Monograph & Serial Costs in ARL Libraries, 1986–2011." http://www.arl.org/storage/documents/monograph-serial-costs.pdf.
Beall, Jeffrey. 2015. "Beall's List of Predatory Publishers 2015." *Scholarly Open Access: Critical Analysis of Scholarly Open-Access Publishing.* http://scholarlyoa.com/2015/01/02/bealls-list-of-predatory-publishers-2015.
Berger, Monica, and Jill Cirasella. 2015. "Beyond Beall's List: Better Understanding Predatory Publishers." *College and Research Libraries News* 76, no. 3: 132–35.
Bird, Claire. 2010. "Continued Adventures in Open Access: 2009 Perspective." *Learned Publishing* 23, no. 2: 107–16.
Bjork, Bo-Christer, Mikael Laakso, Patrik Welling, and Patrik Paetau. 2014. "Anatomy of Green Open Access." *Journal of the Association for Information Science and Technology* 65, no. 2: 237–50.
Bohannon, John. 2015. "Editor Quits Journal over Pay-for-Expedited Peer-Review Offer." *Science*, July 15, 2015. http://news.sciencemag.org/scientific-community/2015/03/editor-quits-journal-over-pay-expedited-peer-review-offer-updated.
Budapest Open Access Initiative. 2012a. "Frequently Asked Questions." http://legacy.earlham.edu/~peters/fos/boaifaq.htm.

————. 2012b. "Ten Years on from the Budapest Open Access Initiative: Setting the Default to Open." http://www.budapestopenaccessinitiative.org/boai-10-recommendations.

Centro ASK, Università Bocconi. 2011. "PEER Economics Report." Milan: European Union. http://www.peerproject.eu/fileadmin/media/reports/PEER_Economics_Report.pdf.

Committee on Publication Ethics. n.d. "Code of Conduct for Journal Publishers." http://publicationethics.org/files/Code%20of%20conduct%20for%20publishers%20FINAL_1_0.pdf.

Dallmeier-Tiessen, Suenje, Robert Darby, Bettina Goerner, Jenni Hyppoelae, Peter Igo-Kemenes, Deborah Kahn, Simon Lambert, Anja Lengenfelder, Chris Leonard, Salvatore Mele, Malgorzata Nowicka, Panayiota Polydoratou, David Ross, Sergio Ruiz-Perez, Ralf Schimmer, Mark Swaisland, and Wim van der Stelt. 2011. "Highlights from the SOAP Project Survey: What Scientists Think about Open Access Publishing." *arXiv.org.* http://arxiv.org/ftp/arxiv/papers/1101/1101.5260.pdf.

Eisen, Michael. 2013. "The Past, Present and Future of Scholarly Publishing." *It Is NOT Junk.* http://www.michaeleisen.org/blog/?p=1346.

Elsevier. 2015a. "Journal Specific Embargo Periods 2015." http://www.elsevier.com/data/assets/pdf_file/0005/78476/external-embargo-list.pdf.

————. 2015b. "Pricing Policy." http://www.elsevier.com/about/policies/pricing-policy.

Fister, Barbara. 2015. "Public Research. Not Too Much." *Inside Higher Ed.* https://www.insidehighered.com/blogs/library-babel-fish/publish-research-not-too-much.

Fruin, Christine, and Fred Rascoe. 2014. "Funding Open Access Journal Publishing: Article Processing Charges." *College & Research Libraries News* 75, no. 5: 240–43.

Gargouri, Yassine, Vincent Larivière, Yves Gingras, Les Carr, and Stevan Harnad. 2012. "Green and Gold Open Access Percentages and Growth, by Discipline." *arXiv.org.* http://arxiv.org/abs/1206.3664.

Gentil-Beccot, Anne, Salvatore Mele, and Jens Vigen. 2010. "SCOAP3: A New Publishing Model for High-Energy Physics." In *Towards Open Access Scholarship: Selected Papers from the Berlin 6 Conference,* edited by Cornelius Puschmann and D. A. Stein, 41–50. Dusseldorf, Germany: Dusseldorf University Press.

Lewis, David W. 2012. "The Inevitability of Open Access." *College & Research Libraries* 73, no. 5: 493–506.

Matthews, Christine M. 2012. *Federal Support for Academic Research.* Washington, DC: Congressional Research Service.

Open Society Institute. 2002. *Read the Budapest Open Access Initiative.* http://www.budapestopenaccessinitiative.org/read.

Pan, Denise, and Yem Fong. 2010. "Return on Investment for Collaborative Collection Development: A Cost-Benefit Evaluation of Consortia Purchasing." *Collaborative Librarianship* 2, no. 4: 183–92.

Public Library of Science. 2015. "Publication Fees." https://www.plos.org/publications/publication-fees.

Rinaldi, Luc. 2015. "Does Peer Review Do More Harm than Good?" *Maclean's.* http://www.macleans.ca/news/canada/does-peer-review-do-more-harm-than-good.

The Royal Society. 2015. "350 Years of Scientific Publishing." https://royalsociety.org/publishing350.

Salo, Dorothea. 2008. "Innkeeper at the Roach Motel." *Library Trends* 57, no. 2: 98–123.

Scholarly Publishing and Academic Resources Coalition. 2007. "Open Access." http://www.sparc.arl.org/issues/open-access.

————. 2011. "SPARC." http://www.sparc.arl.org/sites/default/files/fundsinaction.pdf.

————. 2014. "Open Access Funds in Action." http://www.sparc.arl.org/sites/default/files/OA%20Funds%20in%20Action%20attachment%202014%20%281%29.pdf.

Scholarly Publishing and Academic Research Coalition Europe. 2015. "The Open Access Citation Advantage Service." http://sparceurope.org/oaca.

Shumaker, David. 2012. *The Embedded Librarian: Innovative Strategies for Taking Knowledge Where It's Needed.* Medford, NJ: Information Today.

Solomon, David J., and Bo-Christer Bjork. 2012. "Publication Fees in Open Access Publishing: Sources of Funding and Factors Influencing Choice of Journal." *Journal of the American Society for Information Science and Technology* 63, no. 1: 98–107.

Sponsoring Consortium for Open Access Publishing in Particle Physics. 2015. "SCOAP3 Facts and Figures." http://scoap3.org/files/Facts-Figures1.pdf.

Suber, Peter. 2012. *Open Access.* Cambridge, MA: MIT Press.

Sutton, Caroline. 2013. "OASPA's Response to Request for Input—Finch Report: Survey of Progress, 14 June 2013." http://oaspa.org/oaspas-response-to-request-for-input-finch-report-survey-of-progress.

Swan, Alma. 2012. "Policy Guidelines for the Development and Promotion of Open Access." *United Nations Educational, Scientific and Cultural Organization.* http://unesdoc.unesco.org/images/0021/002158/215863e.pdf.

Swan, Alma, and John Houghton. 2012. "Going for Gold? The Costs and Benefits of Gold Open Access for UK Research Institutions: Further Economic Modelling." *UK Open Access Implementation Group.* http://repository.jisc.ac.uk/610.

Terry, Jennifer. 2011. "ALA Announces 2011 Winner of L. Ray Patterson Copyright Award." *ALA News.* http://www.ala.org/news/press-releases/2011/04/ala-announces-2011-winner-l-ray-patterson-copyright-award.

U.S. Department of Education, National Center for Education Statistics. 2014. "Academic Libraries: 2012 First Look." http://nces.ed.gov/pubs2014/2014038.pdf.

Ware, Mark, and Michael Mabe. 2012. *The STM Report: An Overview of Scientific and Scholarly Journal Publishing.* The Hague: International Association of Scientific, Technical, and Medical Publishers. http://www.stm-assoc.org/2012_12_11_STM_Report_2012.pdf.

Willinsky, John, and Juan Pablo Alperin. 2013. "The Academic Ethics of Open Access to Research and Scholarship." In *Common Ground at the Nexus of Information Literacy and Scholarly Communication*, edited by Stephanie Davis-Kahl and Merinda Kaye Hensley, 25–33. Chicago: Association of College & Research Libraries.

Xia, Jingfeng, Sarah B. Gilchrist, Nathaniel X. P. Smith, Justin A. Kingery, Jennifer R. Radecki, Marcia L. Wilhelm, Keith C. Harrison, Michael L. Ashby, and Alyson J. Mahn. 2012. "A Review of Open Access Self-Archiving Mandate Policies." *Libraries and the Academy* 12, no. 1: 85–102.

Chapter Five

Library Expertise Driving Pedagogical Innovation

The Role of Libraries in Bringing "Open" to the Classroom and to the World

William M. Cross

"University Bookstore Was Just Robbed of $20,000. Culprit Was Seen Taking a Sweatshirt and Three Textbooks."

AN ARMS RACE IN THE COLLEGE BOOKSTORE

A version of this fake news headline makes the rounds every year on social media as new students grapple with the high cost of textbooks (see figure 5.1). This sticker shock stems from textbook prices that have risen more than 82 percent since 2002—triple the rate of inflation—and a staggering 800 percent in the past thirty years (U.S. Government Accountability Office 2013, 6). This rise, which eclipses comparable bubbles in medical services and housing prices, means that current students can expect to spend an average of $1,200 on textbooks each year (U.S. PIRG Education Fund and the Student PIRGS 2014). These numbers reflect a broken marketplace where a small group of for-profit publishers control 80 percent of the market, and purchasing decisions are made by faculty while students pick up the bill (Senack 2015).

On top of their regular course loads, new college students are forced to take a crash course in applied textbook research; the National Association of College Stores estimates that 82 percent of students research their course materials through multiple outlets before purchasing them. In addition to

71

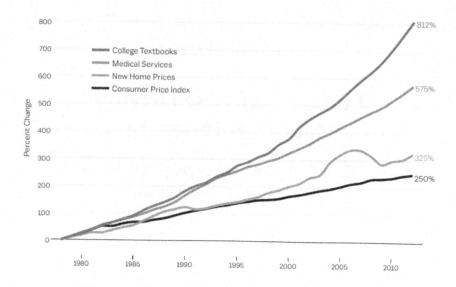

Figure 5.1.   Changes in the prices of books, services, houses, and the CPI.

seeking out used books, many students rent from such vendors as Amazon and Chegg (Parry 2013), share or pirate books (Raschke and Shanks 2011, 53), or rely on the sale of inexpensive international editions—a practice reviewed and upheld by the Supreme Court in the *Kirtsaeng v. Wiley* case that reaffirmed the "central role of libraries in the American way of life" (Band 2014, 14).

The result is an arms race in the college bookstore, with students seeking alternative channels to acquire textbooks while publishers work to plug leaks in their captive marketplace. The rapid release of new editions makes used books obsolete, removing a once-reliable source of affordable materials (Perry 2013). Publishers have also experimented with fully digital works that cannot be resold, most notoriously when Wolters Kluwer's Aspen Casebook Series briefly implemented a system where law students were asked to give up all property rights in their property law casebooks (Chant 2014; Patrice 2014).

This arms race does significant harm to students, particularly those of more modest means who may be priced out of equal participation in higher education. Increasingly, students are choosing courses based on textbook cost rather than substance (Ward 2015) and delaying their textbook purchases to determine the extent to which a title is used in class, setting them back days or weeks in assigned readings (Morris-Babb and Henderson 2012, 150; Reynolds 2011, 180–81). Further, an estimated 65 percent of students admit that they have simply muddled through a course without the assigned textbook because it was too expensive, even though the majority recognized that this presented a "significant concern" for their ability to successfully complete the course (U.S. PIRG Education Fund and the Student PIRGS 2013). Indeed, one recent study found that 10.6 percent of students withdrew from a course and 7.2 percent "frequently or occasionally" failed a course because they could not afford the course text (Morris-Babb and Henderson 2012, 150).

This environment, where commercial publishers leverage faculty incentives to exploit a captive academic market, sounds immediately familiar to anyone who has studied or worked to support open access. Indeed, such scholars as Peek (2012) have written about the way the textbook affordability crisis mirrors the journal pricing crisis and represents an opportunity for similar library involvement. She notes, "Librarians responded to the journal crisis in a number of ways with some becoming involved with the open access movement. It is with this same concern with affordability and access to knowledge that librarians have become involved with [open education] initiatives."

Open education has much in common with open access; the future of academic libraries should include work to transform the way learning objects are created, used, and shared, just as they currently work to change the way scholarship is made and shared. Like open access, open education has an emphasis on removing barriers to the "five Rs": retention, reuse, revision, remixing, and redistribution.

Library support for open access goes further, however, using the open and digital environment to power a revolution in the quality of scholarship and redefine the role of libraries in the scholarly lifecycle. Data mining, visualization, and the digital humanities all reflect the transformative effect of library efforts around "scholarly communication," and each is powered in part by open access. The movement, in short, has enlisted libraries both to remove barriers to access and to power innovation.

Thus far, library efforts around open education often do not mirror librarians' transformative OA work. *Open education* is an increasingly familiar phrase in the media (Mulhere 2015; Senack 2015) and academic literature (Bell 2012; Gallant 2015; Lyons and Hendrix 2014) but one that remains overlooked in many libraries. While institutional repositories proliferate and funds are set aside to support gold open access fees, open education has often remained a tangential concern for many academic libraries, consigned to the corner with open software or altmetrics as a niche issue covered in a brief LibGuide or left to a handful of advocates across campus (Bueno-de-la-Fuente, Robertson, and Boon 2012). Even in cases where librarians do engage with open education, they often present themselves as external advocates, working to persuade others, rather than as partners in the enterprise.

Both OA and open education are about disrupting dysfunctional business models, and both should also be about innovation that brings libraries into the academic life cycle as partners to advance the mission of the institution and the community. In each case, faculty members may play a central role, but libraries can create powerful change by working alongside faculty, administration, and external funders to coordinate efforts in service of society. As with open access, librarians can also stake their own claim in the open education conversation by providing infrastructure and expertise that increase both the quality and the availability of these open materials.

This chapter introduces open educational resources (OERs), a phenomenon that has evolved significantly in the past decade to encompass a wide variety of materials and approaches. It describes the current OER environment and libraries' current role as an ally and driver of OER adoption. Finally, it proposes an expanded role for libraries. In addition to a support role, this chapter suggests that libraries can play a much more active role in open education by using library expertise to support OERs that transform pedagogy, generating resources that support improved educational outcomes and empower instructors. By doing so, librarians can benefit students, faculty, institutions, and their own missions.

OPEN EDUCATION

Although open education in North America can trace its roots back at least to the 4-H clubs of the early 1900s and the Smith-Lever Act of 1914, which created the Cooperative Extension Services connected to land-grant universities, the modern open education movement began with UNESCO's 2002 Forum on the Impact of Open Courseware for Higher Education in Developing Countries (Wiley, Bliss, and McEwen 2014). The forum brought together an international group of experts on the "development and practice of higher education in their respective countries" (UNESCO 2002, 1) for three days of discussion and deliberation that culminated in a final report on OERs that was released to the world.

In their final report, forum participants offered two major definitions of the term *open education* that point to two overlapping but distinct definitions of *openness*. The official definition, emphasizing the importance of digital transformation, is the "open provision of educational resources, enabled by information and communication technologies, for consultation, use and adaptation by a community of users for non-commercial purposes" (UNESCO 2002, 24). Participants built on this goal later in the document, adding a second definition: OERs should be a "universal educational resource available for the whole of humanity" (UNESCO 2002, 28). These two definitions, focusing respectively on cost savings for a particular community and accessibility on a global scale, reflect the overlapping missions of open education.

In the subsequent years, a variety of definitions have refined these ideas. The Scholarly Publishing and Academic Resources Coalition (SPARC) follows David Wiley (2010), one of the leading lights in open education, in defining the practice in terms of the now-standard 5R formulation familiar to open access advocates. Others, such as Wenk (2010), emphasize not just legal use and revision but also the social and cultural ability to "enjoy the benefits of using" and "apply knowledge acquired from" OERs. Further definitions have been proposed that add nuance (Atkins, Brown, and Hammond 2007; Rhoades, Berdan, and Toven-Lindsey 2013), and the term remains fluid today, with different varieties of OERs hewing more or less closely to particular definitions.

In most cases, however, there is general agreement that an OER must be open in both the gratis (no cost) and *libre* (no restrictions) senses (Suber 2012, 65–75), that some form of open licensing—most often Creative Commons (Educause 2010)—should be used, and that these resources must support the educational objectives of students and instructors. The 2012 Paris declaration probably represents the closest we have to a consensus definition of *open educational resources*: "teaching, learning and research materials in any medium, digital or otherwise, that reside in the public domain or have been released under an open license that permits no-cost access, use, adaptation and redistribution by others with no or limited restrictions" (Paris declaration 2012).

Three Revolutions: Textbooks, Courses, and Materials

While a general, if fluid, definition of *open* can be described, defining the parameters of *educational resources* is more complex. Rice professor Richard G. Baraniuk argues that open education is a "perfect storm . . . powering three revolutions that promise to reinvent the way educators produce and disseminate educational materials and fundamentally change the relationship students have with content" (Baraniuk 2012, 1). Baraniuk's "three revolutions"—textbooks, courses, and certification—are slightly different than my own. His emphasis on certification is commendable and points to significant work being done by scholars with training, badging systems, and related practice. Those concerns, however, are somewhat tangential to the thrust of this chapter and elide the significant distinct work being done in higher education related to course materials as modular learning objects. Baraniuk's complementary revolutions emphasize the diversity in OER models (see table 5.1).

OpenCourseWare

At the same time UNESCO's participants were shaping their definitions of *openness* in the early 2000s, MIT was preparing to announce OpenCourse-Ware (OCW), a project that made open versions of MIT courses—including syllabi, lecture notes, assignments, and exams—available to anyone with access to the Internet. These courses were some of the earliest digital education materials to reject the then-ubiquitous dot-com gold rush in favor of academia's public good-focused mission (Abelson 2008). Indeed, their focus on openness in service of the public good was greeted as the "Big Bang in the knowledge universe" and "one of the few beacons of enlightened thinking in an age where the darkness of oppression and proprietary small-mindedness threatens the liberties of free thinkers" (Abelson 2008, 171).

The OCW model, which provides not just learning objects like textbooks but also an entire suite of course materials, has continued to develop, with recorded lectures supplementing lecture notes, more complete rubrics, and a wider selection of courses. In recent years, the OCW model has been linked with the popular practice of offering massive open online courses (MOOCs). MOOCs have been a hot topic, engendering both avid support (Pool 2015; Wu 2013) and deep skepticism (Rhodes, Berdan, and Toven-Lindsey 2013; Kalman 2014). In particular, the commercial and proprietary nature of many MOOCs has led such open education advocates as David Wiley (2015) to lament, "The primary fallout of the brief, blindingly brilliant popularity of MOOCs was to persuade many people that, in the educational context, 'open' means open entry to courses which are not only completely and fully copyrighted, but whose Terms of Use are more restrictive than that of the BBC or *New York Times*."

Because MOOCs are often free in the gratis sense but closed in the *libre* sense and often use a "freemium" model of selling upgrades, credentials, and

Table 5.1.   Types of OERs

Type of Resource	Characteristics	Examples
Open Courses	Unified materials that are designed to work together to present a complete course	MIT OpenCourseWare, Coursera, EdX, Khan Academy
Open Learning Objects	Modular resources that can be combined to meet a variety of learning objectives	MERLOT II, OER Commons, OpenStax CNX
Open Textbooks	Textbook designed as a complimentary material for a particular course or topic	OpenStax, Open Textbook Library, OpenSUNY Textbooks

supporting materials (Porter 2015), they push against the boundaries of "openness" in open education and serve as a reminder that the tension raised in the original UNESCO document remains a live issue across the open education landscape.

Despite these debates about different flavors of openness, however, such open courses as OpenCourseWare remain an important part of the OER environment. MIT's project has been joined by open courses at Michigan, Tufts, and many more, each offering full courses designed by respected faculty members. Today, such third-party services as Khan Academy (Storm 2011) and the MOOCs described previously remain some of the most popular and widely adopted instances of open education.

Open Course Materials and Learning Objects

One of the strengths of *libre* open courses is that they need not be adopted whole cloth. Instructors who want more than a one-size-fits-all approach can disassemble the courses, taking the best materials from any number of OERs and remixing them into their own courses. This approach, grounded in the use of such learning objects as lesson plans, assignments, videos, and exams, is also supported by OERs that are specifically designed to be modular. Developing reusable and sharable quizzes, lesson plans, and activities is a core practice at all levels of education, and the digital environment lends itself to gathering, sharing, and evaluating these resources.

These open course materials are often tagged with metadata and stored individually in a larger repository, such as the Multimedia Educational Repository for Learning and On-line Teaching (MERLOT), a collection of peer-reviewed online higher education learning materials, cataloged by registered members and supported by a set of faculty development services. Launched in the mid-1990s by the California State University system (Cafolla 2006), MERLOT is a consortium of more than forty institutions, systems, and smaller consortia, as well as an "active global community" with twenty-three editorial boards peer-reviewing the quality of materials and fifty distinct "teaching commons," customized sites for particular educational communities (Hanley 2015, 36). Other well-respected collections, such as OER Commons (Anew 2011) and Open Course Library, also leverage Creative Commons licensing to offer course materials of all types.

As with OpenCourseWare, repositories of learning materials provide valuable resources but also have significant limitations. Questions about assessment of quality, appropriateness of fit in distinct educational environments, and lack of a critical mass of available content and interoperability across repositories (Clements and Pawlowski 2012; Davis et al. 2010) mean that, while open learning objects are an important part of the puzzle, they do not represent the entire picture.

Open Textbooks

Increasingly, OERs are also packaged in the form of a textbook, including such supplemental materials as test banks, interactive homework, and study guides (Frith 2009). This model is appealing to instructors who value openness but also prefer an OER with unified content and quality that has been vetted by peers in the field. These instructors can find complete, peer-reviewed open textbooks at such sites as the Open Textbook Library, which aggregates and rates open textbooks. Openstax, an initiative that has grown out of Connexions at Rice University, uses a different model, investing significant resources in the creation of high-quality open resources and then selling add-ons (Chen 2012). Other projects at the State University of New York (Pitcher 2014) and Oregon State (Sutton and Chadwell 2014) have focused on leveraging library expertise and partnerships with a university press to generate high-quality textbooks.

The challenges in this space can be seen in the rise and fall of FlatWorld-Knowledge. The open textbook publisher was initially praised as a revolutionary company that offered a "sustainable model for the future of textbook publishing" (Shelsted 2011) and was prominently featured in Chris Anderson's *Free: The Future of a Radical Price* (2009). A victim of their own success, they were forced in 2013 to begin charging for their materials due to financial pressures stemming from the high cost of creation and support (Howard 2013). Open textbooks remain an attractive and important part of the OER landscape today, but the high cost of production, along with stiff competition from commercial textbooks offering a similar type of resource, still present major challenges.

While these three models represent the most common flavors of OER, the environment is diverse and rapidly expanding, with new players of all sizes regularly entering the field. Taken together, these resources act as points on a continuum of OERs that make up a robust and diverse ecosystem of educational materials. As with OA, commercial publishers are investigating ways to enter the OER marketplace through value-added services. Also like OA, libraries have a significant role to play.

LIBRARIES AS ALLIES IN OPEN EDUCATION

Open education is a natural fit for library engagement because support for academic materials "reflects libraries' enduring roles as crafters of academic collections" and preservers of resources (Scola 2013). The library also plays a central role as an "advocate for access to information and a key campus player in student learning [by] providing access to learning materials through reserve collections and services" (Massis 2013).

As a result, many academic libraries have become "natural allies" in the OER environment (Kleymeer, Kleinman, and Hanss 2010). Significantly, however, most libraries have remained allies rather than becoming full partners, largely focusing on secondary value-added services, such as the description, preservation, and promotion of OER materials (Bueno-de-la-Fuente, Robertson, and Boon 2012). Within this context, library support takes a variety of forms. In her review of the landscape, Okamoto (2013) identifies four distinct roles that libraries have begun to investigate: advocacy, promotion, and discovery; evaluation, collection, preservation, and access; curation and facilitation; and funding (see table 5.2). All of these roles have provided important, and in some cases transformative, services for open education that offer a blueprint for libraries looking to support open education.

Building Knowledge about OERs: Advocacy, Promotion, and Discovery

As described earlier, educators have access to a wide variety of outstanding materials that can replace expensive commercial textbooks, from modular learning objects to holistically designed open courses. Nevertheless, when a recent survey of faculty attitudes toward OERs was released in 2014, the results were sobering: "[M]ost faculty remain unaware of OER, and OER is not a driving force for faculty decisions about which educational materials to adopt" (Allen and Seaman 2014, 2).

To address this information gap, many libraries are working to build knowledge about and understanding of OERs. As they do with open access, libraries create web pages and guides that offer information for finding and evaluating OERs (Jenson and West 2015; Belliston 2009, 286) and advocate for open education as an academic value (Massis 2013; Raschke and Shanks

Table 5.2. Library Roles

Library Role	Characteristics	Examples
Building Knowledge	Advocacy, Promotion, and Discovery	UMass-Amherst LibGuide, SPARC's Impact Stories
Collecting	Evaluation, Preservation, and Access	MERLOT II, Open Textbook Network
Development	Curation and Facilitation	NCSU's Alt-Textbook Project
Funding	Incentivization and Acquisition of Third-Party Content and Resources	Temple's alt-textbook grant program, Open Textbook Library's paid peer review program

2011). The University of Massachusetts-Amherst's open education site (UMass-Amherst) is a good example of this approach, offering an impressive suite of resources, including videos introducing the topic, informational pages targeting such specific stakeholders as faculty and students, a guide to finding and using the most popular OER repositories, and comprehensive information on advocacy for open education. Libraries at such universities as UMass-Amherst, Temple, and North Carolina State also use these sites to promote specific OER projects (discussed later), as well as materials generated in partnership with the library. Describing open resources, Martin (2010) writes,

> The value libraries can add by directing patrons to open resources is immense. Students save time and money in acquiring assigned course materials, educators discover engaging teaching resources, researchers stay on the cusp of information discovery, and libraries benefit not only by saving on subscription costs but also by promoting their own institution's intellectual capital. (190)

Libraries committed to supporting open education can train reference staff (Robertson 2010), continue to create improved finding aids (Cakmak et al. 2012, 1004), and utilize metadata and cataloging skills to improve discoverability of high-quality, relevant resources (Belliston 2009, 286; Robertson 2010, 4). Where they have been engaged, libraries have been successful on each of these fronts, and they are equipped to expand these efforts.

Collecting OERs: Evaluation, Preservation, and Access

Along with providing information about and advocacy for OERs, libraries are also working to support evaluation of and access to high-quality materials. Allen and Seaman (2014) explain, "The most significant barrier to wider adoption of OER remains a faculty perception of the time and effort required to find and evaluate it" (2). By harnessing their rich expertise and historical role in collections, libraries are making OERs easier to understand and rely on. Large-scale repositories like MERLOT and the Open Textbook Library, as well as library-based projects, already rely on library expertise, but any library can do similar work on a smaller scale to evaluate, archive, and make discoverable OERs created both in-house and globally.

A recent report on libraries and OERs reached a similar conclusion, suggesting that "libraries have a history of managing resources—whether physical or digital—in a way that facilitates in their discovery, dissemination, usage, intellectual property licensing, and preservation" (Kazakoff-Lane 2014, 30). With an increased emphasis in this area, these same skills can be used to "facilitate the awareness, visibility, and preservation of OERs in the most efficient manner for higher education institutions" (Kazakoff-Lane

2014, 30). Many libraries are already doing this important work, and many more should begin to do so in the coming years.

Development of OERs: Curation and Facilitation

Some libraries are also taking a more active role in facilitating the creation of OERs. By supporting acquisition and use of materials with copyright and licensing guidance (Robertson 2010), marshaling materials in special collections (Ress 2015), supporting instructional design (Belliston 2009), and offering similar expertise that goes beyond libraries' collections and advocacy work, libraries can make significant contributions to creating better OERs. Leveraging library expertise to contribute to OERs is a significant theme in the literature (Belliston 2009, 285–86; Kazakoff-Lane 2014, 27) and a handful of libraries have put this expertise to work, generating new OERs built directly on library expertise (Kleymeer, Kleinman, and Hanss 2010; Metz-Weisman 2012; Sutton and Chadwell 2014).

Despite this well-documented potential to deploy library expertise in the creation of OERs, however, a recent ARL report concludes, "In most instances, libraries have not systematically assessed how they might aid with OER capacity building," even though numerous scholars have demonstrated that "libraries are in a good position to provide this help" (Kazakoff-Lane 2014, 26). As with collecting OERs, libraries are doing good work but have the potential to be doing much more in OER creation.

Funding OERs: Incentivization and Acquisition of Third-Party Content and Resources

One area where libraries have been increasingly active in past years has been offering funding to support open education and particularly the creation of OERs. Inspired by the Temple Libraries' Alt-Textbook Project (Bell 2012), libraries have begun to provide seed grants to fund faculty who replace closed, commercial textbooks with open alternatives. In 2013, UMass-Amherst followed suit with their own Open Education Initiative, referred to as their "million-dollar idea" based on total savings for students. Other institutions, such as Emory and North Carolina State (Billings et al. 2015), have also created pioneering, well-regarded alt-textbook programs.

As with support for collections and advocacy, these funding efforts fit naturally with the historic role of libraries. As North Carolina State University Libraries director Susan Nutter wrote when announcing the NCSU Libraries' Alt-Textbook project,

> Academic libraries have always been a powerful way to reduce the financial burden of a university education by pooling key resources for everyone to use. The Alt-Textbook grants offer an innovative way to leverage that advantage in

the digital age while at the same time giving our faculty a powerful tool to tailor their course materials to the exact needs of their students. (NCSU Press Release 2014)

One challenge that libraries involved in this effort must grapple with is balancing the obvious benefits of in-hand cost savings with their desire to drive the global and environmental changes at the heart of openness. The underlying tension for MOOCs—that they are free for students but not truly open—exists for library-funded alt-textbooks as well. A faculty member who replaces a five-hundred-dollar introductory textbook with a set of institutionally subscribed journal articles can collectively save students tens of thousands of dollars each year but does little to actually change the larger educational marketplace.

Most institutions, after all, already have some form of electronic reserves, which come with their own challenges around technical support (Konicek, Hyzny, and Allegra 2002) and legal analysis (Hansen, Cross, and Edwards 2013). Dispensing library funds to incentivize a move from textbooks to e-reserves is unlikely to have a substantial effect on textbook prices; in the fifteen years since e-reserves began to proliferate, textbook prices have continued to climb. In fact, high-profile awards to latecomers may antagonize instructors who moved to e-reserves years earlier.

Of course, *openness* is always a complex term. Even Creative Commons–licensed materials (the standard in the field) may not be considered fully open if they include restrictions—for example, on commercial use or derivative works. Recognizing this complexity, Frydenberg and Matkin (2007) identify an aspirational goal of making materials "very available," which they note can have "degrees of meaning" (5–6). Although they focus primarily on balancing technical challenges to openness, questions of "open to which community" similarly require a careful consideration of competing values. Libraries looking to build the profile of a program and support students in a clear and concrete manner would be wise to encourage and trumpet cost savings, even when they require openness that is less than complete. But they must also endeavor to make resources that are truly open in a transformational way and that can be sustained regardless of journal subscription decisions.

No matter how they are generated, these savings are only one part of the power of alt-textbook projects. Bell (2012) identifies four significant outcomes of library involvement in these projects: cost savings, improved student learning based on tailored curricular resources, support for pedagogical experimentation, and seeding an institutional culture of openness. Each of these outcomes contributes to "opening a door," so that faculty, students, and the entire academic community can "cross the threshold towards our preferred future for scholarly communications" (Bell 2012, 5). The potential to open this door should be an invitation for libraries to move beyond their role as allies and take their place as full partners in open education.

WE NEED TO BE PARTNERS

Leveraging expertise and resources in the ways described here has been a powerful method for libraries to raise the profile of OERs, help students stay afloat in a broken marketplace, and support such important projects as the Open Textbook Library and the Oregon State Open Textbook Initiative. In order to reap the full rewards of open education, however, librarians need to be more than eager allies. They must be true partners.

As with open access, libraries can partner with other campus stakeholders to make works that are not just more affordable but also actually transformative. Libraries' expertise with legal, digital, and design practice, as well as their position on campus, suggests that deeper library involvement in OER initiatives would be of "great benefit to those [OER] projects not yet engaged with them" (Bueno-de-la-Fuente, Robertson, and Boon 2012, 7). Despite this potential, scholars have found that the importance of library involvement is not widely understood in the academic community. Even in cases where other participants in a specific project do value the library's contributions, library participation is still not widespread, and a "significant lack of awareness exists both from OER initiatives with regards to library activities and from libraries about the resources released by OER initiatives" (Bueno-de-la-Fuente, Robertson, and Boon 2012, 7). In order to maximize the cost-saving power of OERs and to use open education to improve pedagogy in the same way that open access has powered transformational scholarship, libraries must bring their expertise to bear.

Free and Better

Understandably, the primary focus for OERs so far has been on reducing costs. Cost savings based on library efforts are not fool's gold: Real students benefit directly from these savings, and library programs can reap the benefits of a high-profile program that demonstrates clear institutional value and engenders significant goodwill. Further, rampant increases in textbook costs create critical challenges that price too many students out of higher education and threaten the core mission of colleges and universities.

At the same time, however, there is another important role that libraries can play in the OER environment. Just as open access focuses on both reducing costs and improving scholarship, open education should also drive improvements in the quality of instruction. There is ample space for such improvement in the current environment, in part because commercial print textbooks are often less than ideal tools for student learners and faculty instructors.

Whether they are conscious of the toll expensive textbooks take on student learning or not, many faculty instructors find OERs appealing for an entirely different reason. In many cases—especially for instructors working in specialized or technical areas—there is no high-quality textbook available at any price. Boutique courses may not have the market power to attract a textbook author or publisher. Technical courses, labs, and distance education classes often require hands-on learning that is not well supported by a standard textbook. In courses that are grounded in experiential learning, many instructors find that the "less I use the book, the more they learn" (Ruth 2005).

Reliance on commercial textbooks can also be constraining for an instructor, forcing her to use a one-size-fits-all resource that may be stale or ill-suited to her dynamic and individualistic teaching style. As one instructor writes, "I was frustrated as a young teacher with what I thought was the dated quality of my textbooks and the lack of a system for collecting the best stuff that veteran teachers knew from around the country" (O'Hanlon 2008). Similarly, the homogenous nature of publisher-approved materials may "promote values (overtly and covertly) that maintain social and economic hierarchies" (Hickman and Porfilio 2012, xi) and crowd out more diverse voices of individual instructors and students.

Legal barriers to the creation of instructional materials also limit the ability of instructors to create rich materials, reducing instructors to "hired hands" lacking a "sense of ownership" over the curriculum and the classroom (Sizer 1984). An OER that can be freely reconfigured and remixed "puts ownership of curriculum directly back into the hands of teachers, both encouraging them to reflect on how the materials might be redesigned and improved and empowering them to make these improvements directly" (Robinson et al. 2014).

Frustration with static, one-size-fits-all materials that "present ideas didactically as discrete facts to be accepted, rather than as clues of principles to be discovered and explored" (Ruth 2005) has only grown in light of the trend toward participatory education. Even when a well-regarded print textbook exists, it can still act as an artifact impeding effective instruction. Despite a trend toward participatory learning and a desire to move away from the outdated "sage on the stage" role, many instructors feel trapped with a textbook that "emphasizes facts over thinking" and "looks at information as rare and static rather than abundant and dynamic" (Ward 2015).

Whether replacing a print text with hands-on exercises; stale materials with up-to-date resources; or dry recitations of fact with dynamic, student-centered courses, OERs tailored to the style of the instructor and the needs of the course are better for both students and instructors. By supporting OERs, libraries can help generate education that transforms students from passive consumers of generic content into active participants in a personalized environment (Wiley and Hilton 2009, 3–5).

In light of these pedagogical advantages, it should be no surprise that a growing body of literature suggests that OERs lead to improved learning outcomes as compared to closed, commercial textbooks. Studies of students using open chemistry (Robinson et al. 2014), psychology (Hilton and Laman 2012), and literacy (Pawlyshyn et al. 2013) materials show improved learning outcomes in terms of retention and mastery. Case studies at both Houston Community College (Hilton and Laman 2012) and Virginia State University (Qidong, Griffin, and Xue 2009) also demonstrate that classes using open textbooks have higher grades and better course completion rates.

Certainly, cost savings are a part of this equation: Students cannot learn from textbooks they cannot afford to buy. However, early studies of OERs that are not customized reveal that, while adopting an OER whole cloth does generate significant cost savings, it often leads to only limited improvements in learning outcomes. A 2012 study by Wiley, Hilton, Ellington, and Hall reached exactly this conclusion and suggests that "student test scores will improve when professional development is provided to teachers to help them understand the new activities and pedagogies made possible by the open textbooks" (276).

Institutions that have adopted OERs have begun to investigate open education as a model for innovation in teaching (Petrides et al. 2011) that is more collaborative and interactive. This new model can be enabled and accelerated through partnership with librarians, who bring expertise that fills important gaps in the creation of learning materials so that they can be, as Mercy College describes its OERs, "Free and Better" (Mondelli and Wiley 2015).

Library Expertise Adds Value

Instructors developing OERs can be expected to possess deep disciplinary knowledge, but many lack skills in technical design and coding, intellectual property and licensing, organization and discoverability, and other areas of strength for academic libraries. By engaging with the OER community, libraries have an important opportunity to partner with instructors to generate innovative pedagogical resources.

As with open access two decades ago, librarians are well positioned today to take the lead in open education, in part because they are embedded in the space. Quill West, a thought leader in OER, notes that "librarians have become the OER experts on campus" (Jenson and West 2015). As discussed earlier, librarians currently offer information, workshops, and consultation—as well as advocacy—on the power of OERs. While librarians' roles vary from campus to campus, faculty who are aware of OERs often view librarians as potential OER leaders on campus (Jenson and West 2015). Indeed, a recent workshop put a fine point on this issue with the title "Libraries Leading the Way" (Community College Consortium for Open Educational Resources 2013).

As it has always been, the library is a fertile space on campus for collaboration across disciplines and is "uniquely positioned to work with faculty on curricular change" (Lippincott, Vedantham, and Duckett 2014). This trusted position is grounded in a long history of engagement and support. Librarians remain the campus stakeholders best positioned to partner meaningfully with faculty to develop innovative assignments and assist students in learning. Recent forays into library publishing (Howard 2013; Sutton and Chadwell 2014) and digital scholarship (McCullough 2014; Zhao 2014) have further strengthened valuable skills that align libraries even more closely with these efforts, particularly when librarians combine their skills on a project.

While a single librarian can do important work in this space, librarians can collaborate with instructors as a team to support participants as they "assess their own information needs, identify useful resources, and develop skills in finding, evaluating, accessing, managing, synthesizing, and using information in an online learning environment" (Mahraj 2012). Indeed, one can expect a team-based approach to be quite powerful, both as a safeguard against overcommitment by any single librarian and because the range of expertise that may be brought to bear necessarily extends beyond any single realm (see table 5.3). As described by Lippincott, Vedantham, and Duckett (2014), many different library staff members—often working in teams and leveraging library spaces—can engage with faculty to promote pedagogical and curricular change.

Libraries are also well positioned to fill gaps in faculty knowledge necessary to create transformative OERs. A recent study by the Washington State Board for Community and Technical Colleges found that "faculty who successfully adopted OER needed institutional support in their adoption efforts" (Chae and Jenkins 2015). Along with traditional library services, such as locating and curating materials, the study identified a number of areas where faculty need support. Based on a review of the literature, faculty needs and library expertise overlap heavily in three areas crucial for the development of OERs: instructional design, copyright and licensed resources, and digital materials.

Instructional Design

Library instruction has been a core component of librarianship for more than a century (Farmer 2011), and librarians have increasingly made instructional design an integral part of modern librarianship. Librarians trained in this area can add significant value and improve student outcomes (Kalyuga 2011;

Table 5.3.   Library Expertise for Building OERs

Type of Librarian	Expertise	Role in OER Development
Collections, Acquisition, and Subject Specialist	Acquisition, Developing Collections, Relationships	Licensing Content, Tailoring Materials, Negotiating Use
Reference and Instruction	Identification, Instructional Design, Information Literacy	Course Design, Discovery of Content, Updating Pedagogy
Special Collections	Preservation, Rare Materials, Exhibits	Locating Unique Materials, Sustainability
Digital Libraries	Web Design, Hosting, Streaming Media, Specific Platforms	Creating Digital Materials, Web Hosting, New Formats and Tools
Scholarly Communication	Open Licensing, Fair Use and Copyright Exceptions, Open Culture, Meeting Legal Rules	Using Third-Party Material, Incorporating Open Materials, Accessibility

Paas, Renkl, and Sweller 2003) by designing course materials that encourage collaboration and developing curricula that reflect the need to communicate effectively across various media (Jenkins 2009; Thomas and Brown 2011). Although these skills are central to fostering mastery of course materials and preparing students to put what they learn into practice, they are often not included in the training of faculty instructors, particularly those who have been out of school for years or decades.

These skills are also too often missing from closed, commercial textbooks, which often reflect older models based in a standard curriculum (Jolls 2015; Leland and Kasten 2002). One scholar writes, "The world has moved on from that model. But in far too many cases, education hasn't, treating students as empty vessels that need filling rather than as distinct individuals who need guidance in learning on their own" (Ward 2015). Librarians with expertise in instructional design can serve as an antidote to this "information-first" rather than "learning-first approach" (Ward 2015). To do so, however, they must be deeply involved as partners in course design, working to develop and refine lessons, assignments, and materials.

Copyright and Licensed Resources

Librarians can also bring important expertise in such legal issues as licensing and copyright. Managing copyright and licensing materials is, of course, a central role of libraries (Metz-Wiseman 2012), and the same knowledge used to license resources for the institution can inform individual licensing from rights holders and managing open licensed materials from the Creative Commons (Billings et al. 2012).

Similarly, libraries' investment in copyright expertise, driven by the rise of scholarly communication librarians (Radom, Feltner-Reichert, and stringer-stanback 2012), can be brought to bear when engaging with copyright issues and licensed materials to create OERs. Such scholars as Sizer (1984) and Apple (1995) have documented the way that legal uncertainty has contributed to the deskilling of instructors, who are cut out of the design process by professional textbooks that are designed to be "teacher proof." Robinson et al. (2014) observe, "Although teachers have historically exercised a significant amount of autonomy once the classroom door was closed, the potentially illegal nature of redesigning curriculum . . . prevents these efforts from being widely viewed and valued" (348). Many students also find copyright to be a source of confusion that inhibits collaboration and creativity (Education for Change 2012).

A librarian with expertise in understanding licenses, navigating technical copyright exceptions like the TEACH Act, and developing sophisticated fair use strategies can empower an instructional partner to develop her own tailored materials. As with instructional design, however, librarians are best positioned to do so when they are deeply involved in the concrete practice of creation rather than acting as an "ally" offering general advice about abstract questions.

Digital Materials

Libraries also increasingly have deep expertise in digital issues that may vex instructors. Simple skills, such as creating strategies for web hosting and optimized web design, are staples in most library schools (Lamb and Johnson 2013; Peterson 2006) but may be outside the comfort zone of faculty instructors (Kale 2014). Awareness of current design issues like accessibility and expertise with collaborative digital skills, grouped under the umbrella term *Web 2.0* (Al-Daihani 2009; Arlitsch et al. 2014), can also be of great value, making subject-rich materials more robust and effective.

Librarians also have important expertise in information seeking, evaluation, synthesis, and management skills that Kop et al. (2011) identify as crucial to successful learning in today's information-rich, self-directed digital environments. Many students, however (Beetham et al. 2009; Hampton-Reeves 2009), including so-called digital natives (Trinder et al. 2008), lack a sophisticated understanding of digital literacy.

Many students also operate in a "learning grey market" (White et al. 2012, 14) by using such sources as social media and Wikipedia without revealing them to instructors, thus short-circuiting critical engagement with these sources and creating a disconnect between the sources they are taught to use and those that they actually rely on.

In response, scholars have called on instructors to adopt a "pedagogy 2.0" approach (Lee and McLoughlin 2010; McLoughlin and Alam 2014) that "attempts to overcome the limitations of existing teaching and learning models, by emphasizing the connectivity enabled by social software tools" (McLoughlin and Alam 2014, 128). To do so, however, instructors require support in these areas (McLoughlin and Alam 2014, 134). These are the skills that librarians have in abundance and are trained to provide. The ability of librarians to fill these gaps and power transformative OERs "should be a rallying cry to librarians to get involved" (Mahraj 2012).

CONCLUSION: A TIPPING POINT FOR LIBRARIES AND OER

The nascent open education movement has already begun to challenge traditional, commercial textbooks, but so far, library efforts have been designed to support rather than partner and have focused primarily on cost savings. As with open access, academic libraries can be partners and act as a transformational force in open education by breaking down a socially harmful commercial monopoly and by adding significant value to the work done by instructors. In order to do so, librarians must stand up and take our place as partners in open education. As Micah Vandegrift and Stewart Varner have urged in the context of the digital humanities, librarians must "[e]mbrace the calling of digital work in contrast to the vocation of servitude."

A library-centric OER program can develop relationships to reduce the costs that are pricing too many students out of higher education. These efforts can also engage and empower instruction, a role often devalued or left out of institutional support for open access in favor of support focused primarily on access to research. Most significantly, library OER programs can seed real transformation in instruction, driving improved outcomes for students and faculty, particularly in innovative, interdisciplinary areas where no good textbook exists at any price. As Cormier and Siemens (2010) argue, the "true benefit of the academy is the interaction, the access to the debate, to the negotiation of knowledge—not to the stale cataloging of content."

By doing so, libraries can conserve resources, speed innovation (Mahraj 2012), and demonstrate their value—as well as the value of "open"—in the classroom, just as they have done in labs, faculty offices, and reading rooms with open access. They can also revitalize the image of the library on campus, connecting with the most motivated and innovative faculty and shining a spotlight on the library's services and expertise.

There is no better time for librarians to make their presence felt. The Babson survey, which revealed many faculty members' unfamiliarity with

OERs, also includes an important and hopeful note: Although between 65 and 75 percent of faculty were unaware of OERs and only 2.7 percent cited cost as the most important criterion when selecting teaching resources, faculty members do appreciate the concept of OER, and when it is introduced, they are willing to give it a try (Allen and Seamen 2014, 2). They are particularly likely to engage with open education when OERs have "proven efficacy"—faculty members' number-one cited priority.

OERs built with library expertise do exactly that by improving instructional design, supporting empowered remixing, and connecting learners with digital literacy skills. Some faculty members may adopt OERs for altruistic reasons of cost, especially when incentivized with a seed grant. Many, many more will do so when we can demonstrate that OERs are superior resources tailored to their teaching and powering improved learning outcomes. As one full-time mathematics faculty member reports, "I must admit that I do not pay much attention to the origins of material. My focus is upon content, accuracy, and usability" (Allen and Seamen 2014, 16).

Given these findings, as well as the 2015 Horizon Report's statement that "broader acceptance into higher education hinges on the issue of awareness and accessibility," the central question for librarians interested in open education is "who will introduce the remaining 66%–75% of this country's faculty to OER?" (Wiley 2015). It is incumbent on librarians to use our expertise to help create the examples of OER that will form an impression for a generation of instructors. By doing so, we can make OERs that are both free and better and stake our claim as valued partners in core academic practice.

REFERENCES

Abelson, Hal. 2008. "The Creation of OpenCourseWare at MIT." *Journal of Science Education and Technology* 17, no. 2.

Al-Daihani, Sultan. 2009. "The Knowledge of Web 2.0 by Library and Information Science Academics." *Education for Information* 27, no. 1: 39–55.

Allen, Elaine, and Jeff Seaman. 2014. "Opening the Curriculum: Open Educational Resources in U.S. Higher Education, 2014." *Babson Survey Research Group, Pearson.* http://www.onlinelearningsurvey.com/reports/openingthecurriculum2014.pdf.

Anderson, Chris. 2009. *Free: The Future of a Radical Price.* New York: Hyperion.

Anew, Susan A. 2011. "OER Commons." *Choice: Current Reviews for Academic Libraries* 49, no. 3: 567.

Apple, M. W. 1995. *Education and Power.* New York: Routledge.

Arlitsch, Kenning, Patrick Obrien, Jason A. Clark, Scott W. H. Young, and Doralyn Rossmann. 2014. "Demonstrating Library Value at Network Scale: Leveraging the Semantic Web with New Knowledge Work." *Journal of Library Administration* 54, no. 5: 413–25.

Atkins, Daniel E., John Seely Brown, and Allen Hammond. 2007. "A Review of the Open Educational Resources (OER) Movement: Achievements, Challenges, and New Opportunities." Report to the William and Flora Hewlett Foundation, i–84. http://www.educause.edu/Resources/AreviewoftheOpenEducationalRes/162444.

Baldi, Stefan, Hauke Heier, and Anett Mehler-Bicher. 2003. "Open Courseware and Open Source Software—Learning from Experience?" *Communications of the ACM* 46, no. 9: 105–7.

Band, Jonathan. 2014. "The Impact of the Supreme Court's Decision in *Kirtsaeng v. Wiley* on Libraries." *Library Copyright Alliance Issue Brief.* http://www.librarycopyrightalliance.org/storage/documents/issue-brief-kirtsaeng-post-analysis-02apr13.pdf.

Baraniuk, R. 2012. "Open Education: One Perfect Storm Yields Three Revolutions." *Visiones de Telefonica.* http://www.visionesdetelefonica.cl/wp-content/uploads/2012/10/05-Richard-Baraniuk-Open-education.pdf.

Bell, Steven J. 2012. "Coming in the Back Door: Leveraging Open Textbooks to Promote Scholarly Communications on Campus." *Journal of Librarianship and Scholarly Communication* 1, no. 1: eP1040.

Belliston, C. Jeffrey. 2009. "Open Educational Resources." *College & Research Libraries News* 70, no. 5: 284–303. http://crln.acrl.org/content/70/5/284.full.pdf+html.

Billings, M. S., S. C. Hutton, J. Schafer, C. M. Schweik, and M. Sheridan. 2012. "Open Educational Resources as Learning Materials: Prospects and Strategies for University Libraries." *Research Library Issues* 280: 2–10.

Billings, Marilyn, Sarah C. Hutton, Jay Schafer, Charles M. Schweik, and Matt Sheridan. 2015. "Libraries Leading the Way on the Textbook Problem." *Proceedings of the Charleston Conference.* http://docs.lib.purdue.edu/charleston/2014/Communication/3.

Bueno-de-la-Fuente, Gema, R. John Robertson, and Stuart Boon. 2012. "The Roles of Libraries and Information Professionals in Open Educational Resources (OER) Initiatives." *Cetis LLP Publications.* http://publications.cetis.org.uk/2012/492.

Cafolla, Ralph. 2006. "Project MERLOT: Bringing Peer Review to Web-Based Educational Resources." *Journal of Technology and Teacher Education* 14, no. 2: 313–23.

Cakmak, T., Ozel, N., and Yilmaz, M. 2012. "Open Educational Resources and Academic Libraries: Reflections from Turkey." *Global Journal on Technology* 1: 1002–6. http://www.world-education-center.org/index.php/P-ITCS/article/view/791.

Cape Town Declaration. 2007. http://www.capetowndeclaration.org.

Chae, Boyoung, and Mark Jenkins. 2015. "Qualitative Investigation of Faculty Open Educational Resource Usage in the Washington Community and Technical College System: Models for Support and Implementation." *Washington State Board for Community and Technical Colleges.* https://drive.google.com/file/d/0B4eZdZMtpULyZC1NRHMzOEhRRzg/view.

Chant, Ian. 2014. "Law Profs Revolt after Aspen Casebook Tries to Get around First Sale Doctrine." *Library Journal* (May 21). http://lj.libraryjournal.com/2014/05/academic-libraries/law-profs-revolt-after-aspen-casebook-tries-to-get-around-first-sale-doctrine.

Chen, A. 2012. "Rice U. Hopes Mix of Grants and 'Add Ons' Will Support Free Textbooks." *Chronicle of Higher Education Blogs: Wired Campus.* August 14. http://chronicle.com/blogs/wiredcampus/rice-u-hopes-mix-of-grants-and-add-ons-will-support-free-textbooks/38823.

Clements, K. I., and J. M. Pawlowski. 2012. "User-Oriented Quality for OER: Understanding Teachers' Views on Re-use, Quality, and Trust." *Journal of Computer Assisted Learning* 28: 4–14.

Community College Consortium for Open Educational Resources. 2013. *Libraries Lead the Way: Open Courses, Open Educational Resources, and Open Policies.* http://oerconsortium.org/2013/09/19/libraries-lead-the-way-open-courses-open-educational-resources-and-open-policies.

Cormier, Dave, and George Siemens. 2010. "Through the Open Door: Open Courses as Research, Learning, and Engagement." *EDUCAUSE Review.* http://er.educause.edu/articles/2010/8/through-the-open-door-open-courses-as-research-learning-and-engagement.

Davis, H. C., et al. 2010. "Bootstrapping a Culture of Sharing to Facilitate Open Educational Resources, Learning Technologies." *IEEE Transactions* 3, no. 2 (August 14): 96–109. http://ieeexplore.ieee.org/xpl/articleDetails.jsp?arnumber=5210093.

Education for Change. 2012. " Researchers of Tomorrow: The Research Behaviour of Generation Y Doctoral Students." http://www.jisc.ac.uk/media/documents/publications/reports/
2012/Researchers-of-Tomorrow.pdf.

Educause. 2010. "7 Things You Should Know About Open Educational Resources." http://
net.educause.edu/ir/library/pdf/ELi7061.pdf.

Frith, Jordan. 2009. "The Open Revolution: An Environmental Scan of the Open Textbook
Landscape." http://www.academia.edu/402432/E_Open_Revolution_An_Environmental_
Scan_of_the_Open_Textbook_Landscape.

Frydenberg, Jia, and Gary Matkin. 2007. "Open Textbooks: What? Why? How? When?" http://
wwwstaging.hewlett.org/uploads/files/OpenTextbooks.pdf.

Gallant, Jeff. 2015. "Librarians Transforming Textbooks: The Past, Present, and Future of the
Affordable Learning Georgia Initiative." *Georgia Library Quarterly* 52, no. 2: article 8.
http://digitalcommons.kennesaw.edu/glq/vol52/iss2/8.

Gallaway, Teri Oaks, and James B. Hobbs. 2015. "Open Access for Student Success." *Enhancing Teaching and Learning in the 21st-Century Academic Library: Successful Innovations
That Make a Difference* 2, no. 1.

Grant, Sarah. 2015. "Are Savvy Students Sabotaging Big Textbook? College Kids Are Study-
ing Smarter—and Cheaper—Threatening the Textbook Industry's High Prices." *Bloomberg
Business*. http://www.bloomberg.com/news/articles/2015-08-26/are-savvy-students-
sabotaging-big-textbook-.

Hanley, Gerald L. 2015. "MOOCs, MERLOT, and Open Education Systems." In *MOOCs and
Open Education around the World*, edited by Curtis J. Bonk, Mimi Miyoung Lee, Thomas
C. Reeves, and Thomas H. Reynolds, 34–40. New York: Taylor & Francis. http://
publicationshare.com/moocsbook/TOC_Preface_MOOCs_Open_Ed_book_by_Bonk_Lee_
Reeves_Reynolds.pdf.

Hansen, David, William Cross, and Phillip M. Edwards. 2013. "Copyright Policy and Practice
in Electronic Reserves among ARL Libraries." *College & Research Libraries*.

Hart Research Associates. 2015. "Falling Short? College Learning and Career Success." https://
www.aacu.org/sites/default/files/files/LEAP/2015employerstudentsurvey.pdf.

Hickman, Heather, and Brad J. Porfilio, eds. 2012. *The New Politics of the Textbook: Critical
Analysis in the Core Content Areas*. Rotterdam, Netherlands: Sense.

Hilton, John, III, and Carol Laman. 2012. "One College's Use of an Open Psychology Textbook." *Open Learning: The Journal of Open, Distance and e-Learning* 27, no. 3: 265–72.

Howard, Jennifer. 2013. "For New Ideas in Scholarly Publishing, Look to the Library." *Chronicle of Higher Education.* http://chronicle.com/article/Hot-Off-the-Library-Press/136973.

Jenkins, Henry. 2009. *Confronting the Challenges of Participatory Culture.*With Ravi Puru-
shotma, Margaret Weigel, Katie Clinton, and Alice J. Robison. Cambridge, MA: MIT Press.
https://mitpress.mit.edu/sites/default/files/titles/free_download/9780262513623_
Confronting_the_Challenges.pdf.

Jenson, Kristi, and Quill West. 2015. "Open Educational Resources and the Higher Education
Environment: A Leadership Opportunity for Libraries." *College & Research Libraries
News*. http://crln.acrl.org/content/76/4/215.full.

Jolls, Tessa. 2015. "The New Curricula: Propelling the Growth of Media Literacy Education."
Journal of Media Literacy Education 7, no. 1: 65–71. http://digitalcommons.uri.edu/jmle/
vol7/iss1/7.

Kale, Ugur. 2014. "Can They Plan to Teach with Web 2.0? Future Teachers' Potential Use of
the Emerging Web." *Technology, Pedagogy & Education* 23, no. 4: 471–89.

Kalman, Yoram M. 2014. "A Race to the Bottom: MOOCs and Higher Education Business
Models." *Open Learning* 29, no. 1: 5–14.

Kalyuga, Slava. 2011. "Informing: A Cognitive Load Perspective." *Informing Science: The
International Journal of an Emerging Transdiscipline* 14: 33.

Kazakoff-Lane, Carmen. 2014. "Environmental Scan and Assessment of OERs, MOOCs and
Libraries: What Effectiveness and Sustainability Means for Libraries' Impact on Open Edu-
cation." http://www.ala.org/acrl/sites/ala.org.acrl/files/content/publications/whitepapers/
Environmental%20Scan%20and%20Assessment.pdf.

Kleymeer, Pieter, Molly Kleinman, and Ted Hanss. 2010. "Reaching the Heart of the University: Libraries and the Future of OER." Paper presented at the 7th annual Open Education Conference, November 2–4, Barcelona, Spain. http://deepblue.lib.umich.edu/bitstream/handle/2027.42/78006/ReachingtheHeartoftheUniversity-KleymeerKleinmanHanss.pdf?sequence=1.

Konicek, Kathy, Joy Hyzny, and Richard Allegra. 2002. "Electronic Reserves: The Promise and Challenge to Increase Accessibility." *Library Hi Tech Journal* 21, no. 1: 102–8.

Kop, R., and Carroll, F. 2011. "Cloud Computing and Creativity: Learning on a Massive Open Online Course." *European Journal of Open, Distance and E-Learning* (Special Issue on Creativity and OER). http://www.eurodl.org/?p=special&sp=articles&article=457.

Lamb, Annette, and Larry Johnson. 2013. "Riding the Winds of Change: New Directions for Libraries and Web Development Tools." *Teacher Librarian* 40, no. 5: 58–63.

Lee, Mark J. W., and Catherine McLoughlin. 2010. "Beyond Distance and Time Constraints: Applying Social Networking Tools and Web 2.0 Approaches to Distance Learning." In *Emerging Technologies in Distance Education*, edited by George Veletsianos, 61–87. Edmonton, AB: Athabasca University Press.

Leland, Christine, and Wendy C. Kasten. 2002. "Literacy Education for the 21st Century: It's Time to Close the Factory." *Reading & Writing Quarterly: Overcoming Learning Difficulties* 18, no. 1.

Lippincott, Joan, Anu Vedantham, and Kim Duckett. 2014. "Libraries as Enablers of Pedagogical and Curricular Change." *Educause Review*. http://er.educause.edu/articles/2014/10/libraries-as-enablers-of-pedagogical-and-curricular-change.

Lorenzen, Michael. 2001. "A Brief History of Library Instruction in the United States of America." *Illinois Libraries* 83, no. 2: 8–18.

Lyons, Charles, and Dean Hendrix. 2014. "Textbook Affordability: Is There a Role for the Library?" *Serials Librarian* 66, nos. 1–4: 262–67.

Mahraj, Katy. 2012. "Using Information Expertise to Enhance Massive Open Online Courses." *Public Services Quarterly* 8, no. 4: 359–68.

Martin, Rebecca A. 2010. "Finding Free and Open Access Resources: A Value-Added Service for Patrons." *Journal of Interlibrary Loan, Document Delivery & Electronic Reserve* 20, no. 3: 189–200.

Massis, B. E. 2013. "Textbook affordability: The Library's Role." *New Library World* 114, no. 3/4: 179–83. doi: 10.1108/03074801311304087.

McCullough, Heather. 2014. "Developing Digital Scholarship Services on a Shoestring." *College & Research Libraries News* 75, no. 4: 187–90.

McLoughlin, Catherine E., and Sultana Lubna Alam. 2014. "A Case Study of Instructor Scaffolding Using Web 2.0 Tools to Teach Social Informatics." *Journal of Information Systems Education* 25, no. 2: 125–36.

McNichol, Sarah. 2015. "Digital Literacy and the Challenges of Open Educational Resources." *figshare*. http://dx.doi.org/10.6084/m9.figshare.1512333.

Metz-Wiseman, Monica. 2012. "Textbook Affordability Crisis and the Academic Library: Exploring Alternatives." Session presented at the Electronic Resources and Libraries Conference, Austin, TX.

Mondelli, Vicoria, and David Wiley. 2015. *ELI Webinar: Searching for "Free and Better": Evaluating the Efficacy of Open Educational Resources.* http://www.educause.edu/eli/events/eli-annual-meeting/2015/searching-free-and-better-evaluating-efficacy-open-educational-resources.

Morris-Babb, M. 2012. "An Experiment in Open-Access Textbook Publishing: Changing the World One Textbook at a Time." *Journal of Scholarly Publishing* 43, no. 2: 148. http://dx.doi.org/10.3138/jsp.43.2.148.

Mulhere, Kaitlin. 2015. "Is This the Solution to Crazy High Textbook Prices?" *Time*. http://time.com/money/4017003/high-text-book-prices-solution.

NCSU Libraries. 2014. "NCSU Libraries Offering Grants to Help Faculty Develop Free or Low-Cost Open Textbook Alternatives" (press release).

New Media Consortium. 2015. "NMC Horizon Report—2015 Higher Education Edition." http://www.nmc.org/publication/nmc-horizon-report-2015-higher-education-edition/.

O'Hanlon, Charlene. 2008. "Content, Anyone?" *The Journal: Transforming Education through Technology*. http://thejournal.com/%20Articles/2008/05/01/Content-Anyone.aspx.

Okamoto, Karen. 2013. "Making Higher Education More Affordable, One Course Reading at a Time: Academic Libraries as Key Advocates for Open Access Textbooks and Educational Resources." *Public Services Quarterly* 9: 267–83.

Paas, Fred, Alexander Renkl, and John Sweller. 2003. "Cognitive Load Theory and Instructional Design: Recent Developments." *Educational Psychologist* 38, no. 1: 1–4. http://dx.doi.org/10.1207/S15326985EP3801_1.

Parry, M. 2013. "Students Get Savvier about Textbook Buying." *Chronicle of Higher Education* (Jan. 27). http://chronicle.com/article/Students-Get-Savvier-About/136827.

Patrice, Joe. 2014. "Casebook Publisher Has Aggressive New Plan to Rip Off Law Students." *Above the Law*. http://abovethelaw.com/2014/05/casebook-publisher-has-aggressive-new-plan-to-rip-off-law-students.

Pawlyshyn, Nancy, Dr. Braddlee, Linda Casper, and Howard Miller. 2013. "Adopting OER: A Case Study of Cross-Institutional Collaboration and Innovation." *EDUCAUSE Review*. http://er.educause.edu/articles/2013/11/adopting-oer-a-case-study-of-crossinstitutional-collaboration-and-innovation.

Peek, Robin. 2012. "Textbooks in Turmoil." *Information Today* 29, no. 5: 26.

Peterson, Kate. 2006. "Academic Web Site Design and Academic Templates: Where Does the Library Fit In?" *Information Technology & Libraries* 25, no. 4: 217–21.

Petrides, Lisa, Cynthia Jimes, Clare Middleton-Detzner, Julie Walling, and Shenandoah Weiss. 2011. "Open Textbook Adoption and Use: Implications for Teachers and Learners." *Open Learning: The Journal of Open, Distance and e-Learning* 26, no. 1: 39–49.

Pitcher, K. 2014. "Library Publishing of Open Textbooks: The Open SUNY Textbooks Program." *Against the Grain* 26, no. 5 (2014): 22–24.

Pool, Rebecca. 2015. "Long Live the MOOC." *Research Information* 78: 22–26.

Porter, Sarah. 2015. "The Economics of MOOCs: A Sustainable Future?" *Bottom Line: Managing Library Finances* 28, nos. 1–2: 52–62.

Qidong, Cao, Thomas E. Griffin, and Bai, Xue. 2009. "The Importance of Synchronous Interaction for Student Satisfaction with Course Web Sites." *Journal of Information Systems Education* 20, no. 3: 331–38.

Radom, Rachel, Melanie Feltner-Reichert, and kynita stringer-stanback. 2012. *ARL Spec Kit 332: Organization of Scholarly Communication Services*. http://publications.arl.org/Organization-of-Scholarly-Communication-Services-SPEC-Kit-332.

Raschke, Greg, and Shelby Shanks. 2011. "Water on a Hot Skillet: Textbooks, Open Educational Resources, and the Role of the Library." In *The No Shelf Required Guide to E-Book Purchasing*, edited by Sue Polanka, 52–57. Chicago: ALA TechSource.

Ress, Sunghae. 2015. "Special Collections: Improving Access and Usability." *Reference Librarian* 56, no. 1: 52–58.

Reynolds, R. 2011. "Trends Influencing the Growth of Digital Textbooks in US Higher Education." *Publishing Research Quarterly* 27: 178. doi:10.1007/s12109-011-9216-5.

Rhoads, R. A., Berdan, J., and Toven-Lindsey, B. 2013. "The Open Courseware Movement in Higher Education: Unmasking Power and Raising Questions about the Movement's Democratic Potential." *Education Theory* 63: 87–110. doi:10.1111/edth.12011.

Richter, Thomas, and Maggie McPherson. 2012. "Open Educational Resources: Education for the World?" *Distance Education* 33, no. 2: 201–19.

Robertson, R. J. 2010. "What Do Academic Libraries Have to Do with Open Educational Resources?" (Theme: Long-Term Sustainability of Open Education Projects' First Steps to Start Up). *Open Ed 2010 Proceedings*. http://hdl.handle.net/10609/4847.

Robinson, T. Jared, Lane Fischer, David Wiley, and John Hilton III. 2014. "The Impact of Open Textbooks on Secondary Science Learning Outcomes." *Education & Educational Research* 43, no. 7: 341–51.

Ruth, Geoff. 2005. "No Books, No Problem: Teaching without a Text." *Edutopia*. http://www.edutopia.org/teaching-without-text.

Scola, N. 2013. "Joint Action on Textbook Costs by Faculty and Students at Brooklyn College." Clarion. http://www.psc-cuny.org/clarion/march-2013/joint-action-textbook-costs-faculty-and-students-brooklyn-college.

Senack, Ethan. 2015. "Textbooks Cost a Lot. Here's Why." *Huffington Post*. http://www.huffingtonpost.com/ethan-senack/textbooks-cost-a-lot-here_b_8065762.html.

Shelstad, J. 2011. How Flat World Knowledge Is Transforming College Textbook Publishing." Publishing Research Quarterly 27: 254. doi:10.1007/s12109-011-9222-7.

Sizer, T. R. 2004. *Horace's Compromise: The Dilemma of the American High School*. New York: Houghton Mifflin.

Stacey, Paul. 2007. "Open Educational Resources in a Global Context." *First Monday* 12, no. 4: 7.

Storm, M. 2011. "Khan Academy." *Choice: Current Reviews for Academic Libraries* 48, no. 5: 866.

Suber, P. 2012. *Open Access*. Cambridge, MA: MIT Press.

Sutton, Shan C., and Faye A. Chadwell. 2014. "Open Textbooks at Oregon State University: A Case Study of New Opportunities for Academic Libraries and University Presses." *Journal of Librarianship and Scholarly Communication* 2, no. 4.

Thomas, Douglas, and John Seely Brown. 2011. *A New Culture of Learning: Cultivating the Imagination for a World of Constant Change*. CreateSpace.

Trinder, K., Guiller, J., Margaryan, A., Littlejohn, A., and Nicol, D. 2008. "Learning from Digital Natives: Integrating formal and informal learning" (final project report). Higher Education Academy, UK. http://www.academy.gcal.ac.uk/ldn/LDNFinalReport.pdf.

UNESCO. 2002. "Forum on the Impact of Open Courseware for Higher Education in Developing Countries: Final Report." www.unesco.org/iiep/eng/focus/opensrc/PDF/OERForumFinalReport.pdf.

UNESCO. 2012. Paris Declaration. http://ru.iite.unesco.org/files/news/639202/Paris%20OER%20Declaration_01.pdf.

U.S. Government Accountability Office. 2013. "College Textbooks: Students Have Greater Access to Textbook Information." http://www.gao.gov/assets/660/655066.pdf.

U.S. PIRG Education Fund and the Student PIRGS. 2014. "Fixing the Broken Textbook Market." http://www.uspirg.org/reports/usp/fixing-broken-textbook-market.

Vandegrift, M., and Varner, S. (2013). "Evolving in Common: Creating Mutually Supportive Relationships between Libraries and the Digital Humanities." *Journal of Library Administration* 15, no. 1: 67–78. DOI:10.1080/01930826.2013.756699.

Walz, Anita R. 2015. "Open and Editable: Exploring Library Engagement in Open Educational Resource Adoption, Adaptation and Authoring." *Virginia Libraries* 61, no. 1: 23–31.

Ward, Doug. 2015. "Why You Ought to Think Twice before Assigning a Pricey Textbook." *Chronicle of Higher Education*. http://chronicle.com/article/Why-You-Ought-to-Think-Twice-/232877.

Wenk, Bruno. 2010. "Open Educational Resources (OER) Inspire Teaching and Learning." Paper presented at the IEEE EDUCON Education Engineering 2010—The Future of Global Learning Engineering Education, Madrid, Spain. http://www.ieec.uned.es/Investigacion/Educon2010/SearchTool/EDUCON2010/papers/2010S02G04.pdf.

White, D., Silipigni, L., Lanclos, D., Le Cornu, A., and Hood, E. 2012. "Digital Visitors and Residents" (progress report). http://www.jisc.ac.uk/media/documents/projects/visitorsandresidentsinterim%20report.pdf.

Wiley, David. 2015. "The MOOC Misstep and the Open Education Infrastructure." In *MOOCs and Open Education around the World*, edited by Curtis J. Bonk, Mimi Miyoung Lee, Thomas C. Reeves, and Thomas H. Reynolds, 3–11. New York: Taylor & Francis.

Wiley, David, T. J. Bliss, and Mary McEwen. 2014. "Open Educational Resources: A Review of the Literature." In *Handbook of Research on Educational Communications and Technology*, edited by Michael Spector, M. David Merrill, Jan Elen, and M. J. Bishop, 781. New York: Springer.

Wiley, David, and John Hilton III. 2009. "Openness, Dynamic Specialization, and the Disaggregated Future of Higher Education." *International Review of Research in Open and Distance Learning* 10, no. 5.

Wiley, David, John Hilton III, Shelley Ellington, and Tiffany Hall. 2012. "A Preliminary Examination of the Cost Savings and Learning Impacts of Using Open Textbooks in Middle and High School Science Classes." *International Review of Research in Open and Distributed Learning* 13, no. 3: 262–76. http://www.irrodl.org/index.php/irrodl/article/view/1153/2256.

Wiley, D. 2010. "Openness as Catalyst for an Educational Reformation." *Educause Review* 45, no. 4: 15–20. http://www.educause.edu/EDUCAUSE+Review/EDUCAUSEReviewMagazineVolume45/OpennessasCatalystforanEducati/209246.

Wu, Kerry. 2013. "Academic Libraries in the Age of MOOCs." *Reference Services Review* 41, no. 3: 576–87.

Zhao, Linlin. 2014. "Riding the Wave of Open Access: Providing Library Research Support for Scholarly Publishing Literacy." *Australian Academic & Research Libraries* 45, no. 1: 3–18.

Chapter Six

A Measured Approach

Evaluating Altmetrics as a Library Service

Hui Zhang and Korey Jackson

The emergence of altmetrics has drawn the attention of academic libraries as a new and effective approach for capturing the types of impact often ignored by traditional citation-based metrics. At Oregon State University Libraries, before investing in a full-scale implementation of altmetrics services, we conducted an assessment survey of faculty and other researchers in order to determine whether such products were as valuable to researchers as traditional bibliometrics (including h-index and journal impact factor). Based on the survey results, this chapter seeks to understand best practices for the introduction and implementation of altmetrics services. The results reveal a mixture of both enthusiasm and suspicion toward altmetrics as an impact measure. Ultimately, we find that, while academic libraries are in the best position to act as intermediary providers of altmetrics services, there is much need for refinement of altmetrics evaluation techniques and a more robust set of best practices for institution-wide implementation.

INTRODUCTION

The term *altmetrics* has already become familiar to many librarians, and as more libraries and journal publishers add altmetrics data to their scholarly content, the term is finding currency among researchers as well. But the actual practice of altmetrics—which we define as the "tracking of multichannel, online use and conversation around a discrete piece of scholarship"—has yet to gain wide acceptance among scholars, in part because scholarly and administrative motivations for adoption have not yet appeared. Librarians, on the other hand, especially those who have experienced the limitations of traditional bibliometrics, have been more apt to tout the potential benefits of the "alt" movement in impact metrics. These benefits have two primary beneficiaries: (1) scholarly venues outside the traditional academic journal (e.g., data and software repositories, blogs, non-peer-reviewed online publications) and (2) scholars who might be more likely to contribute to these venues (graduate students, researchers working in fields with clear public contribution mandates, software developers, and all scholars broadly invested in widening the focus of "what counts" as viable scholarship) (Haustein et al. 2014; Sud and Thelwall 2014).

With these benefits in mind, Oregon State University (OSU) Libraries and Press has begun looking to add altmetrics tracking to our institutional repository services (more on this process later). While Chamberlain (2013) and Piwowar and Priem (2013) have reported that scholars are already beginning to include altmetrics data in their CVs, the practice is by no means widespread, and general acceptance of altmetrics impact indicators is by no means assured. Before committing funds to a particular service, we wanted to be sure that such a service would actually benefit our faculty members and other local researchers and that these stakeholders had a clear investment in the overall efficacy and value of altmetrics.

The purpose of this study is not only to assess whether publicizing altmetrics data would benefit campus researchers but also to better understand researcher awareness of altmetrics and overall attitudes toward this relatively new model of assessing impact; if scholars expressed high degrees of skepticism about (or ignorance of) altmetrics services, then the net gain from introducing yet more data into local scholarly assessment practices would be doubtful. While the study is locally motivated, we are equally interested in how this emergent form of impact data has taken hold among scholars more broadly and what it represents as a trend to researchers who find themselves increasingly subject to data-driven evaluation—evaluation that results in decisions as crucial as who is hired into a new position, who receives tenure or promotion, and who is terminated from a position. To summarize, our research questions are:

1. What is the overall perception of altmetrics services and data among researchers (research associates, junior and senior faculty)?
2. How do rank (faculty and other) and departmental affiliation affect support (or lack thereof) for alternative metrics?
3. What benefits would result from OSU Libraries subscribing to specific altmetrics services for its institutional repository content?

What follows is a brief history and explanation of altmetrics practices and services and an overview of contemporary use cases for institutional adoption of various services. We then move on to a discussion of our survey methodology, a presentation of our findings, and finally a discussion of those findings and how they have affected our decision to support and implement altmetrics at OSU.

ALTMETRICS OVERVIEW

One of the major reasons for altmetrics' perceived lack of trustworthiness is the basic fact that it is so new to the bibliometrics scene. The term *altmetrics* was coined in 2010 by Jason Priem, a graduate student at the University of North Carolina and cofounder of Impactstory, an altmetrics service provider. Early on, the term became a token of semiradical dissent, due in part to its popularization in "Altmetrics: A Manifesto" (Priem et al. 2010), where the authors pushed for an expansion of the definitions of both *scholarship* and *metrics*. Ultimately, the manifesto concludes that the new networked world has forced a dramatic change in scholarly communication—seen in the profusion of alternate sites for publication (blogs, social networks, disciplinary and institutional repositories) and types of scholarly output (blog posts, datasets, other online dialogs)—and that this change demands a commensurate expansion of the tools used to assess scholarly merit.

On the surface, the argument is uncontroversial. It seems only fair to expand metric tools as the realm of scholarly production expands. But altmetrics has met with a mixed reception in both the scholarly and bibliometrics communities. For conservative elements in academic and publishing spheres, the *alt* in *altmetrics* tends to imply a worrisome either/or relationship with more traditional citation metrics rather than a more measured both/and relationship. And for true-blue radicals in the academy, altmetrics looks uncomfortably like an extension of the same neoliberal fixation on "outcomes assessment" that gave rise to administrators' overreliance on numbers to measure knowledge in the first place (Kansa 2014). The picture is not all hand-wringing and anxiety, however. As Haustein et al. (2014) have shown, librarians are starting to take notice: Of those they surveyed (all members of the 2012 Science and Technology Indicators Conference), a full "72% valued download counts, while a third saw potential in tracking articles' influence in blogs, Wikipedia, reference managers, and social media" (1145). Numbers like these represent strong positive growth in the rate of adoption of various altmetrics indicators.

To better understand altmetrics as a practice, we can turn to Tananbaum (2013), who offers a pithy definition in "Article-Level Metrics: A SPARC Primer." He writes that altmetrics (and specifically article-level metrics, which represent one subset of the genre) "open the door to measures of both the *immediacy* and the *socialization* of an article" (4, emphasis in original).

Unlike such instruments as h-index, which require long periods of citation history to be effective and accurate, altmetrics services tend to track scholarship's immediacy—its initial entry into the scholarly conversation and its uptake in popular news, social media, online citation managers, and the like. This kind of circulation data also accounts for the idea of the socialization of scholarship: how it is shared not only by scholars but also by pundits, policy makers, and the public at large.

Like most categories of "process," altmetrics is not any one general operation. It is much more accurate to define it as a diverse set of citation-tracking activities performed by a diverse set of actors. At the time of writing, the field of altmetrics services is dominated by three major players: Plum Analytics, Altmetric, and Impactstory. There are, of course, other services that make up the larger practice of alternative metrics tracking, particularly article-level metrics (ALM)—as the name suggests, ALMs represent similar kinds of usage data allied with a particular publisher's corpus of articles. ALM services are now being offered by the likes of the Public Library of Science (PLOS), Elsevier's citation database Scopus, Nature Publishing Group (publisher of the journal *Nature*, among others), and BioMed Central. But the three previously mentioned organizations represent the core of the market for non-publisher-specific services aggregating data on the use and discussion of various types of scholarship.

Services

It might be useful to explore these three altmetrics services briefly, as each has a slightly different mission and set of services to offer. There are of course macrolevel similarities: All provide tracking for different categories of user interaction with online scholarship (download counts, mentions in social media, references in online citation managers, etc.), and all offer some kind of visual shorthand for representing the numbers behind these various metrics.

For instance, Plum Analytics (which since 2014 has been part of EBSCO Information Services) has billed itself as a comprehensive metrics tracker, focusing not just on alternative sites for citation but also on typical in-journal citations. Plum Analytics' PlumX Metrics service, which is promoted specifically for institutional repositories (IRs), cuts a wide swath through the crowded terrain of publication types, locations, and categories of use. In order to make sense of the types of interactions being tracked, Plum Analytics breaks them down into five categories:

1. **Usage:** including numbers of clicks, downloads, and views of an article within various public and institutional repositories (DSpace, EB-

SCO, ePrints, PLOS, figshare, etc.), as well as the number of libraries holding a particular publication

2. **Captures:** including bookmarks and favorites from sources like Delicious, YouTube, and Slideshare, number of forks in GitHub, and number of saves by readers in scholarly networks like Mendeley and ResearchGate

3. **Mentions:** including number of blog posts discussing an article, number of comments about an article on Facebook, and number of Wikipedia links to an article

4. **Social media:** including number of times an article has been like or shared on Facebook and Google Plus and number of tweets mentioning an article

5. **Citations:** including CrossRef, PubMed Central, Scopus, and Social Science Research Network (SSRN)

Whereas Plum Analytics is primarily geared and marketed to institutions—providing large-scale synopses of departmental and university-wide research impact—Impactstory is focused squarely on the individual scholar. Indeed, their tagline, "Your CV, but better," is a clear indicator of the audience they envision. Users begin building their scholarship profile by creating an account linked to author identifiers (such as ORCID) and can then upload scholarly works to that profile page. The resulting page organizes material into types, such as article, dataset, figure, and software. Impactstory also tags each uploaded scholarly contribution with a series of badges according to subgroup, including "Cited" and "Highly Cited" (based on Scopus data) or "Saved" and "Highly Saved" (based on Mendeley and Delicious data).

Having gotten its start as the product of a hackathon in 2011, Impactstory is also more forthright about seeking to change the academic incentives and rewards culture. As their "About" page states, one express aim of the Impactstory tool is to "build a new scholarly reward system that values and encourages web-native scholarship." Though categorized less explicitly than on Plum, a similar set of research use and citation data is also available through the service. Impactstory also expands on the types of scholarship represented, featuring information about articles, datasets, figures, posters, slide decks, and software products. Finally, Impactstory differs from both Plum Analytics and Altmetric in that it is a 501(c)(3) nonprofit corporation, a status that contributes to its overall commitment to openness in terms of both its own transparency and its promotion of open science, open access, and open source materials.

Founded in 2011, Altmetric is probably best known for its signature "donut" scoring mechanism. The Altmetric donut represents a numeric score compiling several different inputs, including Twitter, Facebook, and other social media sources; blogs; citation managers like Mendeley and CiteULike;

major media outlets; and other sources like Wikipedia, F1000, and YouTube. Unlike Plum and Impactstory, Altmetric is attempting to cover all potential consumer bases, offering different service packages for institutions, researchers, and publishers: Almetric for Institutions is an application that displays impact figures for all research articles associated with a particular institution; Altmetric Explorer is their baseline system for tracking various mentions and uses of individual articles; and Altmetric API allows for embedding of an Altmetric score on any website associated with the particular article being tracked.

Games

One point worth mentioning relative to altmetrics' overall trustworthiness is the potential for unscrupulous researchers to game altmetrics scores. Many social media sites and citation managers like Mendeley and ResearchGate allow users to upload and share academic publications. All of the previously mentioned altmetrics services extract such data as number of downloads, views, and registered readers from these sites—data that ultimately becomes part of the final altmetrics score. Because such indicators are harvested automatically from the web, most of them are vulnerable to gaming (i.e., activities used by authors for self-promotion or boosting popularity) and spam (i.e., usage statistics being polluted by a software agent or web bot).

Previous studies reveal how various social impact indicators have been manipulated. Thelwall (2012) argues that authors and even journal editors could inflate the usage statistics of individual articles by repeatedly downloading them with the help of either human or computer agents. Additionally, although captures, such as bookmarks of an article made by users in Mendeley, are a relatively reliable impact indicator used by altmetrics-scoring mechanisms, gaming these article bookmarking features with fake profiles or simply by asking colleagues and other users to bookmark articles is yet another low-tech method of gaming final scores. Another common gaming approach is a kind of link farming in which all occurrences of various types of article metadata (e.g., title, DOI) are extracted to dummy web pages and used to inflate the final tally. There is also the broader issue of counting such mentions as a significant research metric in the first place. The majority of article mentions appearing on research journal websites are found in tables of contents or other similar descriptive lists and thus have no fundamental citation impact (Kousha and Thelwall 2007; Vaughan and Shaw 2003). Finally, within the sphere of social media, altmetrics is especially prone to being gamed due in large part to the kinds of preexisting spam that already infect platforms like Twitter and Facebook. Mass following, creation of multiple accounts or bot accounts, and repeated posting and duplicate updates are all examples of practices that produce misleading altmetrics.

Fortunately, the National Information Standards Organization (NISO) is currently at work on strategies to detect altmetrics gaming and spamming techniques. NISO (2014) recommends "[m]aking all altmetrics data openly available via a standardized API and/or download, a centralized altmetrics data clearinghouse, and audits for altmetrics data" as a set of operations that would help to reduce the vulnerability of altmetrics data to gaming (9). While NISO's efforts are still young and obviously rely on wholesale adoption by major players within the marketplace, there is reason to expect that the near future of altmetrics assessment will be a much more accurate one.

Case Studies

Rather than creating their own altmetrics harvesters for scholarship collections, most academic libraries and many publishers subscribe to services like the ones discussed earlier. We offer the following case studies as models of the ways in which both higher education institutions and publishers have implemented such third-party services.

Along with the Smithsonian Institute, the University of Pittsburgh Library System was one of two pilot institutions for Plum Analytics' harvester toolset PlumX (Howard 2013). Having successfully completed the pilot, the university now offers altmetrics tracking for all scholarly works deposited in their institutional repository, D-Scholarship, which houses a variety of material types, including documents, software, data, and images. At the bottom of each D-Scholarship publication landing page, a viewer can see associated altmetrics (e.g., number of downloads and Twitter mentions) embedded under descriptive metadata. At the time of writing, the University of Pittsburgh's PlumX account covers a total of 74,874 artifacts in the IR, predominantly government documents (approximately 37,000), articles and other papers (approximately 20,000), and theses and dissertations (approximately 6,000) (University of Pittsburgh 2015). In an interview conducted in early 2013, Timothy Deliyannides, director of the Office of Scholarly Communication and Publishing and head of Information Technology for the University of Pittsburgh, emphasized that the purpose of providing altmetrics is to offer a complete view of the impact of all intellectual outputs, including "gray literatures," such as presentation slides and software (Enis 2013). In this sense, PlumX was not implemented with any express purpose of changing how fundamental tenure and review processes work at the university but rather to provide a more granular snapshot of the impact of faculty and departmental scholarship in its many forms and in the many channels where it has taken hold. As Deliyannides puts it, "We're not really on a crusade to change any of the university's normal processes for tenure or review. . . . But we hope people will think of new ways to use this data. We do feel it's valid data and something that hasn't been gathered or reported before" (Howard 2013).

In a similar move, Wiley Journals, a major publisher of scholarly journal content, began in May 2013 to pilot the use of Altmetric services for a number of its subscription and open access journals (Warne 2014). By Wiley's own account, the results of the six-month pilot were positive—enough so that they decided in 2014 to deploy Altmetric tracking across all of its 1,500 journals. As a publisher, Wiley's primary motivations for adding altmetrics were less about measuring research impact and more about increasing readership and author submission rates. For this reason, much like our current study, Wiley was concerned with user attitudes about altmetrics implementation. As Warne (2014) summarizes,

> A major objective of our pilot was to assess reader and author views of altmetrics. . . . During the pilot we ran a poll of website visitors. 65% felt the metrics were useful with a further 23% indicating that they were somewhat useful. 77% of readers responding to the survey agreed or strongly agreed that altmetrics enhanced the value of the journal article. 50% agreed, or strongly agreed that they were more likely to submit a paper to a journal that supports altmetrics.

On the landing page of an article in Wiley's Online Library, users can click the "donut" thumbnail badge, which brings them to a dedicated metric page with detailed data and an overall Altmetric score for that article. While the Altmetric score is just one indicator of the quantity of attention the publication has received, it is an aggregate of several different sources. The "Score" page offers several modes for understanding the score with more granularity, including comparisons with all Wiley articles, with that particular journal's articles, and with articles of a similar age. The page also shows the geographic origins of the various input sources.

Starting in 2014, Oregon State University Libraries (OSUL) began adding an embedded Altmetric badge to the web page of each open access journal article deposited into ScholarsArchive@OSU, the university's IR. The implementation at OSUL first parses the article identifier (either as a DOI or a DSpace handle) from a metadata record and extracts metrics using the Altmetric API. Only when the article has garnered enough attention to receive an Altmetric score larger than zero will it trigger the display of the Altmetric badge.

In 2014, OSUL had a pilot Altmetric Explorer test covering all scholarly works deposited in ScholarsArchive@OSU—more than 50,000 repository items in total. Altmetric Explorer targets the needs of the individual author to measure and monitor the social impact of his or her works. The institutional edition of Explorer, Altmetric for Institutions, allows librarians or administrators to group authors by academic (i.e., departmental) affiliation in order to demonstrate the overall research impact of that group. During the pilot, library staff were able to use the tool to identify the top publications (those with the highest degree of web attention) at the university. The IR librarian notified corresponding authors in order to motivate further self-deposit of article content into the IR; to date, faculty self-deposit has increased following the introduction of altmetrics at OSUL. While this kind of outcome is certainly positive, there are still too many variables to trace direct causation. With this in mind, the next phase—which could take shape as a full subscription to Altmetric for Institutions or another similar service—will require further evidence to make a fully informed decision.

Survey Methodology

A total of 304 researchers were identified based on having authored publications indexed in Web of Science; this list was previously generated by library staff in an effort to promote open access and encourage authors to deposit their publications in the university's IR. The researchers on the list come from various academic rankings—instructor, assistant professor, associate professor, full professor, and emeritus faculty—and all have authored at least one journal article since 2013. The rank and normalized OSU school/college affiliation (i.e., all acronyms or abbreviations resolved to that school/college's full name) of each person were obtained from the university database. The survey was conducted using the online survey software Qualtrics and issued by staff at OSU's Survey Research Center (OSU-SRC). The solicitation of participants continued for five weeks.

The survey questionnaire was designed to be concise and free of field-specific jargon. For instance, the word *altmetrics* was replaced by *web usage*, a term defined by such examples as number of downloads, Twitter mentions, and inclusion in citation managers like Mendeley. The survey begins with six straightforward multiple-choice questions asking for participants' familiarity with bibliometrics (journal impact factor and h-index in particular) and social web tools like Twitter, Facebook, and reference managers. Next, participants answer five multiple-choice questions designed to ascertain their perceptions of altmetrics and its relative importance to their fields of study. The questions cover various aspects of altmetrics, such as which types of scholarship (journal articles, software, datasets, etc.) are most effectively measured by altmetrics and which originating institutions for altmetrics data (institutional repository/library, publisher, funding agency, etc.) are most trustworthy. The questionnaire concludes with two open-ended questions asking for participants' general comments, concerns, and opinions about altmetrics.

All the harvested survey responses were stored in Qualtrics and accessible to the two PIs and OSU-SRC staff. The answers to the multiple-choice questions were analyzed using cross-tabulation analysis, a popular method that is effective for categorical data. The columns and rows of a cross-tabulation table represent two different variables (such as "faculty rank" and answers to "How important is web usage as a measure of an article impact?" respectively), and the cells report the frequency counts and percentages corresponding to both variables. For instance, eight assistant professors consider web usage as a "somewhat important" measure, which constitutes 36.4 percent of all qualified respondents. The power of cross-tabulation analysis is its capacity to provide granular insight into the relationship between such variables as perception of altmetrics, faculty rank, and affiliation.

Results

Out of the 304 faculty members who were contacted to participate in the survey, 69 completed the survey, for a response rate of 22.7 percent. Faculty rank and affiliation in the e-mail list were used to group questionnaire responses for purposes of comparison. By affiliation, the greatest number of completed responses were received from the College of Agricultural Sciences (n = 16). An inadequate number of responses were received from Ocean and Atmospheric Sciences (n = 2); the College of Earth, Ocean, and Atmospheric Sciences (n = 1); the College of Education (n = 1); the College of Pharmacy (n = 3); and the College of Veterinary Science (n = 1). Therefore, these affiliations were not considered in the analysis. By title, the greatest number of responses were received from assistant professors (n = 22), followed by full professors (n = 17). For clarification, the designation "other researcher" refers to graduate students, postdoctorates, and research associates.

PERCEPTIONS OF BIBLIOMETRICS AND ALTMETRICS

Responses to the following five survey questions were used to answer our first research question concerning overall perception of altmetrics and bibliometrics:

Q1. How likely are you to rely on citation metrics, such as journal impact factor, when deciding which journals to publish in?
Q2. How likely are you to include your h-index or other measures of scholarly productivity in your CV or promotion dossier?
Q6. How important is citation count as a measure of an article's impact in your field?
Q7. How important is web usage (e.g., number of downloads, Twitter mentions, inclusion in citation managers like Mendeley) as a measure of an article's impact in your field?

Q8. In your opinion, does including web usage (e.g., number of downloads, Twitter mentions, inclusion in citation managers like Mendeley)
along with citation count create a more trustworthy measure of an
article's impact?

Fifty percent of responding faculty reported they were "somewhat likely" to
depend on journal impact factor in their selection of journals for research
submission. Another 28 percent were "very likely" (see figure 6.1). Thirty-
two percent were "very likely," and 19 percent were "somewhat likely" to
include their h-index or other measures of scholarly productivity in their CV
(see figure 6.2). For purposes of measuring the impact of journal articles, 88
percent of respondents reported that citation count is "very important" or
"somewhat important" (see figure 6.3), whereas only 37 percent reported that
they consider altmetrics (i.e., web usage) either "very important" or "somewhat important" (see figure 6.4). Forty percent of researchers agreed that
combining altmetrics with citation count creates a more trustworthy measure
of impact than citation count alone (see figure 6.5). It is also worth noting
that almost a quarter of respondents selected "not sure/does not apply," indicating that many researchers are still uncertain or undecided about altmetrics,
even in combination with more traditional bibliometrics.

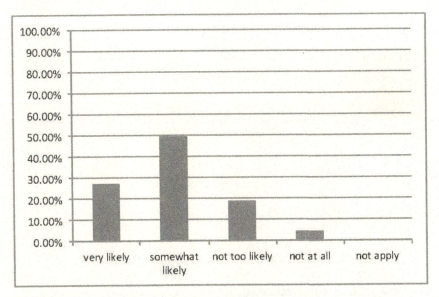

**Figure 6.1.   Q1. How likely are you to rely on citation metrics, such as journal
impact factor, when deciding which journals to publish in?**

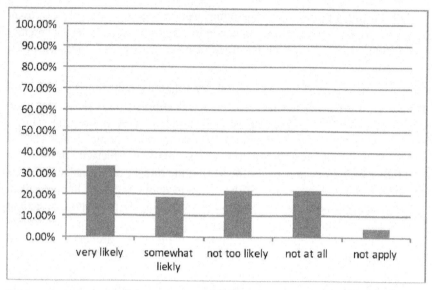

Figure 6.2. Q2. How likely are you to include your h-index or other measures of scholarly productivity in your CV or promotion dossier?

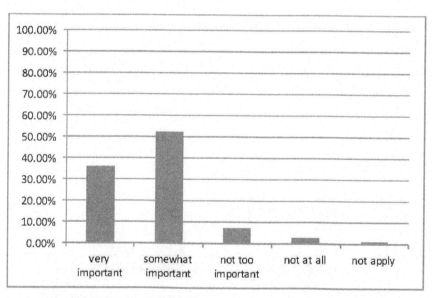

Figure 6.3. Q6. How important is citation count as a measure of an article's impact in your field?

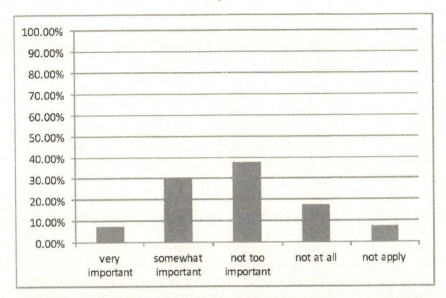

Figure 6.4.   Q7. How important is web usage (e.g., number of downloads, Twitter mentions, inclusion in citation managers like Mendeley) as a measure of an article's impact in your field?

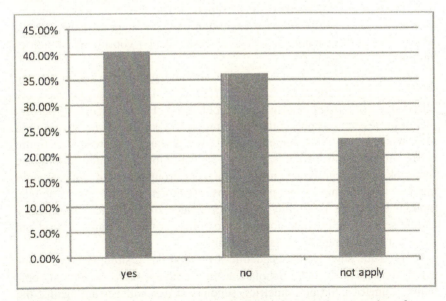

Figure 6.5.   Q8. In your opinion, does including web usage (e.g., number of downloads, Twitter mentions, inclusion in citation managers like Mendeley) along with citation count create a more trustworthy measure of an article's impact?

Effects of Faculty Rank and Affiliation

Answers to the same five questions are separated into both rank and affiliation to provide more granular analysis. We designated the following four categories related to rank: assistant professor (asst), associate professor (asso), full professor (prof), and other researcher (other). School/college affiliations are subdivided into the following: College of Agriculture Science (coll agri sci), College of Engineering (coll engi), College of Liberal Arts (coll lib arts), College of Business (coll business), College of Forestry (coll forestry), College of Public Health and Human Sciences (coll PHHS), and College of Science (coll sci).

When asked about the importance of citation count, an overwhelming majority of faculty across all ranks reported that it was either a "very important" or "somewhat important" (results combined as "important" in figure 6.6) measure of article impact in their respective fields. The same trend is also observed across colleges (see figure 6.7).

The results also suggest that faculty rank has little impact on perceptions of altmetrics (see figure 6.8). There are only slight variations across rank, with a majority of faculty in all four ranks reporting that altmetrics are either "not too important" or "not at all important" (again combined as "not important" for the sake of analysis) for measuring article impact. Likewise, respondents from across the seven colleges reported that altmetrics were "not important" to their fields, with the exception of the College of Liberal Arts, where 57.1 percent (four out of seven respondents) considered altmetrics "important" (see figure 6.9).

Looking at the question of whether combining altmetrics with citation count would make for an overall more trustworthy impact measure, there are observable differences in answers by faculty rank. For instance, 47.1 percent of full professors responded that offering both types of metrics was a good idea, whereas only 36.4 percent of the other researchers agreed (see figure 6.10). Overall, however, this roughly eleven-point differential among the four ranks is not significant enough to make a strong assertion that academic ranking has an impact on perceptions of altmetrics. We can conclude, though, that there is slightly more acceptance of altmetrics' importance among senior faculty when compared to colleagues in the ranks of graduate student, postdoctorate, or research associate.

The results suggest that academic affiliation has a stronger effect compared to professional rank: Scholars at three colleges favor the idea of combining altmetrics and bibliometrics, scholars at two colleges are against the idea, and scholars at the final two colleges are undecided (see figure 6.11). It is hard to conclude, however, that college affiliation (and, by extrapolation,

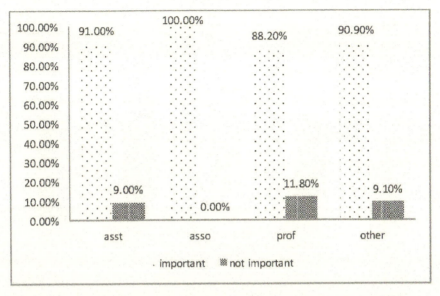

Figure 6.6. Q.6. How important is citation count as a measure of an article's impact in your field? (by faculty rank)

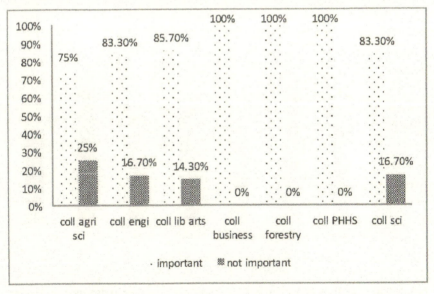

Figure 6.7. Q.6. How important is citation count as a measure of an article's impact in your field? (by faculty affiliation)

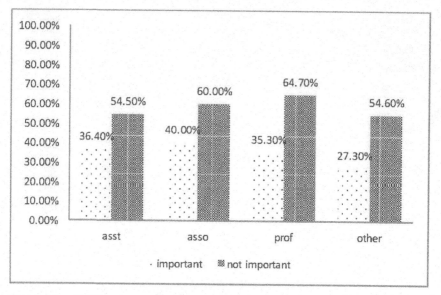

Figure 6.8.   Q7. How important is web usage (e.g., number of downloads, Twitter mentions, inclusion in citation managers like Mendeley) as a measure of an article's impact in your field? (by faculty rank)

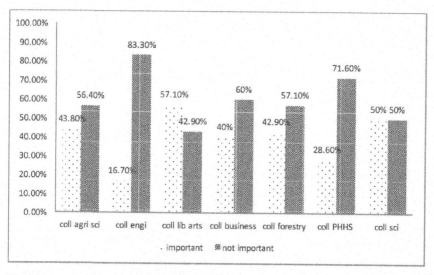

Figure 6.9.   Q7. How important is web usage (e.g., number of downloads, Twitter mentions, inclusion in citation managers like Mendeley) as a measure of an article's impact in your field? (by faculty affiliation)

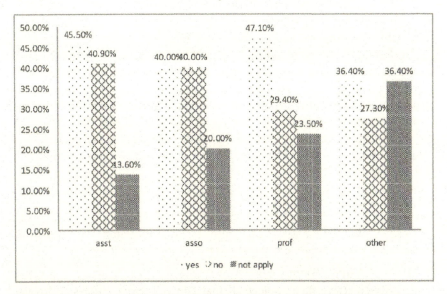

Figure 6.10.   Q8. In your opinion, does including web usage (e.g., number of downloads, Twitter mentions, inclusion in citation managers like Mendeley) along with citation count create a more trustworthy measure of an article's impact? (by rank)

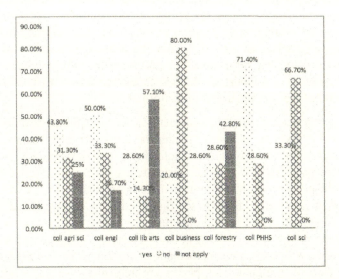

Figure 6.11.   Q8. In your opinion, does including web usage (e.g., number of downloads, Twitter mentions, inclusion in citation managers like Mendeley) along with citation count create a more trustworthy measure of an article's impact? (by affiliation)

research field) has a significant impact because its effects are relatively inconsistent. For instance, faculty from the College of Business and the College of Public Health and Human Sciences strongly disagree on Q8 (In your opinion, does including web usage [e.g., number of downloads, Twitter mentions, inclusion in citation managers like Mendeley] along with citation count create a more trustworthy measure of an article's impact?); 80 percent of the former selected "No," while 71.4 percent of the latter selected "Yes." Despite this discrepancy, they are of similar opinions regarding the other questions (even Q6 and Q7, which address the isolated importance of bibliometrics and altmetrics).

Altmetrics Services at OSU

The survey takers were asked the following three questions as a means of understanding how the library might provide altmetrics as a service:

Q9. Which of the following types of scholarship are effectively measured by web usage data? Select all that apply: journal articles, software, datasets, slides and posters, books and book chapters, white papers and tutorials, and other.

Q10. Please indicate how much you trust each of the following sources as providers of web usage data: institutional repository (library), publisher, funding agency, research database, and other.

Q11. What would motivate you to include web usage data in your CV or dossier? Select all that apply: funding agency encourages use of this information, department encourages use of this information, university promotion and tenure guidelines encourage use of this information, and peers engage in use of this information.

For Q9, 60.9 percent of the respondents selected "journal articles," with "white papers and tutorials" and "books and books chapters" as the second- and third-most selected types of scholarship (30.4 percent and 29 percent selected, respectively). It is not surprising to see "software," "datasets," and "slides and posters" at the bottom of the content types that are effectively measured by altmetrics tracking (see figure 6.12), as these types of scholarship are likely still unfamiliar to some research fields.

Institutional repositories (library) were selected as the most trusted source of altmetrics, with the highest percentage of respondents (46.4 percent) saying they trust them a great deal. Next were publishers, with 31.9 percent of respondents reporting that they would trust this venue a great deal. Research databases and funding agencies were regarded as the least reliable providers of altmetrics, garnering "trust a great deal" responses 24.6 percent and 21.7 percent, respectively (see figure 6.13).

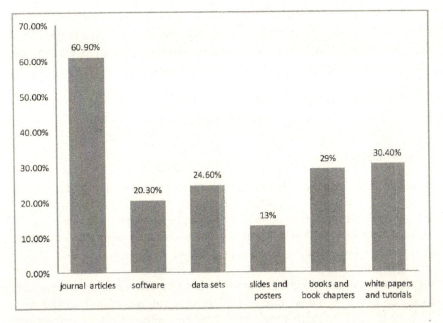

Figure 6.12.   Q9. Which of the following types of scholarship are effectively measured by web usage data?

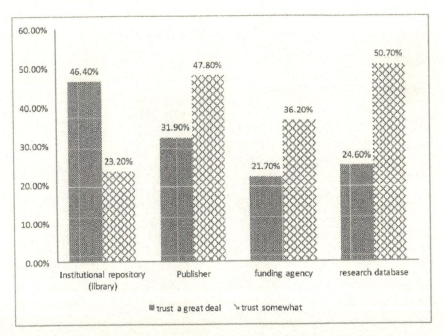

Figure 6.13.   Q10. Please indicate how much you trust each of the following sources as providers of web usage data.

Faculty report that the largest motivator for inclusion of altmetrics in their CVs or dossiers would result from encouragement within university promotion and tenure guidelines (68.1 percent). Motivation from peers was the second-most influential factor, with a 56.5 percent selection rate (see figure 6.14).

DISCUSSION

Limits of Study

Graduate students and junior researchers, such as postdocs and research associates, are likely underrepresented in the survey due to how the survey participants were recruited. Among the 304 researchers at OSU who received the survey invitation, 202 were faculty members (assistant professors, associate professors, or full professors), 64 were graduate students or postdocs, and 25 were categorized as assistant or associate instructors (it is worth noting that the response rate for the last two groups was null). This recruitment approach produced a high response rate of 22.7 percent (69 out of 304 candidates), with the tradeoff being that the results predominantly reflect the perceptions of faculty rather than other types of researchers (graduate students, postdocs, etc.). It would be valuable to conduct a similar survey focusing on graduate

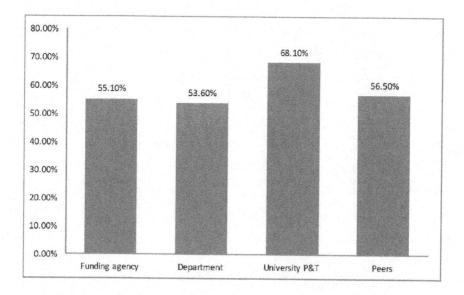

Figure 6.14.   Q11. What would motivate you to include web usage data in your CV or dossier?

students and compare their perceptions of altmetrics with results from faculty. It would be similarly valuable to explore responses from higher-level administrators (department heads, deans, and provosts), especially because these positions carry a great deal of weight when it comes to the overall research agenda and promotion and tenure guidelines within each college and at the university in general.

Additionally, this study only examines the impact of faculty rank and affiliation on perceptions of altmetrics, to the exclusion of several other worthwhile factors. For instance, the source of funding can be vital, especially as funding agencies have begun emphasizing that sponsored projects should demonstrate broad social impact as part of the research results. These kinds of requirements often make researchers more receptive to altmetrics and more likely to include altmetrics indicators in addition to citation counts. While this level of comprehensiveness is outside the scope of this chapter, such a large-scale study conducted with the collaboration of the library community could prove useful to institutions interested in adopting altmetrics products and services.

Longevity and Trust

Most of the faculty members who participated in the survey considered traditional citation count the most important and trusted measure of impact, despite the well-documented weaknesses of this method (Roemer and Borchardt 2015; Wilsdon et al. 2015; Wouters et al. 2015). The limitations of citation count include the lack of context (e.g., when, where, and why an article is cited), lack of capacity to credit newer types of scholarship (e.g., software, datasets), and lack of capacity for tracking the many ways a research product can be used outside of citation (e.g., sharing or hyperlinking in a blog post, mentions in news articles or on Wikipedia).

Given these limitations, we might ask why citation count is still considered the most reliable indicator of research impact. Based on our survey results, it appears that time is the key factor behind the dominance of traditional bibliometrics in scholarly communication. Figure 6.15 shows a correlation between the longevity and the perceived trustworthiness of a given metric strategy.

In this graph, the y axis represents respondents' reported levels of trust in certain metric types. The x axis indicates how long a given metric has been actively available (in years). For instance, the graph demonstrates that the "citation" metric has been in existence for approximately fifty-one years and maintains a corresponding trustworthiness of 88 percent. The longevity of each metric has been determined using the following information:

Citations (citation count): *Science Citation Index* became commercially available in 1964, fifty-one years prior to the study.

JIF (journal impact factor): *Journal Citation Reports* began publication in 1975, forty years prior to the study.

H-index: Jorge Hirsch first published his paper "An Index to Quantify an Individual's Scientific Research Output" in 2005, ten years prior to the study.

Altmetrics: "Altmetrics: A Manifesto" was published online in 2010, five years prior to the study.

The data do suggest a trend whereby the longer a bibliometrics service has been in existence, the more it is generally trusted by scholars. While this is obviously only a very general pattern and does not take into account variables like commercial viability and marketing, it does suggest that, if a new metric instrument can maintain active use and continue to demonstrate some kind of market value, then it stands a fair chance of being more readily adopted—and becoming increasingly trusted—within the academic community.

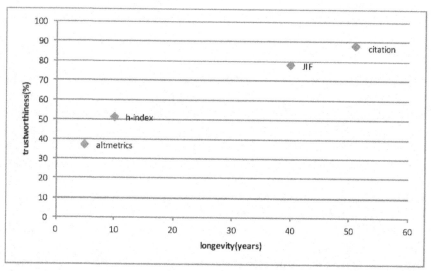

Figure 6.15.　Correlation of history and trust for major impact metrics.

Faculty Concerns with Altmetrics

The survey contained two open-ended questions allowing respondents to address questions and concerns they had about the use of altmetrics impact measures (again, referred to as "web usage" in the survey). Overall, we were surprised by both the number of responses and the depth of the input these questions generated. Answers spanned nearly eighty comments and generated, in total, more than three thousand words. We have tried to synthesize these concerns here (for selected quotations from this series of responses, please see appendix B).

Self-Promotion

In general, researchers were highly suspect of the utility of social media when it comes to scholarly impact. Many suspected that scholars, publishers, and other institutions would take advantage of social media outlets like Twitter and Facebook, falsely inflating both their altmetrics scores and the corresponding appearance of impact. One respondent questioned "how Twitter mentions can be a measure of impact," stating that there are "too many reasons why an article could have a Twitter mention, many of which are not related to scholarly impact."

Researchers were also anxious that altmetrics would force them to self-promote. Because social media sites are important sources for altmetrics data, the implication was that a researcher should be active on several platforms (Twitter, Mendeley, ResearchGate, etc.) to demonstrate impact. There was concern that such activity would impinge on actual research time and would not, in the end, do much to reflect the quality and usefulness of the scholarship.

Gaming and Spamming

Likewise, there was a good deal of concern over the potential for altmetrics numbers to be gamed or otherwise falsified. One respondent brought up the particular issue of bot downloads used to inflate download scores; this same researcher opined that "web usage data are highly suspect, no matter what the source, as long as bots are not excluded from downloading." In another comment, the respondent worried that "[l]arger groups and those with bigger public relations budgets will begin to dominate the market," their scholarship moving to the top of the list simply because it has been "promoted through various means."

Favor to Certain Fields over Others

There was also some apprehension about certain fields garnering more attention than others because of mainstream media popularity or general funding rates. One of the responses provided the following detailed scenario:

> The size of a given research community is often directly related to the amount of funding available in that area. In this regard, people who work in areas of "politicized science" are often deemed more relevant, and given a higher profile, simply because they're working on a more "popular" topic that catches the public's attention and pushes a particular political agenda. If people who

work in these areas receive more citations and downloads than someone in a less competitive field, what does this metric actually measure? . . . To measure all scientists, from both hard and soft disciplines on the same scale of productivity is ridiculous . . . Some structural biologists may spend years preparing a single manuscript, while a computational scientist may publish 12 papers in that time.

This last concern is especially acute when taking into account differences in the level of national funding and mainstream media attention between applied sciences and various forms of humanistic studies.

Lack of Meaningful Peer Review

The overall lack of peer review of online scholarship (e.g., presentations, blogs, and articles) was also a concern in the responses. As one respondent put it, the "lack of critical review of the majority of web-based materials prior to publication" could lead to the unfortunate scenario in which a "totally bogus article from any source" becomes accepted scholarship as a result of a high altmetrics score. The follow-on to this issue was general misgiving about altmetrics becoming a means of promoting and rewarding lower-quality research. Another respondent expressed "concern that papers that are published in lower impact journals, because they are simply not as strong or rigorous, could go on to be perceived to be more important or 'trustworthy' due to high social media exposure."

Providing Altmetrics as a Library Service

We were impressed with the level of knowledge many respondents had about altmetrics and the general operations of altmetrics services. The concerns expressed here are both legitimate and, in most cases, highly informed. That said, despite these concerns, there is still hope—and a good deal of it—for the future of altmetrics as a library service. Indeed, anxieties about altmetrics were counterbalanced by a fair amount of enthusiasm for new methods of measuring scholarly impact. Several respondents were hopeful about the fuller picture of impact offered by altmetrics indicators. One representative comment offered the opinion that altmetrics are a "good addition to more 'traditional' metrics," while another respondent was "supportive of alternative web-based metrics to supplement traditional citation metrics."

In addition to this kind of faith in the potential for altmetrics coming from the faculty and researcher ranks, there is also the fact that major national organizations and indexers have begun to support and refine the development of altmetrics. EBSCO, which acquired Plum Analytics in January 2014, has begun including usage statistics for articles and books across their various databases (EBSCO Information Services and EBSCO Discovery Service).

EBSCO (2014) describes the benefits of the relationship: "The article-level data from these databases will allow Plum Analytics' product PlumX to provide usage statistics on articles and books from tens of thousands of providers. This collaboration marks the first time the wealth of information about the actual usage per article such as abstract views, downloads, etc. can be measured across publishers."

In a similar move, at the end of 2013, Elsevier began displaying Altmetric badges for the top three rated articles from thirty-three of their titles (Huggett and Taylor 2014). This kind of support, while obviously motivated by commercial interest, speaks volumes about publisher investment in these types of services and, as a corollary, their perception that altmetrics stand to become a useful value-add to authors, readers, and scholarly communication consumers in general.

Based on the results of the survey, analysis of the faculty comments, and the general trend in the larger scholarly communication environment, we recommend implementation of altmetrics services at OSU Libraries. While we do not single out a specific provider, in all likelihood such implementation will take the form of subscription to a tool like Impactstory, Altmetric Explorer, or Plum Analytics' PlumX harvester (each of which maintains a back-end harvesting engine of various altmetrics data and a front-end display of an aggregate score based on this data). Acknowledging, however, that any implementation should be approached carefully, we offer the following best practices for the service:

- Display both altmetrics data and traditional citation indicators.
- Provide context for understanding the numbers behind a particular altmetrics score. Offer thoroughgoing answers to the "what and why" of altmetrics, including an introduction to what actually comprises altmetrics scores—where data are collected, how numbers are calculated, and how to interpret the results—and the overall rationale for implementation.
- Create a transparent interface for feedback about the service. We want to make sure that any researcher who has questions or concerns about the display of altmetrics data or methods for harvesting this data has access to a librarian who can answer such questions.
- Customize the suite of altmetrics indicators based on feedback from the local scholarly community.

In general, these practices point to a need for proper introduction to and interpretation of altmetrics as a service from a neutral third party; right now, the academic library is best placed to be such a mediator. For one, libraries represent a natural intermediary, already standing as they do between users and researchers on the one hand and service providers on the other. Libraries also have the potential to be a neutral but invested partner in creating a customized product that better serves both its users and scholarly communication writ large. Academic librarians are also in the best position to fill the information gap—which is one source of the trust gap revealed in the responses to our open-ended questions—by providing detailed information about altmetrics without any necessary agenda regarding their eventual use (in spaces like promotion and tenure review). Our survey results support this proposition, with 46 percent of responding scholars seeing the university library as the most trustworthy source for altmetrics services.

Thinking for a moment about why the library is trusted to serve in such an intermediary capacity, we might point out the fact that libraries have long served as both a space for information expertise and a zone free from any overt political or market-based agenda. Librarians may seek to change certain aspects of information dissemination, but ultimately such change is motivated by a desire to improve the accuracy, discoverability, and accessibility of information. To "improve" in this case means not only to widen the circle of discovery but also to create an information landscape that is culturally more inclusive. In the context of altmetrics, such inclusivity is about expanding both the genres of scholarship and the modes by which it is measured and evaluated.

CONCLUSION

In many ways, what we describe here is a desire to implement altmetrics "ahead of the curve"—to future-proof evaluation metrics in a dynamic scholarly environment by adopting and adapting tools that better serve scholars, their readers, and ultimately their careers. While faculty and other researchers involved in our study were not unilaterally in support of altmetrics, the fact that they expressed enthusiasm for new supplements to traditional citation count suggests the need to experiment with alternatives.

That said, librarians should not be satisfied with simply acting as passive consumers of vended products. As a neutral partner to the scholars we serve, we are well placed to voice concerns about everything from the accuracy of the source to ambiguity in the final score and vulnerability to nefarious actors. We suggest that more librarians be involved in informing policy around best practices, standards, and contextualization of altmetrics service products. While several members of the academic library community have served on standards committees sponsored by the likes of NISO, further involvement in this process can only help to strengthen altmetrics products and, finally, the ecosystem in which they can best succeed.

APPENDIX A: SURVEY QUESTIONNAIRE

Q1. How likely are you to rely on citation metrics, such as journal impact factor, when deciding which journals to publish in?

- Very likely (1)
- Somewhat likely (2)
- Not too likely (3)
- Not at all likely (4)
- Not sure/does not apply (5)

Q2. How likely are you to include your h-index or other measures of scholarly productivity in your CV or promotion dossier?

- Very likely (1)
- Somewhat likely (2)
- Not too likely (3)
- Not at all likely (4)
- Not sure/does not apply (5)

Q3. Do you maintain at least one active social media account (such as Facebook, Twitter, Instagram, etc.)?

- Yes (1)
- No (2)

Q4. Do you maintain at least one active reference manager account (such as ResearchGate, Mendeley, etc.)?

- Yes (1)
- No (2)

Q5. How important is open access to you and your scholarship?

- Very important (1)
- Somewhat important (2)
- Not too important (3)
- Not at all important (4)
- Not sure/does not apply (5)

Q6. How important is citation count as a measure of an article's impact in your field?

- Very important (1)
- Somewhat important (2)
- Not too important (3)
- Not at all important (4)
- Not sure/does not apply (5)

Q7. How important is web usage (e.g., number of downloads, Twitter mentions, inclusion in citation managers like Mendeley) as a measure of an article's impact in your field?

- Very important (1)
- Somewhat important (2)
- Not too important (3)
- Not at all important (4)
- Not sure/does not apply (5)

Q8. In your opinion, does including web usage (e.g., number of downloads, Twitter mentions, inclusion in citation managers like Mendeley) along with citation count create a more trustworthy measure of an article's impact?

- Yes, overall (1)
- No, overall (2)
- Not sure/does not apply (3)

Q9. Which of the following types of scholarship are effectively measured by web usage data? Select all that apply.

- Journal articles (1)
- Software (2)
- Data sets (3)
- Slides and posters (4)
- Books and book chapters (5)
- White papers and tutorials (6)
- Other (describe below) (7)

Q10. Please indicate how much you trust each of the following sources as providers of web usage data (see figure 6.16.).

Q11. What would motivate you to include web usage data in your CV or dossier? Select all that apply.

- Funding agency encourages use of this information (1)
- Department encourages use of this information (2)

- University promotion and tenure guidelines encourage use of this information (3)
- Peers engage in use of this information (4)

Q12. What concerns do you have about web usage data as a trustworthy measure of article impact?

Q13. What else would you like to say about the use of alternative web-based metrics as a supplement to traditional citation metrics?

	Trust a great deal (1)	Trust somewhat (2)	Trust very little (3)	Do not trust at all (4)	Not sure/Does not apply (5)
Institutional repository (library) (1)	O	O	O	O	O
Publisher (2)	O	O	O	O	O
Funding agency (3)	O	O	O	O	O
Research database (4)	O	O	O	O	O
Other (describe below) (5)	O	O	O	O	O

Figure 6.16.

APPENDIX B: RESPONSES TO OPEN-ENDED QUESTIONS

1. First, I think that web usage data are highly suspect, no matter what the source, as long as bots are not excluded from downloading.
2. I have no idea if the statistics on web usage are reliable. Just because someone visits a web-page does not mean the page content had any "impact."
3. It could be manipulated too easily.
4. Just because an article or dataset gets a lot of hits does not make it useful. It could be that it's receiving that attention because it's ungodly awful. Web usage data does nothing to inform *how* the article is being used.
5. Just because people download data and publications, it doesn't mean they actually use it.
6. Might be possible to game the system. Numbers would have to be taken with a grain of salt.
7. Some articles in my field have their impact very slowly—Philosophy is, in general, a slow-moving field—and gain a reputation over time.
8. The size of a given research community is often directly related to the amount of funding available in that area. In this regard, people who

work in areas of "politicized science" are often deemed more relevant, and given a higher profile, simply because they're working on a more "popular" topic that catches the public's attention and pushes a particular political agenda. If people who work in these areas receive more citations and downloads than someone in a less competitive field, what does this metric actually measure? Pragmatism? To measure all scientists, from both hard and soft disciplines on the same scale of productivity is ridiculous. . . . Some structural biologists may spend years preparing a single manuscript, while a computational scientist may publish 12 papers in that time. . . . A difference in the number of other researchers citing this work is indicative of multiple factors, none of which may accurately portray an equitable difference in the caliber or global import of the work being produced. Furthermore, in research . . . the impact of a paper should not always be measured on its immediate impact. . . . Paradigms and regimes of knowledge can change. . . . Good ideas can be missed, buried, forgotten, and then rediscovered.

9. We will increasingly be *flooded* with information promoting various people's scholarship. Authors will essentially become promoters of their own individual scholarship. Larger groups and those with bigger public relations budgets will begin to dominate the market. "Good scholarship" will not necessarily emerge to the top but rather the scholarship that gets promoted through various means. I can also envision that there will be large cabals created to partake in activities like this.

10. Web usage data says more about self-promotion than about the scientific merit of a publication.

11. As a supplement I suppose it would be fine, but it would be a very concerning path for me if we were to start to emphasize web-based metrics over citation metrics in the absence of meaningful peer review.

12. I am very supportive of alternative web-based metrics to supplement traditional citation metrics.

13. I like the idea that they are used as a supplement to provide a bit more info. I also like that there is no delay as there is for citations dependent on the review and publication process. I would like to see public scholarship, such as blogs, have some (even if small) consideration in P&T.

14. I think it would be great to have additional measures of impact above and beyond citation indices and h-indices. However, a metric that is just a count of something is not likely to be very useful. A useful metric also has to carry some evaluatory weight. Number of downloads, for example, could become a measure of the popularity of a

field but not tell you much about the impact of a particular study. On the other hand, something that tracks citations through time and across disciplines would be a nice complement to CI and h-index.

15. The lack of critical review of the majority of web-based materials prior to publication can fool a web-based metric into implying a totally bogus article from any source is a measure of exceptionally good performance. Hence, web-based metrics are by their nature intrinsically flawed due to a lack of actual thought involved in generating the measure of performance.

REFERENCES

Chamberlain, Scott. 2013. "Consuming Article-Level Metrics: Observations and Lessons." *Information Standards Quarterly* 25, no. 2: 4–13.

EBSCO. 2014. "PlumX Includes Usage Statistics from EBSCO Databases." https://www.ebsco.com/news-center/press-releases/plumx-includes-usage-statistics-from-ebsco-databases.

Enis, Matt. 2013. "As University of Pittsburgh Wraps Up Altmetrics Pilot, Plum Analytics Announces Launch of Plum X." *Digital Shift*. http://www.thedigitalshift.com/2013/02/research/as-university-of-pittsburgh-wraps-up-altmetrics-pilot-plum-analytics-announces-launch-of-plum-x.

Haustein, Stefanie, Isabella Peters, Judit Bar-Ilan, Jason Priem, Hadas Shema, and Jens Terliesner. 2014. "Coverage and Adoption of Altmetrics Sources in the Bibliometric Community." *Scientometrics* 101, no. 2: 1145–63.

Howard, Jennifer. 2013. "New Metrics Providers Help Keep Libraries in the Research-Tracking Game." *Chronicle of Higher Education*. http://chronicle.com/article/New-Metrics-Providers-Help/139555.

Huggett, Sarah, and Mike Taylor. 2014. "Elsevier Expands Metrics Perspectives with Launch of New Altmetrics Pilots." *Elsevier*. https://www.elsevier.com/authors-update/story/publishing-trends/elsevier-expands-metrics-perspectives-with-launch-of-new-altmetrics-pilots.

Kansa, Eric. 2014. "It's the Neoliberalism, Stupid: Why Instrumentalist Arguments for Open Access, Open Data, and Open Science Are Not Enough." *London School of Economics and Political Science*. http://blogs.lse.ac.uk/impactofsocialsciences/2014/01/27/its-the-neoliberalism-stupid-kansa.

Kousha, Kayvan, and Mike Thelwall. 2007. "How Is Science Cited on the Web? A Classification of Google Unique Web Citations." *Journal of the American Society for Information Science and Technology* 58, no. 11: 1631–44.

National Information Standards Organization (NISO). 2014. "Alternative Metrics Initiative Phase 1 White Paper." http://www.niso.org/apps/group_public/download.php/13809/Altmetrics_project_phase1_white_paper.pdf.

Piwowar, Heather, and Jason Priem. 2013. "The Power of Altmetrics on a CV." *Bulletin of the American Society for Information Science and Technology* 39, no. 4: 10–13. doi:10.1002/bult.2013.1720390405.

Priem, Jason, Dario Taraborelli, Paul Groth, and Cameron Neylon. 2010. "Altmetrics: A Manifesto." *Altmetrics*. http://altmetrics.org/manifesto.

Roemer, Robin Chin, and Rachel Borchardt. 2015. *Meaningful Metrics: A 21st-Century Librarian's Guide to Bibliometrics, Altmetrics, and Research Impact*. Chicago: ACRL/ALA.

Sud, Pardeep, and Mike Thelwall. 2014. "Evaluating Altmetrics." *Scientometrics* 98, no. 2: 1131–43.

Tananbaum, Greg. 2013. "Article-Level Metrics: A SPARC Primer." *SPARC*. http://www.sparc.arl.org/resource/sparc-article-level-metrics-primer.

Thelwall, Mike. 2012. "Journal Impact Evaluation: A Webometric Perspective." *Scientometrics* 92, no. 2: 429–41.

University of Pittsburgh. 2015. "PlumX Dashboard." https://plu.mx/pitt/g.

Vaughan, Liwen, and Debora Shaw. 2003. "Bibliographic and Web Citations: What Is the Difference?" *Journal of the American Society for Information Science and Technology* 54, no. 14: 1313–22.

Warne, Verity. 2014. "Wiley Introduces Altmetrics to Its Open Access Journals." *Exchanges*. http://exchanges.wiley.com/blog/2014/03/19/wiley-introduces-altmetrics-to-its-open-access-journals.

Wilsdon, James, Liz Allen, Eleonora Belfiore, Philip Campbell, Stephen Curry, Steven Hill, Richard Jones, Roger Kain, Simon Kerridge, Mike Thelwall, Jane Tinkler, Ian Viney, Paul Wouters, Jude Hill, and Ben Johnson. 2015. *The Metric Tide: Report of the Independent Review of the Role of Metrics in Research Assessment and Management*. Higher Education Funding Council for England. doi:10.13140/RG.2.1.4929.1363. http://www.hefce.ac.uk/media/HEFCE,2014/Content/Pubs/Independentresearch/2015/The,Metric,Tide/2015_metric_tide.pdf.

Wouters, Paul, Mike Thelwall, Kayvan Kousha, Ludo Waltman, Sarah de Rijcke, Alex Rushforth, and Thomas Franssen. 2015. *The Metric Tide: Literature Review (Supplementary Report I to the Independent Review of the Role of Metrics in Research Assessment and Management)*. Higher Education Funding Council for England. doi:10.13140/RG.2.1.5066.3520. http://www.dcscience.net/2015_metrictideS1.pdf.

Chapter Seven

Engaging Undergraduates in Scholarly Communication

A Case Study in Intellectual Entrepreneurship at Illinois Wesleyan University

Stephanie Davis-Kahl

Intellectual entrepreneurship (IE) is a useful frame for librarians in general and has special resonance when considering issues of and advocacy for open access and public access. As Professor Richard Cherwitz, founder of the Intellectual Entrepreneurship Consortium at the University of Texas, Austin, states, "The aim of intellectual entrepreneurship is to educate 'citizen-scholars'—individuals who own and are accountable for their education and who utilize their intellectual assets to add to disciplinary knowledge and as a lever for social good" (Cherwitz 2000).

IE serves as a bridge between academia and community, connecting the two entities and creating a reciprocal relationship between students, who apply their knowledge, and community partners, who benefit from students' involvement and provide a real-world outlet for learning. The "social good" quality of IE aligns with the social justice motivation behind open access and public access, and the "disciplinary knowledge" aspect of IE aligns with efforts to bolster public support for liberal education and higher education; it also connects directly to librarians' work with information literacy, data management, reference/consultation models, and collection development. Librarians are agents of IE themselves by training and ethos—"a good heart and an organized mind" (Gorman 1982). The mission of libraries is to provide access to information and knowledge, as well as an environment in which user choices are protected—all of which align with knowledge and social good. As intellectual entrepreneurs, librarians are perfectly situated to help students and faculty develop as intellectual entrepreneurs in their own right, in thought as well as in deed. This chapter discusses the opportunities for bringing together scholarly communication and IE, specifically for an undergraduate population at a liberal arts college.

WHAT IS INTELLECTUAL ENTREPRENEURSHIP?

IE is a major initiative founded and led by professor of rhetoric Richard Cherwitz at the University of Texas at Austin. The program is characterized by a broad approach to defining the word *entrepreneurship*. As Beckman and Cherwitz note,

> idiosyncratic definitions of entrepreneurship also underscore a fundamental tension with the term. A conscious acknowledgement of the problems with defining entrepreneurship in material/financial terms has spawned these grammatical shifts, broader conceptions of what entrepreneurship could mean for higher education and a need for overarching philosophy of practice. (Beckman and Cherwitz 2008, 90)

IE is grounded in the belief that higher education can and should play a positive role in community development and outreach, and through IE, students can connect their classroom experiences and learning with issues in their communities. IE is a way of envisioning higher education and community engagement as mutually beneficial and increasingly necessary. There are several types of entrepreneurship, as shown in figure 7.1, created by Professor Jeanne Koehler, Southern Illinois University School of Medicine.

Diversity within the definition and concept of *entrepreneurship* only strengthens Beckman and Cherwitz's argument that entrepreneurship includes, but goes beyond, a definition focused on the business world. Figure 7.1 demonstrates the scholarship that has been devoted to expanding and extending definitions of *entrepreneurship*. In searching the literature of various disciplines, we see that entrepreneurship is present in such varied fields as art and design (Levick-Parkin 2014), higher education (Chia 1996; Jansen et al. 2015), anthropology (Fayolle, Linan, and Moriano 2014), literary studies (Haveman, Habinek, and Goodman 2012), medicine (Eyre et al. 2015), psychology (White, Thornhill, and Hampson 2007), management (Ogilvie 2015), and urban studies (Freire-Gibbs and Nielsen 2014). IE as a philosophy is an alluring combination of the pragmatic and the ideal. It is

> premised on the belief that intellect is not limited to the academy and entrepreneurship is not restricted to or synonymous with business. Entrepreneurship is a process of cultural innovation. While the creation of material wealth is one expression of entrepreneurship, at a more profound level entrepreneurship is an attitude for engaging the world. Intellectual entrepreneurs, both inside and

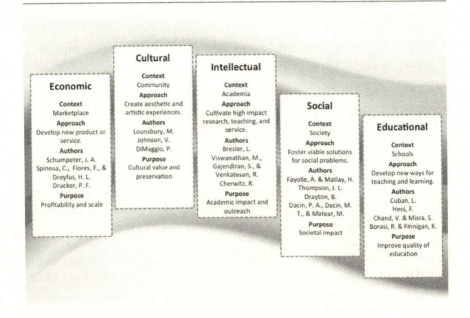

Figure 7.1.   Types of entrepreneurship. *Source: Koehler 2011*

outside universities, take risks and seize opportunities, discover and create knowledge, innovate, collaborate and solve problems in any number of social realms: corporate, non-profit, government, and education. (Intellectual Entrepreneurship Consortium n.d.)

IE speaks at once to "humanist traditions . . . the liberal arts . . . [and] the need for thought and reflection in the midst of the world of action" (Beckman and Cherwitz 2008, 98). It speaks also to pedagogy and teaching, to creating environments in which students are "agents of change who own, are accountable for and put their knowledge to work for the betterment of themselves and society" (Beckman and Cherwitz 2008, 99). It is characterized by words we hear often in higher education, especially when discussing outcomes for students—*discovery, engagement, integrative thinking, collaboration, ownership*, and *action*—and is conceived as an environment where the student moves from the classroom into the community and back again, bringing together what they know and what they do with community partners. As Cherwitz states,

> Complex problems cannot be solved by any one academic discipline or institution. Answers demand collaboration and joint ownership of learning among universities and the public and private sectors. Such an approach rejects the

typical elitist sense of "service," where universities are the sole proprietors of knowledge, contributing to society by promising "access" and "knowledge transfer." (Cherwitz 2005, 69)

Intellectual Entrepreneurship and the Framework for Information Literacy in Higher Education

The idea of educating citizen-scholars who collaborate with communities to solve problems resonates strongly with the ethos of librarianship. To a profession that prides itself on positive community engagement, providing access to information without barriers, promoting discovery and creation of new knowledge through ethical and informed information-literate practices of research, IE is extremely compelling. IE also fits well with the framework for information literacy in higher education (hereinafter referred to as the framework), which was adopted by the Association of College and Research Libraries (ACRL) in early 2016. The introduction to the framework notes that today, "students have a greater role and responsibility in creating new knowledge, in understanding the contours and the changing dynamics of the world of information, and in using information, data and scholarship ethically" (ACRL 2016). This statement echoes IE's focus on students as active participants in the community, partners with specific knowledge who are invested in the community's health and success.

IE and the vision of information literacy (IL) presented by the framework intersect in several ways. First, both of them stress learning and behavior— IE by emphasizing disciplinary knowledge, and the framework by focusing on "knowledge practices," which it defines as "demonstrations of ways in which learners can increase their understanding of these information literacy concepts" (ACRL 2016). Second, both aim for a shift in what the framework calls "knowledge dispositions," which are "ways in which to address the affective, attitudinal, or valuing dimension of learning" (ACRL 2016), either directly in response to students' experiences in the community (IE) or during the research process (the framework). Third, both IE and the framework are discipline-neutral. Both the main definition of *IE* and the six concepts that make up the framework can be applied to any and all disciplines, as well as interdisciplinary studies. Both also function as student-centered foundations for learning, application, practice, and experimentation, and both emphasize integration. The framework's definition of *IL* is based on integration: "Information literacy is the set of *integrated abilities* encompassing the reflective discovery of information, the understanding of how information is produced and valued, and the use of information in creating new knowledge and participating ethically in communities of learning" (ACRL 2016, emphasis mine). IE, by insisting on a reciprocal and equal relationship between knowledge and experience, also uses integration as an indicator of success. Fourth, both

IE and the framework can be put into practice anywhere in the curriculum, with any level of undergraduate or graduate student. Both the framework and the philosophy behind IE undergird *High-Impact Educational Practices*, a set of educational experiences espoused by the American Association of Colleges and Universities (AAC&U) that have been shown through the work of George Kuh and others to significantly engage students (Kuh 2008). Finally, both IE and the framework rely on student agency to participate, reflect, and improve themselves and their work in the classroom, IE with its focus on students' ownership of their experiential learning process, and the framework with its focus on metacognition, defined by Merriam-Webster as "awareness or analysis of one's own learning or thinking processes" (Merriam-Webster 2015). It could be argued that, in order for IE to be fully realized, the dispositions in the framework must be mastered, and for the framework to be fully mastered, students must apply their knowledge as set forth in the definition of *IE*. It seems, therefore, that the two are linked inextricably and serve to improve one another.

Intellectual Entrepreneurship and Scholarly Communication

The "social good" element of IE provides the strongest connection to scholarly communication advocacy for open access (OA) and public access (PA). Sharing the products of state or federally funded faculty research is a vital form of social good enacted by both OA and PA. Another connection is the strong advocacy for fair use as a social good. The movement to educate the public about their rights as readers and users of content through the creation of Creative Commons licenses is another vital contribution toward legal and ethical use of information in all formats and serves as a teaching opportunity for librarians, faculty, and students in curricular and cocurricular experiences. Large-scale efforts to open content, such as textbooks, data, images, journals, and monographs, all fulfill IE's integration of disciplinary knowledge for the social good philosophy and, thanks to reuse and share-alike licenses, encourage expanding and extending scholarship in the hands of the public. Similar to IE, scholarly communication advocacy efforts in OA and PA, as well as author rights, serve to educate and shift behavior and attitudes in the hopes that faculty and researchers will take ownership of their work. Beckman and Cherwitz (2008) state that "discovery is a privilege shared by the university community" (93), and scholarly communication advocacy seeks to extend that privilege directly to the public.

Case Studies

At Illinois Wesleyan University (IWU), we are fortunate to have a number of opportunities to connect scholarly communication education and advocacy with information literacy in the framework of IE. The following are short case studies that illustrate examples of positive collaboration with faculty, departments, and schools; risk and experimentation; application of disciplinary knowledge; and open sharing of undergraduate work to benefit the community. The examples align well with IE, as they show students engaging deeply with a specific topic within or across disciplines to identify and create new interpretations and knowledge that they then share with their scholarly and artistic communities, either locally or globally.

Undergraduate Research

The Council for Undergraduate Research (CUR) defines *undergraduate research* as an "inquiry or investigation conducted by an undergraduate student that makes an original intellectual or creative contribution to the discipline" (Council for Undergraduate Research n.d.). Gerald Graff (2006), professor of English and educational studies at the University of Illinois at Chicago, states, "'Research' is best defined simply as work that enters the current conversation of a particular field in a significant way." At IWU, a deep and vibrant tradition of undergraduate research fulfills both of these definitions. Departmental honors is one such example. The program requires a 3.50 grade point average in the major, a proposal approved by a faculty research advisor, and a commitment by three faculty members to serve as the student's research committee. The student defends the project at the end of the year, receives a notation on his or her transcript, and is expected to deposit the final project in Digital Commons @ IWU, the institutional repository. It is a common practice for students working toward honors to participate in the John Wesley Powell Undergraduate Research Conference (also known as JWP), an annual event that celebrated its twenty-seventh anniversary in 2016. Honors students usually give a presentation on their findings or present a poster to share their methods and conclusions with an audience of faculty, fellow students, parents, alumni, board of trustees members, and members of the community.

Students have the option to share their JWP presentations and posters via Digital Commons @ IWU; workshops sponsored by the JWP committee teach students about this opportunity and introduce them to the permissions form that allows IWU to distribute their work, while they retain copyright. Students are encouraged to confer with their faculty advisors for advice on sharing their work, and they often consult the scholarly communications librarian for guidance as well. The conference is an excellent opportunity for students to share their work through the repository, and most choose to do so. Every year, however, a number of students elect not to share their work, some because they are working with faculty on projects that will eventually be published in the professional literature, and others for personal reasons; others decide to embargo their work for a few years.

There are also faculty who require their students not only to present at the conference but also to deposit their work in Digital Commons. One example is Professor Leah Nillas in educational studies. Senior students in the department are required to undertake a major research project as part of their student teaching in order to fulfill state requirements for the teacher credential. Professor Nillas requires her students to create a poster based on their research and present it at the JWP conference; all teachers who supervised the students during student teaching are invited to the presentation, so that students may share their results and publicly thank their supervising teachers. The teaching opportunities related to scholarly communication issues here are mainly focused on providing clarity regarding the roles, rights, and responsibilities of the students in relation to the university and include reviewing the permissions form to clarify student roles and responsibilities for using others' work ethically and to ascertain that students understand their role and rights as copyright holders.

Student work in the Schools of Music and Art presents interesting challenges for the repository but also offers new opportunities for students to critically consider whether to share their work openly. In the past, the conference's art and music events were not as well attended as the poster and oral presentations. Creating a collection expressly for fine arts was an early goal in the development of Digital Commons @ IWU due to the excellent quality of student work, the potential for expanding the reach of the that work, and the capacity of the platform to integrate video and images. Again, informing and educating students about their roles, rights, and responsibilities is key; allowing them to consider and reflect on the pros and cons of sharing their work gives them the agency to manage their own artistic identities and voices. The music students especially are given several options to share and archive their work via video- or audiotaped performances hosted in the repository, PDFs of their scores hosted in the repository, the same PDFs added to the library's collection, or all of the above. These options are included in the permissions form designed especially for music students and developed in collaboration with composition faculty. Art students are given similar options—a recording of their presentation on video or audio, plus a transcript to improve discoverability of their work. Finally, we ask permission to host images of the students' works in the repository. By working with art and music students to discuss options for sharing and by sharing different forms of their work, it is our hope that we educate them on positive models of permissions and rights; give them a vocabulary for advocating for their creators' rights in the future; and build goodwill between the library, the school, and their students and alumni.

Curricular Opportunities

Another example of the intersection between IE and scholarly communication advocacy is via the formal curriculum. Two courses at IWU in the social sciences, Creating a Sustainable Society and Visual and Ethnographic Methods, are significant in this regard. In both courses, students work to gain specialized skills and knowledge in the disciplines, and they interact with community members to apply their knowledge and skills to issues within the community or to explore the lives and professions of community members. Both courses carry with them the expectation of a major final project and the requirement that the product of the work be shared with the community. The professors who teach both courses select projects that result in high-quality research and writing for inclusion in Digital Commons @ IWU.

Visual and Ethnographic Methods is an upper-division course offered in the Anthropology Department. The course description states that "analysis of the production of visual ethnographic material from the turn of the century to the present is followed by hands-on training in ethnographic interviewing and culminates with student-produced ethnographic films" (Illinois Wesleyan University Catalog 2015, 129). Students in the course produce not only short films but also posters for the JWP conference and photo-essays. Professor Rebecca Gearhart selects a few essays each year for inclusion in Digital Commons and has revised her standard Institutional Review Board proposal for the course so that participating community members who serve as research subjects understand that the information about them collected by students is openly accessible via the repository. The social good element demonstrated in this example is educating the campus community about members of our external community; the diversity of professions, experiences, and life histories portrayed in the photo-essays helps to break the campus bubble we often reference in discussions of our students' campus experience and connects with IE's ideal of sharing discoveries: "Perhaps the most important part of the IE ethos is bringing a discovered idea—one which is owned by an individual or group—to a community which will benefit from this innovation" (Beckman and Cherwitz 2009, 23).

By agreeing to share their work openly via Digital Commons, the students are sharing their discoveries beyond the campus community with the potential of sharing beyond even the local community. The students' choice to share completes the final phase of the scholarly communication cycle: dissemination, with an understanding of their rights and responsibilities as researchers and as copyright holders, because they have made an important contribution to their discipline and community.

Creating a Sustainable Society, the senior seminar course for environmental studies, provides majors with the chance to match their coursework with a "real-world" sustainability challenge in the local community. According to the course description, "[a]pplying the subfield perspective they have acquired in earlier coursework, each student will research and write a substantial paper on the seminar topic and present his or her findings orally. Taken collectively, these individual works will provide a multidisciplinary analysis of the seminar topic" (Illinois Wesleyan University Catalog 2015, 176). By asking students to build on the foundation of past coursework (i.e., scaffolding to a capstone experience), the course requires students to grapple with the integration of research methods, writing skills, and real-world issues encountered in the Bloomington-Normal community. Similar to Visual and Ethnographic Methods, students' research and the community partnership culminate in a presentation to community organizations and with a paper, some of which are selected for inclusion in our institutional repository.

There have been projects that have brought about significant social change in our community, such as "Growing Food Justice in West Bloomington, Illinois" by Daniel Burke (2008), class of 2009. Burke's paper discusses food insecurity writ large and the food desert in West Bloomington and ultimately led to an internship with the Heartland Local Food Network. During his internship, he developed and implemented a plan to provide residents of Bloomington-Normal who receive benefits from the Supplemental Nutrition Assistance Program (SNAP) easier access to our local farmer's market via a grant-funded point-of-sale machine for the farmer's market. Thanks to his efforts and the community's support, now anyone can use cash, credit cards, or SNAP cards to purchase tokens to use at the farmer's market as payment. The course often deals with similar issues of social justice, and students in the course are often involved in our campus Action Research Center.

Not only does Creating a Sustainable Society pose a significant IL challenge for students, who seek out and use scholarship from various disciplines to inform their work, but the projects also pose challenges at times for the students whose work is selected for deposit in Digital Commons. Pursuing permissions for images and text used in presentations to community members offers an excellent teachable moment for locating Creative Commons–licensed images and for best practices in requesting permissions from rights holders. In addition, education about the responsibilities and rights of researchers is a key aspect of students' dissemination of their work after the coursework is completed.

Undergraduate Journals

Illinois Wesleyan University currently has six undergraduate journals, four of which are long-standing publications sponsored by departments and hosted in the institutional repository. In general, undergraduate journals are an increasingly high-interest area for academic libraries, especially as library

publishing programs become more prevalent. Undergraduate journals connect with several of the AAC&U's *High-Impact Educational Practices*—
collaborative projects, undergraduate research, capstone projects, and intern-
ships. Sharon Weiner and Charles Watkinson of Purdue University published
an article in the *Journal of Librarianship and Scholarly Communication*
about their assessment of undergraduate journals. In their study, they found:

> The assessment showed that student authors benefitted from experiencing the
> full spectrum of the scholarly publishing process. Notably, students gained
> knowledge of important information literacy concepts. These learning gains
> and the demonstrated influence of JPUR [*Journal of Purdue Undergraduate
> Research*] on student career and scholarly aspirations clearly show that publi-
> cation of an undergraduate research journal supports university priorities for
> student success as well as the Libraries' strategic priorities of information
> literacy and scholarly communication. (Weiner and Watkinson 2014, 1)

Each undergraduate journal at IWU has its own identity, traditions, and mission; this chapter focuses on the *Undergraduate Economic Review* (*UER*)
because of its strong and collaborative partnership with the library. The *UER*
has an interesting history and is a stellar example of IE and scholarly communication advocacy efforts. The *UER* has its roots in collaboration; before
the *UER* was developed, Illinois State University, located about a mile away
from our campus, and IWU published a joint undergraduate research journal
called the *University Avenue Undergraduate Journal of Economics*. That
journal ceased publication in 2004, and the *UER* was created to "support and
encourage high quality student research in all areas of economics by publishing the best undergraduate papers from across the world" (Garg 2004, 14).
The *UER* is sponsored by the Department of Economics at IWU, with infrastructure for submission, review, and publishing provided by the Ames Library at IWU through our institutional repository, Digital Commons @ IWU.
Submissions are open to any undergraduate student in economics in the
world. The journal has had submissions from Mexico, England, China, and
India, to name a few. It is a born-digital, open access journal, and all authors
retain copyright in their work. Editorial processes are run by the student
editorial board, which is led by a senior economics major selected by the
faculty as the editor-in-chief.

The journal, while run by students, is advised by two faculty members.
Professor Michael Seeborg, the Robert S. Eckley Distinguished Professor of
Economics, and I, in my capacity as scholarly communications librarian and
the library liaison to the department, serve as managing faculty coeditors and
advisors to the editorial board. Professor Seeborg contributes his substantial
disciplinary expertise, and I advise from my perspective as a librarian, liaison, and open access advocate. My goal is to teach and educate students
about their contributions to the overall open access movement through their

work on the *UER*. The editorial board meets throughout the year to discuss marketing the journal to increase submissions; different types of research to feature in the future; and, most recently, the possibility of including data with articles.

Most of our reviewers are drawn from the Economics Department's senior seminar, and also include younger students who have excelled at writing in the department—each fall, we meet as a group and review the criteria for publication as well as the mission of the journal and its history, and I give a presentation and lead a discussion about scholarly publishing; the tension and stressors on the scholarly publishing environment (as well as generally within higher education and for libraries); and how open access, while not without its own challenges and issues, is a way to achieve the mission of research—to contribute to the common good by sharing knowledge. It is a new topic for the majority of the students, and it is often a thought-provoking conversation for them.

Professor Seeborg and I, in collaboration with Professor Robert Leekley, the advisor for the *Park Place Economist*, designed and deployed a survey to better understand the costs and benefits to students' participation in the two economics journals. Our results echoed the Weiner and Watkinson study. Peer-reviewing had a significant impact on students' learning in three specific areas: It offered a model for students' writing in general, it helped them learn about new applications of economic concepts, and it helped them to learn about other areas of economics. In addition, 63 percent of students said they gained a better understanding of open access; in fact, Jake Mann, who served as editor-in-chief from 2011 to 2012, wrote the journal's open access statement during his term. Further, in a bepress webinar broadcast in 2013, then-editor-in-chief Skye Song stated:

> As a reviewer, my critical thinking and writing skills improved substantially through reviewing the articles. . . . And the critical thinking and writing skills I gained through my work with the UER proved beneficial for my own coursework, because I remember when there were group projects—oftentimes I found myself the designated proofreader and trusted by my peers to make the final edits for the papers. Now, two years later, as the editor-in-chief, although my responsibilities have moved away a little bit from reviewing articles, I have taken on other responsibilities, such as recruiting and managing reviewers and editors, assigning any editorial tasks, reviewing reports by the editors to make final decisions on articles, maintaining communications with authors, faculty members from other institutions, and answering inquiries. Therefore, this role has greatly enhanced my leadership and teamwork skills, as well as my communication and organization skills. (quoted in Davis-Kahl and Seeborg 2013)

What began as an experiment with Professor Seeborg and the *UER* is now a fully formed partnership that represents IE's mission to create experiences for students to use their disciplinary knowledge for the public good. The presentation at the beginning of the year stresses the *UER*'s contribution to the economics discipline and to the open access movement as a model for undergraduate students and faculty to disseminate their work. The experience of working with the journal opens up the opportunity to embed scholarly communication education and advocacy directly into the curricular and extracurricular experience for students. Further, in participating in the journal, students *integrate* past coursework from their majors, from IWU's writing program, and from the various IL sessions they have participated in from their first year. Bringing all these elements together embodies the integrative aspects of IE for students. If our goal is to educate a knowledgeable, engaged, and information-literate citizenry, then we must not only embed topics of open access, public access, and author rights into our work with undergraduates; we must also do so in ways that connect with disciplinary knowledge and lived experiences.

Benefits for Undergraduates, Libraries, and Institutions

Bringing together IE and scholarly communication education and advocacy has several benefits. Building on existing curricula and partnerships between faculty, departments, and the library can create new ways to foster and share information between the university and the community. Using the repository as an outlet for student work requires a high level of relationship development with faculty to create trust and to dispel concerns about OA, many of which are born out of myth and misperception. Using the repository can encourage different conversations between faculty, students, and librarians that extend IL instruction and has the potential to give librarians a new role on campus as experts in copyright as well as open access advocates. Sharing student work, especially work done in partnership with the local community, can help demonstrate intellectual, creative, and scholarly achievements, the marketing of skills, and adherence to the ethics and conventions of the discipline. For prospective students and their parents, showcasing products of IE experiences in the repository can help to promote the university as a place that values student-centered learning and the accomplishments of students and speaks to the achievements of a liberally educated student at IWU. Finally, students who choose to share their work do so after making an informed decision about why sharing with a wider community is beneficial and part of their learning experience.

There are also challenges to using IE to embed scholarly communication education and advocacy into student experiences. Unfamiliarity with the term *intellectual entrepreneurship* or a distrust of entrepreneurship in general could be a stumbling block for librarians wishing to frame their work in this way. Regarding open access, there are still many faculty members who are unfamiliar with open access or still view it as anathema to true scholarship, equating it with predatory or vanity publishing. There may also be strong concern regarding the sharing of undergraduate work specifically, even work that has been designated as honors, as too unpolished to share with the discipline at large.

CONCLUSION

Chambliss and Takacs (2014) state that "students best learn skills in a supportive community, with relationships that value and encourage those students and those skills. *The real people involved*—not the abstract 'programs'—are crucial" (133). IE helps students to find and own their voices, in part due to the relationships formed with faculty through courses; with community partners through experiential learning; and with librarians as experts in open access, copyright, and author rights. Open access advocacy for scholarship arising out of IE experiences with community partners teaches students about their agency over the products of their scholarship, communicates the certification of a significant academic achievement, and finally acknowledges that their research has had meaning and value within the local communities.

REFERENCES

Association of College & Research Libraries (ACRL). 2016. "Framework for Information Literacy in Higher Education." http://www.ala.org/acrl/standards/ilframework. Accessed October 3, 2015.

Beckman, Gary D., and Richard A. Cherwitz. 2008. "Intellectual Entrepreneurship as a Platform for Transforming Higher Education." *Metropolitan Universities* 19, no. 3: 88–101.

———. 2009. "Intellectual Entrepreneurship and the Role of the Business School." In *Handbook of University-Wide Entrepreneurship Education*, edited by G. Page West III, Elizabeth J. Gatewood, and Kelly G. Shaver, 21–34. Cheltenham, UK: Edward Elgar.

Burke, Daniel. 2008. "Growing Food Justice in West Bloomington, Illinois." *Outstanding Senior Seminar Papers*. Paper 5. http://digitalcommons.iwu.edu/envstu_seminar/5.

Chambliss, Daniel F., and Christopher G. Takacs. 2014. *How College Works*. Cambridge, MA: Harvard University Press.

Cherwitz, Richard A. 2005. "Faculty Forum: Intellectual Entrepreneurship." *Academe* 91, no. 4: 69.

Chia, R. 1996. "Teaching Paradigm Shifting in Management Education: University Business Schools and the Entrepreneurial Imagination." *Journal of Management Studies* 33, no. 4: 409–28.

Council for Undergraduate Research. n.d. "Fact Sheet." http://www.cur.org/about_cur/fact_sheet. Accessed October 4, 2015.

Davis-Kahl, Stephanie, and Michael C. Seeborg. 2013. "Building an Outstanding Student Research Journal in the IR." http://digitalcommons.bepress.com/webinars/34. Accessed October 4, 2015.

Eyre, Harris A., Timothy Lindsay, James A. Churchill, Oliver Cronin, and Arlen Meyers. 2015. "Fostering Creativity and Innovation in the Health System: The Role of Doctors-in-Training in Biomedical Innovation and Entrepreneurship." *Medical Journal of Australia* 203, no. 2: 68–70.

Fayolle, Alain, Francisco Linan, and Juan A. Moriano. 2014. "Beyond Entrepreneurial Intentions: Values and Motivations in Entrepreneurship." *International Entrepreneurship and Management Journal* 10, no. 4: 679–89.

Freire-Gibb, Lucio Carlos, and Kristian Nielsen. 2014. "Entrepreneurship within Urban and Rural Areas: Creative People and Social Networks." *Regional Studies* 48, no. 1: 139–53.

Garg, Mahi. 2004. "A New Beginning: The *Undergraduate Economics Review*." *Park Place Economist* 12. http://digitalcommons.iwu.edu/parkplace/vol12/iss1/8. Accessed October 4, 2015.

Gorman, Michael. 1982. "A Good Heart and an Organized Mind." In *Library Leadership: Visualizing the Future*, edited by Donald E. Riggs, 73–83. Phoenix: Oryx Press.

Graff, Gerald. 2006. "Confusions about Undergraduate Research." http://geraldgraff.com/graff_articles/On_Defining_Research.pdf.

Hatch, Rachel. 2009. "Pioneering Work by Alumnus Helps Low-Income Access to Fresh Foods." http://digitalcommons.iwu.edu/news/358. Accessed October 4, 2015.

Haveman, Heather A., Jacob Habinek, and Leo A. Goodman. 2012. "How Entrepreneurship Evolves: The Founders of New Magazines in America, 1741–1860." *Administrative Science Quarterly* 57, no. 4: 585–624.

Intellectual Entrepreneurship Consortium. n.d. "About IE." http://www.ut-ie.com/about-ie.html.

Jansen, Slinger, Tommy van de Zande, Sjaak Brinkkemper, Erik Stam, and Vasudeva Varma. 2015. "How Education, Stimulation, and Incubation Encourage Student Entrepreneurship: Observations from MIT, IIIT, and Utrecht University." *International Journal of Management* 13, no. 2: 170–81.

Koehler, Jeanne. 2011. "Broadening Scientific Engagement through Teacher's Entrepreneurial Endeavors." Presentation, Illinois Wesleyan University.

Kuh, George D. 2008. "High-Impact Educational Practices: A Brief Overview." *Association of American Colleges & Universities*. https://www.aacu.org/leap/hips. Accessed October 4, 2015.

Levick-Parkin, Melanie. 2014. "Creativity, the Muse of Innovation: How Art and Design Pedagogy Can Further Entrepreneurship." *Industry and Higher Education* 28, no. 3: 163–69.

Merriam-Webster. 2015. "Metacognition." http://www.merriam-webster.com/dictionary/metacognition.

Ogilvie, Timothy. 2015. "How to Thrive in the Era of Collaborative Services Entrepreneurship." *Research Technology Management* 58, no. 5: 24–33.

White, Roderick E., Stewart Thornhill, and Elizabeth Hampson. 2007. "A Biosocial Model of Entrepreneurship: The Combined Effects of Nurture and Nature." *Journal of Organizational Behavior* 28, no. 4: 451–66.

Chapter Eight

Sharing the Spotlight

Open Access Publishing and Undergraduate Research

Genya O'Gara and Laura Drake Davis

Academic libraries are continually reshaping services, policies, and staff to support the rapidly evolving fields of scholarly research and communication. Ensuring broad access within the ever-changing information environment is a central aim of libraries, one that leads many librarians to align with the open access goals of unrestricted access and unrestricted reuse of research.[1] The emerging digital research and publication needs of faculty and graduate students have prompted many college and university libraries to provide more direct support for the creation, dissemination, and curation of scholarly, creative, and educational works through library publishing activities.[2] But as libraries transform to meet campus needs and wrestle with the difficult questions of open access, creator rights, and the future of publishing, where is the undergraduate in this conversation? Those students we encourage to become critical thinkers, future researchers, authors, and information-literate navigators of this realm hold an essential place in the open access landscape.

With the rapid expansion of library services, many academic libraries across the country are working closely with campus stakeholders, not just to preserve research, but also to publish and disseminate it in both print and digital formats. The challenges posed by government mandates to make grant-funded research and associated data publicly available, the movement in the academy toward open access publications and open educational resources, and the crisis in serials and publishing are being met by libraries with the adoption of repository and publication platforms and the expansion of specialized library staffing. In this process, academic libraries engage closely with faculty and graduate students as both producers and users, while the undergraduate is often treated as an unconsulted consumer. Undergraduates have largely been left out of the open access conversation, aside from calls for greater incorporation of scholarly communication discussions into library instruction and information literacy initiatives.

The undergraduate stake in open access publishing and undergraduate research is significant and growing. These students are intimately aware of the cost of education and the resources it requires and are "highly attuned to issues of social justice and civic engagement"—issues that infuse current conversations about open access and the shifting modes of scholarly communication (Davis-Kahl 2012, 212). From a practical perspective, the dissemination of undergraduate scholarship through open access publishing is an opportunity for students to enhance their future graduate study and employment opportunities. If librarians are eager to promote open models for scholarship in support of a core professional ethos of broad information dissemination, then we must include undergraduate students as key contributors rather than as afterthoughts. New roles for libraries as publishers of open scholarship create the opportunity to enlist students early in their academic careers with real-world experience, so that they might become "effective advocates for access to their own work, or for access to research that can aid them in becoming informed and critical researchers, consumers, and citizens" (Davis-Kahl 2012, 212). As we grapple with these quicksilver issues, now is the time for thoughtful engagement with the undergraduate community.

The open access publishing opportunities available to universities with a focus on undergraduate research are both numerous and complex. Institutions nationwide are embarking on a multitude of student publication projects, with varying approaches to the development, support, and infrastructure for this emerging area. Libraries are more often than not the primary point of support for these student publication projects.[3] This chapter delineates the successes and challenges James Madison University (JMU) encountered in the first year of this process, including disciplinary differences in attitudes toward publishing undergraduate research; student, faculty, and institutional concerns, including ongoing research, plagiarism, and institutional liability; the risks associated with the open distribution of subpar student research; accessibility of platforms; library staffing models; the potential of undergraduate publications to build and elevate institutional and student profiles; and student learning opportunities.

Our examination of JMU's initial efforts in this arena is informed by a survey of the current landscape and literature, with a focus on library publishing efforts, undergraduate research, and the role of open access. The chapter articulates lessons learned during the process and how these lessons may be reflected or applied to other ongoing undergraduate open access publishing efforts across the country. Though the long-term institutional and educational benefits of engaging undergraduates in open access publishing are numerous and perhaps even crucial, so, too, are the many challenges that libraries face in attempting to engage undergraduates and campus communities in these efforts.

THE LANDSCAPE

Academic Libraries and Open Access Publishing

Open access publishing efforts in academic libraries are both numerous and varied, with no two institutions approaching this evolving field in the same manner. Perhaps it is not surprising, then, that the Library Publishing Coalition's "About Us" page defines *library publishing* in part as being "distinguished from other publishing fields by a preference for Open Access dissemination as well as a willingness to embrace informal and experimental forms of scholarly communication and to challenge the status quo" (Library Publishing Coalition 2016). In recent years, the move to support and publish within open access arenas (including journals and institutional and subject repositories) has gained momentum in many disciplines due to better alignment of the values of open access publication with institutional and disciplinary research priorities and a greater understanding among academics of the extraordinarily high subscription costs of the journals and publications to which they have contributed their intellectual work.

Because an academic library's mission is firmly tied to that of its institution, it is crucial to appreciate the dramatic and rapid changes taking place in the academy's perception and adoption of the open access model in order to understand the space that library publishing of undergraduate research occupies. A 2011 study of OA activity showed that, between 1993 and 2009, OA journal publishing—measured in both total number of journals and total article output—had increased tenfold. Approximately 19,500 OA articles were published in 2000; by 2009, that number had increased to 191,850 (Laakso et al. 2011). As of August 2015, more than 10,500 titles were listed in the Directory of Open Access Journals (http://doaj.org).

Growing faculty support for open access publication across disciplines is a crucial factor in the acceptance of open access publications by the academy and, therefore, by the student population. Conley and Wooders (2009) clearly articulate this changing trajectory in their thorough examination of economics publications over the last two decades. They note a steady disciplinary shift toward open access as a preferred publication option and show how the cost burden of publication has changed dramatically as publications have moved online. The cachet of publishing with a major press has significantly diminished due to current purchasing models that bundle publications as well as the constant and ongoing mergers of presses and platforms. In a shift from early perceptions of the viability of OA, Conley and Wooders (2009) conclude that open access publishing today is not only more cost efficient but also more in keeping with the values of the academy.

The adoption of OA has also been field specific, often tied directly to the disciplinary communication cultures that naturally shape the practices of both faculty and students. In chemistry, for example, an OA e-print model collapsed under pressure from the American Chemical Society, while in physics, arXiv (http://arxiv.org), an open access repository of scientific pre-prints, has thrived, reinforcing sharing as the disciplinary norm in that field. In other words, "scholarly publishing mechanisms are deeply interdependent with historically embedded communication cultures, collaboration patterns, and attitudes toward openness (sharing) and closure that mitigate the power of exit and voice, strengthening existing infrastructures with strongly enforced institutional loyalty" (Lagoze et al. 2015).

The enthusiasm and skepticism open access engenders within the academy are apparent today, as they have been throughout the history of the OA movement. Open access publishing is challenged by the complexities of copyright transfer procedures that did not evolve sensibly from a paper-based world to a digital one, as well as by funding, tenure, and promotion decisions that are tied to publication in "established flagship 'high-end' journals" and a lucrative, multibillion-dollar academic publishing industry (Joseph 2013, 1). Still, despite substantial obstacles, acceptance of open access continues to grow, as do the options for easily implementable OA platforms and open licenses (Creative Commons n.d.).

As adoption has grown, so, too, has the centrality of academic libraries within this new publishing model. In a report analyzing current trends in OA and library publishing, Chadwell and Sutton (2014) predict that academic libraries will be the predominant disseminator of scholarly research articles in the near future. Trends they cite in support of this vision include government mandates to make the outputs of grant-funded research freely available, the codification and implementation of open access policies by grant-awarding agencies and universities, and the implementation of institutional repositories and publication platforms. They conclude that these developments, coupled with emerging economic realities for libraries, publishers, and universities, will create an environment in which library staff take on new roles focused on OA publishing and dissemination.

If, as predicted, the repository model of article publishing becomes the norm across disciplines, then library-supported repositories will expand their focus from preserving manuscripts of articles published in journals to publishing original content through the repository. A fuller transition to this model is predicated on increasing support and subsidies from scholarly societies, libraries, universities, and foundations, as seen in such successful open access ventures arXiv (https://arxiv.org). In this vision, academic libraries provide the technical and staffing infrastructure, redirecting the high subscription dollars formerly allocated to "big deals" and huge bundled packages to support for open access publishing. SCOAP^3 (Sponsoring Consortium for Open Access Publishing in Particle Physics) provides an active example of the type of partnership between libraries, research centers, and funding agencies that can support a library-centric economic model for OA publishing (http://scoap3.org). Indications of viability can also be seen in the formation of the Library Publishing Coalition (http://librarypublishing.org); the work of the Confederation of Open Access Repositories (www.coar-repositories.org); and the growth of hosted solutions for open source publishing systems, including such commercial platforms such as Digital Commons (http://digitalcommons.bepress.com). Academic library publishing of open access materials starts with repositories that are focused on disseminating original research from their own institutions for which there is no suitable publication venue, as well as its associated scholarly products and data.

Unsurprisingly, the futures of open access and library publishing will be entwined, as library publishing services evolve to provide full support for open access and the platforms for dissemination that faculty and scholars need (Chadwell and Sutton 2014). The 2012 Institute of Museum and Library Services (IMLS)–funded report *Library Publishing Services: Strategies for Success* concludes that publishing has indeed become a core activity of North American academic libraries and examines ways in which it could be supported. Some of its recommendations for libraries (modified for brevity) include:

- reallocating funds from existing library budgets to serve [unaddressed] faculty and institutional publishing needs
- committing to professional development for existing staff and to filling new library publishing positions with personnel who have new competencies and perspectives
- using OA business models and fee-based service provision to align the value in publishing services with the strategic goals of the academic library and its home institution
- treating academic publishing support as a holistic endeavor by assuming responsibility for acquiring a comprehensive understanding of editor and author needs
- leveraging existing partnerships with university presses to meet requirements beyond the mere "bare bones" of software and content hosting (Mullins et al. 2012)

The implications for changes in scholarly communication as the structures, platforms, and supports shift are numerous. Support for open access efforts and studies of this publishing landscape in the library literature have until recently focused on the needs of faculty and graduate researchers, the serials crisis, new business models, and the growing expectation that research be open. Academic library engagement in open access publishing is not, however, prompted solely by these motivations.

Undergraduate Research and Publishing

The Association of College and Research Libraries (ACRL) has "charged academic libraries with educating students about the economics of the distribution of scholarship as part of the information literacy mission" (Fruin 2013). Librarians involved with student-run journals repeatedly say that working with undergraduates as authors, editors, and publishers can be an important tool to teach them about all of the economic, technical, and legal aspects of scholarly publishing, as they are charged to do by the ACRL (Fruin 2013).

The benefits for students of engaging in research and publication at the undergraduate level are well detailed in the literature (Burks and Chumchal 2009; Craney et al. 2011; Kuh 2008). Purdue University Libraries' assessment of their undergraduate research publishing efforts demonstrated, through analysis of student and faculty feedback and journal metrics, a direct connection between student authorship and an "increased rate of student degree completion and future employment, or study" (Weiner and Watkinson 2014). Despite the positives, however, cautions about the overall role of undergraduate research and the publication of that research are numerous in the literature as well. Arguments against its utility include worries about the quality or perceived quality of "undergraduate only" journals; apprehension that publication in these journals will preclude later publication in top disciplinary journals; doubt about students' ability to peer-review each other's work; concerns about appropriate coauthorship and attribution; a lack of faculty and peer mentorship throughout the life cycle of the publication process; and, an often cited concern, the potential for inappropriate early publication of research that is in process with faculty (Gilbert 2004; Siegel 2004).

Many institutions avoid undergraduate open access publishing because rights are murkier, and issues of quality, workflow, sustainability, editorial turnover, and longevity are more challenging with student publications. This fact has not, however, stalled libraries; a survey by the Library Publishing Coalition found that 57 percent of the responding libraries publish student journals (Fruin 2013). Students clearly have an important role to play and should be engaged early on with issues related to open access, public access, creator rights, and the economics of publishing (Davis-Kahl 2012). Undergraduates in particular are highly cognizant of educational costs, from textbooks to student loans. Development of a holistic approach to educating and creating awareness around scholarly communication issues in the curriculum, in the library, and on campus is key, but perhaps even more important to the future scholarly landscape is the development of a culture of sharing. Although there are many challenges, as noted by Davis-Kahl (2012); Fruin (2013); and Hensley, Shreeves, and Davis-Kahl (2014), the benefits of undergraduate student publishing and open access research are significant. Libraries have the opportunity, "in collaboration with departments and teaching faculty," to "provide the infrastructure and expertise to build upon the undergraduate research experience to support student publishing in the form of journals." Even acknowledging the depth of involvement and the high degree of "faculty-librarian-student dedication, time commitment, and investment of financial and human resources" such a commitment would require, one might still conclude that the rewards outweigh the heavy investment (Davis-Kahl 2012). Examples of librarian-faculty collaborations in undergraduate publishing abound and include Illinois Wesleyan University's *Undergraduate Economic Review*, *Journal of Purdue Undergraduate Research*, *Tulane Undergraduate Research Journal*, and *Undergraduate Journal of Mathematical Modeling: One + Two*, to name just a few. These efforts encourage critical thinking, link up with the ACRL's mandates about information and data literacy skills, engage undergraduates directly in real-world publishing, and give students an opportunity to participate in professional communication via critical peer review. Student reviewers of these publications learn about open and public access, how their work fits into the scholarly communication cycle, and global open access efforts. Open access publishing endeavors also give libraries the opportunity to work with students on research production, archiving, and the publication of less-traditional materials, such as the oral history publications at the University of Washington, Bothell, and Cascadia College Library (Hattwig, Lam, and Freiberg 2015).

Publishing student work remains controversial, even in light of recent successes, particularly when it comes to electronic theses and dissertations (ETDs) and other works submitted by undergraduates. A recent study reviewing 150 university and library policies related to the deposit of student work in institutional repositories led its authors to the conclusion that "in their enthusiasm for OA, universities and libraries across the US are cajoling, arm-twisting, or even coercing students into in effect surrendering the copyright to their dissertations and theses, sometimes with the threat that students cannot graduate if they disagree" (Hawkins, Kimball, and Ives 2013, 32). Mandatory submission of ETDs, the authors argue, creates a false dichotomy by pitting the "principles of open access" against the "intellectual property rights of researchers."[4] Particularly in light of the unequal power relationship between universities and students, Hawkins, Kimball, and Ives (2013) found that the policies reviewed in their study effectively forced students to give up their intellectual property rights. Concerns with open access and ETDs are not limited to the ethics of mandated deposit and can vary widely between disciplines. The American Historical Association's (2013) recommendation of a six-year embargo on ETDs is one highly contested example of a specific disciplinary concern. The association reasoned that making doctoral dissertations available electronically compromises future publishing opportunities—even though surveys of academic publishers and their willingness to consider work derived from OA ETDs does not appear to bear this out (Waugh and Keralis 2013).[5]

These are not easy questions for libraries or students to grapple with, and the implications are twofold for undergraduate publications. Libraries that establish local OA mandates or urge such mandates may feel they are "contributing to a greater openness of scholarship and enabling global access to that scholarship, while at the same time creating structures that reduce the amount of control local researchers and faculty have over the disposition of their own work" (Anderson 2015). This nuanced view is perhaps the perfect perspective for libraries participating directly in the publication of undergraduate work because it embraces all of the complex issues that are implicated. In the chapter "Exploring the Intersections of Information Literacy and Scholarly Communication," Duckett and Warren (2013) ask the question, "Why not teach students that the modern library is engaged in a challenging real-time experiment about rights rather than the simple procurement of stuff—and that the outcome is far from predetermined?"

According to studies thus far, libraries with successful undergraduate OA publishing initiatives address research areas and populations that are currently not well represented by traditional or established publications and that directly align with their universities' larger goals. In the case of James Madison University, this alignment consisted of supporting the university's goal of promoting undergraduate research in an engaged university. In a similar way, the *Journal of Purdue Undergraduate Research* supports the university's larger goals in the area of undergraduate recruitment by advertising "Purdue as a place where undergraduates are involved with innovative research early and often" and stating that the "professional electronic edition of the journal will reach global audiences (this impact will be tracked using usage analysis tools), strengthening Purdue's ability to attract outstanding international students" (*Journal of Purdue Undergraduate Research* n.d.).

Even in the face of continued debate, there is a growing recognition that the benefits for undergraduates and libraries involved in OA publishing initiatives are greater than the challenges. This is particularly true when the challenges are weighed against the potential to catalyze long-term shifts in scholarly communication by empowering students to take control of their intellectual property, to break down walls across disciplines, to foster collaboration and communication, to support information literacy, and to position students as valued players within the rapidly shifting information economy. As Miller and Booth (2014) write, "OA work at the undergraduate level has important pedagogical implications. It challenges traditional hierarchical dynamics in academia and publishing and gives student authors space to assert their intellectual agency." Early engagement may spur future disciplinary shifts in scholarly communication practices, equipping students with a deep understanding of the library, publishing, and research landscape.

JMU's foray into undergraduate open access publishing is in line with other contemporary library publishing efforts but has had a specific focus from the beginning on undergraduate research. Acknowledging the complexities raised for both libraries and undergraduate researchers, JMU took the plunge into the deep end of the publishing pool in 2013.

CASE STUDY

JMU is a masters-level comprehensive institution, where the majority of the approximately 20,000 students are undergraduates. JMU prides itself on providing undergraduate students with high-level research opportunities as part of the student experience; in its "Core Qualities," JMU describes itself as a "community committed to academic rigor and teaching excellence combined with the intentional engagement of students and faculty in meaningful research and experiences of other scholarly endeavors" (James Madison University n.d.).

In the fall of 2012, JMU's Libraries and Educational Technologies Department (LET) appointed a scholarly communication task force to survey the environment across campus. In particular, the group was charged with identifying new and growing scholarly communication trends on campus and pinpointing unmet campus needs that had developed in response to the growth of digital scholarly outputs produced across disciplines. The group understood from the outset that the university's emphasis on undergraduate research and engagement would likely identify a different set of needs than those of a doctoral research institution. The task force engaged units across campus in structured conversations about what scholarship was being produced and what support was needed.[6] They found that needs differed between students and faculty, as well as across disciplines and colleges. Additionally, research outputs at JMU include everything from databases, datasets, and digital text and images to audiovisual materials, visualizations, and animations, particularly in more recent works of scholarship. These outputs reside alongside such traditional publications as journal articles and books. Individual groups had conflicting reactions to issues of open access, publication of student work, undergraduate research, and granting agency requirements for depositing works in repositories. There were some areas of agreement. Most groups wanted a centralized place to highlight JMU scholarship (both faculty and undergraduate research); open access publication platforms enabling peer review; a space to house grant-funded data for which there was no appropriate subject repository; and a home for nontraditional research outputs not slated for traditional publication, such as conference proceedings and video portfolios. The task force ultimately published a report with specific recommendations for the LET. Of the nine recommendations made by the task force, four were particularly relevant to JMU's initial steps into open access publishing of undergraduate research. These were:

1. implement repository services and define policies for hosting and managing the repository, while designating relevant individuals with corresponding responsibilities
2. implement an online publishing platform by determining needs, identifying appropriate technology, and collaborating with other campus organizations
3. develop programs to support student research by implementing mechanisms to identify CUR (Council on Undergraduate Research)–defined research, investigating the needs of students and faculty and expanding partnerships with other organizations on campus
4. collaborate with the institution to develop programs and systems to support, promote, educate about, and recognize research, scholarship, and creative expression (Scholarly Communication Task Force 2013).

As a result of these recommendations and findings, JMU Libraries and Educational Technologies acquired bepress's Digital Commons platform in early 2013 to begin to address the interdepartmental campus needs. A new digital collections unit within LET was formed, a digital collections librarian hired, and technical services staff retrained and assigned to the unit. The first task of this unit was to oversee the launch of JMU Scholarly Commons on the Digital Commons platform, broadly conceived as a repository and publication space for JMU campus scholarship. This launch took place in the fall of 2014, and the space was initially populated with a few representative collections to illustrate the capabilities of the platform. The strategy for JMU Scholarly Commons was phased due to small staff and a focus on encouraging campus adoption. The initial focus was on gathering content from across all campus populations identified by the task force. The phased implementation strategy for different collections required that, in addition to working with specific stakeholders (faculty, honors program, undergraduate researchers, graduate school), the platform would need to be tested and marketed for a variety of formats. These formats included journal publications, ETDs, conference publications, archival manuscript collections, and individual works of scholarship.

As JMU Scholarly Commons was preparing to launch, the *James Madison Undergraduate Research Journal* (*JMURJ*) was in the process of reforming. Initially established in 2007, *JMURJ* was the brainchild of two undergraduate physics students, Casey Boutwell and Laurence Lewis. Boutwell and Lewis describe their goals for the new undergraduate research journal:

> We envisioned a forum where undergraduate researchers could come together to share ideas and collaborate on new projects. Our vision was the James Madison Undergraduate Research Journal (JMURJ). . . . JMURJ provides the structure of peer review with giving undergraduates the authority to run a self-sustaining journal. It is a publication for undergraduates, by undergraduates. (Boutwell and Lewis 2009)

The first issue of *JMURJ* was published in the spring of 2009 and consists of thirteen articles on a variety of subjects, including international relations, public health, animal science, and history (Boutwell and Lewis 2009). Following the publication of this inaugural issue, momentum stalled due to a lack of ready student successors to the initial team. It seemed that Boutwell and Lewis's vision of an interdisciplinary publication could not be sustained.

In the fall of 2013, four years following the publication of the inaugural issue, efforts to resurrect *JMURJ* began in concert with a newly offered course, Developing an Undergraduate Research Journal (Mowey 2014). The course was a recurring seminar in the Honors Program and aimed to create a sustainable publication focused on undergraduate research at JMU. A call for submissions was disseminated in the dining halls on table tents, in the student newspaper, and on flyers posted on department bulletin boards, bringing *JMURJ* to the attention of the libraries. *JMURJ*'s focus on undergraduate research, technical infrastructure requirements, and need for a peer-review workflow aligned perfectly with the campus needs that JMU Scholarly Commons was acquired to address.

The digital collections librarian met with a member of the *JMURJ* student editorial board late in the fall 2013 semester and introduced JMU Scholarly Commons as a potential hosted solution for the journal. Benefits of the partnership between the libraries and the journal included greater exposure through open access publishing, improved workflow structure, and library staffing support to assist in streamlining the peer-review process. The discoverability of materials within the Digital Commons platform was particularly appealing to the editors and advisors of *JMURJ*. Specifically, the *JMURJ* team appreciated the fact that subscribing institution members could easily search the materials of all Digital Commons instances from their local library search interface and that all included materials were completely indexed by Google Scholar. For these reasons, *JMURJ* chose to utilize JMU Scholarly Commons to publish and distribute the journal.

In volume 1 (2014), *JMURJ*'s student editors and faculty advisors state their adherence to the principles of open access sharing of undergraduate student research: "The journal affirms our university's enduring commitment to undergraduate research in all its forms and offers JMU students a forum for their excellent scholarship" ("From the Editors" 2014). Outreach efforts to solicit content for *JMURJ* addressed the diversity of research produced across disciplines, as illustrated in figure 8.1.

Providing specific examples of research as *JMURJ* defines it is crucial to ensuring that students on campus know whether their work is eligible for submission. *JMURJ* has been proactive in its recognition of the variety of forms and formats research can take. Their broad characterization of research is consistent with the aims of its founders, who defined *research* as a "systematic study directed toward fuller human understanding, or making an original, intellectual and creative contribution to a discipline" (Boutwell and Lewis 2009, 4).

The structure of *JMURJ* has required addressing issues of workflow, training, and engagement with library publishing staff. In its current state,

Figure 8.1.   Advertisement for *James Madison Undergraduate Research Journal*
Source: "What Is Research?" n.d.

JMURJ consists of a student editorial board, two faculty advisors, and an advisory board comprising faculty members across disciplines. In keeping with Boutwell and Lewis's original vision, the student editorial board is responsible for all decision making, with the faculty advisors serving in a consultative capacity. Members of the student editorial board generally serve for one term consisting of two consecutive semesters. Terms are staggered, with a portion of the board serving from fall to spring and others serving from spring to fall. The result is that students are assigned yearlong projects in pairs: Partner 1 in her/his second semester mentors partner 2 in her/his first semester on the job; after a semester shadowing the experienced partner, partner 2 becomes a mentor during her/his second semester. This ensures some consistency in practice and fosters continuity for the publication, as half of the student board rotates off each semester.

As with many student-produced publications, the transient nature of the student body poses unique challenges for publications such as *JMURJ*. While the pairing of student editors in a mentor–mentee relationship addresses specific tasks and provides some consistency in the transfer of knowledge, the personal connection with library publishing support is sometimes lost during these transitions. Although not crucial to the operation of either *JMURJ* or JMU Scholarly Commons, these relationships facilitate consultation between the student editors and the JMU Scholarly Commons administrator to ensure that the full capabilities of the platform are being utilized. The brevity of the student editors' terms poses the threat of lost knowledge, more so than on a faculty or more traditional research publication. For example, the primary upload of materials in a new issue occurs during the spring semester; a student shadowing during one spring semester upload will have rotated off the editorial board by the time the next upload occurs the following academic year. This weakness in the production calendar is not easily overcome with a frequently rotating editorial board.

The faculty advisors oversee the production of *JMURJ* as a whole and must consider all aspects of the publication, including the editorial process, design, publicity, and ultimately distribution. However, advisors need not be proficient in the manual process of uploading content to *JMURJ*. Student editors assigned to work with JMU Scholarly Commons set up new issues, maintain the current editorial board's information, and upload content. Documentation for these processes is provided to *JMURJ* editors and advisors, and consultation with library staff is encouraged.

JMURJ maintains a page for the publication on the JMU website that is separate from JMU Scholarly Commons (www.jmu.edu/jmurj). Created prior to *JMURJ*'s partnership with JMU Scholarly Commons, this page contains detailed information on submitting content, social media feeds, and marketing materials and is maintained in conjunction with the JMU Scholarly Commons site, even though there is some redundancy in the information on the two pages. Current and past issues are also available from the *JMURJ* website, and they include links to individual items in JMU Scholarly Commons, allowing for one set of usage statistics to be captured for the 2014 and 2015 issues. For example, in the 2015 issue, Juliana Garabedian's article "Animating Gender Roles: How Disney Is Redefining the Modern Princess" had 1,002 downloads from the time of upload in February 2015 through June 30, 2015. This article was the number-one performing article within JMU Scholarly Commons during the spring 2015 semester.

The challenges and successes experienced with *JMURJ* are consistent with JMU's other undergraduate publishing efforts, not all of which are "traditional publications." The MADRush Undergraduate Research Conference (MADRush) publishes a "best of" series that is judged by JMU faculty for a top prize and publication in JMU Scholarly Commons. Papers submitted to MADRush are received from undergraduate students enrolled at JMU and other institutions in a multitude of disciplines. JMU Scholarly Commons also hosts the Middle Eastern Communities and Migrations Student Research Paper Series (MECMSRPS), a series of student research papers produced in 2010. In September 2014, the most downloaded paper in the Digital Commons network series of Near and Middle East Studies papers was a JMU undergraduate student paper titled "Nationalism in Afghanistan: A Descriptive Analysis" by Jawan Shir Rasikh. In addition to these publications, the libraries work with other groups across the JMU campus to provide a publishing venue for such undergraduate research products as articles, presentations, and exceptional examples of undergraduate research. Providing a venue for these research products leads to challenges in working with student populations, including informing students and faculty about open access; Creative Commons licensing; rights and responsibilities; assessing the sustainability of programs and publications associated with undergraduate research; and, in consultation with faculty members, evaluating the appropriateness of select undergraduate research for wider publication on the JMU Scholarly Commons publication platform.

OBSERVATIONS AND LESSONS LEARNED

Open Access

Recognition of open access and a keen awareness of creators' rights are important components of the student learning experience. *JMURJ* founders Boutwell and Lewis were keenly aware of potential implications of undergraduate publishing in this new venue and insisted that the authors retain the copyrights to their individual works:

> We were initially concerned that we may limit authors' ability to submit in
> external technical journals if we published their articles in JMURJ. . . . [W]e
> allow the author to retain the copyright of their work. By keeping the power
> with the students we provide a venue for ownership of their potential. JMURJ
> provides an opportunity for self-actuated success. (Boutwell and Lewis 2009,
> 5)

The consideration of author/creator rights is key to OA publishing models—
particularly those where the library serves as a publisher to campus constituents. Boutwell and Lewis's consideration of these rights provided a guide-
post for *JMURJ*.

The Role of Early Adopters

When the LET first contacted *JMURJ*'s editorial board, JMU Scholarly
Commons had not yet been launched; *JMURJ* was the first publication to
participate in the new publishing services. This partnership came at a crucial
time for both parties in establishing processes and workflows. Student editors
responding to the initial inquiry were excited to be part of this new service
and saw the advantages for publishing and streamlining processes; however,
after they consulted with colleagues on the student editorial board and faculty advisors, they were hesitant to adopt the full functionality of the Digital
Commons platform. They were especially concerned about the built-in submission and double-blind peer review functionality. Part of this concern was
due to *JMURJ*'s role as an early adopter and the inexperience of the library
staff with the newly acquired Digital Commons platform. But from the outset, *JMURJ* saw the advantages of open access distribution with enhanced
discovery beyond what was offered through the JMU website—a testament
to the value of open access and their commitment to the goals of Boutwell
and Lewis. Regular meetings with *JMURJ* allowed the libraries, student
editors, and faculty advisors to review workflow and functionality and ultimately streamline the processes of the publication while still maintaining the
goals of the course. The lesson for both parties was that assuming the role of
early adopter requires a deep level of comfort in the iterative process of
developing new workflows.

Institutional Alignment and Student Work

The publication of student work is a delicate area requiring careful naviga-
tion. With the initial launch of Scholarly Commons, the director of collections; the digital collections librarian; a faculty research fellow in the Center
for Instructional Technology; and the assistant director of systems, R&D,
were asked to present on library publishing initiatives to multiple campus
groups. The audiences included the College of Math and Science; campus

associate deans; the Academic Research Council; and the university's president, vice provost, and members of the advancement team. Attendees responded positively to the promotion of JMU's values through engaged publishing efforts focused on undergraduate student research, as well as to the early statistics on use of student research papers. However, concerns were raised about the ownership of student intellectual property, students' grasp of copyright implications, undergraduate research based on ongoing faculty research, and the selection process for included materials. The potential for plagiarism and concerns about the quality of the work being showcased were also mentioned. Although enthusiasm for the initiative ultimately far outweighed the concerns, it is important to highlight the intermingling of excitement and trepidation on campus surrounding library publishing efforts and undergraduate research.

Working with Student Authors, Editors, and Editorial Boards

Working with student editorial boards requires knowledge and tolerance of the publishing process, student schedules and work habits, and student editorial staff turnover each semester. Student authors must be trained in the publishing process, including peer review, feedback, and the additional editing that is often needed after initial submission; such training requires a great deal of staff time. Submitters who do not internalize this process can be slow to respond to requests following the initial submission. Similarly, consideration of quality, rights, and the implications of wide distribution of scholarship noted throughout this chapter are generally hampered by limited knowledge of the issues surrounding open access publishing. Undergraduate student authors are often willing to share their scholarship but are not always informed of the consequences of that sharing. In telephone interviews with repository administrators at other institutions, this concern emerged as a recurring theme. At Butler University, Minnesota State University, Mankato, and Wright State University, staff indicated during telephone interviews in August 2015 the need to better inform student authors and editorial boards regarding the implications of widely distributed, freely accessible scholarship, as well as authors' responsibility for due diligence in attributing sources and obtaining permission for the use of copyrighted material.

As might be expected, interaction with members of the student editorial board can be limited by their class and activity schedules. Students often request consultations after standard work hours, with an increase in such requests as deadlines approach, which puts added pressure on library staff.

The most significant challenge in working with student editorial boards is the high turnover in staffing. *JMURJ* presents a particular challenge, with half of the editorial board leaving each semester. While efforts have been made to counterbalance this predictable attrition, the potential for loss of processes, key contacts outside the immediate organization, and institutional memory for the publication is still high.

Working with Faculty in Open Access Publishing Initiatives

Faculty advisors, often a student publication's one consistent element over time, are key to ensuring a commitment to publishing through open access channels. The faculty role is frequently somewhat hands off at JMU, where publications are often (purposefully) student managed with minimal intervention from the faculty, and the Scholarly Communication Task Force found that students require "further mentorship within disciplines about the research and publishing process" (Scholarly Communication Task Force 2013, 8). Managing the rotation of new student editors, communicating expectations, providing supplemental guidance to students serving in the role of mentor, and ensuring progress toward publication within established deadlines is labor intensive even for the most dedicated faculty members, but faculty influence is still difficult to overstate even for such publications as *JMURJ*, whose faculty advisors assume a more hands-off role.

The Scholarly Communications Task Force also determined through interviews and focus groups across campus that faculty definitions of *scholarship* are influenced by departmental tenure and promotion requirements. As noted previously, the founders of *JMURJ* articulated a broad definition of scholarship that does not adhere to traditional disciplinary norms based on established tenure requirements. Faculty advisors to *JMURJ* must put their disciplinary expectations aside and inspire the undergraduate student editors to maintain an open mind about what constitutes research and scholarship.

Establishing and Maintaining a Library Publishing Program

Since the launch of JMU Scholarly Commons in 2014, interest across campus from students, faculty, and administration has increased. In addition to the current student research products in JMU Scholarly Commons (*JMURJ* and the *Madison Historical Review*, the "Best Paper Series" from the MADRush Undergraduate Research Conference, and honors projects), more individuals and groups on campus are recognizing the value of open access distribution of scholarship through JMU Scholarly Commons, leading to many requests for publishing services. Due to staffing constraints, the services provided by the libraries, and the Digital Collections unit specifically, do not include the review or upload of individual items. However, the Digital Collections unit does assist in establishing sites, configuring submission forms in consultation with editors and conference organizers, initial testing of sites, and training editors and conference organizers, all of which represent a significant investment of resources. The Digital Collections unit at JMU currently consists of one full-time faculty, one full-time classified, one part-time wage position, and shifting numbers (one to three) of undergraduate and graduate student staffing throughout the year. Though maintaining the repository and publishing platform is a primary function of the unit, it is not its only function. The unit is also responsible for the development of digital preservation standards, consultation with special collections on digital objects, and the digitization and reformatting of archival materials. With limited staffing, the unit has created detailed documentation to provide training to new users and is currently producing on-demand video tutorials to supplement initial training sessions.

Despite these activities, demand for services is still far beyond current staffing abilities, and therefore projects must be chosen with care. University administration has responded positively to the progress JMU Scholarly Commons has made during its first year toward meeting the goals identified in the Scholarly Communication Task Force report. Positive campus reactions to the increased distribution, in both downloads and prominence, of individual student works, such as Jawan Shir Rasikh's "Nationalism in Afghanistan: A Descriptive Analysis," help to highlight the need for further staffing.

Experiences similar to those encountered with *JMURJ* are not unique to JMU. Repository managers at other institutions share similar experiences with undergraduate research, open access, and institutional commitment to OA publishing opportunities for undergraduate students. Heidi Southworth, digital initiatives librarian at Minnesota State University, Mankato, indicated in an interview on August 21, 2015, that, while open access publishing opportunities do provide undergraduate students with increased opportunities for global access to their work, which they can then reference in resumes and applications for continuing their education, there are still challenges. These challenges include informing undergraduate students about what online, open access publishing actually means after materials are ingested—taking into account considerations of copyright, online permanence, and use by others. Franny Graede, scholarly communications librarian at Butler University, also emphasized in an interview on August 21, 2015, the need to inform students about rights and permissions. Both Southworth and Graede indicated that gaining the support of high-level university administrators who can provide sustained support is key to the success of any open access publishing program.

CHALLENGES TO UNDERGRADUATE OPEN ACCESS PUBLISHING

The challenges faced by open access advocates in higher education are numerous and well documented. For librarians, these challenges often relate to concerns about creators' rights and faculty concerns about discipline-specific tenure requirements and open access. Academic libraries also face pressures to serve as a publication platform for campus content, provide repositories to meet the open data requirements of grant-funded research, and staff and resource these platforms, all while continuing to provide access to expensive journals, databases, and other licensed research outputs required by members of the campus community. Libraries actively supporting and engaged in the open access publication of undergraduate research must also educate undergraduates, who have often had little exposure to issues facing the disciplines with changing modes of scholarly communication. These issues include complex, publication-specific challenges, such as copyright, embargoes, open access, peer review, and electronic distribution on a global scale. Academic library participants in student journal publications must also overcome the challenge of ever-changing student participants.

Ensuring the sustainability of both student-managed open access publications and the institutional human and fiscal resources to provide open access publishing platforms is a significant hurdle. While student-managed publications enable the student to take a hands-on approach to the publishing process, the rate of turnover on student editorial boards is a challenge. High turnover requires a substantial recurring investment to train and educate students in the workflow and publishing process, as well as open access and intellectual property issues, such as the impact of global distribution. This training must take place on at least an annual basis, if not more frequently.

Instructing undergraduate students in author agreements is another challenge many institutions face. At JMU, the libraries have been successful in recruiting content creators to publish in JMU Scholarly Commons, but as noted, they have also encountered some resistance across publications to utilizing the full capabilities of the platform, especially with regard to submission of student materials. For many existing publications, students submit their scholarship via e-mail to a publication e-mail address, often without a formal submission agreement indicating the terms of publication. The importance of a well-written submission agreement outlining the terms of distribution, ownership of the intellectual content, and use of copyrighted materials, including the correct permission and attribution of those copyrighted materials, cannot be overstated. Despite ongoing efforts to stress the necessity of this documentation, undergraduate students favor the ease of submitting items via e-mail over addressing intellectual property concerns by uploading directly to a publishing platform that incorporates a formal agreement directly with the submission. This preference has created an additional layer of work in obtaining these agreements postsubmission and review.

The opportunities for informing students, particularly undergraduates, of the issues associated with open access publishing need to be increased. Incorporating these concepts into information literacy instruction and integrating them into individual courses, especially those that serve as laboratories for the creation of open access publications, is key. A series of examples of the incorporation of these two topics can be seen in the compiled essays of *Common Ground at the Nexus of Information Literacy and Scholarly Communication* (Davis-Kahl and Hensley 2013). These efforts will succeed only in partnership with faculty and with administrative support.

As noted by Hawkins, Kimball, and Ives (2013), students may feel pressure to meet faculty, class, or institutional requirements for publication. Because of the power imbalance between universities and students, it is imperative that they have a nuanced understanding of both intellectual property rights and the implications of making research open and available on a global scale. In imparting this understanding, academic libraries can excel: They value the importance of open information to enrich citizens; the education of students is a priority for them; they have an intimate understanding of the cost and value of information resources; and they do not seek a financial return on the intellectual outputs of their campuses.

RECOMMENDATIONS

Although the challenges of openly publishing undergraduate content are numerous, so are the rewards. Students have the opportunity through open access publishing to participate in a community of practice and improve on the quality and depth of their work. As Miller and Booth (2014) state,

> The raised stakes of public readership can augment the urgency and impact of collaboration with librarians on issues of source use and robust argumentation. Writing for a wider audience also acts as a springboard for the cultivation of a student's voice and expertise, expanding the meaning of an assignment far beyond securing a good grade. And the larger and more realistic the audience these students address, the more compelling the experience.

Bibliographic instruction at libraries should incorporate discussions of open access and the utility of wide distribution of personal scholarship. This training is an important element in educating students about quality scholarship and research practices.

Identifying appropriate opportunities for undergraduates to contribute to the body of open access scholarship frequently requires developing relationships among campus departments, centers, institutes, and councils. The honors program and the Academic Research Council at JMU are often tuned in to scholarship across campus that could benefit from partnership with library publishing services. Ongoing observation of campus trends and new initiatives is also key. As with *JMURJ*, the opportunity to partner with JMU Scholarly Commons was identified through *JMURJ*'s campus-wide marketing campaign. Library publishing programs should be constantly on the lookout for existing publications, some of which are known only within the authoring departments or colleges.

If opportunities for undergraduates to contribute to the body of open access scholarship in existing outlets do not exist, then the creation of an additional outlet is an option. Conley and Wooders (2009) recommend that new open access publications focus, as they did, on disciplinary areas that are not currently well served by publishers. The formation of the *Journal of Undergraduate Ethnic Minority Psychology*, described by Harrell and Cothran (2015), is an example of an OA publishing outlet being created based on observed needs in underserved areas.

Contributions by the undergraduate population to open access literature have the potential to enhance the profile of the parent institution by highlighting the quality of undergraduate research. As a comprehensive institution, JMU prides itself on exceptional undergraduate research opportunities and aims to be a leader in the engaged university model, promoting an active global citizenship beginning at the undergraduate level. This goal corresponds with the aim of promoting open access student scholarship, although it may be the job of the libraries to make the connection apparent.

Capturing all student scholarship for any university is not practical, particularly with necessarily limited resources to ensure consistently high-quality work. Therefore, selectivity based on institutional needs, active collection development policies, and a clear understanding of available staffing resources is a must. Libraries should build these collections and publications as carefully as they do any other part of a library collection. As demand for open access publishing accelerates, advocating for program growth, including staffing and infrastructure, is fundamental for creating a sustainable open access publishing program.

FUTURE RESEARCH

The recognition of undergraduates as viable researchers continues to grow within the academy, as do the number of institutions focusing on undergraduate research and open access publication platforms. Further research on the role of undergraduates as scholarly contributors to the academy within the open access movement and in library publishing initiatives is needed to enable academic libraries to mindfully develop these areas.

The establishment of best practices based on wide-ranging studies and analysis of the plethora of case studies and existing publications is a necessary next step. Assessments linked to student outcomes, such as the recent study by Purdue, are crucial. Long term, we need to examine the differences in expectations about open research that exist between students and faculty.

It will be useful as well to measure the impact on acceptance to graduate schools, job success, and disciplinary engagement when undergraduates contribute to OA publications.

The current population of undergraduates is accustomed to freely sharing content online but is not always aware of the impact of such actions. Examination of the avenues in which undergraduate scholars freely share research beyond those discussed here is an area that also requires attention and further study.

Additionally, further study into the role of faculty and academic libraries in student-managed open access publications, particularly those publications that follow a "publication as laboratory" model, would be valuable. Studies such as these will be crucial in informing the development of curricular engagement in publishing modules and the role of libraries. They will add to current and future conversations about open access research and its underlying principles.

CONCLUSION

As Miller and Booth (2014) write, open access publishing "challenges traditional hierarchical dynamics in academia and publishing and gives student authors space to assert their intellectual agency." It also has the potential "to shift paradigms in a way that empowers all scholars—not just those with 'Ph.D' appended to their names" (Miller and Booth 2014).

Ultimately, the institutional and educational benefits of engaging undergraduate students in open access publishing outweigh the challenges libraries face in doing so. This early engagement is crucial to the longer-term adoption of open access, both within and outside the academy's walls. It is also crucial to the development of students' comfort in navigating the retention of intellectual property rights in an information-based economy. Libraries partnering with faculty, student groups, or university presses to publish research in open access journals are providing undergraduate students with a real-world opportunity to explore the legal and economic ramifications of the right to information through direct experience.

As scholarly publishing continues to react and evolve in response to changing modes of sharing, government mandates, and research norms, and as universities encourage undergraduate researchers across disciplines to take a more active role in scholarly communication, there will be additional opportunities for libraries to partner and collaborate in the development of these publications. "When open publication is integral to the teaching and learning process, it can show students what it means to participate in a community of practice and improve the quality and depth of their work" (Miller and Booth 2014). Libraries have an opportunity now as publishers of undergraduate open access research materials to mobilize students in this important conversation.

NOTES

1. The Public Library of Science (n.d.) definitions of *unrestricted access* and *unrestricted use* are used.

2. The Library Publishing Coalition (2016) on the "About Us" page on their website defines *publishing* and notes that library publishing "requires a publishing process, presents original work not previously made available" and is "distinguished from other fields by a preference for Open Access dissemination as well as a willingness to embrace informal and experimental forms of scholarly communication."

3. Bepress's Undergraduate Research Commons is one example of the growth in the publication of undergraduate research. This portal highlights more than seven hundred undergraduate research publications currently published by universities and colleges (Undergraduate Research Commons n.d.).

4. The authors quote and refer to the "Denton Declaration: An Open Access Manifesto" (Keralis 2012).

5. Waugh and Keralis (2013) note, "A 2011 survey of academic publishers found that 82.8 percent of responding journal editors, and 53.7 percent of responding university press directors were willing to consider work derived from Open Access ETDs."

6. The task force met with all of the colleges, academic research groups, the Office of Sponsored Programs, the honors program, and the Faculty Research Council.

REFERENCES

American Historical Association. 2013. "American Historical Association Statement on Policies Regarding the Embargoing of Completed History PhD Dissertations." *AHA Today.* http://blog.historians.org/2013/07/american-historical-association-statement-on-policies-regarding-the-embargoing-of-completed-history-phd-dissertations.

Anderson, Rick. 2015. "A Quiet Culture War in Research Libraries—and What It Means for Librarians, Researchers and Publishers." *UKSG Insights* 28, no. 2: 21–27. http://doi.org/10.1629/uksg.230.

arXiv. n.d. http://arxiv.org.

Boutwell, Casey, and Laurence Lewis. 2009. "Creating the JMURJ: The Men behind the Mystery." *James Madison Undergraduate Research Journal* (Spring): 4–7. http://issuu.com/jmurj/docs/jmurj.com.

Burks, Romi L., and Matthew M. Chumchal. 2009. "To Co-Author or Not to Co-Author: How to Write, Publish, and Negotiate Issues of Authorship with Undergraduate Research Students." *Science Signaling* 2, no. 94: tr3.

Chadwell, Faye, and Shan C. Sutton. 2014. "The Future of Open Access and Library Publishing." *New Library World* 115, nos. 5–6: 225–36.

COAR: Confederation of Open Access Repositories. n.d. https://www.coar-repositories.org.

Conley, John P., and Myrna Wooders. 2009. "But What Have You Done for Me Lately? Commercial Publishing, Scholarly Communication, and Open-Access." *Economic Analysis and Policy* 39, no. 1: 71–87.

Craney, Chris, Tara McKay, April Mazzeo, Janet Morris, Cheryl Prigodich, and Robert de Groot. 2011. "Cross-Discipline Perceptions of the Undergraduate Research Experience." *Journal of Higher Education* 82, no. 1: 92–113.

Creative Commons. n.d. "About the Licenses." https://creativecommons.org/licenses.

Cullen, Rowena, and Brenda Chawner. 2011. "Institutional Repositories, Open Access, and Scholarly Communication: A Study of Conflicting Paradigms." *Journal of Academic Librarianship* 37, no. 6: 460–70.

Davis-Kahl, Stephanie. 2012. "Engaging Undergraduates in Scholarly Communication Outreach, Education, and Advocacy." *College & Research Libraries News* 73, no. 4: 212–22.

Davis-Kahl, Stephanie, and Merinda Kaye Hensley. 2013. *Common Ground at the Nexus of Information Literacy and Scholarly Communication.* Chicago: Association of College & Research Libraries.

Digital Commons. n.d. http://digitalcommons.bepress.com.

Directory of Open Access Journals (DOAJ). 2016. https://doaj.org.

Duckett, Kim, and Scott Warren. 2013. "Exploring the Intersections of Information Literacy and Scholarly Communication [Two Frames of Reference for Undergraduate Instruction]." In *Common Ground at the Nexus of Information Literacy and Scholarly Communication*, edited by Stephanie Davis-Kahl and Merinda Kay Hensley, 25–44. Chicago: Association of College & Research Libraries.

Farney, Tabatha A., and Suzanne L. Byerley. "Publishing a Student Research Journal: A Case Study." *Portal: Libraries and the Academy* 10, no. 3 (2010): 323–35.

"From the Editors." 2014. *James Madison Undergraduate Research Journal* 1. http://commons.lib.jmu.edu/jmurj/vol1/iss1/2.

Fruin, Christine. 2013. "The New Scholars: Library Publishing of Undergraduate Research Journals." Durham, NC: Association of Southeastern Research Libraries. http://ufdc.ufl.edu/IR00003861/00001/pdf.

Gilbert, Scott F. 2004. "Points of View: Should Students Be Encouraged to Publish Their Research in Student-Run Publications? A Case against Undergraduate-Only Journal Publications." *Cell Biology Education* 3, no. 1: 22–23.

Harrell, Martika, and D. Lisa Cothran. 2015. "Meeting the Need: Developing an On-line, Open Access Journal Focused on Ethnic Minority Undergraduate Students." *Journal of Undergraduate Ethnic Minority Psychology* 1, no. 1: 1. http://www.juempsychology.com/volume-1.

Hattwig, Denise, Nia Lam, and Jill Freidberg. 2015. "Student Participation in Scholarly Communication and Library Digital Collections: A Case Study from the University of Washington Bothell Library." *College & Undergraduate Libraries* 22, no. 2: 188–208.

Hawkins, Ann R., Miles A. Kimball, and Maura Ives. 2013. "Mandatory Open Access Publishing for Electronic Theses and Dissertations: Ethics and Enthusiasm." *Journal of Academic Librarianship* 39, no. 1: 32–60.

Hensley, Merinda Kaye, Sarah L. Shreeves, and Stephanie Davis-Kahl. 2014. "A Survey of Library Support for Formal Undergraduate Research Programs." *College & Research Libraries* 75, no. 4: 422–41.

James Madison Undergraduate Research Journal. n.d. http://www.jmu.edu/jmurj.

James Madison University. n.d. "The Madison Plan: Strategic Plan 2014–2020." http://www.jmu.edu/jmuplans/jmu-strategic-plan/index.shtml.

Joseph, Heather. 2013. "The Open Access Movement Grows Up: Taking Stock of a Revolution." *PLoS Biology* 11, no. 10: e1001686. http://journals.plos.org/plosbiology/article?id=10.1371/journal.pbio.1001686.

Journal of Purdue Undergraduate Research. n.d. "About This Journal." http://docs.lib.purdue.edu/jpur/about.html.

Keralis, Spencer D. C. 2012. "The Denton Declaration: An Open Data Manifesto." *Open Access @ UNT.* http://openaccess.unt.edu/denton-declaration.

Kuh, George D. 2008. *High-Impact Educational Practices: What They Are, Who Has Access to Them, and Why They Matter.* Washington, DC: Association of American Colleges and Universities.

Laakso, Mikael, Patrik Welling, Helena Bukvova, Linus Nyman, Bo-Christer Bjrk, and Turid Hedlund. 2009. "The Development of Open Access Journal Publishing from 1993 to 2009." *PloS One* 6, no. 6: e20961.

Lagoze, Carl, Paul Edwards, Christian Sandvig, and Jean-Christophe Plantin. 2015. "Should I Stay or Should I Go? Alternative Infrastructures in Scholarly Publishing." *International Journal of Communication* 9: 20.

Library Publishing Coalition. 2016. "About Us." http://www.librarypublishing.org/about-us.

Miller, Char, and Char Booth. "Open Access as Undergraduate Pedagogy." 2014. *Academic Newswire.* http://lj.libraryjournal.com/2014/03/opinion/backtalk/open-access-as-undergraduate-pedagogy-backtalk.

Mowey, Melissa. 2014. "Students Re-Establish Undergraduate Research Journal." *James Madison University News.* http://www.jmu.edu/news/2014/02/11-jmurj-reestablished.shtml.

Mullins, James L., Catherine Murray Rust, Joyce L. Ogburn, Raym Crow, October Ivins, Allyson Mower, Daureen Nesdill, Mark Newton, Julie Speer, and Charles Watkinson. 2012. *Library Publishing Services: Strategies for Success, Final Research Report.* Washington, DC: SPARC.

Potvin, Sarah. 2013. "The Principle and the Pragmatist: On Conflict and Coalescence for Librarian Engagement with Open Access Initiatives." *Journal of Academic Librarianship* 39, no. 1: 67–75.

Public Library of Science (PLOS). n.d. "The Case for Open Access." https://www.plos.org/open-access.

Scholarly Communication Task Force. 2013. "Final Report and Recommendations." http://sites.jmu.edu/scholarlycommunication/files/2013/09/ScholarlyCommunicationsReport_9-2-13.pdf.

SCOAP³—Sponsoring Consortium for Open Access Publishing in Particle Physics. n.d. http://scoap3.org.

Siegel, Vivian. 2004. "Points of View: Should Students Be Encouraged to Publish Their Research in Student-Run Publications? Weighing the Pros and Cons of Undergraduate-Only Journal Publications." *Cell Biology Education* 3, no. 1: 26–27.

SPARC. 2016. "What Are Article-Level Metrics?" http://www.sparc.arl.org/initiatives/article-level-metrics.

Suber, Peter. 2015. "Open Access Overview." http://legacy.earlham.edu/~peters/fos/overview.htm.

Tomaszewski, Robert, Sonia Poulin, and Karen I. MacDonald. 2013. "Publishing in Discipline-Specific Open Access Journals: Opportunities and Outreach for Librarians." *Journal of Academic Librarianship* 39, no. 1: 61–66.

Tulane Undergraduate Research Journal. n.d. https://library.tulane.edu/journals/index.php/celt/index.

Undergraduate Economic Review. n.d. http://digitalcommons.iwu.edu/uer.

Undergraduate Journal of Mathematical Modeling: One + Two. n.d. http://scholarcommons.usf.edu/ujmm.

Undergraduate Research Commons. n.d. "About the Undergraduate Research Commons." http://undergraduatecommons.com/about.html.

Waugh, Laura, and Spencer Keralis. 2013. "The Value of Open Access to Undergraduate Research." *Eagle Feather* 10. http://eaglefeather.honors.unt.edu/2013/article/287#.VdetY0b4afa.

Weiner, Sharon A., and Charles Watkinson. 2014. "What Do Students Learn from Participation in an Undergraduate Research Journal? Results of an Assessment." *Journal of Librarianship and Scholarly Communication* 2, no. 2: eP1125.

"What Is Research?" n.d. *James Madison Undergraduate Research Journal.* http://www.jmu.edu/research/whatisresearch.shtml.

Chapter Nine

Open Access Implications for Information Literacy

Rachel Elizabeth Scott

The availability of OA resources has grown at an unprecedented rate since the signing of the Budapest Open Access Initiative in 2002. Since then, governmental agencies, universities, libraries, and other stakeholders have introduced or expanded initiatives to make OA content available and accessible. In a memo dated February 22, 2013, the U.S. Office of Science and Technology Policy announced that all "digitally formatted scientific data resulting from unclassified research supported wholly or in part by Federal funding should be stored and publicly accessible to search, retrieve, and analyze" (White House 2013). The European Union's Horizon 2020 program requires that funded publications and research data be deposited in OA repositories (European Commission 2014). Libraries across the world have worked together to secure OA rights for several academic titles in the Knowledge Unlatched pilot project (Montgomery 2014).

As excellent resources become more easily searched and increasingly freely available outside of library databases and integrated library systems, the role of the library in the discovery process is changing, with an emphasis on disintermediation, allowing the user to access resources directly, without librarian intervention (Asher, Duke, and Wilson 2012; Griffiths and Brophy 2005; Rempel, Buck, and Deitering 2013). As traditional research evolves and is more frequently conducted outside of library platforms, librarians will need to address newly arising information literacy considerations. OA has immediate and manifold implications for how users at all levels discover and make use of information. This chapter uses the "Framework for Information Literacy for Higher Education" to discuss how librarians can engage undergraduate students in the use, understanding, evaluation, and creation of OA resources. By incorporating OA resources and platforms into information literacy instruction and workshops, librarians have an opportunity to add value and insight during this transitional period.

TRANSITIONAL TIMES

Both librarians' perceptions of OA and the national guidelines for information literacy are undergoing major changes. A decade ago, librarians and teaching faculty were optimistic about yet skeptical of OA resources. A 2006 national survey of academic librarians found a gap between stated support for OA and lack of action (Palmer, Dill, and Christie 2009). Some librarians were reluctant to add OA resources to catalogs due to their perceived instability and concerns about their quality (Schmidt and Newsome 2007) and descriptive metadata (Beall 2009). Faculty did not see advantages to freely disseminating their work and thought that OA models might negatively impact research quality and undermine existing publishing models, among other concerns (University of California 2007).

The proliferation of high-quality OA resources, OA's demonstrated benefit in the dissemination of scholarship and uptake of findings (Eysenbach 2006; Houghton et al. 2009; Lawrence 2001), and the standardization of OA metadata (for example, Open Archives Initiative) have led librarians and teaching faculty to champion OA resources more readily. Librarians often go beyond adding OA content to their integrated library systems (ILS), discovery platforms, and e-resource access and management services (ERAMS); they increasingly maintain institutional repositories and publish content (Brown 2013; Cullen and Chawner 2011). Librarians also incorporate OA into information literacy sessions; a 2012 survey reported that the primary way in which librarians introduce open access to college students is via information literacy sessions (Keane 2012). Nonetheless, in information literacy sessions, some librarians are reluctant to leave the security of library platforms to find and use OA resources. Perhaps this is related to Kulhthau's (2004) observation: "The bibliographic paradigm is based on certainty and order, whereas the user's constructive process is characterized by uncertainty and confusion" (8). OA resources add complexity to the information landscape and, when incorporated, will necessarily change the way librarians conduct information literacy instruction. Embracing the complexity and constructive nature of research relates to the recent reenvisioning of information literacy guidelines.

The Association of College and Research Libraries' (ACRL) "Framework for Information Literacy for Higher Education" (referred to as "framework") was approved in its third draft on February 2, 2015. The framework replaces the ACRL's information literacy competency standards for higher education

(IL standards) as the national guidelines on information literacy in higher education. Instead of discrete competencies and outcomes, the new document is comprised of six "frames" (threshold concepts), each with a definition and discussion, "knowledge practices" (ways in which learners can increase their understanding), and "dispositions" (ways in which to address the affective, attitudinal, or valuing dimension of learning).

The IL standards, adopted in 2000, were criticized for being too skills based, prescriptive, and constraining (Jacobs 2008; Owusu-Ansah 2003). Several alternate or complementary models were proposed, including the possibility of not maintaining a national information literacy policy (Cowan 2014; Pawley 2003). In response to the skills-oriented approach perpetuated by the IL standards, Jacobs and Berg (2011) propose "appreciative inquiry" and "critical information literacy" to "reengage with the possibilities and potentials within information literacy to meet larger social goals" (385). Critical information literacy has been widely espoused in library literature and practice (Elmborg 2006; Jacobs 2008; Swanson 2004). Dewey (2010) advocates creation literacy, the "ability to create and disseminate new knowledge in meaningful ways in our global networked society" (5), and Bruce (1997; Bruce, Edwards, and Lupton 2006) uses phenomenographic methods (i.e., qualitative evaluation of individuals' conceptions) to investigate users' information literacy experiences and understandings.

In their work, Jacobson and Mackey (2013; Mackey and Jacobson 2011) propose metaliteracy, an "overarching and unifying framework that builds on the core information literacy competencies while addressing the revolutionary changes in how learners communicate, create, and distribute information in participatory environments," as an alternate model to "advance critical thinking and reflection in social media, open learning settings, and online communities" (Jacobson and Mackey 2013, 84). The learning objectives identified by Mackey and Jacobson, current cochair of the ACRL Information Literacy Competency Standards for Higher Education Task Force, bear some similarity to the six frames of the framework.

The framework draws heavily on Meyer and Land's (2003) characteristics of threshold concepts, which "represent a transformed way of understanding, or interpreting, or viewing something without which the learner cannot progress." Threshold concepts have gained traction in information literacy over the past several years (Blackmore 2010; Hofer, Townsend, and Brunetti 2012) and have been adopted as the conceptual "framework behind the framework." The frames, or threshold concepts, are iterative and represent interconnected concepts. Unlike the IL standards, the framework is flexible and not prescriptive: "The framework . . . grows out of a belief that information literacy as an educational reform movement will realize its potential only through a richer, more complex set of core ideas" (ACRL 2015, 2). The framework defines *information literacy* as a "spectrum of abilities, practices, and habits of mind that extends and deepens learning through engagement with the information ecosystem." OA relates to this definition not just as a type of resource or new platform to search but also as a multifaceted component of the complex information ecosystem. Open access is ideology, product, and process.

In the following sections, each of the six frames—"Authority Is Constructed and Contextual," "Information Creation as a Process," "Information Has Value," "Research as Inquiry," "Scholarship as a Conversation," and "Searching as Strategic Exploration"—are evaluated with respect to OA resources, services, platforms, or publishing processes. Each section concludes with a suggested activity to engage students in active learning about open access. As in the framework, frames are presented in alphabetical order and are not meant to be comprehensive; users are encouraged to customize and adapt according to local needs.

AUTHORITY IS CONSTRUCTED AND CONTEXTUAL

> "Information resources reflect their creators' expertise and credibility, and are evaluated based on the information need and the context in which the information will be used. Authority is constructed in that various communities may recognize different types of authority. It is contextual in that the information need may help to determine the level of authority required."—ACRL 2015, 4

OA resources differ from traditionally published sources in many respects, but those differences do not necessarily change how OA resources should be evaluated by readers with respect to authority. The typical starting point when considering authority is the author. Although tenure-track authors may have historically avoided OA (University of California 2007), there is considerable evidence and increasing buy-in that OA benefits research dissemination (Cullen and Chawner 2011; Eysenbach 2006). Altmetrics and more diverse ways of measuring impact (Bollen et al. 2009) are making OA publication more attractive to established researchers. Although tenure requirements have historically persuaded academic experts to pursue publication in traditionally published journals, it is no longer the case that the credibility of the author should be questioned because an article was published in an OA journal or can be found in an institutional repository.

When evaluating the authority of a source, one substantial difference between OA and traditionally published resources is the source or publication. For many readers, the medium is the message (McLuhan 1964); it is hard to separate the content from the platform on which it is presented. The perceived prestige of a journal, monographic series, or publisher still carries significant authority in the minds of expert and novice researchers alike. While conducting instruction, librarians often reiterate that, before an article is published in an elite journal, it is extensively edited and the content, style, and methodology are vetted by experts in the field. Do OA resources go through such rigorous processes of editing and examination? Depending on the resource in question, they may. The great variety of OA publishing and archiving options that exist, from peer-reviewed journals and discipline-specific archives to library publishing and personal archiving, are detailed throughout this volume and are beyond the scope of this chapter.

Because of the wide array of OA publication options, proving that the quality of OA resources suffers would be challenging. OA publications and platforms that "publish" material, as opposed to hosting prepublished materials or archiving unpublished works, often employ editors and have editorial boards and peer-reviewing processes to ensure the consistency and quality of articles. Because OA increases the number of downloads and citations to the resource (Eysenbach 2006; Lawrence 2001), one might suppose that the increase in reader scrutiny and usage would be a mechanism of quality control.

Another consideration when evaluating authority is the evidence provided. Evidence should be evaluated case by case and not generalized by document type. However, digital repositories can host more detailed data than most traditionally published sources, which is an advantage for some OA resources. Instead of a few select charts or graphs, a researcher can upload whole datasets and allow readers to see the data in context. In Public Library of Science (PLoS), for example, datasets and file sets in various file formats are presented as "supporting information" within the article and also linked in figshare, a digital data repository. This opportunity for increased context and evidence can lend authority.

As with all aspects of evaluation, appropriateness of source should be considered; OA and freely available sources should not be automatically rejected because they are not traditionally published. Instead, readers must learn to base their evaluative decisions on their specific needs. When considering authority, it is useful to ask what role privilege plays. OA resources have provided a platform for student researchers and other marginalized groups that may have been excluded from traditional publishing platforms and media. Projects like the academic/popular magazine *Harlot* and the *Queer Zine Archive Project* provide the space for previously disenfranchised groups to assume an authorial and authoritative voice and to gain confidence as content creators and authors.

Indicators of authority, like author credentials and publication type, are often explicit in platforms for traditionally published resources like article databases. OA resources that include similar, albeit superficial, information would likely be useful teaching tools to librarians and undergraduate users. OA resources that employ citation network maps can help make visible the contextual nature of authority within a particular discipline.

In an instructional setting, the librarian could assess "Authority Is Constructed and Contextual" by having students work in groups to identify the evidence that an author uses to assert authority in an assigned OA article. Ideally, articles with accompanying datasets should be chosen. The students would collaborate to expand their understanding of authority in written documents by answering open-ended questions; for example, identify several examples of evidence in the article and explain how the author uses them to assert authority:

- Is there any disagreement among evidence provided?
- Why include different types of evidence?
- How does the source (publication/platform) influence your perception of the article's authority? Who can publish in this source?

Corresponding outcomes for this assignment might state:

- The student will evaluate the author's use of sources.
- The student will differentiate between various types of evidence.
- The student will explain how the evidence provided lends authority to the article.

INFORMATION CREATION AS A PROCESS

"Information in any format is produced to convey a message and is shared via a selected delivery method. The iterative processes of researching, creating, revising, and disseminating information vary, and the resulting product reflects these differences."—ACRL 2015, 5

Most information literacy practitioners appreciate the importance of teaching how information is produced and emphasizing the various processes entailed. The iterative, or complex and repetitive, nature of knowledge production is often a source of frustration to undergraduate students. Project Information Literacy identifies four ways in which college research is different from high school research, all of which emphasize the complexity and extensive processes involved in information creation. Not only are there more sources to consider and more freedom in conducting research, but also the sources must be searched in more and different ways and then evaluated (Head 2013). Those who work with undergraduate students have recognized that disagreement or ambivalence surrounding a topic can confuse or upset students. Cousin (2009) notes that "some students protect themselves from the troubling aspects of their subject by remaining within a common sense understanding and/or by defending themselves from journeying too far into the subject" (204). Searching one platform to find all of the needed sources and ignoring complexity and dissent are trademarks of novice research; experts engage in the time-consuming processes of researching, drafting, revising, soliciting input, and revising again.

The information creation process begins with the identification of an unanswered question of interest. Research, or finding out how others have started to answer this or related questions, is a natural response. Searching the user's native or preferred platforms is discussed in more depth later, but it is worth mentioning that the librarian should allow students to begin their information creation process in an authentic way, even if it is searching Google. Although there is still no single search box that retrieves all relevant results and presents them in a meaningful way, the web optimization of many OA repositories, journals, and platforms means that students increasingly find high-quality results searching the open web with a search engine. The librarian can add value by teaching more sophisticated research strategies, such as making use of controlled vocabularies and subject-specific platforms, and advising on the value of and differences between various platforms.

Students should be taught to ask about the audience for and purpose of the information. The author's intent in creating information, whether to persuade, inform, entertain, share research results, meet tenure requirements, or a combination of several reasons, has implications for how the reader should understand and make use of the information. One should not interpret a "Hey girl" meme, for example, as indicating Ryan Gosling's romantic interest or use it to provide evidence thereof. The audience for OA resources is far more inclusive and harder to identify than it is for traditionally published materials. The purpose for the information, however, may or may not differ from traditionally published materials. For example, the OA requirement for NIH-funded research is due to its purpose, namely to improve human health.

The information creation processes for OA resources may or may not differ from those for traditionally published resources. One of the established benefits of OA is accelerating the dissemination of research (Eysenbach 2006), which renders traditional publishing timelines outdated. In light of OA resources, information literacy librarians should no longer claim that peer-reviewed or high-quality scholarly material takes years to publish (Virginia Tech 2016). Depending on the subject, methodology, and other factors, a scholarly article may be written and published within a single year. Researchers may negotiate rights to upload or deposit prereview or final versions in institutional repositories or on a personal webpage at the point of, or even before, publication.

Another part of the information creation process is editing and reviewing the information. This process, too, may or may not differ for OA resources. When teaching students about the editing and reviewing processes entailed in the production of scholarly articles, it is important for librarians to emphasize how the editorial work involved strengthens the end product and not focus on the prestige of being published in a high-impact journal.

The potential for increased information dissemination is an opportunity afforded by digital platforms, some of which are OA. Scholars can post drafts for feedback or collaboration and archive various iterations to show their creation process. Social media is frequently embedded in digital platforms, making it easy to blog, tweet, retweet, and upload research findings and to interact socially with the information. Librarians should discuss the various ways in which digital platforms make information creation social and the implications of this; by so doing, they can highlight the processes involved in information dissemination.

One way to teach and assess "Information Creation as a Process" would be to pair students to read and examine the submission requirements for an OA journal and the comments offered from a peer reviewer to a potential author. Depending on the examples provided, ask students to answer some of the following questions:

- What is the importance of knowing one's audience as one begins the information creation process?
- Describe the role of informal and academic peer review in information creation.
- Does soliciting input from others encourage diverse approaches? Does it complicate the information creation process? How?

Outcomes for this assignment might state:

- The student will identify several steps in the information creation process.
- The student will brainstorm a list of ways in which peer review influences information creation.

INFORMATION HAS VALUE

"Information possesses several dimensions of value, including as a commodity, as a means of education, as a means to influence, and as a means of negotiating and understanding the world. Legal and socioeconomic interests influence information production and dissemination."—ACRL 2015, 6

This frame has several obvious connections to OA. Even when there is no download or usage fee for the end user, information is treated as a commodity by publishers and vendors. In an information economy, information has power, influence, and the means to exclude or empower. Accordingly, it is of utmost importance to teach students about the economics of publishing and the various ways of valuing information.

Much time and work goes into scholarly publications, regardless of their eventual price tag. Authors must conduct preliminary research; plan, prepare for, and execute a study; manage the resulting data; write up the results; ensure that the paper is edited and reviewed; and secure publication, hosting, archiving, and dissemination for the final product. Traditionally, publishers provided editing and publishing services and in return retained partial rights to the content published in their journals. The cost was passed on to readers, who had to pay to access content or secure access through an institutional subscription or license.

Traditional funding models are more uniform than OA models. OA has varied funding models and sometimes combines one or more of the following models. Some OA resources, such as PLoS, charge author-side fees; some, like arXiv, are subsidized by institutions, including universities, government agencies, libraries, or learned societies; some, such as *Plant Physiology*, rely on membership dues; others are supported by a traditionally published journal—*postmedieval FORUM*, for example, is the OA supplementary issue to *postmedieval*; and others rely on volunteer labor.

OA and hybrid publishing models are sometimes described in terms of colors. Articles published in OA journals, which may or may not be peer-reviewed, are gold. Yellow journals allow for the archiving of draft or pre-print papers but not published versions. Blue journals allow only postprint and not preprint drafts to be archived. Both preprints and postprints may be archived in the case of green journals. White journals do not support archiving (Laakso 2014, 479). Of course there are various combinations and exceptions: Traditional journals may allow authors to pay a fee in order for their article to be OA, in which case it is gold OA. Green OA articles are typically but not always deposited after having been traditionally published and represent a sort of hybrid approach. The diversity and flexibility of OA models may help scholarly journals remain viable in this transitional period.

Just as OA resources are published differently, they are also typically licensed differently from traditional publications. Instead of employing traditional copyright protection, OA resources often allow the author to choose a more open license, such as the various Creative Commons (CC) licensing options. This freedom provides the end user with varying levels of permissions when using the content.

The most open CC license, "Attribution," allows users to distribute the item commercially and modify it, as long as the original item is properly cited. The most restrictive CC license, "Attribution-NonCommercial-NoDerivs," allows end users only to download and share in noncommercial settings. Managing intellectual property is one means of making explicit that information has value. The librarian could ask students to upload papers to their personal spaces on an institutional hosting server or photos to Flickr and go through the process of selecting a Creative Commons license and embedding the license in the platform. Requiring students to go through the process of choosing a license for their work will help them to understand what the symbols mean and appreciate their import.

It should also be reiterated in instructional settings that OA resources are licensed so that they are open to public viewing and downloading. OA resources present the librarian with an opportunity to discuss ethical information use in a way that traditionally published resources do not. A book on the shelf or an article in a subscription database has obviously been procured by the library. A PDF in Google Scholar, however, may be a legitimately licensed copy of the article or may have been illegally posted. Illegally downloading or distributing copyrighted material is easier in a digital environment; students need to learn to distinguish legitimate repositories from illegal file-sharing networks and to eschew the latter.

Allowing students to encounter paywalls is a great way to demonstrate legal and socioeconomic influences on information dissemination. Specifically, it teaches them that vendors treat information as a commodity and demonstrates that traditionally published content is prohibitively expensive for many. Librarians have advocated for freedom of access, not only to OA resources, but also to physical and digital collections and all of the technologies required to access them, from the Internet to assistive technologies. This advocacy must be based in an understanding of the costs and value of information to our various constituents.

Not only does the information itself have value, but the platform hosting it can also provide value and utility. In a digital context, whether OA or traditionally published, the platform provides several amenities. Social media plug-ins, citation trackers and network maps, link resolvers/DOIs for cited or citing articles, author ID services (e.g., ORCiD), RSS feeds for new publications, and thesauri and linked controlled vocabularies all add value to the raw content, as well as facilitate discovery and access. Web optimization of OA metadata adds value in the large-scale and expeditious dissemination of content, which not only facilitates widespread sharing of information but also contributes to the prestige and research mission of scholars and their host institutions.

One approach to teaching and assessing "Information Has Value" for students in nursing or health sciences would be to ask them to read and respond to the memo "Increasing Access to the Results of Federally Funded Scientific Research" (White House 2013). The librarian can help them to visualize the difference between open and closed access by demonstrating what it looks like when an OA version of the article has been posted to PubMed Central and what it looks like when an article is behind a paywall and requires the user to purchase content. Questions one might ask students to discuss include:

- What is the federal government's role in making information (equally) accessible to its constituents?
- How might making research open access foster innovation?
- Why does this policy deal primarily with science and technology research?

Especially in the case of the second question, responses may be formatted in a concept map or other visual representation of the information. Outcomes for this assignment might state:

- The student will evaluate the government's role in information policy.
- The student will list ways in which OA fosters innovation.
- The student will analyze differences in OA policy for different disciplines.

RESEARCH AS INQUIRY

"Research is iterative and depends upon asking increasingly complex or new questions whose answers in turn develop additional questions or lines of inquiry in any field."—ACRL 2015, 7

Experts understand that knowledge is advanced through the answering of unresolved questions by means of increasingly sophisticated methods. However, students sometimes conflate scholarly research with their casual research process of finding answers to known questions using a search engine, and as Head (2013) points out, the "cognitive skills needed for scholarly inquiry are very different than finding ready-made answers using a Google search" (34). How should the librarian address this challenge? Gelfand and Palmer (2013) are opposed to the "limiting nature of defining information literacy instruction as an activity by which librarians deposit knowledge about the location, evaluation, and use of information into students" (17–18). Instead of teaching where to point and click or how to search a given database, librarians must emphasize that research is a nonlinear process that depends on posing increasingly complex questions as one synthesizes existing information. Doing so will mark a shift in the way many librarians teach: Instead of teaching tools, librarians will outline processes and propose strategies.

Questions posed in the research process should be authentic to each student. However, as students develop a deeper understanding of how research is conducted in their areas, they should be more open to revising their strategies. Research processes vary considerably among disciplines. The methodologies and required skills are often discipline specific. Accordingly, techniques introduced by the librarian should be faithful to the way in which research is conducted in the particular discipline.

One can begin to understand how scholars in various disciplines engage in inquiry by evaluating some discipline-specific OA resources and comparing their funding and review models. For example, arXiv was an early adopter of the OA model. Its quick and overwhelming success reveals how researchers in natural sciences and math value rapid dissemination of their findings and near-immediate access to recently compiled data.

PLos Biology, a peer-reviewed OA journal, retains some aspects of traditional publishing while taking advantage of OA attributes. It is high profile and indexed in all relevant and reputable indexes, including PubMed, MEDLINE, Scopus, Web of Science, Chemical Abstracts Service, Embase, and PsycInfo. Most authors pay a fee and retain copyright to their work; doing so ensures that their readers will have fewer barriers to access. This model demonstrates how biomedical researchers have balanced the need for traditional publication systems with the expanded need for access.

OA humanities projects are more difficult to generalize because there are not yet primary repositories as in the sciences. However, recent developments, such as burgeoning digital humanities research and the momentum of the Open Library of Humanities, suggest that this may be changing. The Open Library of Humanities is an OA gold repository that relies on library subsidies. Because most humanities research is "unfunded and rests upon institutional support" (Eve 2014, 1), the Open Library of Humanities has necessarily sought an alternative funding model to the author-pays model used by PLoS. Additionally, humanities scholars seem to assign greater importance to peer review and less importance to immediacy than do physical science researchers; as literature professor Martin Eve (2014) says, "since arXiv is not a journal and has no review criteria . . . but is a pre-print repository, it is not 'trusted' to carry content of a reviewed quality in the same way as journals with gatekeeping policies or modes of post-review and weighting" (3).

"Research as Inquiry" may best be taught and assessed within the context of a discipline-specific OA platform. The librarian can help students identify an OA resource in their disciplines and investigate it to answer several open-ended questions:

- What types of questions are researchers in your field asking? Write down a few, and see what connections you can identify.
- What is the scope of these questions, and how are larger and smaller questions treated?
- What research methods are employed? List a few, and consider their effectiveness for learning about and understanding the content.

Answering these questions will develop students' recognition of appropriate research questions and their scopes. Students will identify the various research methods employed in the disciplines and appreciate how the methods employed determine the conclusions drawn. Some outcomes for this lesson might be:

- Students will identify research questions investigated in a discipline-specific OA repository.
- Students will evaluate research methods employed in a discipline-specific OA repository.

SCHOLARSHIP AS A CONVERSATION

"Communities of scholars, researchers, or professionals engage in sustained discourse with new insights and discoveries occurring over time as a result of varied perspectives and interpretations."—ACRL 2015, 8

Scholarship evolves in public and private conversations held in both traditional and informal settings. The egalitarian platforms on which OA relies foster educational equity and encourage a more diverse group to participate in the conversation of scholarship. Digital platforms enable participation and sustain discourse in ways that were previously impossible: Authors can post early drafts or data and quickly get feedback from readers around the world. Collaborative projects are now frequently international in scope because the ongoing discourse necessary for scholarship can be easily sustained via digital technologies.

Previously, scholars sustained these conversations via published research, conferences, and other oral and written communications. Opportunities to engage in scholarly discourse have proliferated. Scholars were early adopters of the LISTSERV format; H-Net, for example, connects scholars in history to discuss their research, recent publications/reviews, positions, and conferences. Researchers have also made good use of online forums to solicit feedback, find collaborators, and connect with their peers.

Part of teaching "Scholarship as Conversation" to undergraduate students is encouraging them to take on the mantle of scholars. Undergraduates may begin to connect with this concept when they acknowledge the work of published authors by citing them. This concept may, however, not be explicit, and the librarian should explain that in-text citations and works-cited lists are one way to acknowledge the scholars with whom one has engaged throughout the research process. Students need to understand that listing works cited—in addition to integrating them into the paper—reveals much about their understanding of the discourse surrounding their topics.

Students may initially be reluctant to see themselves as scholars. They may more readily identify with the role of content creators and copyright holders. As previously mentioned, asking them to license some content (essay, picture, recording) that they have created may help them to appreciate some of the choices entailed in scholarly content creation. Two other chapters in this volume deal with undergraduate engagement in OA and publishing and should be consulted for best practices and context.

Introducing undergraduate students to some of the more casual venues for scholarly communication may also help to ease them into some of the sustained discourse on which scholarship relies. Showing various iterations or drafts of a document in an OA repository may make clear to some students how others' varied perspectives and interpretations play into the revisions of an article or document.

In order to address "Scholarship as Conversation" in the classroom, the librarian might challenge students to make this conversation visible. For example, one might ask students to choose one of the following:

- Use citation network software to map linked citations, and note OA and proprietary sources with different color nodes.
- Make a concept map of conflicting and converging ideas around a given research question.
- Create a comic strip to represent various individuals' contributions to a scholarly conversation.

An outcome for the first idea is: Students will map scholarship networks and indicate whether they are OA or proprietary.

SEARCHING AS STRATEGIC EXPLORATION

"Searching for information is often nonlinear and iterative, requiring the evaluation of a range of information sources and the mental flexibility to pursue alternate avenues as new understanding develops."—ACRL 2015, 9

One of the hallmarks of advanced researchers is their persistence. They employ iterative and nonlinear processes to ensure that they have conducted a comprehensive search of all relevant and useful sources and then do further browsing and reading. This trait can be challenging to instill in undergraduate users and may be best addressed at the point of need. When the student does not successfully identify the desired information, the librarian might recommend a discipline-specific OA repository or database, suggest ways to incorporate new information into the search and evaluate the appropriateness of results, or introduce new strategies to employ. One such strategy is to stop and brainstorm a list of stakeholders who might produce information on the topic and then search accordingly. Another is to make use of the platform's built-in vocabularies, facets, and structural metadata to refine one's search. It is imperative to reiterate to students that the process is not linear and clean but requires reevaluation, flexibility, and time.

Librarians have historically used library catalogs and databases as their primary platforms during information literacy instruction. This practice has been increasingly called into question, both for its perpetuation of the library as an "information bank" (Elmborg 2004) or "depository of knowledge" (Kopp and Olson-Kopp 2010) and because "academic research should be connected to students' existing practices rather than set separate from (and better than) them" (Purdy and Walker 2013). Situating information literacy instruction in undergraduate users' preferred search platforms, likely search engines, will require much more flexibility on the part of the librarian and will engage both the student and the librarian in the evaluation of resources, some of which will be OA.

OA resources are sometimes but not always differently located and accessed than traditionally published materials. OA resources are increasingly easily added to library platforms; whole collections of OA content can be activated on the backend of EBSCO's EDS, for example (EBSCO 2014). Due to the optimization of metadata and indexing in Google Scholar, OA resources are even easier to find outside library platforms. The expanded and accelerated discovery of OA materials in a user's native or preferred search platform has meant that researchers can read and build on the findings of others with limited restriction.

"Searching as Strategic Exploration" may be taught by comparing a discipline-specific OA repository, discipline-specific database, and search engine. Librarians can have students begin their research in each of these settings by trying out multiple searches and noticing the various results. Ask students to reflect on the process and the differences:

- Did your first search work equally well in all three platforms? Explain.
- How did you revise your search to find more relevant results? What role did the specific platform play in this process?
- Explain the biggest challenge or frustration you encountered and how/whether you overcame it.

Outcomes for this lesson might include:

- Students will list differences in the functionality of an OA repository, database, and search engine.
- Students will evaluate differences in the results/content found in an OA repository, database, and search engine.
- Students will identify and employ a search strategy to improve search results.

CONCLUSION

Cousin (2009) suggests that the "overwhelming strength of threshold concepts is precisely in the opportunities for co-inquiry it presents between subject experts, students and educational researchers" (211). Librarians can best appreciate users' needs by engaging in inquiry alongside them. When working with students to teach them about open access, librarians must be sensitive to differences of student familiarity, interest, and expertise. Only by asking students what is new and hard or what is not making sense can we address the challenges in ways that allow the student to begin to make sense of complex material.

Considering the information literacy implications for open access frame by frame has revealed some themes. Both the OA landscape and research are messy and complex. Indeed, the variety of processes and products makes generalizing tricky in either instance. This does not mean, however, that they are unknowable. By familiarizing oneself with OA resources, platforms, and their purpose, librarians will better integrate them into our information literacy programs and advocate for their continued support and use. As with the establishment of institutional repositories and undergraduate research publications, information literacy instruction provides another opportunity for librarians to be leaders in the OA landscape.

REFERENCES

Asher, Andrew D., Lynda Duke, and Suzanne Wilson. 2012. "Paths of Discovery: Comparing the Search Effectiveness of EBSCO Discovery Service, Summon, Google Scholar, and Conventional Library Resources." *College & Research Libraries* 74: 464–88.

Association of College and Research Libraries (ACRL). 2015. "Framework for Information Literacy for Higher Education." http://www.ala.org/acrl/standards/ilframework.

Beall, Jeffrey. 2009. "Free Books: Loading Brief MARC Records for Open-Access Books in an Academic Library Catalog." *Cataloging & Classification Quarterly* 47, no. 5: 452–63.

Blackmore, Margaret. 2010. "Student Engagement with Information: Applying a Threshold Concept Approach to Information Literacy Development." Paper presented at the third Biennial Threshold Concepts Symposium: Exploring Transformative Dimensions of Threshold Concepts, Sydney, Australia, July 1–2.

Bollen, Johan, Herbert Van de Sompel, Aric Hagberg, and Ryan Chute. 2009. "A Principal Component Analysis of 39 Scientific Impact Measures." *PloS ONE* 4, no. 6: e6022.

Brown, Mark L. 2013. "The Role of the Research Library." In *The Future of Scholarly Communication*, edited by Deborah Shorley and Michael Jubb, 157–68. London: Facet.

Bruce, Christine. 1997. *The Seven Faces of Information Literacy*. Adelaide, Australia: Auslib Press.

Bruce, Christine, Sylvia Edwards, and Mandy Jean Lupton. 2006. "Six Frames for Information Literacy Education: A Conceptual Framework for Interpreting the Relationships between Theory and Practice." *Innovation in Teaching and Learning in Information and Computer Sciences* 5, no. 1: 1–18.

Budapest Open Access Initiative. 2002. "Read the Budapest Open Access Initiative." http://www.budapestopenaccessinitiative.org/read.

Cousin, Glynis. 2009. *Researching Learning in Higher Education: An Introduction to Contemporary Methods and Approaches*. New York: Routledge.

Cowan, Susanna M. 2014. "Information Literacy: The Battle We Won That We Lost?" *portal: Libraries and the Academy* 14: 23–32.

Cullen, Rowena, and Brenda Chawner. 2011. "Institutional Repositories, Open Access, and Scholarly Communication: A Study of Conflicting Paradigms." *Journal of Academic Librarianship* 37, no. 6: 460–70.

Dewey, Barbara, ed. 2010. *Transforming Research Libraries for the Global Knowledge Society*. Oxford: Chandos.

EBSCO. 2014. "EBSCO Discovery Service (EDS) Partner Database Questionnaire—English." http://support.ebsco.com/knowledge_base/detail.php?id=6431.

Elmborg, James. 2004. "Literacies Large and Small: The Case of Information Literacy." *International Journal of Learning* 11: 1235–39.

———. 2006. "Critical Information Literacy: Implications for Instructional Practice." *Journal of Academic Librarianship* 32, no. 2: 192–99.

European Commission Decision C 4995. 2014. "Horizon 2020: Work Programme 2014-2015." http://ec.europa.eu/research/participants/data/ref/h2020/wp/2014_2015/main/h2020-wp1415-intro_en.pdf.

Eve, Martin. 2014. "All That Glisters: Investigating Collective Funding Mechanisms for Gold Open Access in Humanities." *Journal of Librarianship and Scholarly Communication* 2, no. 3: eP1131.

Eysenbach, Gunther. 2006. "Citation Advantage of Open Access Articles." *PLoS biology* 4, no. 5: e157.

Gelfand, Julia, and Catherine Palmer. 2013. "Weaving Scholarly Communication and Information Literacy." In *Common Ground at the Nexus of Information Literacy and Scholarly Communication*, edited by Stephanie Davis-Kahl and Merinda K. Hensley, 1–24. Chicago: Association of College and Research Libraries.

Griffiths, Jillian R., and Peter Brophy. 2005. "Student Searching Behaviour and the Web: Use of Academic Resources and Google." *Library Trends* 53, no. 4: 539–54.

Head, Alison J. 2013. "Learning the Ropes: How Freshmen Conduct Course Research Once They Enter College." http://projectinfolit.org/images/pdfs/pil_2013_freshmenstudy_fullreport.pdf.

Hofer, Amy R., Lori Townsend, and Korey Brunetti. 2012. "Troublesome Concepts and Information Literacy: Investigating Threshold Concepts for IL Instruction." *portal: Libraries and the Academy* 12, no 4: 387–405.

Houghton, John, Bruce Rasmussen, Peter Sheehan, Charles Oppenheim, Anne Morris, Claire Creaser, Helen Greenwood, Mark Summers, and Adrian R. Gourlay. 2009. *Economic Implications of Alternative Scholarly Publishing Models: Exploring the Costs and Benefits*. London: JISC. https://dspace.lboro.ac.uk/2134/4137.

Jacobs, Heidi L. M. 2008. "Information Literacy and Reflective Pedagogical Praxis." *Journal of Academic Librarianship* 34, no. 3: 256–62.

Jacobson, Trudi E., and Thomas P. Mackey. 2013. "Proposing a Metaliteracy Model to Redefine Information Literacy." *Communications in Information Literacy* 7, no. 2: 84–91.

Keane, Edward P. 2012. "Librarian Viewpoints on Teaching Open Access Publishing Principles to College Students." *Serials Librarian* 63, nos. 3–4: 333–49.

Kopp, Bryan M., and Kim Olson-Kopp. 2010. "Depositories of Knowledge: Library Instruction and the Development of Critical Consciousness." In *Critical Library Instruction: Theories and Methods*, edited by Emily Drabinski, Alana Kumbier, and Maria Accardi, 55–67. Duluth, MN: Library Juice Press.

Kuhlthau, Carol C. 2004. *Seeking Meaning: A Process Approach to Library and Information Services*. Westport, CT: Libraries Unlimited.

Laakso, Mikael. 2014. "Green Open Access Policies of Scholarly Journal Publishers: A Study of What, When, and Where Self-Archiving Is Allowed." *Scientometrics* 99, no. 2: 475–94.

Lawrence, Steve. 2001. "Free Online Availability Substantially Increases a Paper's Impact." *Nature* 411, no. 6837: 521.

Mackey, Thomas P., and Trudi E. Jacobson. 2011. "Reframing Information Literacy as a Metaliteracy." *College & Research Libraries* 72, no. 1: 62–78.

McLuhan, Marshall. 1964. *Understanding Media: The Extensions of Man*. New York: McGraw-Hill.

Meyer, Jan, and Ray Land. 2003. *Threshold Concepts and Troublesome Knowledge: Linkages to Ways of Thinking and Practising within the Disciplines*. Edinburgh: University of Edinburgh.

Montgomery, Lucy. 2014. "Knowledge Unlatched: A Global Library Consortium Model for Funding Open Access Scholarly Books." *Cultural Science* 7, no. 2: 1–66.

Owusu-Ansah, Edward K. 2003. "Information Literacy and the Academic Library: A Critical Look at a Concept and the Controversies Surrounding It." *Journal of Academic Librarianship* 29, no. 4: 219–30.

Palmer, Kristi L., Emily Dill, and Charlene Christie. 2009. "Where There's a Will There's a Way? Survey of Academic Librarian Attitudes about Open Access." *College & Research Libraries* 70, no. 4: 315–35.

Pawley, Christine. 2003. "Information Literacy: A Contradictory Coupling." *Library Quarterly*: 422–52.

Purdy, James P., and Joyce R. Walker. 2013. "Liminal Spaces and Research Identity: The Construction of Introductory Composition Students as Researchers." *Pedagogy* 13, no. 1: 9–41.

Rempel, Hannah, Stefanie Buck, and Anne-Marie Deitering. 2013. "Examining Student Research Choices and Processes in a Disintermediated Searching Environment." *portal: Libraries and the Academy* 13, no. 4: 363–84.

Schmidt, Krista, and Nancy Newsome. 2007. "The Changing Landscape of Serials: Open Access Journals in the Public Catalog." *Serials Librarian* 52, nos. 1–2: 119–33.

Swanson, Troy A. 2004. "A Radical Step: Implementing a Critical Information Literacy Model." *portal: Libraries and the Academy* 4, no. 2: 259–73.

University of California Office of Scholarly Communication and the California Digital Library eScholarship Program. 2007. *Faculty Attitudes and Behaviors Regarding Scholarly Communication: Survey Findings from the University of California*. http://osc.universityofcalifornia.edu/wp-content/uploads/2013/09/OSC-survey-full-20070828.pdf.

Virginia Tech. 2016. "Information Timeline." http://www.lib.vt.edu/help/research/information-timeline.html.

White House. 2013. "Increasing Access to the Results of Federally Funded Scientific Research." http://www.whitehouse.gov/sites/default/files/microsites/ostp/ostp_public_access_memo_2013.pdf.

Chapter Ten

Out of the Archives and into the World

ETDs and the Consequences of Openness

Hillary Corbett

The academic library has long served its institution by housing print dissertations in its archives. Until recently, once a student submitted her final, approved dissertation to the library, it would rarely again see the light of day. Although researchers might learn of a dissertation through the library's catalog or through an index, accessing it was difficult. A university's collection of its students' dissertations was a walled garden in many ways. But with the advent of electronic thesis and dissertation (ETD) programs, a more appropriate analogy would be to a public park—a place where researchers from all over the world can freely access dissertations and master's theses via the library's institutional repository.

Of course, this expanded access to dissertations and theses has come with challenges as well as rewards. Some students have difficulty accepting that, once their dissertation is made publicly available, they no longer have control over how it is used—although the majority of such uses are positive (enhancing scholarly communication, advancing understanding of their fields, and so on), the negative possibilities, such as plagiarism, concern them. Students also are very susceptible to the perception that their openly accessible dissertations are not acceptable as book manuscripts because there is no market for their work if it is already available online.

How does the library gracefully maintain its traditional role as the steward of graduate student research while pushing against the resistance it may encounter to openness? This chapter examines the development of ETD programs and the library's role in managing the need for greater access to graduate student research while tempering concerns about the consequences of openness.

A BRIEF HISTORY OF THE DISSERTATION

The oldest dissertations archived at Harvard University, the oldest institution of higher education in the United States, date from the end of the eighteenth century (Harvard University 2015). While earlier dissertations may have been written, they were perhaps lost in the fire that destroyed the Harvard library in 1764 (Tommase 2007). In Europe, the dissertation has a much longer history: A 2005 exhibition at Leiden University showcased dissertations dating back to 1575. The catalog for that exhibition describes the scholastic *disputatio*, or disputation, a debate that was an essential educational and research method in medieval and early modern universities, serving as both a test of student knowledge and an exercise in logical thought (Weijers 2005). Both students and teachers attended these events, during which other instructional activity halted. Beginning in the mid-1500s, the *disputatio* (by this time also called *dissertatio*) sometimes also took written form. A written *disputatio* or *dissertatio* could be brief—a single-page list of questions or theses to be addressed in an oral conversation—or could include lengthier commentaries and discussions of topics stretching to one hundred pages or more (Freedman 2005).

Authorship of these early written dissertations was not always clear. In some cases, the presider over the *disputatio* (the closest equivalent to the modern dissertation advisor) was identified as the author, particularly in cases where the *disputatio* involved multiple students; in others, a student was named as author. In most cases, however, no record of authorship was made at all. During the course of the sixteenth through eighteenth centuries in Europe, two trends emerged: Students began to be named as authors more frequently, and their dissertations grew in length (doubtless aided by advances in printing technology). Freedman (2005) notes that, beginning in the mid-1600s, the dissertation became a place to communicate new ideas, as well as to demonstrate knowledge of established topics.

We know so much about these early dissertations because they were exchanged among an informal network of European universities whose libraries collected them—a practice of scholarly communication that ensured both dissemination and preservation of knowledge. It was only in 2004 that Dutch universities ceased to participate in this exchange, at which point the Leiden University library contained an estimated 600,000 dissertations— roughly 20 percent of their total print collection. The majority have remained uncataloged, probably because at the outset it was easy enough to locate a particular dissertation if it was shelved by institution; over the centuries, as the collection grew, this prospect became more difficult, but the practice was too entrenched and the volume of material certainly too enormous to catalog retrospectively (Damen 2005). Despite their lack of discoverability, to use a contemporary library buzzword, the existence of these early printed dissertations in modern European libraries serves as a signal of the dissertation's long-standing importance as part of the university's intellectual record and underscores the library's role in preserving and disseminating that record.

FROM PRINT TO ELECTRONIC: THE RISE OF THE ETD

While American institutions haven't had the time to produce as many dissertations as have those in Europe, they have also endeavored to collect and preserve their students' work. In the late 1930s, a new company called University Microfilms International (UMI) expanded its original mission of working with the British Library and began creating preservation copies of dissertations on microfilm for research libraries. In 1951, UMI began publishing *Dissertation Abstracts* as a service to the Association of Research Libraries. *Dissertation Abstracts* became an indispensable resource found in almost every academic library—a necessary tool for researchers to discover the dissertation holdings of distant libraries. UMI also sold copies of dissertations in microform or print to libraries and individuals—often this was the only way to read a dissertation not held locally, libraries being understandably hesitant to send out their archival copies on interlibrary loan (ProQuest 2015; Thistlethwaite 2012, 2).

Despite the increased discoverability of dissertations made possible by centralized microfilming and indexing, the copies of dissertations held in library archives are rarely accessed, compared to dissertations available online. At Northeastern University, print dissertations in the archives were accessed seventeen times during a two-year period. In the same time period, Northeastern's electronic dissertations in its institutional repository were accessed more than 57,000 times. On average, the electronic dissertations were accessed 7,847 percent more than the print, despite the print collection being more than twice as large as the electronic collection.

As enormous as that percentage is, it seems minute compared to that at another institution. In 2009, as West Virginia University transitioned from collecting print dissertations to an ETD program, the library reported that electronic theses and dissertations were accessed a whopping 145,000 percent more than items in the print collection (McCutcheon 2010, 23). While reporting differences may not permit a direct comparison between these statistics, they nevertheless indicate a massive increase in visibility and usage when dissertations are made openly available online.

Virginia Tech was the first institution of higher education to begin requiring electronic deposit of theses and dissertations in 1997. Also in that year, UMI began to create PDFs of all the dissertations they received, in addition to microfilming them (Fox, McMillan, and Eaton 1999, 1). During the late 1990s, improvements in Internet connectivity speeds and networking capa-

Table 10.1.   Access of Print versus Electronic Dissertations at Northeastern University

Format	Number of dissertations in collection	Number of times accessed, July 2013–2015	Accesses per dissertation
Print	2,039	17	0.008
Electronic	916	57,501	62.774

Note: Print usage statistics recorded by Northeastern University Archives and Special Collections. Electronic access statistics recorded by Northeastern's institutional repository platform (Digital Commons).

bilities meant library databases were transforming beyond locally mounted CD-ROMs and early online resources that responded to text commands. Library users began to expect immediate online access to the full text of whatever they had located in their database searches; while text rendered in HTML still downloaded more quickly over slow Internet connections, as speeds improved and broadband Ethernet replaced dialup in many libraries, PDFs became more desirable. The PDF, or portable document format, was becoming the standard for representing word processor–generated documents as attractive digital simulacra, and there was significant uptake of this format in the development of next-generation article databases (Tenopir 1998; Wusteman 1997).[1] UMI, which had already expanded its offerings to include online resources under the ProQuest Direct name in 1996 (ProQuest 2015), doubtless saw the business advantage of creating PDFs of dissertations while it had them under the camera for microfilming. In 2003, ProQuest began accepting electronic submissions of dissertations, with a few early adopters taking advantage of the service; by 2007, the company was actively marketing the service and encouraging institutions to transition away from sending print dissertations for filming (ProQuest 2007).

The Networked Digital Library of Theses and Dissertations (NDLTD) was developed in 1996 to begin serving the same role online that *Dissertation Abstracts* served for physical collections. Virginia Tech, as an early adopter of ETDs, was a key developer. A 2002 article from the Virginia Tech team in the *Journal of Computing in Higher Education* states that NDLTD included federated results from more than 120 universities worldwide (Fox et al. 2002). Unlike *Dissertation Abstracts*, however, NDLTD was created with no commercial interests behind it; rather, its stated mission is "promoting the adoption, creation, use, dissemination, and preservation of electronic theses and dissertations (ETDs) [and] support[ing] electronic publishing and open access to scholarship in order to enhance the sharing of knowledge worldwide." NDLTD was incorporated as a registered nonprofit organization in 2003 and later transitioned to a membership-supported business model

(NDLTD n.d., "Mission"). As of this writing, NDLTD is supported by more than one hundred institutional, consortial, and individual members (NDLTD n.d., "List of Members").[2] Any institution, regardless of membership status, may have its ETD metadata harvested for inclusion in the NDLTD database, which currently includes more than four million records. More recently, another online index, Open Access Theses and Dissertations (OATD), was launched to provide an alternative to NDLTD (Dowling 2013). While OATD contains fewer records than NDLTD (more than 2.4 million at the time of this writing), its initial advantage when it was launched by Wake Forest University in 2013 was a more user-friendly interface. Previously, NDLTD had been hampered by a restrictive architecture that has since been updated. NDLTD and OATD continue to run in parallel, providing different access points to ETDs held worldwide.

NDLTD and OATD aggregate metadata from institutional repositories, where the majority of North American ETDs are found. (Institutions in other countries sometimes make use of national-level ETD repositories, like the British Library's ETHoS service.) Because of the increased visibility of ETDs in discovery services like these, as well as their inclusion in search engine results, some institutions are now choosing to make the ETDs deposited in their repositories—rather than those that are submitted to ProQuest—the copies of record. While many institutions still require their students to submit a copy of their theses or dissertations to ProQuest for inclusion in the ProQuest Dissertations and Theses (PQDT) database, some schools make this submission optional or don't participate in the PQDT database at all. This latter practice is sometimes referred to colloquially as "NoQuest."

There are two central rationales for not participating in the ProQuest submission service. One is that libraries have traditionally held the copies of record of dissertations in their physical archives, so the transition from print to electronic should not mark a shift away from library custody of the copies of record. When ETD programs were initially implemented, many schools perhaps took advantage of the ProQuest service because their institutional repository infrastructures were in their early stages of development and not yet established enough for administrators to entrust them with the long-term preservation of such unique and valuable documents; in addition, most schools already had a well-established relationship with ProQuest as a partner in the preservation of dissertations on microfilm. But the institutional repository is now considered an essential, supported service at most of these institutions, and outsourcing preservation to a commercial entity seems less necessary or desirable. Indeed, the second rationale for turning away from ProQuest is the commercial nature of its service; while the company has long maintained that students retain their copyrights and only grant a nonexclusive distribution license, institutions who choose to opt out of the ProQuest service sometimes do so because they want to distance themselves from the commercialization of their students' work through inclusion in a subscription database. Gail Clement and Fred Rascoe (2013) sum up this movement succinctly in their excellent and thorough article on changing practices in ETD management:

> The growing trend in questioning a publishing and archiving policy devised in the age of microfilm should come as no surprise. As many universities succeed in establishing their own campus-based Internet publishing systems, and as an increasing number of reputable scholarly sharing sites proliferate across the World Wide Web, the practice of outsourcing academic publishing and archiving to a commercial, third-party distributor may no longer be as compelling as it was before the Internet. Increasing awareness of, and support for, Open Access, Open Education, and Open Science across American campuses is heightening demand for open access to scholarship in all its forms, from textbooks to the literature of peer-reviewed articles. In this context, ETD management and publishing systems that impede open access to graduate works may appear counter to stakeholder values.

NEW ROLES FOR THE LIBRARY IN THE ETD ENVIRONMENT: SUPPORTING THE GRADUATE SCHOOL

At universities that have transitioned from accepting print dissertations and theses to accepting electronic-only submissions, the library's traditional role as the cataloger and archiver of student research output has expanded. As illustrated in the previous section, once print dissertations and theses were shelved in the closed stacks of the archives, there was little more for the library to do except retrieve them for interested readers on a very infrequent basis. ETD programs, by contrast, involve the library more substantially for several reasons. Libraries find themselves fielding questions from students and graduate school staff regarding the submission process, the need for embargoes, and especially the impact that open access will have on their work. This process is often cyclical, with upticks in queries coming as each graduation date approaches. But as the conversations on the ETD-L electronic discussion list show, new questions and concerns arise throughout the year (see http://listserv.vt.edu/cgi-bin/wa?A0=ETD-L). In an environment where graduate students are essentially releasing the fruits of their labors to the world rather than consigning them to the shelves of the archives, issues of copyright and fair use, plagiarism, and the publishing pressures on newly minted academics take on much greater significance.

The changing nature of ETDs themselves also prompts input and assistance from the library. Change in academe is often slow, but some libraries are now seeing dissertations and theses that diverge from the traditional PDF format, especially from such programs as the digital humanities, that do not lend themselves well to research output in that limiting format. The library can support this change by providing a digital environment that permits the inclusion of supplemental files and multimodal display of information in a manner that might better represent the nature of a student's work. While it is ultimately the graduate school that will decide what form or forms an ETD may take, the library's advocacy and demonstration of technical capabilities can effect change that will further the transformation of the ETD beyond the PDF and lead to greater innovation in the presentation of research output.

The library has an essential role to play as communicator and coordinator in an ETD environment. In institutions where the graduate school or individual colleges are working directly with ProQuest to manage the submission process, the library can serve as a facilitator. Librarians are experts at working with vendors in general and most likely already have a well-established working relationship with ProQuest that dates back to the days of shipping unbound dissertations to UMI to be microfilmed and maintaining a standing order to *Dissertation Abstracts*. The library can help graduate school staff who may be uncertain about whom they should contact to make changes to their submission interface, for example, or who have billing questions. The library may also want to serve more generally as a conduit of information between the graduate school and ProQuest, especially if there are multiple people on campus involved with approving ETD submissions. The workability of this arrangement will probably depend on campus organizational culture, but at Northeastern University we have found that it is effective for the library to serve as a main point of communication with ProQuest for resolving questions and concerns.

In a large institution, where each school or college may have its own requirements for formatting and submission, there is a higher likelihood that graduate students in different departments may receive information about the ETD program that is presented to them either differently or at different points in their studies. A student who hears about the university's ETD program only as part of the graduate student handbook she receives on the first day of her degree program will almost certainly have forgotten all about it by the time she is ready to submit her dissertation and may not understand why, after graduation, her dissertation comes up in a Google search for her name. "Why is my dissertation in Google?" is probably the most common question received from Northeastern University graduates about the ETD program. Because the library isn't able to forcibly insert itself into the internal operations of the graduate school or schools, it must be vocal about the requirements and implications of the ETD program where it does have that opportunity. At Northeastern, we found that there was much less confusion from students about finding their dissertations on the open web once we inserted a page of information about our ETD program into the ProQuest submission interface, where they were required to check a box indicating that they had read it before completing the submission process. This page includes an explanation of what an ETD program is, why Northeastern has one, and what its advantages are. The library also provides this information to each graduate school for distribution to students as part of the ETD formatting guidelines, if they want to include it there, and it is available on the library's website (see   http://library.northeastern.edu/get-help/theses-dissertations). Even just reassuring students that ETD programs are now very common across the world can help alleviate concerns that open access to theses and dissertations isn't some harebrained scheme cooked up by their particular library.

NEW ROLES FOR THE LIBRARY IN THE ETD ENVIRONMENT: SUPPORTING STUDENTS

Most current graduate students are digital natives—they grew up in an era saturated with digital technologies and are accustomed to finding the vast majority of the information they need online. Yet they still express anxieties over allowing the information they created—their theses or dissertations—to exist on the open web. Sometimes these anxieties can be exacerbated by negative statements they may hear from their advisors ("Isn't someone in China going to plagiarize my dissertation and pass it off as his own?") or from professional societies or disciplinary associations. In 2013, the American Historical Association (AHA) issued a highly debated statement that students should embargo their dissertations for six years because otherwise no publisher would want to work with them (American Historical Association 2013). Many commentators pointed out that a dissertation is usually so far removed from being an accepted book manuscript that it is essentially a different publication. Indeed, a study found that the majority of journal editors and university press directors in the humanities and social sciences either welcomed or were willing to consider manuscripts based on openly accessible ETDs (Ramirez et al. 2012). Master of fine arts students, who do generally produce publishable works as their theses, perhaps have a valid concern here and have argued for the ability to embargo their work until their manuscripts have been formally published.

In other cases, such as patent applications, embargo periods are also appropriate, and in such situations, most institutions permit ETDs to be embargoed for set time periods, such as six months or one year. Indefinite embargoes, however, while they may seem desirable to the student who is fearful of diminished publishing opportunities, are rarely necessary. Situations that might require an indefinite or permanent embargo, such as the inclusion of privileged corporate or government information, should be avoided. The goal of ETD programs, after all, is to expand readership of theses and dissertations rather than create access barriers. The library has an important role to play here in guiding students and advisors to consider what goes into an ETD before it has been completed and approved, when substantive changes become more difficult. After all, the ETD is intended as a public and final record of a student's work, a tradition dating back to the medieval *disputatio*. Students are already taught how to report on research in a way that does not reveal identifying information about subjects; the library can enhance this standard component of graduate education by offering advice on how to produce an ETD that can be released to a worldwide audience without permanent restriction. Permanent or indefinite embargoes should be reserved for rare situations, such as a threat to the student author's personal safety, and should be considered by the graduate school carefully on a case-by-case basis.

Librarians who have experience advocating for open access to research output can play an important role in debunking certain concerns outright and providing good reasons why the advantages of openness far outweigh the potential for harm. As part of Open Access Week programming in 2013, the Boston College Libraries facilitated a panel discussion in response to the American Historical Association statement; the panel included an executive editor from Harvard University Press as well as faculty members and a current PhD student (Boston College Libraries 2013). Harvard University Press had responded in favor of immediate open access after the AHA statement was issued, and this opinion was represented by the editor on the panel. Jane Morris, Boston College's scholarly communications librarian, reported that the panel was successful in addressing the concerns AHA had raised about open access to dissertations. Regularizing this type of outreach to graduate students, faculty, and administrators will ensure that stakeholders are well informed about the true implications of open access to theses and dissertations. Indeed, the ETD program, with its impressive access statistics, serves as an important illustrative example in the library's open access advocacy. Not only is it obvious that these works receive much more readership than their closed access counterparts, but they also directly increase the institution's academic impact.

Library or graduate school websites often address student concerns about potential plagiarism or copyright infringement, assuring them that there is no difference in their intellectual property rights when their dissertations or theses are made available online as opposed to existing only in print. However, all authors, not just graduate students, must accept that, once their work is released to the world, plagiarism is a possibility regardless of format. And plagiarism, after all, does not reflect poorly on the creator of the original work but on the plagiarist and whomever vets the plagiarist's work. Expressions of fear about plagiarism often specifically mention China and India as hotbeds for this kind of activity, where young researchers are pressured to publish in English despite limited proficiency in order to obtain academic prestige and where unethical publishers aid and abet plagiarism and other forms of research deception. Those with something to gain may be playing up these concerns; see, for example, a 2011 white paper from a company that produces plagiarism detection software (iThenticate 2011). In truth, there is no proof that wholesale plagiarism of ETDs is taking place in these countries or elsewhere. Jeffrey Beall (2014), a prominent critic of open access publishing, asserts that ETDs are "increasingly used as a source for plagiarized journal articles" but provides only one example, of an American dissertation that had been plagiarized by Indian scholars, to back up this claim. If anything, it is easier to prove original authorship when a work is publicly posted, with its date of deposit clearly stated. So, a savvy plagiarist who did not want to be discovered would be wise to choose a less-visible source to copy!

In an ETD environment, intellectual property issues can also seem more crucial, although, as with plagiarism, the rules are not any different than in a print environment. Students must still determine that their usage of others' intellectual property falls within fair use or else seek permission. However, the increased visibility of ETDs over print theses and dissertations creates heightened anxiety about "doing the right thing" because rights holders' awareness of students' usage of their work is just a Google search away. The ETD can actually serve as an instructional tool in providing more general copyright advice to graduate students. After all, a thesis or dissertation will be the last thing they create in their graduate education, but it exists on a spectrum of authorship that includes journal articles coauthored with lab supervisors, critical response papers in their coursework, project-based websites, and all the work they will produce after graduating if they go on to an academic career. On day one of graduate school, they may not know what other types of work they'll be producing, but they all know they'll be writing a thesis or dissertation at the end if their program requires it. Getting students to think about writing for a public audience through the medium of the ETD can also help them to think about how their other academic writing should conform to best practices regarding copyright and fair use.

As anyone who has offered copyright education in an academic setting knows, there is a range of misconceptions held by scholars at all levels. A grad student may say, "My advisor told me anything used for academic purposes doesn't require permission, but I thought I should check with you," or, "If I got these images from the Internet, it's okay to include them in my dissertation, right?" Uncertainty is understandable—copyright law can be confusing to the layperson—but ideally students shouldn't get to the point of putting the finishing touches on their theses or dissertations before they start thinking about these questions. Copyright advisory to grad students is essential throughout their enrollment. ETDs already deposited in the institutional repository can serve as excellent examples to illustrate when permission is needed for reuse of others' work and when a determination of fair use may be made. Librarians who offer instruction and outreach to grad students should always include copyright and fair use as part of their sessions, so that students have a good handle on when they might need to seek permission by the time they get to the stage of writing their theses or dissertations. Such instruction will give them a higher level of confidence that they have nothing to fear regarding the public release of their ETDs on the open web.

While the risk of being plagiarized by others is not the student's responsibility, the risk of infringing on the intellectual property rights of others is. The responsibility for performing a fair use analysis and seeking permission if necessary ultimately rests with the student author. Neither graduate schools nor libraries have the time to review every page of every ETD when submitted; ProQuest reviews appendixes for copyrighted survey instruments and the like, but they do not review the full texts of ETDs either. This understanding may bring about a change in perspective for students who have grown up in a culture where "everything on the Internet is free." Libraries already do their best to disabuse students of this notion through copyright outreach as well as open access advocacy that highlights, for example, how much e-journal subscriptions actually cost, but such a distinction may only become personally relevant when they themselves are publishing their scholarship on the Internet via their ETDs.

Libraries may already be receiving queries from graduate students in the social sciences and humanities who are seeking advice on where to publish articles. (In the sciences, students more frequently serve as primary authors on articles coauthored by their faculty advisors or lab supervisors; in those cases, the senior authors likely determine where articles are submitted.) A search for this topic across the LibGuides platform shows dozens of guides created by libraries to help answer the question of where to publish (see http://libguides.com/community.php?m=s&it=0&search=where+to+publish).

Some address topics like journal impact factor or acceptance rate, while others emphasize the importance of being aware of predatory publishers. This latter point has particular relevance to the ETD program. While vanity publishers have been contacting students for decades about having their dissertations published for a fee, the increase in online availability of ETDs has likely resulted in a corresponding increase in these solicitations—after all, improved discoverability makes everyone's work easier, even the vanity publishers.

Libraries and graduate schools can help students to avoid falling prey to vanity presses and other predatory publishers, whose primary interest is in making money rather than advancing scholarship. Highlighting the problem in student-facing materials related to the ETD program is certainly a good idea (for an example, see the University of Massachusetts at Amherst's Lib-Guide for ETD authors, available at http://guides.library.umass.edu/content.php?pid=110362&sid=832620). Establishing a policy of not displaying students' e-mail addresses publicly with their ETDs and advising students not to include their contact information in their PDFs will make it more difficult for predatory publishers to contact students. And creating a feedback loop between the library and the graduate school about student queries regarding suspect publishers will permit both parties to be better informed and able to track trends in publisher contacts. Naturally, some publisher outreach to students may be completely legitimate. The library, especially its scholarly communication librarians and subject specialists, is well positioned to offer advice on whether a publisher's solicitation is aboveboard or suspect, and it should promote this service to the graduate school and its students. While open access to a student's dissertation or thesis will not damage her academic reputation, publishing it for a fee with a vanity press may have negative consequences, and the library can help ensure that she does not fall prey to such a solicitation.

NEW ROLES FOR THE LIBRARY IN THE ETD ENVIRONMENT: MARKETING AND ADVOCACY

In the print environment, dissertations and master's theses were not a focal point of the library's marketing efforts. Perhaps the collection in the archives might have been mentioned if it happened to contain works by prominent alumni—Nobel Prize winners, presidential candidates, and the like—but it was otherwise largely relegated to the background. By contrast, the library's collection of ETDs is highly promotable. Not only does it represent a significant library investment in terms of infrastructure, but it also illustrates the institution's commitment to making its research output more accessible and the value it places on graduate research in particular. In the broadest sense, as mentioned earlier, ETDs can serve as a cornerstone of the library's advocacy for open access. ETDs have local relevance, and their usage statistics are a compelling argument for the advantages of wider availability of research.

While the actual content of most dissertations and theses might be too specialized for a general audience, such as the recipients of a library supporters' newsletter, interest in reading the ETDs themselves is not necessary for understanding the significance of making this kind of research output more accessible worldwide. Impressive download statistics should certainly be promoted, as they reflect positively on the library's hard work in developing and maintaining the repository. It is also worth noting to university-level marketing staff that open access increases citation rates by 50 percent or more, a phenomenon first reported in Eysenbach (2006). Thus the ETD program also becomes an important tool for the university to market its graduate programs to prospective students who are keen to make their scholarly mark on the world. The success of the ETD program may be used for internal advocacy purposes as well; for example, to help convince university administrators to provide financial support for an open access publishing fund or to encourage faculty to consider adopting an open access policy.

The ETD program's achievements in expanding access to dissertations and theses can also be used to market a retrospective digitization program to alumni. Some institutions have either undertaken or are planning digitization of their print dissertation holdings in order to provide greater access as well as a more complete picture of their graduate research output over time. Librarians who advocate for open access are well versed in explaining how the advantages of increased accessibility outweigh any perceived disadvantages, and they can put this expertise to good use in outreach to alumni about digitization projects. Some alumni may balk at having their theses or dissertations retrospectively digitized and made available because of fears that their early, less-polished writings might detract from their scholarly reputations or perhaps reveal youthful opinions or outdated theories they would prefer to keep in seclusion on the archives shelf. But feedback from institutions that have undertaken retrospective digitization indicates that the majority of alumni are quite pleased to have their dusty old dissertations revived on the web. While Northeastern University has not yet embarked on a comprehensive digitization project, we have digitized older dissertations upon author request, and these authors have provided positive feedback on the outcome. Those who went on to establish academic careers have been pleased to be able to simply point prospective readers to their dissertations in our repository, as opposed to having to send photocopies or scans upon request. And they are interested in and surprised at the attention their digitized dissertations get, as evidenced in the download reports they receive. These success stories are marketing gold to library communications staff.

CONCLUSION

The library's role as the steward of graduate student research output has expanded significantly since the days of print archives. In addition to continuing its primary mission of safeguarding dissertations and theses in order to preserve the institutional record, something it has been doing for centuries, the library has now taken on additional roles as coordinator, advisor, and champion. Regular assessment of the services the library provides in support of the ETD program is essential, as is regular communication with the graduate school, students, and other stakeholders. With greater accessibility comes increased need for management and cultivation—to return to the metaphor introduced at the beginning of this chapter, a public park serves everyone, and their needs and uses will sometimes be unanticipated. But it is clear that the consequences of openness in an ETD environment are overwhelmingly positive for student authors and their institutions.

NOTES

1. Although the PDF standard was first released by Adobe in 1993, it wasn't until 1996, when the more functional version 2.0 was released (accompanied by the free release of Acrobat Reader software), that it saw wide uptake. See https://en.wikipedia.org/wiki/Portable_Document_Format.

2. Northeastern University is an NDLTD member.

REFERENCES

American Historical Association. 2013. "Statement on Policies Regarding the Option to Embargo Completed History PhD Dissertations." https://www.historians.org/jobs-and-professional-development/statements-and-standards-of-the-profession/statement-on-policies-regarding-the-option-to-embargo-completed-history-phd-dissertations.

Beall, Jeffrey. 2014. "Open Access Theses and Dissertations Increasingly Used as a Source for Plagiarized Journal Articles." http://scholarlyoa.com/2014/01/16/open-access-theses-and-dissertations-increasingly-used-as-a-source-for-plagiarized-journal-articles.

Boston College Libraries. 2013. "Open Access Week Events at Boston College University Libraries." *Boston College Libraries Newsletter* 14, no. 4. http://www.bc.edu/libraries/newsletter/2013fall/lh_oa.html.

Clement, Gail P., and Fred Rascoe. 2013. "ETD Management and Publishing in the ProQuest System and the University Repository: A Comparative Analysis." *Journal of Librarianship and Scholarly Communication* 1, no. 4: 1–29.

Damen, Jos. 2005. "Five Centuries of Dissertations in Leiden: A Mirror of Academic Life." In *Hora Est! On Dissertations*, 11–22. Leiden: Leiden University Library. http://www.ascleiden.nl/Pdf/horaestklein.pdf.

Dowling, Thomas. 2013. "Open Access Theses and Dissertations—oatd.org." Message posted April 4 to http://listserv.vt.edu/cgi-bin/wa?A0=ETD-L.

Eysenbach, Gunther. 2006. "Citation Advantage of Open Access Articles." *PLoS Biology* 4, no. 5: e157.

Fox, Edward A., Marcos André Gonçalves, Gail McMillan, John Eaton, Anthony Atkins, and Neill Kipp. 2002. "The Networked Digital Library of Theses and Dissertations: Changes in the University Community." *Journal of Computing in Higher Education* 13, no. 2: 102–24.

Fox, Edward A., Gail McMillan, and John L. Eaton. 1999. "The Evolving Genre of Electronic Theses and Dissertations." Paper presented at the thirty-second Hawaii International Conference on System Sciences, Maui. http://scholar.lib.vt.edu/theses/presentations/ETDgenre2.pdf.

Freedman, Joseph S. 2005. "Disputations in Europe in the Early Modern Period." In *Hora Est! On Dissertations*, 30–50. Leiden: Leiden University Library. http://www.ascleiden.nl/Pdf/horaestklein.pdf.

Harvard University. 2015. "History." http://www.harvard.edu/history.

iThenticate. 2011. "Pressure to Publish: How Globalization and Technology Are Increasing Misconduct in Scholarly Research." http://cdn2.hubspot.net/hub/92785/file-5414706-pdf/media/pressure-publish-free-white-paper.pdf.

McCutcheon, Angela M. 2010. "Impact of Publishers' Policy on Electronic Thesis and Dissertation (ETD) Distribution Options within the United States." PhD diss., Ohio University, Athens. http://rave.ohiolink.edu/etdc/view?acc_num=ohiou1273584209.

NDLTD. n.d. "List of Members." http://www.ndltd.org/about/membership.

———. n.d. "Mission, Goals, and History." http://www.ndltd.org/about.

ProQuest. 2007. "Submitting Graduate Works to UMI Dissertation Publishing." https://web.
archive.org/web/20070412085236/http://www.proquest.com/products_umi/dissertations/
submittinggrad.shtml.
———. 2015. "History & Milestones." http://www.proquest.com/about/history-milestones.
Ramirez, Marisa, Joan T. Dalton, Gail McMillan, Max Read, and Nancy H. Seamans. 2012.
"Do Open Access Electronic Theses and Dissertations Diminish Publishing Opportunities in
the Social Sciences and Humanities? Findings from a 2011 Survey of Academic Publishers." *College & Research Libraries* 74, no. 4: 368–80. http://digitalcommons.calpoly.edu/
lib_fac/98.
Tenopir, Carol. 1998. "Linking to Full Texts." *Library Journal* 123, no. 6: 34, 36.
Thistlethwaite, Polly. 2012. "Publish. Perish? The Academic Author and Open Access Publishing." In *Media Authorship*, edited by Cynthia Chris and David Gerstner. New York: Routledge. http://academicworks.cuny.edu/gc_pubs/86.
Tommase, Jennifer. 2007. "Tale of John Harvard's Surviving Book." *Harvard Gazette*. http://
news.harvard.edu/gazette/story/2007/11/tale-of-john-harvard%E2%80%99s-surviving-
book.
Weijers, Olga. 2005. "The Medieval *Disputatio*." In *Hora Est! On Dissertations*, 23–27. Leid-
en: Leiden University Library. http://www.ascleiden.nl/Pdf/horaestklein.pdf.
Wusteman, Judith. 1997. "Formats for the Electronic Library." *Ariadne* 8. http://www.ariadne.
ac.uk/issue8/electronic-formats.

Chapter Eleven

Open Access and the Graduate Author

A Dissertation Anxiety Manual

Jill Cirasella and Polly Thistlethwaite

The process of completing a dissertation is stressful—deadlines are scary, editing is hard, formatting is tricky, and defending is terrifying.[1] (And, of course, postgraduate employment is often uncertain.) Now that dissertations are deposited and distributed electronically, students must perform yet another anxiety-inducing task: deciding whether they want to make their dissertations immediately open access (OA) or, at universities that require OA, coming to terms with openness. For some students, mostly in the humanities and some of the social sciences, who hope to transform their dissertations into books, OA has become a bogeyman, a supposed saboteur of book contracts and destroyer of careers.

At a panel discussion about dissertations and access at the Graduate Center of the City University of New York (CUNY), Kathleen Fitzpatrick, director of scholarly communication at the Modern Language Association, expresses regret that students must decide about access to their dissertations at that stressful time:

> I have thought for quite a while that it's a shame that graduate students have to make this decision about the future disposition of their work at what is really a moment of peak anxiety for them. . . . You don't know what's coming and yet here you are suddenly having to make this long-term decision about the disposition of the document and what might become of it over the Internet. (cited in Smith-Cruz 2014, clip 3)

This chapter examines the various access-related anxieties that contribute to that "moment of peak anxiety." It is a kind of diagnostic and statistical manual of dissertation anxieties—a "Dissertation Anxiety Manual," if you will—describing anxieties surrounding book contracts, book sales, plagiarism, juvenilia, the ambiguity of the term *online*, and changes in scholarly research and production.[2]

In our examination, we primarily cite blog posts, news articles, and other nonrefereed sources because this is where most of the debate about OA dissertations occurs and where anxieties are most freely aired. (Of course, anxiety-laced articles feed anxieties among graduate students, advisors, and publishers, creating a vicious circle of misgivings and misinformation about OA.) There are relatively few peer-reviewed articles on these issues; we hope this chapter inspires researchers to study them in depth and over time.

ANXIETIES ABOUT FINDING BOOK PUBLISHERS

The top anxiety about OA dissertations appears to be the fear that the dissertations' ready online availability adversely affects prospects for turning them into first books. (This anxiety does not, for the most part, apply to students in the sciences, where journal articles, not books, are the primary units of scholarship.) Of course, most scholars care less about publishing a book and more about what a book makes possible, or at least easier, in today's academic climate. They believe that publishing a dissertation-based book is required, or at least desired, for finding and keeping a tenure-track academic job, becoming a known scholar, and earning tenure. In short, they feel, rightly or wrongly, that their short- and long-term livelihoods depend on being able to publish their dissertations as books.

This cascade of anxieties is not new, but it shot to the fore of academia's consciousness when the American Historical Association (AHA 2013) released a statement urging universities "to adopt a policy that allows the embargoing of completed history PhD dissertations in digital form for as many as six years" (para. 1). The AHA (2013) justified its call for six-year embargoes with an assertion that an "increasing number of university presses are reluctant to offer a publishing contract to newly minted PhDs whose dissertations have been freely available via online sources" (para. 1) and a reminder that "[h]istory has been and remains a book-based discipline" (para. 3). However, both of those claims generated controversy—the first for not being clearly supported by the evidence and the second for failing to see beyond the status quo.

Is it true that an "increasing number" of university presses are biased against manuscripts based on OA dissertations—or is it a rumor based on superficial logic and "anecdotes, ghost stories, and fear" (Patton 2013, para. 23)? There are certainly some publishers who are explicit about their prejudice. For example, Charles Backus, director of Texas A&M University Press, said that, because of the increase in online availability of dissertations, his press has become "much more reluctant to consider works based on dissertations than in the past" (Howard 2011, para. 16). And the University of Manchester Press explicitly states on their website their disinclination to publish dissertation-based books:

> Because PhD theses are increasingly freely and widely available in digital repositories, our policy is that we will not consider books based on theses for publication. In a small number of cases, where the research is of exceptionally high quality and broad appeal, we can consider a book that takes thesis research as its starting point and expands upon it significantly, on the strict understanding that it must have been entirely rewritten and restructured for a wider audience. (Manchester University Press n.d.)

Of course, many students do not communicate directly with presses while they are writing their dissertations. Rather, they rely on the advice of their advisors and other senior scholars, most of whom matured academically in a pre-OA world and many of whom have heard anecdotes—or third-party retellings of anecdotes—about difficulties publishing dissertation-based books. They, like former AHA president William Cronon (2013), worry that OA dissertations "*might* [italics his] make it more difficult for early-career colleagues to find publishers" and favor preemptively closing dissertations over facing what *might* happen (para. 28). Or, as Kathleen Fitzpatrick puts it, "with all kinds of good intentions, advisors . . . have a tendency to persuade graduate students and others that we should really be more conservative" (cited in Smith-Cruz 2014, clip 3).

Are these well-intentioned encouragements to temporarily or permanently restrict access well founded? That question loops us back to the question of whether an increasing number of publishers are exhibiting prejudice against OA dissertations. Clearly some publishers are. But there seem to be many more with no such prejudice.

For example, Philip Leventhal, senior editor at Columbia University Press, says, "In my time at Columbia, it's never come up that we've decided not to publish a book because it was available online" (cited in Smith-Cruz 2014, clip 4). Also, Doug Armato (2013), director of the University of Minnesota Press, revealed that his press "would consider, have considered, and indeed regularly publish, single-authored books that are revised from 100% previously available material" (para. 4). Columbia and Minnesota are not outliers: Prompted by the AHA statement to investigate the situation, Peter Berkery, executive director of the Association of American University Presses, queried fifteen press directors and reports, "I haven't found one person who has said if it is available open access, we won't publish it" (cited in Cohen 2013, para. 19).

Some presses are more than merely willing to publish books based on OA dissertations—they actively credit openness for leading them to publishable dissertations. For example, Harvard University Press's assistant editor Brian Distelberg is "always looking out for exciting new scholarship that might make for a good book." For him, "to whatever extent open access to a dissertation increases the odds of its ideas being read and discussed more widely, I tend to think it increases the odds of my hearing about them" (cited in Harvard University Press 2013, para. 5). Indeed, Harvard University Press (2013) sums up their sentiment thus: "If you can't find it, you can't sign it" (para. 6).

Furthermore, some presses appreciate that openness promotes conversation and useful revision. Leventhal explains that "you get a response and you get feedback, and that will in turn help shape your project" (cited in Smith-Cruz 2014, clip 4). Indeed, the value of public conversation in shaping the minds and works of junior scholars has been acknowledged for centuries. For example, Renaissance humanist Colluccio Salutati considers *disputatio*, or public scholarly debate, essential to training the mind and refining claims; he considers it "absurd to talk with oneself between walls and in solitude" (cited in Covey 2013, 546).

Rather than countering mere anecdote with anecdote, we should also look at data. As mentioned previously, there are not yet many research studies investigating the effect of OA on prospects for publishing dissertation-based books (for those interested, the field is wide open!), but there is one recent study of note: "Do Open Access Electronic Theses and Dissertations Diminish Publishing Opportunities in the Social Sciences and Humanities? Findings from a 2011 Survey of Academic Publishers" (Ramirez et al. 2013). The authors received responses from fifty-three university presses, with 9.8 percent indicating that manuscripts derived from OA theses and dissertations are "always welcome," 43.9 percent considering such manuscripts "on a case-by-case basis," and 26.8 percent welcoming them "only if the contents and conclusions are substantially different" from the thesis or dissertation (374).

Graduate students might initially be alarmed that only 9.8 percent "always welcome" such manuscripts, but it is important to remember that publishers consider *all* manuscripts on a case-by-case basis. Similarly, just about all publishers expect dissertation-based manuscripts to differ significantly from the original dissertation or work with authors to overhaul the manuscript before publishing it (see, for example, Harvard University Press 2013; Smith-Cruz 2014; and especially Wissoker 2013). This is because a dissertation, as long and sophisticated as it might be, is nevertheless a student work written for a specific audience, not a book written for broader consumption.

Therefore, it is reasonable to combine the groups who answered "always welcome," "on a case-by-case basis," and "only if the contents and conclusions are substantially different." Doing so, we see that fully 80.5 percent of respondents are willing to consider manuscripts based on OA theses and dissertations—certainly not every respondent but the overwhelming majority.[3]

ANXIETIES ABOUT BOOK SALES

As both anecdotes and research have shown, most publishers do not discriminate against manuscripts based on dissertations, even OA dissertations. They understand the distinctions between a dissertation and a book and the in-depth and inevitable revising, reframing, and rewriting that separate them. William Germano (2005), former editor at Columbia University Press and Routledge and a scholar of the book, writes in *From Dissertation to Book*, "To the new PhD's eager question—'What do I do now that I'm done?'—[there are] answers rather than an answer. . . . The key to any of them, though, is revision" (1). Similarly, Patrick Alexander, director of Penn State University Press, tells the *Chronicle of Higher Education*, "The best advice I could give students . . . is to remember that books and dissertations are two distinct species" (cited in Howard 2011, para. 23).

However, some publishers do discriminate against book proposals that spring from dissertations, and those who do are driven by anxieties of their own: dismay at shrinking per-title sales, fears about libraries' purchasing habits, and concerns about staying financially afloat. Jerome Singerman, senior editor at the University of Pennsylvania Press, puts it this way: "Although university presses are nonprofit institutions, we are totally driven by and reactive to the market. . . . We need to publish in a way that is financially viable . . . and there is a threshold beneath which we just can't go for sales" (cited in Smith-Cruz 2014, clip 5).

If university presses are going to continue in their current form, then they must indeed maintain a certain level of sales. (Whether they will or should stay essentially as they are is an important issue but beyond the scope of this chapter.) So the question must be examined, Do books based on dissertations sell worse than other books?

Some publishers believe so, apparently based primarily on what they have heard about the "approval plans" that libraries set up with book distributors. Approval plans allow libraries to specify the kinds of books they want to receive notification about or even have delivered automatically. Distributors allow libraries to include or exclude books according to many parameters, including publisher, subject, whether a book is a textbook, and whether it is based on a dissertation.

The existence of the dissertation parameter has spooked some university press editors and directors, who believe that libraries are increasingly excluding dissertation-based books from their approval plans and doing so "on

grounds they can already get the material through dissertation databases"
(Ramirez et al. 2013, 376). Singerman describes the situation even more
starkly, saying that the distributor Yankee Book Peddler (now known as YBP
Library Services) marks any book it determines to be based on a dissertation
as a "do-not-buy title" (cited in Smith-Cruz 2014, clip 5).

However, what these publishers have heard—what they think they
know—is wrong. There is little evidence that libraries are increasingly excluding dissertation-based books from approval plans or that the libraries that
do exclude such books do so because the original dissertations are available
online. And distributors, whose businesses are based on selling books, certainly do not brand dissertation-based books with some kind of fatal do-not-
buy stamp.

Michael Zeoli, a vice president at YBP, dispels several myths surrounding approval plans and dissertation-based books. First, "there is no stand-
alone term 'dissertation'": YBP's approval plans distinguish between "unrevised dissertations" and "revised dissertations" (Zeoli 2013, para. 4). Admittedly, few libraries purchase unrevised dissertations, but the same is not true
for revised dissertations. Zeoli also reports that revised dissertations published by university presses sold almost as well as other university press
books. He also found that libraries bought revised dissertations from university presses in considerably larger numbers than revised dissertations from
commercial presses, evidence that librarians respect the selection judgments
of university presses and value their intensive editorial work. In 2015, Zeoli
examined more recent sales figures for university presses and found that
revised dissertations were selling, on average, just as well as the presses'
other books: "I took the new title output of revised dissertations for 1 year for
a dozen U.S. university presses spanning types from high-end prestigious to
small presses with a regional focus. Surprisingly, the *average* number of
units sold for revised dissertations was identical to the number of titles sold
for other titles: 83" (personal communication, September 3, 2015). Not surprisingly, the exact balance between revised dissertations and other books
varied by press. Zeoli saw that some presses sold fewer revised dissertations
than other books and some sold more. But, "[i]n general, the numbers were
fairly close, as the average reveals" (personal communication, September 3,
2015). However, he also learned that, on average, revised dissertations sell
less well in the first ninety days after publication. YBP's buyers initially
purchase stock for the first ninety days, so they do indeed sometimes tell
publishers that revised dissertations sell fewer copies (personal communication, September 3, 2015). Even though these books catch up over time, the
phenomenon of the first ninety days may scare publishers.

Zeoli believes that the rise in demand-driven acquisitions (DDA) of e-
books is a more significant development to watch and that it affects library
sales much more than the accessibility of dissertations: "The real impact on

sales has been the dramatic growth of content flowing into DDA pools in libraries and triggering into a sale at a very low rate (and even then, more often as a loan or rental than as a purchase). The debate over dissertations really doesn't even rise to the level of 'footnote' in terms of impact on publisher sustainability" (personal communication, September 3, 2015). As for the supposed prejudice against revised dissertations in approval plans, Zeoli (2013) dispels that myth too: "Having written many Approval Plans over 15 years, I know that libraries do not punish this category of books anymore [*sic*] than others, at least not when published by university presses" (para. 10). Still, some libraries do exclude both unrevised and revised dissertations from their approval plans; Kevin Smith (2013b) summarizes some of the reasons:

> Many academic libraries, especially at smaller institutions that do not have a mandate to build a research collection, will exclude books based on revised dissertations from their approval plan because such books are likely to be very expensive and very narrowly focused. Many libraries simply cannot put their limited funds toward highly-specialized monographs that will not broadly support a teaching-focused mission. (para. 6)

Of course, libraries do not acquire books exclusively through approval plans. Individual librarians also select individual titles, making decisions based on their libraries' collection priorities and researcher populations. Smith (2013b) also addresses the question of whether librarians do what some publishers fear and discriminate against dissertation-based books for which the dissertation is available online:

> In 25 years as an academic librarian, I have never met a librarian who looks for an online version of a dissertation before buying the published, and presumably heavily revised, monograph based on that dissertation. That is just not part of the process; most acquisitions librarians do not even know if there is an online version of the dissertation when they decide about purchasing the monograph; I certainly did not when I made these sorts of decisions. Libraries look for well-reviewed items that fit the curricular needs of their campus. They may ask if the book is over-priced and/or too narrowly focused, and those questions may rule out many revised dissertations these days. But they simply do not, based on my experience and discussions with many of my colleagues (more anecdotal evidence!), look to see if they can get an unrevised version for free. (para. 5)

As Smith acknowledges, his reporting is based on anecdote, not data. But there are many others who support his claims. See, for example, Leonard Cassuto's (2011) informal survey investigating the related question of whether acquisitions librarians discriminate against dissertation-based books whose authors have previously published dissertation findings or excerpts in journals. Spoiler: They don't (para. 11). Librarians know that, given the choice, scholars at all levels prefer to interact with and refer to a published work, not its precursor dissertation, in scholarly conversation. So, if a university press book is well reviewed, then librarians will consider its relevance to their institution's researchers and its affordability without a negative thought about its possible origins as a dissertation.

Nevertheless, sales of university press books have declined precipitously since the 1970s. According to Singerman, "every time you thought it couldn't go lower from where it was, it would go lower." But the decline, according even to Singerman, is due to steeply increasing serials prices and libraries' correspondingly smaller monograph budgets (cited in Smith-Cruz 2014, clip 5). Or, as Kevin Smith (2013a) writes in response to Charles Backus, "Your lunch, Mr. Backus, is being eaten by Elsevier and Wiley, not by ETDs" (para. 6).

As discussed in the previous section, publishers who are wary of OA dissertations are outnumbered by those who are unfazed by them or see them as tools for finding good manuscripts. But it goes further: Some publishers actually favor OA dissertations that have attracted attention online. They interpret buzz surrounding an online dissertation as evidence that there is a market for a book and do not worry about the dissertation potentially pulling buyers away from the book. According to Jim McCoy, director of the University of Iowa Press, "[a]ny dissertation that's on the Internet and has taken on a life of its own, that would be a selling point to me" (cited in Howard 2011, para. 19). Sara Pritchard, formerly of West Virginia University Press, has a similar view, saying of a dissertation-based book on mountaintop-removal coal mining, "We thought it was a good sign that her electronic dissertation was receiving so many hits . . . and that it boded well for sales of her book," which has indeed sold "extremely well" (cited in Howard 2011, para. 20). Granted, publishers will always favor manuscripts on controversial issues, such as mountaintop-removal coal mining, and popular topics, such as the Civil War, because they attract interest beyond the academy (Ramirez et al. 2013). Of course, as pointed out by Harvard University Press (2013), the "proper role of market viability in scholarly publishing" is an "unsettled matter" (para. 7). But that is a discussion for a different venue.

Clearly, anxieties about the effect of OA dissertations on the sales of resulting books have been driven by rumors and accumulated distortions, not actual information about approval plans and library acquisitions. Somehow, almost as in the children's game "Telephone," the existence of dissertation parameters in approval plans turned into a rumor that YBP marks dissertation-based books with a do-not-buy flag and a belief that books based on OA dissertations sell especially poorly. In order to ameliorate this mass misunderstanding and prevent future ones, we must all heed this plea from Cassuto (2011): "If I may presume to advise publishers and librarians, let me ask you to talk to each other. Keep each other informed so that your policies are based on fact, not fear" (para. 23). We must also continue to study the trends and analyze data, not just anecdotes. Without that data, we will, as Rick Anderson (2013) puts it, "continue operating in the realm of inference, anecdote, and fear—none of which generally provides a solid basis for policy" (para. 10).

ANXIETIES ABOUT MISDEEDS

Another fear among dissertation writers and advisors, especially those unfamiliar with OA in general, is that OA dissertations will attract plagiarists, swindlers, and other no-goodniks of the scholarly world. When considering these concerns, we must recall that, before the Internet, interlibrary loan (ILL) and microformats were regarded with the same wariness. As Andrew H. Horn wrote in 1952, the "thing [the graduate student] demands of the university archivist is a promise that his brain child will not be turned over to the library for promiscuous interlibrary lending, lest some literary pirate steal his stuff before he gets it in print himself" (328).

Concerns about ILL-enabled misdeeds were not allowed to interfere with libraries' mandate to collect, preserve, and provide access to dissertations—to the great benefit of today's researchers, whose work requires access to many sources, including the dissertations of earlier generations. Similarly, moral panic about OA-enabled misdeeds cannot be allowed to prevent the collection, preservation, and provision of access to today's dissertations or the modernization and improvement of techniques for accomplishing these tasks (e.g., online submission, digital preservation, and OA distribution). Nevertheless, let us examine the concerns about OA and the scholarly offenses it supposedly encourages: plagiarism, idea theft, and copyright violations, including repackaging for profit.

Without question, texts that are freely available online are easy to plagiarize. And if they are well researched and well written, as dissertations generally are, they are likely to appeal to a would-be plagiarist. However, if the text is online, then it is also easy to identify as the source material of a plagiarized work. As many professors attest, plagiarized papers are often easy to spot; they tend to be marked by patchiness, including sudden changes in style, tense, and even formatting. Once a paper has raised suspicions, a quick Internet search for some fishy phrases often reveals the source—but only if the source is online. So, while openness may make plagiarism easier to commit, it also makes plagiarism easier to detect.

Of course, most dissertation writers are less concerned about plagiarism by students than plagiarism by unscrupulous scholars in their field. These supposed scholars are often craftier plagiarists, more likely to blend in the stolen bits and make a seemingly unified whole. As a result, their creations set off fewer alarms than sloppily plagiarized student papers. But they are still sniffed out, often because another researcher in the field, sometimes the author of the source, recognizes stolen arguments or language (e.g., Sonfield 2014). And, as with student papers, Internet searching can reveal the malfeasance, provided the source is also online.

Because openness is so useful in rooting out plagiarism, it can even provide a deterrent against it. As leading OA expert Peter Suber (2012) puts it, "[n]ot all plagiarists are smart, but the smart ones will not steal from OA sources indexed in every search engine. In this sense, OA deters plagiarism" (24). Furthermore, in cases of authors accusing each other of plagiarism, an online time stamp can serve as arbiter. In fact, a time stamp helped one of the authors of this chapter make a successful case against a researcher who had plagiarized her master's thesis in large quantities. After reporting the plagiarism, she was asked to prove that this person had plagiarized her, not vice versa. To do so, she simply showed that her thesis had been posted online long before the other work was submitted for evaluation. With the question of priority addressed, the investigation continued and found the accused guilty of extensive plagiarism from multiple sources.

Similar to the fear of plagiarism is the fear of idea theft—having ideas from one's dissertation found, stolen, and published by someone else before the dissertation can be turned into an article or book. But the surest way to prevent someone else from taking credit for an idea—either because that person stole the idea or because that person had the idea independently—is to make the idea public as soon as possible, to establish priority (Harnad 2006). If the original work is OA, then someone might try to take credit for its ideas, but the time-stamped original can disprove the appropriator's claims.

Still, some argue that secrecy, which would make appropriation impossible, is preferable to time-stamped sharing. However, total secrecy of doctoral research is rare. For example, many graduate students present their findings at symposia and conferences, and unprincipled academic supervisors, who of course have privileged access to their students' unpublished work, sometimes claim credit for such work (Martin 2013).

Others worry that crooked publishers will "steal" OA dissertations and sell them for profit (Hawkins, Kimball, and Ives 2013, 36). This fear seems to be unfounded, a conflation of two other phenomena: (1) the existence of shady book publishers that sell compilations of OA articles originally published under a Creative Commons Attribution (CC BY) license, which allows commercial reuse (Anderson 2015), and (2) ProQuest's now-discontinued practice of selling dissertations through "third-party retailers," such as Amazon (Straumsheim 2014). The first should not concern dissertation authors, almost none of whom give their dissertations a CC BY license. Unless a publisher is willing to commit flagrant copyright violations, it will not repackage works that are traditionally copyrighted or released under licenses with noncommercial clauses. And the second is neither an OA issue per se nor any longer an issue at all, only a lingering resentment (see "Anxiety about Corporate Collusion," later).

Graduates are more likely to be tricked by e-mail enticements from publishers that sell unedited dissertations (Stromberg 2014). When dissertation authors transfer copyright to such publishers, they relinquish almost all rights to the work, including the right to make derivative works. It is important to note the great distance between what these publishers do and what universities with OA dissertation policies do. Despite alarmist claims that universities require students to "forfeit their intellectual property rights" (Hawkins, Kimball, and Ives 2013, 32), they do no such thing. Rather, universities leave copyright with the author, only requiring a nonexclusive license to distribute the work noncommercially (see Duke University Graduate School n.d.). The rampant confusion on this point highlights the need for rights education by universities, libraries, and publishers.

Of course, those who choose to restrict access to their dissertations are hiding them not just from bad attention but also from good attention. If a dissertation is not OA, then it is much less likely to be read by those who might provide useful feedback, offer career-boosting opportunities, cite it in their publications, bolster the author's scholarly confidence, or silently appreciate the work.

Rebecca Anne Goetz (2013) is just one scholar who found a publisher because her dissertation was OA: "I ended up submitting my manuscript to [Johns Hopkins University] Press *after* American history editor Bob Brugger had read the dissertation and sought me out at a conference to talk about it" (para. 7). And her testimonial about OA goes beyond the benefits it brought her: "As scholars we are supposed to speak to one another, and our written work is supposed to start conversations. Embargoing prevents good conversations from ever getting started" (para. 8).

Download counts do not qualify as conversation, but they do communicate valuable information to authors. Take, for example, Gregory T. Donovan, who not only posted his dissertation online but also used the website's URL as his dissertation title (MyDigitalFootprint.org) to make sure that anyone who saw or heard mention of his dissertation would immediately understand how to access it. In 2013, he reported that his site had had more than three thousand unique visits in the previous year, with more than five hundred PDF downloads. Of course, he did not communicate directly with most of the downloaders, but the numbers nevertheless demonstrated to him "some kind of interest, which just at a personal level motivates me to continue this work, know that there's an audience out there, and know that my scholarship is getting some kind of traction" (cited in Smith-Cruz 2014, clip 6).

Let us close this examination of fear-based opposition to OA with some provocative words from Denise Troll Covey's (2013) compelling article "Opening the Dissertation: Overcoming Cultural Calcification and Agoraphobia." She denounces those who restrict their dissertations out of fear of misuse, saying, "They are hoarders and censors who undermine the values and mission of the university, upset the balance between private interest and public good that copyright was designed to achieve, and impair the online identity critical to their future employment" (551). She argues that those who restrict access and those who advise them to do so are "not good stewards of their discipline" (Covey 2013, 551).

Indeed, stewards bear responsibility for the renovation of their disciplines. Of course, many would counter that scholars have a greater responsibility to themselves than to their disciplines. But even if so, it is not at all clear that they serve themselves well by embargoing their dissertations. Yes, there are some risks in releasing one's dissertation or any other publication to the public. But there are greater risks and lost opportunity costs in hiding it.

ANXIETY ABOUT JUVENILIA

Emotionally exhausted and intellectually insecure at the end of the defense ordeal, some graduate students seek to hide their dissertation from further scrutiny, not wanting to reveal their work until they have transformed it into a more perfect, mature text. Fears that graduate work "isn't ready" for larger audiences reflect a mighty and common fear of being judged on work that is underdeveloped, underreviewed, and undertested.

However, the Association of College & Research Libraries' "Framework for Information Literacy for Higher Education" (2015) highlights that scholarship is an ongoing, unfinished conversation. Scholarship takes place in different venues and consists of a continuum of intellectual iterations, reviews, and revisions. The dissertation is a well-defined venue for the early work of junior scholars, the first iteration of scholarship that may later be revised for a polished appearance in long format. Differences between unrevised and revised scholarly iterations and the venues that contain them are understood by participants in the conversation. Authors fearing exposure of their graduate work not only misjudge their audiences' expectations but also underestimate their readers' competencies.

The dissertation is the culmination of graduate study proposed, constructed, approved, and defended in relationship with a committee of faculty advisors, but it is not selected, shaped, or edited with any audience in mind except the degree-granting institution. Academic press titles are, on the whole, thoroughly transformed, rewritten, and improved from the standard six-chapter dissertation of their inception.

Nevertheless, new academic authors often conflate expectations for the dissertation with those for the book. University of Alabama religious studies professor Michael J. Altman (2013) blogged about why he embargoed his dissertation:

> I have a book project that I'm working on and it is based on my dissertation. The dissertation is a really good dissertation . . . but it isn't as good as the book will be. It doesn't have the kind of sharp teeth I want the final book to have. It was written for an audience of three, not an entire field. And even though I was told to "write for the book" by my advisor, it is still the rough draft of the book. It is a . . . fine dissertation, but it is not my first book. (para. 7)

If the dissertation were truly embraced as a requirement for a degree, as a step in a public scholarly conversation, and not held to the fantastically aspirational standard of publisher-ready copy, then this dilemma would not present itself. Advisors offering dissertation authors encouragement to "write for the book" would do them a greater service by presenting it as advice intended to elicit a reader-friendly style of writing or creativity of argument. Advisory encouragement should constitute a guideline or a challenge to the dissertation author, not a blurred expectation that advisory committees assume the same standards and purposes as academic book publishers.

ANXIETY ABOUT ANYTHING ONLINE

Leonard Cassuto (2011) offers the following as a supposed distillation of the sentiments of editors, or at least the editors he talks to: "Don't make your dissertation available online. Book editors seem unanimous on that point for obvious reasons. Many university libraries routinely add dissertations to their electronic holdings. If yours does, then opt out. If your thesis is already online, then have it taken down" (para. 11).

Of course, *online* could mean many different things. It could describe a dissertation that is immediately posted OA or one that is online in an OA repository but temporarily embargoed or one that is online but available only via ProQuest's subscription database or sales site or one that is submitted to ProQuest but embargoed forever. Are all these varieties of online distribution obviously and equally threatening to all university press editors? Survey evidence and anecdotal reporting both suggest that online distribution does not in itself worry publishers. But OA distribution makes some vocal publishers, often small ones in specialized fields, nervous to varying degrees (Ramirez et al. 2013).

With university press sales on a downward trend for decades and with small presses with small print runs operating on slimmer and slimmer margins, OA dissertations are new complications. But they are not necessarily threats for unstable small businesses. As mentioned earlier, publishers can use download metrics for an OA dissertation to gauge reader interest in the work. In OA repositories, publishers have new tools to establish which works have ready audiences and to identify where on the globe those readers reside. Furthermore, studies indicate that offering a book in full-text downloadable form openly and online does not necessarily cut into print-copy sales (McGreal and Chen 2011). Readers prefer to read long-form writing in hard copy, but online will do for chapter reading or if the hard copy is out of reach (JISC Collections 2009).

Demanding that a dissertation be "taken down" altogether from a university's repository of record is often incompatible with university policies that require dissertations to be available for public review. Advocating that universities remove dissertations from any and all online platforms, presumably with a reversion to paper- and microfilm-based storage and distribution, is advocating for a refusal to modernize. Disengagement from standard forms of scholarly distribution will serve no individual career well. Furthermore, disciplines that fail to embrace new technologies and new methods of scholarly communication imperil their own viability.

Cassuto's distilled warning was cited and promulgated by well-known academic advisor Kathryn Hume (2011), who cautions, in blogger boldface, that "[w]ithout the quality control implied by refereeing, ProQuest 'publication' will not count for tenure. Furthermore, its being there may interfere with your landing a revised version at a reputable press. You could ruin your chances of getting tenure if your thesis is freely available" (para. 2). Now, ProQuest work is actually quite rarely "freely available." Both Cassuto's and Hume's warnings involve a lack of specificity, a sort of fuzzy fear, about the varieties and options of online dissertations that haunt and hype these conversations.

Hume, like Cassuto, fails to distinguish effectively either between ProQuest and OA repository platforms or among the different public access and embargo options that both routinely offer. While ProQuest offers authors (particularly those without an institutional repository) an option to make their dissertations OA for a fee, ProQuest's primary distribution model is subscription- and sales-based. ProQuest's for-profit distribution model hews closely to the company's tradition of print and microfilm distribution.

Producing graduate work that is archived and publicly accessible is a requirement for the PhD. It is not an established threat to publishers or a strike against a productive career. Faculty advisors, especially those who publish their advice, do student authors a disservice by discussing dissertation distribution options without a complete and reliable grasp of the conditions about which they are advising. Advisors recommending takedown to prevent ruinous consequences might better influence students' careers and the future of their disciplines by accurately representing academic publishers' varying opinions about OA dissertations and the roots of their anxieties. They might help student authors to carefully consider online dissertation discovery mechanisms and embargo options and walk them through the consequences of both obscurity and exposure, informed by their knowledge of how publishing, hiring, and promotion works in their disciplines. They could more productively identify the particular publishers who will not consider proposals based on dissertations or unembargoed dissertations instead of painting the entire academic publishing enterprise as antidissertation and anti-OA.

The confusion about posting dissertations online is not solely the result of publisher-inspired advisor fear and misunderstanding. A great deal of OA anxiety is generated by the liberal use of the word *publish* and its attendant (mis)understandings. Hume (2011), again conflating ProQuest with OA, here concerns herself with the notion of publishing: "Once available through any form of open access, be it ProQuest or a university library's public access materials, that dissertation is functionally published" (para. 2). The word *publishing* is commonly used to describe posting to ProQuest or an institutional repository. However, works on these platforms are not "published" in the fullest sense of the word. Dissertations are reviewed by a committee of advisors, and they are formatted and copyedited to a small degree. But they are not curated by a publishing house or evaluated by reviewers unknown to the author.

Also, it is important for new academic authors and their advisors not to conflate copyright concepts with publishing concepts. Traditional academic publishers generally require authors to transfer copyright in their works to them and with it the exclusive license to distribute the work. ProQuest and universities with OA repositories, on the other hand, leave copyright with authors. Both of the latter require a nonexclusive license to archive and distribute the work in perpetuity, but neither demands that authors hand over copyright. Nonexclusive licenses do not prevent a dissertation author from repurposing a work, transferring the copyright to another party, or modifying it and publishing again.

University instructions for submitting graduate work online can further muddle understandings about online platforms and their distribution options. Most North American universities require graduate authors to submit dissertations to ProQuest for the distribution, reproduction, and preservation services they provide.[4] Some require deposit to both ProQuest and an institutional repository, but many of those institutions have devised workflows that allow authors to submit their works online only once through one interface. Staff then copy and transfer the works and associated metadata to the other platform. These procedures are designed to save authors time and effort, but they can also generate further confusion.

For example, at the CUNY Graduate Center, authors are required to deposit in ProQuest, where they specify two sets of embargo options—one for ProQuest and the other for the CUNY institutional repository. Some authors choose to embargo differently for each platform, reflecting their differing preferences for commercial and OA distribution of their work. However, using ProQuest's interface alone for collecting author decisions about two significantly different platforms has led to author uncertainty about embargo and OA conditions for both platforms.

ANXIETY ABOUT CORPORATE COLLUSION

ProQuest's third-party retailer option, begun in 2010 and ended in 2014, confounded a significant number of authors and faculty advisors (Straumsheim 2014). While the option was in effect, authors were offered the chance to accept or decline increased exposure and possible sale, for royalties, of their work on such retailer websites as Amazon. ProQuest also asked (and continues to ask) authors whether they wanted their work to be discoverable by third-party search engines (ProQuest 2015). With third-party retailers frequently discoverable by third-party search engines, student authors were left confused about the resale and discovery factors at play.

Authors who unwittingly allowed third-party sales could ask ProQuest to remove the listing, but removal was usually not immediate due to the lingering discoverable caches of the systems involved. The horror of discovery that ProQuest-deposited dissertations were for sale on Amazon quickly turned to outrage at presumed profit-mongering by two giant corporations. Though ProQuest and Amazon did not attempt to boost sales of dissertations at the expense of author choice, mistrust lingers among authors and advisors, who are uncertain about ProQuest's distribution patterns.

While the real lesson of the third-party retailer option is that authors do not always understand or anticipate the consequences of their choices in this complex and evolving realm, objections to mandatory ProQuest deposit reflect concerns about the potential for author exploitation and loss of author control (Clement 2013). Author choice is at the center of arguments against university mandates for deposit in ProQuest. Jesse Stommel (2015), assistant professor of digital humanities at the University of Wisconsin–Madison, writes,

> Students shouldn't be required by supposedly nonprofit educational institutions to publish their theses or dissertations on corporate platforms like ProQuest. They shouldn't be forced to upload their intellectual property to profit-driven and often predatory sites like Turnitin. Students need to be . . . allowed to make critical decisions about what happens to their work and where it will live. (para. 8)

ProQuest assures authors and ETD administrators that the use of work shared with ProQuest is determined exclusively by authors. Universities may not always make all options and the string of implications that follow from them crystal clear to all authors, but authors can contact ProQuest any time after submission to request or extend an embargo, which makes a dissertation inaccessible to visitors to the ProQuest dissertation database and sales site. ProQuest allows embargoes for any length of time, even unlimited, offering more flexibility than many universities, which often limit authors to two-year repository embargoes, sometimes renewable and sometimes not. Still, students at ProQuest-mandating universities are not afforded the essential choice of whether to license their work to ProQuest in the first place.

ProQuest's long-standing preservation practices are valued by many—ProQuest is the preservation platform contracted by the Library of Congress for copies of record. And ProQuest shares dissertation metadata with more than thirty subject indexes, allowing graduate work to appear in the MLA Bibliography, SciFinder, Sociological Abstracts, ERIC, PsycINFO, and others, thus raising the profile of graduate work for researchers using these traditional library tools (ProQuest n.d., "ProQuest Dissertation and Theses Dissemination," para. 3). ProQuest advertises, "In disciplines where journals are not the primary form of scholarly communication, dissertations offer access to significant primary research that is not published in any other format and they surface seminal ideas from notable scholars" (ProQuest n.d., "ProQuest Dissertation & Theses Global"). ProQuest's long-lived practice of sharing metadata with discipline-based indexes in order to "surface seminal ideas" and often, in turn, to link directly to ProQuest's subscription-based dissertation database seems not to agitate those who worry about the sales of dissertation-based books, even though users of library indexes and databases are a primary market for those books. Links from popular search engines, such as Google Scholar, directly to OA dissertations seem to cause more consternation than ready availability to academic audiences through ProQuest's dissertation database. This incongruity in reasoning is difficult to thoroughly explain, but it may be chalked up to anxieties about new forms of openness in previously closed commercial systems of academic distribution.

Authors like Stommel also object to ProQuest's practice of sharing dissertations with the subscription-based antiplagiarism database Turnitin, referred to by its parent organization iParadigms on the ProQuest submission site (ProQuest allows authors to retract their dissertations after they have been shared with iParadigms, and dissertations embargoed in ProQuest are never shared with any entity). Of course, Turnitin can also mine OA items for inclusion in its bank of texts for plagiarism detection, so ProQuest's contribution of texts to Turnitin only complements what is already available to Turnitin on the open web. Nevertheless, for authors concerned about Pro-

Quest's commercial applications of graduate work, ProQuest's partnership with iParadigms taps anxieties about corporate chicanery.

ANXIETY'S WELLSPRING

As awareness increases about the unsustainability of the academic publishing industry and about the shifts in the technologies of scholarly research and production, so do anxiety and speculation about them. Covey (2013) cites communications scholars Walter J. Ong and James J. O'Donnell, who usefully address previous and current shifts in "technologies of the word" (545). Ong (1977) writes that the "technologies of writing and print and electronic devices radically transform the word and the mental processes" (339). It is the technologically driven shift in these mental processes and the accompanying changes in research and production practices that give rise to anxiety among scholars and publishers trained in print-based systems of research and production. Kathleen Fitzpatrick (2011) follows Ong's observations by exploring claims about the obsolescence of literary forms (e.g., the novel) to find that they indicate more about the anxieties of the claimants, practitioners of print working in an electronic age, than they do about the objects of the claim. Scholars' defensiveness about perceived threats to traditional practice and formats, she argues, works to "re-create an elite cadre of cultural producers and consumers . . . profiting from their claims of marginality by creating a sense that their values, once part of a utopian mainstream and now apparently waning, must be protected" (Fitzpatrick 2011, 2).

Publishers' fears about the unsustainability of their business model and academics' anxieties about shifting research methods, new varieties of scholarly production, more open formats for public scholarship, and ultimately the new skills required for academic success that senior scholars often do not possess lie at the root of anxiety about OA dissertations. Anecdote is the coin of the realm in this anxiety-laden academic conversation. The few survey-based studies of publishers' practices indicate that OA dissertations revised and repackaged appeal to the majority of university presses, with quality and audience being the most important factors. Informed exploration of publisher practices and attitudes, as well as longitudinal data about book contracts and sales, would move the conversation to a more sophisticated level beyond what anecdote can convey.

Anxieties about scholarly production are on display in other academic venues as well—for example, in reaction to new library designs that reduce the prominence of books and secluded individual study spaces within the scene of scholarly production. Designs to accommodate and incorporate new scholarly practices, such as more frequent use of electronic texts and collaborative work spaces, can be construed as threats to the preeminence of traditional scholarly practice—that is, book-based research and single-author, long-form writing (Morris 2012). Will the academy's conservatism stifle innovation in form and method, or will new sensibilities coalesce to encourage invention and variety?

It is this same, anxious group of scholars, steeped in the traditions of print production, who must embrace the changes that worry them. Open access dissertation distribution is a basic element in a cluster of technology-driven scholarly practices waiting to get a foothold. Reflecting her own anxiety that the academy will not reform quickly enough to maintain relevance, Covey (2013) urges, "Only opening other dimensions of the dissertation—the structure, media, notion of authorship, and methods of assessment—can foster the digital literacy needed to save PhD programs from extinction" (543).

Though Covey's anxieties about the extinction of the doctoral degree may appear to be premature or overwrought, she points to crucial issues that must be resolved to stabilize the future for new scholars. If fewer and fewer dissertations become books, will academic review continue to include one- or two-book standards for promotion and tenure? Will the scholarly monograph continue to be the gold standard for academic success? Will solitary authorship of book-length texts continue to be the bread and butter of the humanities and some social sciences? Will biases against open academic production reduce the productivity and relevance of disciplines that are slower to evolve?

Tending libraries and archives is a relentlessly public service. Librarians and archivists seek to engage our constituencies broadly, to share our collective culture deeply. How else but through active, open engagement with our publics, through forthright circulation of our collections, can we excite scholarly conversation and inspire creation of new works? There is no other way we know. Open access advocacy for dissertations and other works does not derive from some ideological fervor alien to librarianship. Rather, it stems from the central and very traditional values of archiving and librarianship, from our professional obligation to provide meaningful access to the world's culture for the people of the world. Supporting open access, the most democratic method of sharing technologically possible in our time, is hardly a radical gesture. It is a librarian's fundamental responsibility.

NOTES

1. This chapter focuses on doctoral dissertations, but much of what is discussed applies to master's theses as well.

2. In addition to the anxieties described in this chapter, there is a looming suspicion about institutions' motives for encouraging or requiring OA dissertations. Some scholars have noticed that OA advocates sometimes refer to theses and dissertations as "low-hanging fruit" for building institutional repositories (Hawkins, Kimball, and Ives 2013; Stone, Comstock, and Glavash 2006). And, indeed, that phrase suggests that the push for openness is more about

boosting repository numbers than about serving scholars and scholarly communication. OA advocates are well advised to refrain from referring to any scholar's arduously produced work as "low-hanging fruit."

3. Admittedly, the situation is different in creative writing. Unlike most academic researchers, many creative writers earn their livelihoods, or at least supplement their incomes, by selling their works to publishers. However, publishers of creative writing generally require authors to give them first publishing rights. If a work has already been published online, then a publisher cannot be given first rights. (For more information, see Association of Writers & Writing Programs n.d.; Kaufka and Bryan 2007; Thomas and Shirkey 2013.)

4. There is a growing number of institutions that offer students a choice to deposit with ProQuest or not. These ProQuest-optional institutions include several high-profile universities, among them MIT, Stanford University, Brown University, Johns Hopkins University, and University of Texas at Austin (Clement n.d.).

REFERENCES

Altman, Michael J. 2013. "Why I Embargoed My Dissertation." http://michaeljaltman.net/2013/07/24/why-i-embargoed-my-dissertation.

American Historical Association. 2013. "American Historical Association Statement on Policies Regarding the Embargoing of Completed History PhD Dissertations." http://blog.historians.org/2013/07/american-historical-association-statement-on-policies-regarding-the-embargoing-of-completed-history-phd-dissertations.

Anderson, Rick. 2013. "Dissertation Embargoes and the Rights of Scholars: AHA Smacks the Hornet's Nest." *Scholarly Kitchen.* http://scholarlykitchen.sspnet.org/2013/07/26/dissertation-embargoes-and-the-rights-of-scholars-aha-smacks-the-hornets-nest.

———. 2015. "CC BY and Its Discontents—A Growing Challenge for Open Access." *Library Journal.* http://lj.libraryjournal.com/2015/02/opinion/peer-to-peer-review/cc-by-and-its-discontents-a-growing-challenge-for-open-access-peer-to-peer-review.

Armato, Doug. 2013. "From MLA 2013: Considering Serial Scholarship and the Future of Scholarly Publishing." http://www.uminnpressblog.com/2013/01/from-mla-2013-considering-serial.html.

Association of College & Research Libraries. 2015. "Framework for Information Literacy for Higher Education." http://www.ala.org/acrl/standards/ilframework.

Association of Writers & Writing Programs. n.d. "AWP Policy on Electronic Theses and Dissertations." https://www.awpwriter.org/guide/directors_handbook_policy_on_electronic_theses_and_dissertations.

Cassuto, Leonard. 2011. "From Dissertation to Book." *Chronicle of Higher Education.* http://chronicle.com/article/From-Dissertation-to-Book/127677.

Clement, Gail P. n.d. "ETDs Freed Here (U.S. Institutions Respecting Student Choice in Disseminating Their ETDs)." https://sites.tdl.org/fuse/?page_id=372.

———. 2013. "American ETD Dissemination in the Age of Open Access: ProQuest, NoQuest, or Allowing Student Choice." *College & Research Libraries News* 74, no. 11: 562–66.

Cohen, Noam. 2013. "Historians Seek a Delay in Posting Dissertations." *New York Times.* http://www.nytimes.com/2013/07/29/business/media/historians-seek-a-delay-in-posting-dissertations.html.

Covey, Denise Troll. 2013. "Opening the Dissertation: Overcoming Cultural Calcification and Agoraphobia." *tripleC: Communication, Capitalism & Critique: Open Access Journal for a Global Sustainable Information Society* 11, no. 2: 543–57.

Cronon, William. 2013. "Why Put at Risk the Publishing Options of Our Most Vulnerable Colleagues?" http://blog.historians.org/2013/07/why-put-at-risk-the-publishing-options-of-our-most-vulnerable-colleagues.

Duke University Graduate School. n.d. "ETD Copyright Information." https://gradschool.duke.edu/academics/theses-and-dissertations/etd-copyright-information.

Fitzpatrick, Kathleen. 2011. *Planned Obsolescence: Publishing, Technology, and the Future of the Academy.* New York: NYU Press.

Germano, William P. 2005. *From Dissertation to Book*. Chicago: University of Chicago Press.

Goetz, Rebecca Anne. 2013. "Do Not Fear Open Access. Embrace It!" http://jhupressblog.com/2013/08/22/on-dissertations-embargoes-books-and-jobs.

Harnad, Stevan. 2006. "Opening Access by Overcoming Zeno's Paralysis." In *Open Access: Key Strategic, Technical and Economic Aspects*, edited by Neil Jacobs. Oxford: Chandos.

Harvard University Press. 2013. "Can't Find It, Can't Sign It: On Dissertation Embargoes." http://harvardpress.typepad.com/hup_publicity/2013/07/cant-find-it-cant-sign-it-on-dissertation-embargoes.html.

Hawkins, Ann R., Miles A. Kimball, and Maura Ives. 2013. "Mandatory Open Access Publishing for Electronic Theses and Dissertations: Ethics and Enthusiasm." *Journal of Academic Librarianship* 39, no. 1: 32–60.

Horn, Andrew H. 1952. "The University Archivist and the Thesis Problem." *American Archivist* 15, no. 4: 321–31.

Howard, Jennifer. 2011. "The Road from Dissertation to Book Has a New Pothole: The Internet." *Chronicle of Higher Education*. http://chronicle.com/article/The-Road-From-Dissertation-to/126977.

Hume, Kathryn. 2011. "The Perils of Publishing Your Dissertation Online." http://theprofessorisin.com/2011/08/24/the-perils-of-publishing-your-dissertation-online.

JISC Collections. 2009. "JISC National E-books Observatory Project: Key Findings and Recommendations." http://observatory.jiscebooks.org/reports/jisc-national-e-books-observatory-project-key-findings-and-recommendations.

Kaufka, Beth, and Jennifer Bryan. 2007. "Workshop: The Case against Electronic Theses." *Poets and Writers* 35, no. 2: 99–102.

Manchester University Press. n.d. "Publishing Your Book with MUP." http://www.manchesteruniversitypress.co.uk/cgi-bin/scribe?showinfo=ip006.

Martin, Brian. 2013. "Countering Supervisor Exploitation." *Journal of Scholarly Publishing* 45, no. 1: 74–86.

McGreal, Rory, and Nian-Shing Chen. 2011. "AUPress: A Comparison of an Open Access University Press with Traditional Presses." *Educational Technology & Society* 14, no. 3: 231–39.

Morris, Edmund. 2012. "Sacking a Palace of Culture." *New York Times*. http://www.nytimes.com/2012/04/22/opinion/sunday/sacking-a-palace-of-culture.html.

Ong, Walter J. 1977. *Interfaces of the Word: Studies in the Evolution of Consciousness and Culture*. Ithaca, NY: Cornell University Press.

Patton, Stacey. 2013. "Scholarly Group Seeks up to 6-Year Embargoes on Digital Dissertations." *Chronicle of Higher Education*. http://chronicle.com/article/Scholarly-Group-Seeks-Up-to/140515.

ProQuest. n.d. "ProQuest Dissertation and Theses Dissemination." http://www.proquest.com/products-services/proquest-dissertation-publishing.html.

———. n.d. "ProQuest Dissertations & Theses Global." http://www.proquest.com/products-services/pqdtglobal.html.

———. 2015. "Submitting Your ETD." http://www.etdadmin.com/GlobalTemplates/ETDAdmin/StudentHelp/submit.html.

Ramirez, Marisa L., John T. Dalton, Gail McMillan, Max Read, and Nancy H. Seamans. 2013. "Do Open Access Electronic Theses and Dissertations Diminish Publishing Opportunities in the Social Sciences and Humanities? Findings from a 2011 Survey of Academic Publishers." *College & Research Libraries* 74, no. 4: 368–80.

Smith, Kevin. 2013a. "ETDs, Publishing & Policy Based on Fear." https://blogs.library.duke.edu/scholcomm/2013/07/24/etds-publishing-policy-based-on-fear.

———. 2013b. "More on the AHA, ETDs and Libraries." http://blogs.library.duke.edu/scholcomm/2013/07/29/more-on-the-aha-etds-and-libraries.

Smith-Cruz, Shawn(ta). 2014. "Dissertation Dilemma: To Embargo or Not to Embargo?" http://gclibrary.commons.gc.cuny.edu/2014/09/22/dissertation-dilemma.

Sonfield, Matthew C. 2014. "Academic Plagiarism at the Faculty Level: Legal versus Ethical Issues and a Case Study." *Journal of Academic Ethics* 12, no. 2: 75–87.

Stommel, Jesse. 2015. "Who Controls Your Dissertation?" https://chroniclevitae.com/news/852-who-controls-your-dissertation.

Stone, Larry, Bill Comstock, and Keith Glavash. 2006. "Harvesting the Low-Hanging Fruit: World Wide Web Access to a Collection of MIT Theses." http://docs.ndltd.org/dspace/handle/2340/164.

Straumsheim, Carl. 2014. "ProQuest Ends Dissertation Sales through Amazon." *Inside Higher Ed.* https://www.insidehighered.com/news/2014/11/12/proquest-ends-dissertation-sales-through-amazon.

Stromberg, Joseph. 2014. "I Sold My Undergraduate Thesis to a Print Content Farm." *Slate.* http://www.slate.com/articles/technology/future_tense/2014/03/lap_lambert_academic_publishing_my_trip_to_a_print_content_farm.single.html.

Suber, Peter. 2012. "Open Access." Cambridge, MA: MIT Press. https://mitpress.mit.edu/books/open-access.

Thomas, William Joseph, and Cynthia Shirkey. 2013. "The Continuing Cautionary Tale of Creative Writing ETDs." *North Carolina Libraries* 71, no. 1: 23–33.

Wissoker, Ken. 2013. "The Relationship between Research and Publication, or Why Libraries Should Buy More First Books than Any Others." http://scholarlykitchen.sspnet.org/2013/07/22/the-relationship-between-research-and-publication-or-why-libraries-should-buy-more-first-books-than-any-others.

Zeoli, Michael. 2013. "Re: Embargoed Dissertations." http://listserv.crl.edu/wa.exe?A2=LIBLICENSE-L;859baf0b.1307.

Chapter Twelve

From Apprehension to Comprehension

Addressing Anxieties about Open Access to ETDs

Kyle K. Courtney and Emily Kilcer

In this chapter, we share both evidence-based arguments and observations of student concerns and behavior from Harvard University's ETD implementation. We then address these concerns with proposed recommendations for forthright information sharing that may ease student anxiety and help them to make more reasoned decisions about the distribution of their dissertations and future work. Let's begin with a tale of two dissertations.

The first dissertation, completed by a graduate student in a microrobotics laboratory at Harvard, addresses the challenges of and successes in developing a robotic bee. The student, who was interviewed as part of an outreach effort by the library's Office for Scholarly Communication, spoke of the importance of making his work openly available in the university's open access (OA) repository, Digital Access to Scholarship at Harvard (DASH). He mentioned the absurdity of the exorbitant cost of some toll-access, peer-reviewed literature and cited the benefits of distributing his thesis publicly through DASH. He felt this choice was an important one because he was providing open access to information from government-funded projects to the taxpaying public, and he was personally benefitting from the increased discoverability of his own research. Since becoming available in DASH almost three years ago, this student's work has been downloaded more than 450 times. Details of the full interview may be found in Dodson (2013a).

The second dissertation, completed by a graduate student in comparative literature, offers a critical reading of Plato's dialogues. This student requested an indefinite embargo at the point of submission, meaning only the metadata associated with the text would be openly available. The embargo was approved by the department chair, contrary to university policy (a standing 1951 corporation policy requires the university librarian and department head to approve longer embargoes; Harvard University Archives 2016). The work does not appear in DASH with the rest of the dissertations from the student's graduating cohort—not because it contains sensitive or risk-based material but out of concern for what open distribution would mean for her future publishing prospects. How would providing open access to her dissertation affect her future in a time where there are more PhDs than there are tenure-track openings (Iasevoli 2015)? Would a book publisher not consider the work because it appeared online first? How would this impact her academic future, her tenure, and her promotion?

One might say these two stories clearly illustrate the differences between disciplinary cultures and needs and that the behavior of both graduates is emblematic of their mentors' and colleagues' behavior. This is undoubtedly true. However, it also illustrates the current state of affairs of electronic theses and dissertations, with all of its pitfalls and opportunities.

As we begin, let's first get our bearings by looking back at the origins of the present-day dissertation, its purpose, its lifecycle, and the behaviors associated with these works.

HISTORY OF THE DISSERTATION

At its heart, the dissertation is intended as a public contribution to the new PhD's field of study. This is a simple concept but one that is tied to the evolution of the history of scholarship.

The dissertation is born out of the medieval tradition in which students established themselves as skilled colleagues to their faculty through "dialectical argument" based on canonical texts (Barton 2005, 36). By demonstrating deft argument rooted in a mastery of rhetorical technique and textual exegesis, students would be recognized as peer scholars.

This oral system shifted with the advent of the printing press. Following this new technology, knowledge became "easier to objectify" (Barton 2005, 40) and share, and authors became valued creators of unique ideas. This shift to authors as creators, coupled with the invention of postal systems, supported the rapid distribution of ideas. Later, this enabled the foundation of the first journal, which made subsequent changes in scholarly communication and education an inevitable byproduct.

By the nineteenth century, led by Humboldt University (Shieber 2011), the modern notion of the PhD was born. There was a profound shift in German universities from mastery of the canon to the production of new knowledge, an effort to which students were expected to contribute: "The dissertation, as a result of such inquiries, was valuable precisely because it would make a valid and useful contribution to scientific knowledge" (Barton

2005, 48). This model crossed the Atlantic and was adopted at U.S. institutions, establishing the dissertation as the pinnacle of a PhD's scholarly endeavor. From its inception, then, at the heart of the conferral of the PhD is an affirmation of an individual's substantial, original, and public contribution to one's field.

In the early days, dissertations were distributed as bound copies. With the arrival of microfilm in the late 1930s, however, dissertations found a new form. In their analysis of ETD management and publication, Clement and Rascoe (2013) note that the benefits the new technology of microfilm afforded—that is, low first-copy costs and on-demand duplication—were ideal for the specialized scholarship that dissertations represented. They further explain that University Microfilms International (UMI), one particular microfilm company, saw an opportunity to leverage this content in an innovative way by targeting libraries as consumers. UMI distributed abstracts along with ordering information to libraries. Copies of the full text could then be purchased on fiche. A handful of universities joined this experimental distribution pilot in the 1930s, and over the next several years, UMI expanded its dissertation-indexing program. A subsequent 1951 Association of Research Libraries report that recommended thesis distribution as a book, article, and micropublication helped to cement UMI's market dominance of theses and dissertations distribution. UMI became the default standard thesis-indexing and -abstracting service for U.S. institutions.

In the 1990s, another disruptive technology, the Internet, shifted the dissertation once more. The physical moved to the virtual. Dissertations, submitted as bound copies for approval and then for preservation in an institution's library or archive following a student's defense, moved to the digital realm. With this shift, the Coalition for Networked Information (CNI) helped launch "one of the first ETD conferences in 1993 in order to explore the potential of electronic theses and dissertations as new forms of scholarly communication and as drivers for the development of digital libraries" (Lippincott and Lynch 2010, 7). CNI also conducted a survey to discover "whether ETD programs were being treated as a way to simply manage paper dissertations by other means (much like the situation today with scientific journal articles, which are distributed and stored digitally, but still conform very close to the historical printed articles in terms of content and organization)" (Lippincott and Lynch 2010, 8).

In 1996, ProQuest launched its "first Internet accessible instance of UMI" (ProQuest 2016b). Today, ProQuest both processes theses and dissertations from more than 700 institutions (ProQuest 2016c) and indexes more than 2.3 million entries (ProQuest 2016a). With their ETD Administrator submission tool and theses and dissertation subscription databases, which are only available to paying subscribers, ProQuest UMI has a relative monopoly on dissertation processing and distribution. The services UMI offers students include a pay-for-OA option, where students can pay ProQuest a fee to distribute their dissertations openly in the theses and dissertations database, and copyright registration, through which UMI assumes responsibility for registration with the Copyright Office. UMI similarly offers institutions services that are spun out of the submission tool, including bound preservation copies and delivery of the electronic files and metadata for distribution in an institutional repository (IR). While this is not a comprehensive list of ProQuest's service offerings, their commercial priorities are clear. Dissertation collection, storage, and distribution have been almost entirely in the control of this commercial vendor since they first emerged in the market.

Another key consideration in the evolution of the scholarly landscape is the appearance of institutional repositories. Over the past decade and more, inspired by Raym Crow's (2002) "Case for Institutional Repositories" and Clifford Lynch's (2003) "Institutional Repositories: Essential Infrastructure for Scholarship in the Digital Age," universities began to invest time and resources on building IRs. Universities recognized the untapped potential—and crucial need—for taking an active role in showcasing the wealth of their scholars' research output by collecting, preserving, and sharing their community's work within these new systems. By serving as the steward to this content and preserving it as an essential piece of their scholarly record, universities began to regain control over the contributions their faculty, students, and staff created. In an environment where publishing houses are either merging or closing and the pricing for content is increasing at a rate higher than inflation (Bosch and Henderson 2012), gathering and distributing content through IRs openly represent a very real, complementary distribution stream to institutions, authors, and readers alike.

Institution-managed ETD programs present a similar opportunity. By pulling the processing and management of dissertations internally, a university can both increase the discoverability and usage of their student's work and regain control of their institution's unique scholarship. Distribution through ProQuest would no longer be essential and could then be an optional service.

Data from a survey by Dorothea Salo (2015) indicates that theses and dissertations are increasingly being included in the material that universities began collecting for distribution in IRs. The earliest ETD collection effort recorded in Salo (2015) started in 1997 at Virginia Tech. Of the one hundred–plus institutions that have provided data on their ETD programs, most require theses and dissertation distribution through both the local IR and ProQuest's indexes. McMillan, Stark, and Halbert (2013) find similar results from their survey, with 69 percent of their respondents indicating that submission to the ETD program, which were managed in house by 66 percent of the institutions surveyed, is mandatory.

The implications of moving from print-based distribution to the often open access distribution in IRs are at the heart of what has become a hot topic in academia these days: access to student work. As academic institutions have established IRs, which have often become a default access point for student work, this new technology has welcomed a broader audience, and in response, some students' anxiety levels have spiked. In what follows, we explore some of the issues students often raise as barriers to OA distribution: from concern about their work being scooped to publication issues and the pressure of their communities' norms of practice. Following the rollout of the university's new ETD submission system, we have learned that the strongest antidote to student anxieties has been a persistent and multifaceted education and outreach effort to ensure that students are making informed and well-considered decisions about their work. We share student stories and offer responses that have helped to allay student concern and instill a confidence in their rights—and responsibilities—as scholars and authors operating in a world where access to content is easier than ever and copyright law, contracts and licensing, and distribution decisions can easily become muddied with misinformation.

OA ETD ANXIETIES AND ANTIDOTES

Writing on the subject of open access to ETDs, Peter Suber (2006) notes,

> Dissertations are not just good, they're largely invisible. Libraries rarely hold dissertations not written by their own students. Dissertations are not well indexed. They're available for purchase, but difficult to evaluate before purchasing. Moreover, many details from dissertations never make it into journal articles, and many dissertation topics are too narrow to justify book publication. In short, dissertations are high in quality and low in accessibility, in fact, I'd say they constitute the most invisible form of useful literature and the most useful form of invisible literature.

The increased access that open distribution through IRs affords student work is powerful: Suber (2006) continues, "By making ETDs visible, OA helps the readers who wouldn't otherwise have ready access. But it also helps the ETD authors, boosting their visibility and impact just as it does for the authors of journal articles." While readers and institutions benefit from opening access to ETDs, it is students who feel the results of this increased access acutely—experiencing the benefits most personally, along with the misgivings and pressures. In this new, open world, the institution has a responsibility to provide comprehensive outreach to students, educating them on author rights, copyright, and open access so they can be empowered to make informed decisions about their work.

The following are some of the most common student concerns that we have encountered in our outreach and education efforts. As much as all of these potential challenges to students and their careers loom during the creation, submission, and distribution of their ETDs, there are as many arguments for opportunities inherent in OA ETDs. Concerted efforts to dispel student anxieties can yield often surprising results; here we identify common student anxieties we have encountered and then share our complementary arguments to address these fears about open distribution.

Understanding that there are differences between fields, this is intended to provide broad-stroke scaffolding for leading conversations or developing resources that may help to ease student fears.

Anxiety: Scooping

A common concern students raise, particularly in STEM fields, is having their work "scooped." The potential downstream results of being scooped range from the scooper receiving the impact of the dissertation's argument (along with the attendant implications for tenure and promotion) to the scooper gaining patent rights to the novel thing within the dissertation (thereby getting rights to commercial exploitation).

In 2011, Kathryn Hume opens her blog post by clearly illustrating the anxiety that students may feel over the prospect of being scooped if one's dissertation is openly available:

> Once upon a time, dissertations were "available" through UMI as microfilm or through Interlibrary Loan as bound copies. . . . Since you knew the material was unusable without permission, you felt free to ignore dissertations, except to make sure that a recent one was not too similar to the one that you hoped to write, lest it get published before yours and scoop you. Yes, such documents were technically "available," but they were definitely not published or easily consultable.

The distinction that Hume draws, while seemingly rooted in an incomplete sense of copyright and fair use, is one that students often raise. If their work is discoverable, then others will use it and be the recipient of the credit for the idea.

Hume and many others see the exclusive availability of bound dissertations in archives and through interlibrary loan as a hurdle that makes them "unusable." Their relative inaccessibility makes them dark literature, effectively, and safer somehow. They are to be consulted only to make sure they are not "too similar to the one that you hoped to write." By extension, rather than being viewed as a valuable contribution to a body of knowledge, openly accessible dissertations become a potential threat.

Underlying this notion of the hidden dissertation, which is not easily "consumed" for fear of scooping, is the idea that one's years of research and writing are best approached as a solitary exercise. Rather than being available for research and study, a hidden dissertation ensures that one's ideas are not easily accessible, thereby curtailing the opportunity for unethical behavior, from improper attribution to losing out on first publication or patenting opportunities.

While this runs counter to the idea of scholarship as an ecosystem that builds on itself incrementally, students have persistent concern over their ideas being available—and usable—before being formally published in a peer-reviewed form. They feel open access distribution of their work makes their ideas vulnerable to misuse and misappropriation.

Antidote: Actual Impact and "Planting of the Flag"

As noted by Gary King, Albert J. Weatherhead III University Professor at Harvard, "when you're a junior faculty member and pretty much throughout your career the thing that people worry about the most is being scooped and the thing that matters the least is being scooped. The thing that matters the most is being ignored" (cited in Dodson 2013b). While one could assert that this is a statement from an established faculty member at the height of his career, the sentiment is one that should be well considered: It is only by sharing work that a researcher establishes herself and has impact in her field.

In addition to fulfilling the obligation of the public contribution to one's field by distributing one's work openly, dissertations that are OA are more visible and, therefore, more likely to be cited. Students who are early-career researchers, in particular, are concerned with the impact of their work. With impact comes tenure and promotion, funding, and prestige.[1] The sooner a student can establish the importance of her work, the better.

While impact is clearly a student concern, the threat of one's ideas being scooped often is enough of a deterrent for students to shy away from OA ETD distribution. To challenge this assumption, students should be reminded that another tangible side effect of providing open distribution to a dissertation is the "planting the flag" phenomenon. By making one's work very publicly available in an IR with a time stamp and permanent link, the student can establish the research within the dissertation as one's own work. The ideas therein become defensible as original should someone, in fact, try to "scoop" the student's ideas. OA ETDs are inherently "safer" in this way.

AUTHOR RIGHTS AND COPYRIGHT: UNTANGLING THE TANGLED WEB

Underlying the fear of being scooped is the unruly world of copyright and author rights. For even the most well-seasoned authors, copyright has the potential to be confusing. Publication agreements tend to have an implied up-front finality to them. More often than not, a student's interest and energies are focused elsewhere, which leads to either an information vacuum or po-tential misapprehension about author rights and contracts and use and reuse of third-party material. This confusion can lead to misinformed decision making that can unnecessarily constrain a student's work.

The best solution is early and often outreach that emphasizes an author's right to amend a publishing agreement; informs the student about fair use, the public domain, and the balance inherent in copyright; and engages with data about publisher practices around dissertations.

Anxiety: High-Risk Contractual Liability

A common fear among students is contractual liability when they have pub-lished all or part of the dissertation in peer-reviewed publications prior to the submission of their complete work for their degrees. Underlying this concern is a certain helplessness.

As suggested in Hume's (2011) assertion about reuse, there is a great deal of insecurity and confusion around the use and reuse of previously published and third-party content in dissertations. There is also a fair amount of misin-formation about and unfamiliarity with licensing agreements, author rights, and scholarly practice. As publishing has shifted into the digital age, there are new considerations when authors sign publishing agreements. While reuse is still a right about which authors should be vigilant when signing publishing agreements, the scope of reuse feels magnified when work is available online. And as early-career researchers, students feel particularly vulnerable.

An example of the scope of this challenge is in fields where it is common practice for a student to use a previously published journal article as a chap-ter in her dissertation. This is often work that is the result of collaboration within a lab group, with the findings being something that is written as a distinct piece from the larger dissertation but is then folded into the disserta-tion as a chapter. For example, at Harvard, the T. H. Chan School of Public Health's dissertations are composed of three separate publications that have already been published or soon will be (Harvard T. H. Chan School of Public Health Registrar's Office 2015). Because of the very nature of these works, understanding the publisher's licensing terms is crucial to reuse in the stu-dent's dissertation and—oftentimes—completion of the degree.

Because journal articles that students produce and then reuse in dissertations are often some of the first work they produce, they may be signing publishing contracts without a confidence in their abilities to negotiate the terms to ensure reuse. Often, they are pleased to be published, are distracted with other pressing deadlines, and don't want to hold up the process to sharing their—and their principal investigator's (PI's)—results. Additionally, they may or may not remember to hold onto their contract. In cases of click-through agreements, which are becoming a standard in the industry, the barrier to amending an agreement is engineered so authors accept the publisher's default terms, whether they best serve their needs or not.

Combined with the stress associated with dissertation defense and a potentially last-minute submission for their degree requirements, students have a high level of concern, which may be reinforced by their PI or colleagues, about contract liability and repurposing their own work. This anxiety persists across disciplines, affecting those students who may only reuse a figure or small extract from their previously published work. Students often perceive this use, and the public display thereof, as asking for trouble.

Antidote: Modern Twenty-First-Century Contracts: New Uses and Negotiation

What is an alternative solution for students who use a previously published work in their dissertations? As much as click-through agreements are de rigueur and as much as amending contracts may seem to be either a tedious or intimidating activity, there is a great deal to be gained by being a well-informed and active participant in this exchange.

Publishers need content, and once a work has been accepted, then the publisher is committed to distributing it. The author, student or otherwise, does have the latitude (and one might assert responsibility) to advocate for terms that best serve her needs.

Publishers do not operate in a vacuum and most certainly understand the collaborative practices of today's researchers. They recognize that authors expect to be able to distribute their work online, on a personal or departmental website, or through an IR. Publishers are aware that content that may be distributed through their journals or monographs may be fodder for a subsequent work by the author or an element in a course site. Publishers also recognize that students may need to reuse their previously published content in a thesis, and many publishers explicitly grant an author this right in their licensing terms.[2]

Because sharing and reuse are easier in the digital world in general, publishers often address these issues in licensing agreements. Before signing any agreement, authors should ensure that they are retaining the rights that they need in their work: to post their work online, use it in conference presentations or teaching, and make use of it in future work (e.g., in theses). In cases where the publisher's terms are less than optimal or don't speak to a particular need of the author, there is a twofold way to remedy the situation: use an addendum or update the contract's language.

Students should be reassured that amending the publishing agreement can be as simple as crossing language out of the contract and updating it with more preferable terms. This assumes that you have the complete language of the agreement and a click-through isn't required. When faced with a click-through agreement, the author should feel comfortable sending the publisher's editor an addendum that enumerates the terms that the author would like to change. Both methods are perfectly reasonable and ensure that the author's future needs for the work are accommodated. Occasionally, institutions will have in-house amendments that authors may use. For those who are looking for help with this sort of request, the Scholarly Publishing and Academic Resources Coalition (SPARC) provides an addendum that serves the needs of most authors well (SPARC 2016).

Again, whether the author amends the agreement or not, the licensing agreement with the publisher is a legally binding contract and should be treated as such. The author should hold onto the reference copy of the agreement once she has secured the rights she would like to maintain over her publication's future.

Anxiety: Future Publication

The other side of the publication coin is student concern around the desire to publish work she has included in her dissertation.

Much as with issues around reuse addressed earlier, these fears are wrapped up in publisher practice and licensing agreements. An additional worry in this arena, however, is the need to publish in high-impact journals or with a reputable monograph publishing house for successful tenure and promotion. The tenure and promotion process is a different discussion, but it is important to recognize that, as early-career researchers, PhD students may have very visceral reactions to institutional policies requiring them to provide open access to their dissertations. Inherent in this response is the notion that a dissertation and future journal article, book chapter, or monograph based on the dissertation are seen as the same document by publishers and that distribution through an IR qualifies as "prior publication," making it a less-likely candidate for publication (see Patton 2013). For publishers, original research drives prestige and subscriptions.

Certainly the scope of this concern depends on the specific discipline and its publication habits. STEM students are most concerned with journal publication, whereas humanities and social science students are looking at long-form publications and the longer timescale of the monograph. Either way, some students may see OA distribution in a repository as a threat to the future life of their research and careers. Students tend to make the assumption that the availability of their dissertations online is comparable to publication—that the very public nature of their works' availability in an IR would prevent their shopping these works to a journal or monograph publisher in the future. This is neither an accurate nor complete picture.

Antidote: Evidence-Based Decision Making

The dissertation is the starting point for future publications, and, as such, students should be reassured that availability in an IR is not equivalent to publication. There is no peer-review process; there is no house style or formatting process. A completed dissertation is not a final product that will be published in the same form.

This is not merely anecdotal. As early as 2001, Gail McMillan shared survey results about STEM publishers and their responses to the question of whether they could consider publishing openly available dissertations. Only 14 percent of the survey respondents indicated that they would not be "willing to accept articles from ETDs" (McMillan 2001). More recently, Ramirez et al. (2013) conducted a survey to explore publisher behavior related to OA ETDs in the social sciences, humanities, and arts. In this study, "75 percent of the respondents representing the social sciences indicated they would either accept or consider, without prejudice, submissions derived from openly available ETDs," with only 4.5 percent reporting they would not consider an ETD for publication (Ramirez et al. 2013, 377). One additional datapoint: MIT Libraries (2016) produced a table illustrating publisher behavior related to new work derived from thesis content; the vast majority of these publishers are similarly responsive to considering OA ETDs.

In light of this data, one can infer that much of the publishing industry will consider publishing dissertations that have been openly distributed in an IR. While this number is not 100 percent, the odds of having a publisher reject a paper because of its open access status is unlikely. Students should be reassured and faculty advisors should be made aware of these trends. As noted by Ramirez et al. (2013), "[p]ublishers recognize that a book or journal article must be adapted to a new audience and conform to peer review, so the final work will be different in many ways from the original ETD" (377). Additionally, the publishing industry is starting to take note of the advantages of open access distribution. Harvard University Press's acquisitions editor noted recently, "If you can't find it, you can't sign it" (Harvard University Press Blog 2013). Open access can help publishers find important voices.

Anxiety: Using Third-Party Material

Another important point of student concern related to copyright is making use of work that is not their own without securing permission. Scholarship is an incremental process, where new ideas are built on the prior work of others. Any dissertation will use content from other scholars and creators, either for reference or as a launching point for commentary or criticism. Well-considered use of such third-party material is most always fair use (which we explore later). This practice of leveraging third-party material to scaffold an argument is standard and speaks to the very nature of scholarship, but students often have concern about making such material in their dissertations openly available.

From the use of figures and images—a particularly sensitive point of concern—to text itself, many students are under the impression that they need to seek permission for every use of third-party material and that, without permission, distributing their use of this content publicly would open them to the specter of litigation. Open access distribution compounds this concern: Some students may perceive their OA ETDs' attendant larger audiences as a threat, particularly if they are worried about being penalized for their fair use of third-party work. Thankfully, this can be addressed by informing students about their rights and offering alternatives for situations where they may not be able to claim fair use.

FAIR USE AND PUBLIC DOMAIN

There is one very powerful provision of copyright law that students should be comfortable exercising: fair use. As a crucial right inside the copyright law, fair use allows for the use of a certain amount of copyrighted material without seeking permission. This may be the student's own work or her use of third-party material. As established earlier, nearly every dissertation includes some example of a fair use of copyrighted works, including brief quotations, figures, or images from other sources. In fact, students often utilize fair use without even realizing it. This is because it is commonplace for quotations or images to appear in a thesis. When you actually mention the phrase and identify a use as "fair" is when some of the concern emerges; however, this is truly a customary doctrine underpinning all scholarship.

Summarizing the fair use statute, there are four factors to consider when determining whether a use of a copyrighted work qualifies for this fair use exemption:

1. For what purpose would the work be used?
2. What is the nature of the work to be used?
3. How much of the work would be used?

4. What effect on the market for that work would the use have?

Applying this four-factor test is not a clear-cut process. Students need to weigh all four factors to decide whether a fair use exemption seems to apply to each proposed use within their work.

Recent court decisions have further emphasized the unique transformative nature of a fair use, especially in nonprofit education research, such as a thesis or dissertation. Courts have boiled down the complex four-factor fair use test into the following two questions:

1. Does the use *transform the material* by using it for a different *purpose*?
2. Was the *amount taken appropriate* to the new *purpose*?

To make a claim of educational, transformative fair use (which is use without the copyright holder's permission), the third-party copyrighted material (image, clip, quote) must be necessary to the student's analysis and serve a different purpose than the original. The image or text should be a part of the dissertation's pedagogical point—in other words, absolutely necessary to prove that particular point in the dissertation. A classic example of transformative use is a quotation from an earlier work in a critical essay to illustrate the essayist's argument.

A question students can ask to measure this transformative use is, Does the user analyze, study, or criticize the third-party copyrighted material? If so, then it may be a transformative fair use. In the words of the Supreme Court, which founded the notion of a transformative fair use, the use of that third-party copyrighted material "adds something new, with a further purpose or different character, altering the first with new expression, meaning or message."

If the use of the work is more aesthetic, that is, simply "window dressing" rather than crucial to the dissertation, then it may not be necessary to the argument and is, therefore, less likely to be a transformative fair use. In such cases where the student's use does not fulfill an important point in the dissertation and is merely a decorative expression and therefore less likely to be a fair use, then the student would need to seek permission from the creator. Occasionally this may be a publisher, if the work is the student's own and the licensing agreement doesn't allow for this sort of reuse.

The "amount taken" factor of fair use is also worth a discussion. How much of the copyrighted material is necessary to prove the argument in the thesis? Students should use no more of a third-party copyrighted work than is reasonably appropriate to serve their educational purposes. Students should understand what amount is reasonable and what may be too much. Obviously, short quotations or clips help the cause for making a fair use. But, again, the four-factor test clearly provides for whatever amount is necessary in the use. If a student needs to use the entire work—for example, a painting—because she is analyzing it from top to bottom, then she should feel comfortable using the whole work. However, if a student can make her point with a forty-seven-second music clip instead of the full two-minute-long song, then she should do that—use only the amount necessary.

This powerful provision and its modern-day transformative test is something that students are often hesitant to use. However, it is a right that serves their scholarship. By exercising this right, they are asserting the balance inherent in copyright law: to both protect copyright holders and promote the creation of new knowledge.

In instances where the student is unable to make a confident fair use of a work but she wants to provide some illustration or flourish, there may be additional options that are free or nearly free of copyright or licensing.

One such solution is the public domain. Works in the public domain are those whose intellectual property rights have expired, have been forfeited, or are inapplicable. While sometimes difficult to ascertain, the rule of thumb in the United States is that materials published before 1923 are in the public domain and therefore can be utilized in any document without permission.

Second, the Creative Commons licensing schema (Creative Commons 2016) offers students a variety of options for using copyrighted materials. Creative Commons licensing allows the copyright holder to release her work to the public for a specific type of use, provided certain licensing restrictions are followed. The advantage for the copyright owner is that she does not have to wait for copyright to expire, and the advantage for the user is that she does not have to seek permission. Everything is included in the license. By way of example, the most basic Creative Commons license is CC BY, which requires simple attribution. Anyone may use the copyrighted work, but according to the license, the creator must be cited in the form she wants. For theses and dissertations, this is a mere extension of a well-established practice for good scholarly work: properly citing your sources.

Last, the open access movement isn't just about ETDs in institutional repositories. Students should be reminded that there are hundreds of open access repositories arranged by institution, subject, or discipline that are available under an open license. This means that the content has the same liberal type of use provisions similar to Creative Commons, with the same attribution standards. You can find a plethora of photos, images, figures, and other work inside any of these repositories.

Admittedly, these sources may not solve all ills; however, when a student may use a substitute in instances where fair use does not apply, public domain, Creative Commons, or open access works may be a preferable solution to removing a reference to an image or text altogether.

Anxiety: Community Practice

The source of the last of the most common student fears around OA ETDs is found in their discipline's attitudes toward this sort of distribution. As discussed previously, throughout the history of the academy, students are immersed in the canons and cultures of their particular fields. As they progress through their studies and gain a mastery of and begin to contribute to their fields, becoming colleagues to their once-mentors, they often inherit the language and habits of those communities. Until such time as they have established their own scholarly identities, students often rely on mentors to help them navigate any number of concerns, including the creation and distribution of their dissertations and other publications.

Students, as newcomers to their fields, look to faculty and other students from their cohorts to help inform them about the mores of their community. This is a powerful force in a student's development and eventual emergence as a scholar. As noted by McMillan (2001), the "majority of graduate student authors at Virginia Tech reported through a survey administered at the end of the ETD submission process that the decision to limit access to their ETDs was based on advice from their faculty advisors." Community impressions about open access, author rights, licensing agreements, citation and reuse, embargoes, and more have a profound effect on many students' decisions.

The nature of these impressions depend greatly on the field. The physics community has different ways of creating and distributing research compared to comparative literature. These cultures are decades in the making and are byproducts of the larger scholarly communication environment in which they operate. Publishers; disciplinary organizations and scholarly communities; and libraries, archives, and cultural institutions help to color these impressions, as well.

By way of example, from one particular submission period: A history of art and architecture student approached the Office for Scholarly Communication to ask for the redaction of images in his dissertation. Because the images were from a very restrictive archive, he had concerns about them being publicly available in his dissertation in DASH, per the recommendation of his mentor. Within an hour after his call, four colleagues from his cohort called with similar concerns. Word of mouth is a powerful, if somewhat blunt, tool.

As much as local communities can affect a student's behavior, so, too, do their parent communities. This is perhaps best exemplified by the very public statement in 2013 by the American Historical Association (AHA) calling for embargoes of at least six years for history dissertations. The reason for doing so relates to the misconception, discussed previously, of an OA ETD being considered a previous publication:

> An increasing number of university presses are reluctant to offer a publishing contract to newly minted PhDs whose dissertations have been freely available via online sources. Presumably, online readers will become familiar with an author's particular argument, methodology, and archival sources, and will feel no need to buy the book once it is available. As a result, students who must post their dissertations online immediately after they receive their degree can find themselves at a serious disadvantage in their effort to get their first book published. (American Historical Association 2013)

As poorly informed as this statement is, it has had a very real impact on discussion on campus and decision making by students. Professional organizations, as representative of a field's perspective, can thus very quickly shape a student's attitudes and behavior.

Similarly, certain professional organizations and archives in the arts and humanities have the power to sway a student's behavior. Another local example is a music PhD who was working with a particular composer's archive in her dissertation. She resisted OA distribution of her work out of fear of the archive cold-shouldering her future use of the work they held if she did so. This is a concern that has been raised on multiple occasions by other students in the arts. For students whose work depends on access to the rich resources in these archives, such a threat can shape a pattern of behavior quickly.

Antidote: Changing the Conversation

Much like with publishers, there is an opportunity when working with estates and archives. While the power dynamic is a bit different, there is still a symbiotic relationship between an archive or estate and its users. Without users, an archive has less use, potentially less funding, and less reason to collect work. Without archives and estates, an incredible richness to scholarship would be lost.

If an archive or estate requires users to sign a consent or permissions form for use of material, then there may be an opportunity to have a conversation at the point of use rather than asking for permission after the fact. It should be noted that use of estate and archival work does fall under the confines of copyright law and fair use, and as such, a student may be able to make an argument for fair use of such work, if applicable.

Some specialized archives or estates do not fully comprehend the copyright law themselves. Some believe an age-old myth that possession of a work constitutes rights in that work. As a result, students may find themselves dealing with a contract that allows them a certain amount of access to a work, only to then be presented with another "permission to publish" contract for when they want to use the material or a copy of the material in their theses or dissertations. Students should be wary of signing these contracts, especially if there are fees involved.

In cases where an archive or estate is being particularly challenging, students may be interested in exploring whether the archive or estate is the rights holder to the work in question. A subject librarian would be particularly well suited to help in this endeavor. If a search reveals that the archive or estate is not the rights holder, then this has downstream implications for whom to contact for permission, such as an heir or executor.

Regardless of these myriad possibilities, there is always space for negotiation. Dissertations are scholarly, noncommercial works, and such a use may be less threatening to a fully commercialized archive or estate. Additionally, these communities may realize the value in bringing new attention to the archive or estate holdings, particularly if their collections are supporting interdisciplinary work that they had not previously considered. In the end, a student always has the potential and should be encouraged to create a well-crafted argument for limited, open use that would benefit both parties.

Last, students should be reminded that these archives or estates may own work from or collect in scholarly fields that a student may spend her life studying. It is important that a student foster good communication from the beginning. Students should be encouraged to be open and honest at all times, especially if they plan on forming long-term academic relationships with the archives or estates for continued access and use.

CONCLUSIONS

ETD programs have become more established, with more institutions mandating the open distribution of dissertations. What was standard practice in the days of distribution through bound copies feels like new, unstable ground. Student research opportunities and professional futures feel a little more vulnerable in an open world.

While these concerns can more often than not be addressed with reasoned approaches, it is the university's place to help students get to the place where they feel confident with decisions they are making about their work and access to it. Once properly informed, students will be empowered to make reasoned choices related to their scholarship—not only for their dissertations but also into their academic futures.

We have not yet addressed the relevance of the strategic embargo. Contrary to the American Historical Association's exhortation otherwise, default lengthy embargoes do not necessarily serve student needs. As Salo (2015) finds, six-month, one-year, and two-year embargoes are common (likely due to these being the default embargo options in ProQuest's submission tool), with the upper limit usually capping at five years, often with provisions for extensions. Shorter embargoes with the potential for an extension afford students the best of both worlds: protection from journal and monograph publishing constraints and the benefit of open access distribution, with its broader audience and increased impact. Rather than requesting lengthy embargoes that may not be necessary, students should be advised to look at the publishers with which they hope to distribute their work, account for revision time, and take the embargoes that will serve their needs and not needlessly constrain their works' use.

We have learned a few lessons from Harvard's relatively recent rollout of an in-house ETD submission system. These mirror some of the key findings of the Council of Graduate Schools (2007) report on "policies and practices to promote student success": articulate expectations, provide resources to scaffold student efforts, and offer comprehensive orientation to help students prepare for their graduate school careers.

We emphasize that crucially important to this effort are strategic partnerships across campus. From program deans and administrators to faculty, registrars, and library staff, it is imperative that constituents who work with students across the institution are aware of, understand the reasons for, and recognize the benefits of the institution's OA ETD program and policies. By ensuring that there is a team of well-informed and engaged people who will help students to consider their options and make the best choices possible for their work, there will be opportunities for education from the beginning of their time in the program to the point of their submission of the dissertations.

Implicit in such a distributed network of support is the idea of sustained education and outreach. While students matriculate through a program, complete one dissertation, graduate, and move on to their careers, faculty and relevant staff sustain a robust OA ETD program. These "expert" contacts need to be easily identifiable and provide documentation and programming that gives students information at their points of need.

Only with their help will it be possible to deliver crucial information to early-career researchers that will not only help them to make reasoned decisions about their ETD but also to form productive habits for their scholarly lives going forward. Having an understanding of author rights and copyright, fair use, and negotiation are crucial to an academic, and by delivering this information early in a researcher's career, universities have the potential to help scholars adopt informed, productive, and open publishing behaviors. By doing so, as Lippincott and Lynch (2010) assert, ETD programs can change the landscape of scholarly publishing.

NOTES

We would like to thank Kevin Smith, Sue Kriegsman, and Arlene Navarro for their invaluable comments, research, and advice.

1. Articles in DASH display individual download statistics. One recent graduate has used his ETD download statistics in his tenure and promotion review; another graduate used her ETD download statistics to convince a museum to launch an exhibit based on her research.

2. For example, see MIT's list of publishers that allow "[r]euse of author's previously published article in author's thesis" (MIT Libraries 2016).

REFERENCES

American Historical Association. 2013. "American Historical Association Statement on Policies Regarding the Embargoing of Complete History PhD Dissertations." *AHA Today*. http://blog.historians.org/2013/07/american-historical-association-statement-on-policies-regarding-the-embargoing-of-completed-history-phd-dissertations.

Barton, Matthew D. 2005. "Dissertations: Past, Present, and Future." *Graduate Theses and Dissertations*. http://scholarcommons.usf.edu/etd/2777.

Bosch, Stephen, and Kittie Henderson. 2012. "Coping with the Terrible Twins | Periodicals Price Survey 2012." *Library Journal*. http://lj.libraryjournal.com/2012/04/funding/coping-with-the-terrible-twins-periodicals-price-survey-2012.

Clement, Gail P., and Fred Rascoe. 2013. "ETD Management and Publishing in the ProQuest System and the University Repository: A Comparative Analysis." *Journal of Librarianship and Scholarly Communication* 1, no. 4: eP1074.

Council of Graduate Schools. 2007. "PhD Completion Project: Policies and Practices to Promote Student Success: Executive Summary." http://www.phdcompletion.org/information/executive_summary_student_success_book_iv.pdf.

Creative Commons. 2016. "About the Licenses." https://creativecommons.org/licenses.

Crow, Raym. 2002. "The Case for Institutional Repositories: A SPARC Position Paper." *ARL Bimonthly Report* 223. http://works.bepress.com/ir_research/7.

Dodson, Thomas. 2013a. "Office Hours: Ben Finio Talks about OA and Science Funding." *YouTube*. https://www.youtube.com/watch?v=LYgYXvDADtM.

———. 2013b. "Office Hours: Harvard Faculty Talk about Open Access." *YouTube*. https://www.youtube.com/watch?v=jD6CcFxRelY.

Harvard T. H. Chan School of Public Health Registrar's Office. 2015. "Dissertation Guidelines: Body of Dissertation." http://www.hsph.harvard.edu/registrar/dissertation-guidelines/#body.

Harvard University Archives. 2016. "Harvard University Archives Mission." http://library.harvard.edu/university-archives/mission.

Harvard University Press Blog. 2013. "Can't Find It, Can't Sign It: On Dissertation Embargoes." http://harvardpress.typepad.com/hup_publicity/2013/07/cant-find-it-cant-sign-it-on-dissertation-embargoes.html.

Hume, Kathryn. 2011. "The Perils of Publishing your Dissertation Online." *Professor Is In*. http://theprofessorisin.com/2011/08/24/the-perils-of-publishing-your-dissertation-online/#.

Iasevoli, Brenda. 2015. "A Glut of Ph.D.s Means Long Odds of Getting Jobs." *NPR Ed*. http://www.npr.org/sections/ed/2015/02/27/388443923/a-glut-of-ph-d-s-means-long-odds-of-getting-jobs.

Lippincott, Joan K., and Clifford A. Lynch. 2010. "ETDs and Graduate Education: Programs and Prospects." *Research Library Issues*, no. 270. http://old.arl.org/bm~doc/rli-270-etds.pdf.

Lynch, Clifford A. 2003. "Institutional Repositories: Essential Infrastructure for Scholarship in the Digital Age." *ARL* 26: 1–7.

McMillan, Gail. 2001. "Do ETDs Deter Publishers?" *College and Research Libraries News* 62, no. 6: 620–21. http://scholar.lib.vt.edu/staff/gailmac/publications/pubrsETD2001.html.

McMillan, Gail, Shannon Stark, and Martin Halbert. 2013. "2013 NDLTD Survey of ETD Practices." Sixteenth International ETD Symposium, Hong Kong. https://vtechworks.lib.vt.edu/handle/10919/50978.

MIT Libraries. 2016. "Publisher Policies: Thesis Content and Article Publishing." *Scholarly Publishing @ MIT Libraries*. http://libraries.mit.edu/sites/scholarly/publishing/publisher-policies-thesis-content-and-article-publishing.

Patton, Stacey. 2013. "Embargoes Can Go Only So Far to Help New PhD's Get Published, Experts Say." *Chronicle of Higher Education News*. http://chronicle.com/article/Embargoes-Can-Go-Only-So-Far/140603/?cid=wc&utm_source=wc&utm_medium=en.

ProQuest. 2016a. "Find a Dissertation." http://www.proquest.com/products-services/dissertations/find-a-dissertation.html.

———. 2016b. "History and Milestones." http://www.proquest.com/about/history-milestones.

———. 2016c. "Submit Dissertations or Theses." http://www.proquest.com/products-services/dissertations/submit-a-dissertation.html.

Ramirez, Marisa L., Joan T. Dalton, Gail McMillan, Max Read, and Nancy H. Seamans. 2013. "Do Open Access Electronic Theses and Dissertations Diminish Publishing Opportunities in the Social Sciences and Humanities?" *College and Research Libraries News* 74, no. 4: 368–80. http://dx.doi.org/10.5860/crl-356.

Salo, Dorothea. 2015. "Institutions Requiring Electronic Thesis/Dissertation Submissions." https://docs.google.com/spreadsheets/d/1VPrZTfW5ejHzRoluo0ttZwkCY6npqMoZUGjRBdYYH-4/edit#gid=0.

Shieber, Stuart. 2011. "Dissertation Distribution Online: My Comments at the AHA." *Occasional Pamphlet*. https://blogs.law.harvard.edu/pamphlet/2011/02/14/dissertation-distribution-online-my-comments-at-the-aha.

SPARC. 2016. "Author Rights: Using the SPARC Author Addendum." http://sparcopen.org/our-work/author-rights/brochure-html.

Suber, Peter. 2006. "Open Access to Electronic Theses and Dissertations (ETDs)." *SPARC Open Access Newsletter*. http://nrs.harvard.edu/urn-3:HUL.InstRepos:4727443.

Chapter Thirteen

Library Services in Critical Thinking, Use, and Evaluation of Open Data

Tara Das

Under the umbrella of open access, local and national governments have started making available the raw data that they collect in the course of providing public services for users to conduct their own analyses. This trend in open data has dovetailed with a trend in data librarianship in academic libraries. Much of open data is derived from government services, which is the focus of this chapter, and so the terms *open data* and *open government data* used interchangeably here. As part of data librarianship, librarians provide services related to data analysis and management. These services have been affected by the availability of open data and the strengths and weaknesses therein.

With more data being made available under the open data movement, users are more likely to find data that are suitable for their research and analysis needs. However, library services in open data do not stop after helping users with data discovery and selection. As part of instruction, librarians can increase user awareness of the socially constructed nature of open data and support its critical evaluation. Because government data do not exist independently of human action—they are collected by humans as part of their workflows and operations—human values and prejudices infuse data. In order for users to draw tenable conclusions from and identify limitations in analysis using open data, academic libraries must extend data librarianship services to incorporate critical evaluation of open data.

With open data, a dataset that is created under particular circumstances and assumptions may be used to answer questions that are not entirely appropriate to ask of it, depending on the nature of data collection and presentation. As Best (2001) argues, "We sometimes talk about statistics as though they are facts that simply exist. . . . All statistics are created through people's actions: people have to decide what to count and how to count it" (27). In following Best, it behooves academic librarians to foster connections with government agencies as part of their services and to understand how government data are created. In this way, they can better understand open data's definitions, strengths, and deficiencies and work with users to critically evaluate open data for their needs. Critical evaluation and careful selection of open data requires literacy that goes beyond understanding how to use data. This chapter (1) provides an overview of open data in the United States; (2) describes specific trends in data librarianship that apply to open data; (3) identifies critical issues with open data; and (4) provides illustrations of library services in critical data librarianship, including advocacy, preservation, and instruction in national and local (specifically New York City) open data.

OPEN DATA IN THE UNITED STATES

On January 21, 2009, President Obama signed a memorandum on transparency and open government. It asked federal agencies to make recommendations for an open government directive that would operationalize principles of transparency, participation, and collaboration in part by providing open data (White House 2009). *Open government data* is defined as having a format that is "platform independent, machine readable, and made available to the public without restrictions that would impede re-use of that information" (Office of Management and Budget 2009). Data are made open and reusable under the premise that government should provide data about activities and programs in order to promote transparency about its operations and policies. The memorandum states, "Transparency promotes accountability and provides information for citizens about what their Government is doing. . . . Executive departments and agencies should harness new technologies to put information about their operations and decisions online and readily available to the public" (White House 2009).

The directive created Data.gov as the home for all federal open government data. The Office of Management and Budget issued the "Open Data Policy" pursuant to executive order 13642, "Making Open and Machine Readable the New Default for Government Information," which was issued May 9, 2013. The policy sets the framework for how the government will manage open data across time (Office of Management and Budget 2013). In addition to complying with open data formats, standards, licenses, and privacy restrictions when creating and collecting data, agencies are expected to create a single data inventory and publish a public data listing that can be harvested and added to Data.gov.

The "Open Data Policy" also details principles that open government data should adhere to: They should be public, accessible, described, reusable, complete, timely, and managed postrelease. Users need to be provided with data documentation so that they can understand the strengths and limitations of the data, as well as how to process the data. "This involves the use of robust, granular metadata . . . through documentation of data elements, data dictionaries, and, if applicable, additional descriptions of the purpose of the collection, the population of interest, the characteristics of the sample, and the method of data collection" (Office of Management and Budget 2013, 5). Federal agencies, however, are not required to provide this detailed documentation with their data.

Currently, there are 164,264 datasets on Data.gov (Data.gov n.d., "Data Catalog"). While Data.gov was developed to store federal government data, state and local governments, universities, and nonprofit organizations can also have their open data discoverable on Data.gov. There are 129,489 federal government datasets; 14,422 state government datasets; 2,860 city government datasets; and 756 county government datasets currently available on Data.gov. The movement to open government data and make it publicly available via online portals has occurred at levels of government below the federal; according to Data.gov, there are forty state and forty-six local (city and county) online portals for open data (Data.gov n.d., "Open Government"). New York City was one of the first local governments to legislate open government data and has its data discoverable on Data.gov in addition to hosting its own online portal for New York City open data.

Similar to President Obama, New York City mayor Michael Bloomberg signed local law 11 of 2012 to open agency data to the public, promoting transparency and accountability of city government services (New York City 2012). As with Data.gov and federal agencies, New York City agencies are required to make their public datasets available by 2018 via a single online portal, now known as NYC Open Data. In order to prioritize public datasets for release to NYC Open Data, city agencies are asked to consider whether a particular dataset can:

- be used to increase agency accountability and responsiveness,
- improve public knowledge of the agency and its operations,
- further the mission of the agency,
- create economic opportunity, or
- respond to a need or demand identified by public consultation. (New York City 2012)

Also pursuant to local law 11, the NYC Department of Information Technology & Telecommunications published an "Open Data Policy and Technical Standards Manual" in September 2012 to guide administration, infrastructure, and data standards for NYC Open Data. Each city agency must have an open data coordinator who is responsible for identifying and supporting the delivery of datasets to the portal (in contrast to Data.gov, datasets are not automatically harvested from agency websites) and addressing public feedback about the agency's public datasets. Although detailed data documentation (e.g., dataset column and value definitions) is not required, the "Open Data Policy and Technical Standards Manual" advises agencies to include data documentation when the column identifiers do not provide a user with enough information to use it effectively. For example, the metadata for a column containing restaurant inspection letter grades should indicate the possible values and their meanings (NYC Department of Information Technology & Telecommunications 2012, 14). Like the policy underlying Data.gov, the NYC open data policy recognizes the importance of metadata specific to data but does not require its inclusion. Currently, there are 1,161 datasets on NYC Open Data (NYC Open Data 2014). Similar to Data.gov, these datasets include reference lists and directories, as well as numeric and geospatial (e.g., maps, shape files) data.

There are some interesting points of contrast, however, between the rules and operations governing Data.gov and NYC Open Data. In library consultations and instruction at Columbia (my university), strategies for searching the portals, with their varying rules, interfaces, and data collections, are shared with users. For instance, the "Open Data Policy" for Data.gov requires agencies to maintain a data inventory using metadata. Any datasets that can be made publicly available from this inventory must be listed in open data format (human- and machine-readable) on an agency website at www.[agency].gov/data, with files also posted at www.[agency].gov/data.json (Project Open Data n.d.). Data.gov harvests these datasets for inclusion in its catalog. Likewise, datasets that are replaced or updated (e.g., with information for additional years) need to have the same title and web address so that Data.gov can replace the current dataset via automated harvesting.

In contrast, the provision of new and updated data from agencies to NYC Open Data is done manually. According to the "Open Data Policy and Technical Standards Manual," NYC Department of Information Technology & Telecommunications (DoITT) staff work with agency open data coordinators to update data on NYC Open Data. City agencies can provide DoITT staff access to their databases for extracting data, or they can publish files to a location that DoITT can access. Data are thus manually transferred to DoITT rather than being harvested automatically. Moreover, while the intent of local law 11 is to make all NYC public government data available through a single online portal, many agencies provide new and updated data on their agency websites. These updates are not always communicated to DoITT staff for upload into NYC Open Data. As a result, users are advised to review agency websites in addition to open data portals that store agency data.

While it may not seem obvious to discuss the rules and operations under-lying open data portals and how they impact data content and search strate-gies with users, it is worthwhile. Such discussion should be incorporated into library consultations and instruction around open data so that users are aware that open data are not some objective entity that exists outside of humans but rather that their creation is affected by human and organizational practices. Agency operations that underlie data collection efforts should be discussed as well to increase this awareness. It cannot be ignored that, with few excep-tions, government data originate from the programmatic, administrative work that agencies do before they are repurposed by users (this concept is further explained later in this chapter). For instance, 311 (the nonemergency counterpart to 911) is New York City's primary source of government infor-mation. Operators respond to nonemergency calls and service requests, and data on 311 calls are considered open government data (NYC Open Data 2014). Data can be accessed through New York City government websites and include information on the date of each call, responding agency, nature of complaint, and resolution. The data are publicly available for analysis and are used to examine the frequency and density of specific complaints by neighborhood location. Using 311 data critically, however, means consider-ing how it is created. Such data are not collected with analysis as the end objective, and their creation and processing are not subject to scientific meth-ods. One must take into account whether 311 calls accurately represent con-ditions as reported. For example, false complaints can be called in to 311. Likewise, because 311 does not collect identifying information about callers, the data cannot easily be cleaned to account for duplicate reports or multiple reports made by the same caller. These critical issues with open data and how library services should address them are considered after first describing trends in data librarianship.

DATA LIBRARIANSHIP IN ACADEMIC LIBRARIES

Data librarians provide research consultation and instruction to support users and their data needs, and open data make this task easier by providing so much data to the public for analysis. Consultation and instruction revolve around finding data, cleaning and analyzing data, and using data analysis and visualization software. Consultation and instruction in data librarianship also require statistical and data literacy—that is, critical thinking skills in evaluat-ing the relevance, quality, and usefulness of statistics or data prior to incor-porating them into one's work. With open data, such evaluation entails dis-cussion about the operations that drive agencies' data collection and presen-tation practices, as well as those that underlie the open data portals that store data collections. Central to these aspects of statistics and data is the notion that numbers are not objective. Statistical and data literacy is akin to information literacy, on which librarians often provide instruction:

> Statistical literacy is an essential component of information literacy. Students must be statistically literate: they must be able to think critically about basic descriptive statistics. Analyzing, interpreting and evaluating statistics as evidence is a special skill. And students must be data literate: they must be able to access, assess, manipulate, summarize, and present data. Data literacy is an essential component of both information literacy and statistical literacy. (Shields 2004, 8)

Beyond supporting users with data-related consultation and instruction, librarians can embed themselves deeper in the open data process with such services as curation, metadata, and data management. Providing these services requires librarians to become involved in the prepublication stages of research, when data is created, and work with government agencies to improve open data. As mentioned earlier, data documentation and data-specific metadata are not required in Data.gov or NYC Open Data, and they are not always available. Nevertheless, they are essential to understanding and using a dataset that one did not create and to interpreting any analysis that uses such a dataset.

Metadata for data can be categorized into four types, according to Gutmann et al. (2004). First, study-level metadata describe the study or data collection, including the objectives, sample or population characteristics, and the variables or indicators that are being measured. Second, file-level metadata summarize the properties of individual data files within the collection. Third, variable-level metadata describe the variables measured in the dataset and how they are defined and coded. Finally, administrative and structural metadata describe the structure and technical aspects of the data so that the data can be properly maintained and preserved over time.

The Data Documentation Initiative (DDI) is a metadata specification that captures the data life cycle for social sciences data, from initial data concept and collection to archiving (DDI 2009). DDI elements capture the purpose of the study, data sources, the methodology behind data collection and processing, and the logical and physical structure of the data. The Inter-university Consortium for Political and Social Research (ICPSR), an established data repository in the United States and a data archive for selected government agencies, recommends that researchers deposit DDI metadata when they deposit their data (ICPSR 2012). The ICPSR also provides a list of nineteen important metadata elements for social science data, which overlap with the DDI specification and include sample and sampling procedures; units of analysis/observation; detailed variable background, description, and definitions; data collection instruments; and coding instruments. Metadata specifications uniquely suited to data include elements that describe the data collection or study context, study purpose, data collection procedures, and variable information. These elements help users understand others' data as if they had created them themselves in order to repurpose it for their research and analyses.

Given librarians' expertise in metadata and data management practices, they can, as part of their services, collaborate with government agencies to facilitate successful sharing and reuse of open data (this type of collaboration is discussed later in this chapter). At Purdue University, for example, librarians assess the suitability of particular research data collections for their library collections and conduct data interviews with the researcher-creators, posing such questions as:

- What is the story of the data?
- How was the dataset created, processed, and analyzed?
- How could the data be used, reused, and repurposed?
- What publications or discoveries have resulted from the data? (Witt and Carlson 2007)

In the case of Purdue University, in order for librarians to appropriately curate data (i.e., store, maintain, and preserve them over their life cycle while ensuring their discovery, retrieval, sharing, and reuse by others), they must have information about their creation, processing, file structure, intended use, and users. That is, they must have metadata from the people who created the data.

In the context of open data and their impact on library services, library advocacy for metadata and data documentation is necessary to improve open data. A dataset cannot be appropriately evaluated, selected, and used—activities that take place during data consultation and instruction—if data about their data are not available. Metadata include the kinds of information that Purdue University librarians glean from their data interviews. In conducting these data interviews, librarians are actively creating metadata by engaging with data creators. This process can be undertaken with government agencies that create open data as well. If such metadata do not exist, then data sharing and reuse becomes problematic, affecting data-related instruction, consultation, and infrastructure in libraries:

> In marked contrast to the digital representation of a book, for example, social science data are seldom easily understood on their own. Put simply, a social science survey rendered in digital format is just a list of numbers, often nothing more. In order for a future content user to make sense of those numbers, extensive metadata must be prepared. . . . If a digital record does not have sufficient metadata to adequately explain its content and relevance, or these metadata cannot be reproduced, it will usually remain unavailable for secondary analysis. (Gutmann et al. 2004, 217)

Because open government data often originate from the programmatic, administrative work of agencies, understanding how these data were created, processed, and used—questions that root the librarian earlier in the data process—is key to strong data librarianship. Understanding the importance of having metadata specific to the data process and documenting data creation, collection, and definitions is central to enhancing library services around open data. In general, understanding the critical issues with open data that have been raised in public administration and law literature is crucial for enhancing library services related to open data.

CRITICAL ISSUES WITH OPEN DATA

Open government data are facilitated through online access, including web portals and computerized systems. As stated in the previous section, governments argue that this access furthers the transparency of their programs and operations. In the public administration literature, Meijer (2009) evaluates modern government transparency as communicated through the Internet, which is a shift from traditional government transparency as contextually experienced through face-to-face interactions in local settings. Transparency through the Internet and computerized systems (e.g. open data) is expected to improve government by increasing its accountability to the people. As Meijer argues, however, while more information is provided with modern transparency, it is computer mediated and not direct. In effect, when numbers are provided to the public, they are divorced from the behaviors in local settings that gave rise to them. Thus open data create more ambiguity about government activities. Meijer asserts that, as a result of modern computer-mediated transparency, information is decontextualized:

> The Internet creates opportunities for presenting information about performance in various ways. The effect of it, however, is that the transparency is taken away from the context that it refers to. [For example,] information about school performance seems interesting but is difficult to interpret without knowledge of the local context. Korean citizens can see how their applications proceed but have no information about the context in which civil servants handle these applications. (Meijer 2009, 259)

Likewise, in disentangling the notions of open government and open data, Yu and Robinson (2012) argue that simply providing access to open data makes government neither open nor transparent. The politics of open government need to be kept separate from the technologies of open data. Open data can be used to create mobile apps, online tools and interfaces, and "improve quality of life and enhance public service delivery, but may have little impact on political accountability" (Yu and Robinson 2012, 180).

The distinction that Yu and Robinson draw between public accountability and service delivery is striking. Academic librarians who work with open data collections should keep it in mind when assessing open data for research and program evaluation. Both the U.S. and New York City governments emphasize innovation and entrepreneurship alongside accountability as benefits of providing open data. The federal "Open Data Policy" emphasizes "engaging entrepreneurs and innovators in the private and nonprofit sectors to encourage and facilitate the use of agency data to build applications and services" (Office of Management and Budget 2013, 9). Data.gov highlights such uses of open data on its website (Data.gov n.d., "Impact"). Likewise, New York City local law 11 of 2012 is intended to "permit the public to assist in identifying efficient solutions for government, promote innovative strategies for social progress, and create economic opportunities" (New York City 2012).

The NYC Open Data portal also provides a selected list of public and private datasets to support the annual NYC BigApps Competition, where teams submit innovative solutions and projects using official New York City datasets that are intended to solve New York City challenges (NYC Open Data n.d.). BetaNYC is a community with more than 2,100 members that includes developers and civic hackers and claims to represent New York City open government data users. A review of the community's open data testimony to the NYC Council (the legislative body for the city), as well as its "Roadmap to a Digital New York City," reveals concerns about the lack of daily and subdaily reports, machine-readable file formats, data standards, and data-sharing protocols, as well as inadequate geocoding or location-based data (Hidalgo and Baek 2014). These concerns stem from a focus on developing applications using open data to visualize government services for the public.

Despite these concerns, by associating open data with open government and focusing on data that further innovative technology solutions, a government can provide data on "safe" routine operations and programs, thus at least giving the appearance that it is open, transparent, and supportive of service delivery via third-party applications. Brito (2008) gives credence to this idea by asserting that government can enable openness and transparency by "making its data available online in useful and flexible formats, [so that] citizens will be able to utilize modern Internet tools to shed light on government activities" (119). Even a government that provides open data can nevertheless remain opaque and unaccountable in its practices. For example, as Yu and Robinson point out, although federal agencies are now required to provide datasets to Data.gov under the "Open Data Policy," many of these datasets were already publicly available online. Thus no new light was being shed on those government programs and operations. Moreover, while agencies packaged some of these datasets into more usable machine-readable formats, critics questioned how these disclosures added to the public's "insight into agency management, deliberations or results." Critics saw the repackaging of old information as providing only "marginal value" and urged the government to make available "public data that holds an agency accountable for its policy and spending decisions." (Yu and Robinson 2012, 198)

A more critical examination of the types of information that government provides is warranted, particularly if open data objectives include enabling a more transparent government that is accountable to its people. Dawes (2010) highlights the multifaceted relationship government has vis-à-vis information, pointing out that "government is also an information collector, producer, provider, and user" that carries out its information-related policies in one of a variety of ways: "by collecting data for the express purpose of publication, by requiring private entities to publish certain kinds of information, or by releasing to the public information collected in the course of government program operations and regulatory activities" (377).

Thus "government data" are not a unitary whole; they are derived from multiple different agencies with different organizational mandates, programs, and policies. Government scientific and statistical agencies (e.g., the United States Census Bureau and the National Center for Health Statistics) have long provided open data before the phrase came into vogue. Such scientific data are produced by government to support its programs and policies, but they have also traditionally been disseminated publicly for research and business purposes; this type of data is collected for publication purposes per Dawes's framework. Agencies provide these datasets for public reuse, and they are derived from formal data collection efforts, such as surveys and censuses. These open government data have been accompanied by detailed documentation and codebooks (i.e., metadata) that describe the data collection background, instruments, definitions, and methodology, as is expected practice in research communities sharing datasets. For instance, the United States Census Bureau (2015) provides code lists, subject definitions, sample design, and questionnaires for the "American Community Survey."

Scientific and statistical data are not the only data types being provided under current open government data initiatives; government information that stems from less-structured data collection undertaken to support agency programs and operations is also provided. Government agencies create information when performing their mandated activities (e.g., legislative hearing transcripts, budgets, crime monitoring reports, and voting records). Such information is now being supplied under open data initiatives and is categorized by Dawes as being collected in the course of government programs and activities. Given that these data reflect government decisions and operations, they can be used to evaluate government effectiveness and facilitate government transparency and accountability. Yet as Dawes and Helbig (2010) point out,

> [i]t is important to remember that these datasets are defined and collected in different ways by different organizations. They come from a variety of different systems and processes and represent different time frames and other essential characteristics. Most come from existing information systems that were designed for specific operational purposes. Few were created with public use in mind. . . . While quickly getting data out in the open is an important goal . . . the value of the data for any particular use depends on making these characteristics easy for users to find and understand. (51)

As stated earlier, it is possible for a dataset created under particular circumstances and assumptions to be used to answer questions that are not entirely appropriate to ask of it. Thus Dawes considers quality metadata to be as important as the open data themselves, particularly when data are collected without publication in mind. Even when these data are essential for evaluating government activities, it is "seldom managed in the structured way that census data or other standard statistics are managed, making it more difficult for others to use and interpret and more subjective to understanding and misused" (Dawes 2010, 378).

If government information in itself is not useful for understanding agency operations, then transforming it into open data format without the quality metadata required to evaluate, use, and interpret it will not add any value. "Opening data that has no adequate information quality can result in discussions, confusions, less transparency, and even in less trust in the government" (Janssen, Charalabidis, and Zuiderwijk 2012, 264). An open data user needs to be provided with detailed descriptions of government information, including objectives, sources of data, and methods of data collection, in order for government to be transparent and accountable. These metadata elements are specific to each dataset, but unfortunately they have not been deemed required elements by open data providers. "In order for users to assess data quality, they need to understand the nature of the data and because data producers cannot anticipate all users and uses, the provision of good quality metadata is as important as the quality of the data itself" (Dawes and Helbig 2010, 57).

Metadata and data documentation are seldom provided when government information is collected in the course of agency operations and provided as open data. Yet "when information collected for one purpose is used for a different purpose, there is potential for misuse, misunderstanding, and misinterpretation" (Dawes, Pardo, and Cresswell 2004, 16). Open data as issued from different agencies cannot be treated as a homogeneous whole. Individual datasets have their own strengths, challenges, and deficiencies. Quality metadata can aid tremendously in minimizing inaccurate understanding of open data and interpretation of analysis using open data across government agency sources. Moreover, "if the content has enduring social, legal, or historical value, metadata is critical to its long term and effective use" (Dawes, Pardo, and Cresswell 2004, 19).

In its recommendations to city council on improving NYC Open Data, BetaNYC includes just one sentence on data documentation: "A majority of the city's data is explanatory for someone who is a subject matter expert. For the City's data to be maximized, datasets must have better documentation" (Hidalgo 2014). Yet, such data are not necessarily understandable, even to subject-matter experts. They may only be understandable to those specific individuals who collected and presented them—a much smaller population of people who can analyze open data and use them for research purposes. If detailed data documentation and metadata were included with open data, then researchers would understand their nature, be able to reuse them appropriately for analysis, and interpret their findings in context, taking into account that the data were collected for specific government purposes using specific definitions. In this regard, open government data could support a public push for policy changes based on analysis and evaluation of open data, in addition to development of applications that leverage open data.

In a response to Yu and Robinson's critique, Weinstein and Goldstein (2012) agree that the notions of open data and open government should be distinguished but argue that open data can still facilitate open government. "Even if initial data releases are inconsequential for accountability, such releases spark a public conversation about what data matter and contribute to changes in norms and practices inside government" (Weinstein and Goldstein 2012, 41). How librarians can contribute to this conversation through collaboration with government officials and advocates is addressed in the next section.

LIBRARY SERVICES AND OPEN DATA: ADVOCACY, METADATA, AND PRESERVATION

Librarians have historically been strong advocates with government on issues of privacy, civil rights, and education. With their expertise in data librarianship, particularly in metadata for the purposes of data sharing and reuse, there are opportunities for librarians to engage in open data advocacy as part of their services. As Janssen, Charalabidis, and Zuiderwijk (2012) argue, "[o]pen data on its own has little intrinsic value; the value is created by its use. The publicizing of data needs to be accompanied by an infrastructure which is able to handle the data in an easy-to-use way to lower the user threshold" (264). With metadata schemas specific to data that emphasize how data are created, collected, and defined, librarians are in an excellent place to share their knowledge with government agencies to strengthen metadata for open data. In New York City, for instance, I have been reaching out to government agencies to create data-specific metadata and data dictionaries for datasets available via NYC Open Data. As previously stated, agencies designate open data coordinators who manage data delivery to NYC Open Data, as well as coordinate communications around open data for their agency. I have been working with open data coordinators to obtain data documentation for specific datasets and with New York City Council to pass legislation that would require agencies to provide data dictionaries on NYC Open Data. Based on these efforts, such legislation was passed in November 2015, requiring data dictionaries and documentation to provide context for each dataset that is available on NYC Open Data. Preserving NYC Open Data in our university data catalog was the original objective of developing library data repository services in open data. Doing so would increase the visibility of these data to our users and minimize the risk of open data loss should specific datasets be dropped from NYC Open Data or should NYC Open Data itself be shut down. With government information, including open government data, in electronic form, preservation and access concerns arise. For instance, library government information collections have moved toward pointing to web links and away from collecting publications. Yet governments, their websites, and individual webpages can shut down, which makes this move toward "pointing" for government collections fraught with risk for libraries, on whom people rely for information. Despite the electronic nature of government information,

> libraries should still be selecting, acquiring, organizing, and preserving information for their user-communities, and providing access to and services for those collections. Libraries do no one a long-term service by simply pointing to resources over which they have no control and which someone else can simply make unavailable literally at the flick of a switch. (Free Government Information 2013)

My close examination of NYC Open Data revealed that it was largely not reusable due to poor data documentation (e.g., definitions of column names and values, descriptions of how the data were collected and cleaned). We did not want to preserve data in our collections that we could not adequately describe to users. This limitation is a common one with open data—particularly open data that were derived from agency internal operations and were not created for the purpose of public research or evaluation. In general, government officials simply want to make data available to meet open data mandates. As stated earlier, local law 11 of 2012 does not require data dictionaries but does require data to be made open (i.e., available on NYC Open Data) by 2018. In their interviews with policy makers who provide open data, Janssen, Charalabidis, and Zuiderwijk (2012) quote one official as stating, "Preferably we can just drop the data and don't have to worry about provenance, enriching, or whatever" (265). Yet, as asserted in the previous section, open data are not just a matter of making data available. They require metadata, including dataset identifiers and descriptions of how data were created and collected, to render them usable. In viewing open data as a means through which government is made transparent and accountable, it becomes clear that detailed metadata also facilitate insight into government programs and operations and support critical evaluation of data. The Sunlight Foundation, whose mission is to make government more transparent, includes metadata in its best practices for open government data.

Documentation of the workflow helps the public and government alike discern qualities about the dataset otherwise unavailable, such as (but not limited to) the sourcing, reliability, rarity, and usability of the data. Additionally, documenting data-creation processes can identify redundancy and areas for workflow and data-creation improvements (Sunlight Foundation 2014, 8). Although the metadata standards and guidelines for providing metadata with open government data do exist, the metadata are not being produced. Here, librarians can collaborate with government agencies to create these metadata. For data that were not collected for release in a structured dataset, librarians can interview government officials who carry knowledge of the programs that gave rise to the data in order to elucidate metadata for open government data. As Davies and Bawa (2012) point out,

> Information may exist instead in the head of a key actor, or "informally" recorded in notes and paper records, which are not comprehensively encoded as structured data. In focusing on getting structured datasets, we gain a lot in terms of the share-ability of formally structured information. But there is also a potential loss or missed opportunity of engaging with the depth of tacit knowledge which is not easily translated, encoded and deciphered in open datasets.

By personally engaging with government officials and the records and archives in their possession, librarians can ascertain the meanings underlying data in a way that is less burdensome for officials and thus strengthen the potential for using open data to keep government accountable. Yet there are challenges in cultivating relationships with government officials, as has been my experience in reaching out to New York City agencies for the information required to create metadata and data documentation for NYC Open Data. The main challenge is that government officials work under tight deadlines, public visibility, and competing priorities. Because metadata standards that are tailored to data were not originally legally required in New York City, responses are sometimes difficult to obtain when soliciting detailed documentation for NYC Open Data.

In spite of its challenges, working closely with government agencies in open data advocacy has multiple benefits. Libraries acquire additional knowledge into how government data are created and disseminated via communication and collaboration, which enhances data librarianship services and collections. Awareness of librarian services in data librarianship grows. With successful outreach, government agencies have value added to their open data via library metadata, data documentation, and data cleaning. These data quality and usability concerns have had lower priority on the government side than has the need to meet legal requirements and navigate internal data use agreements to provide public access to data. In addition, with open data being later stored in a library data catalog or repository, users have access to government data from multiple sources, and there is not a single point of failure. With metadata tailored to datasets, users are also better equipped to appropriately reuse data and interpret results from data analysis.

INSTRUCTION

My colleagues and I have developed workshops based on the experiences we have had with open data. For instance, one workshop, "Finding Free and Open Data," provides a general overview of the open data movement and explains where users can search open data collections and the issues they should keep in mind when using open data. The sociopolitical context in which the open data movement is situated is presented alongside traditional librarianship instruction on where to find data and information. The workshop first asks what open data are by showing what they are not—they are not PDF files (regarded as an anti-open data format); they are not web query programs that give you statistics or maps on command; and they are not restricted data. These are not formats that are platform independent, machine readable, and open to all. We then review the history of open data in the United States and how government leaders have implemented open data policies to strengthen democracy and improve the transparency and accountability of government operations and decisions. Next, we review various open data collections, including Data.gov, NYC Open Data, and UNData, paying special attention to how the operations and policies underlying these portals impact the data provided. Examples of open data uses in research, journalism, and business are covered, followed by an exploration of open data issues, like metadata and data documentation, harmonizing datasets for longitudinal analysis, and data citation. The workshop also discusses how users need not only rely on existing open data but can also proactively open up data via data-scraping tools and Freedom of Information Act (FOIA) requests to government agencies to release information. Examples of this form of open data activism are highlighted, wherein individuals have scraped data or obtained data through open records requests and then made that data open for public use. For instance, the organization BetaNYC, which advocates for open government through technology, has established its own open data portal at data.beta.nyc. It consists of New York City government data that has been scraped from websites (e.g., data scraped from PDF files, which are not amenable to analysis or visualization, and converted into CSV files) or provided from agencies in response to open records requests. The workshop has garnered interest from students and faculty in social work, journalism, business, and the social sciences.

Another workshop, "The Art of the Merge," delves further into harmonizing and merging open datasets for analysis. Merging (or combining) datasets is a common practice because many research questions—particularly longitudinal analyses across multiple years for a specific area or population—may not be completely addressed by one dataset. In addition, there are different types of merges to consider—for example, Does the user want all observations or only the matching observations in the final dataset? The syntax required in different statistical software (SAS, Stata, and R) to clean data and merge datasets is reviewed and explained, but this is not the only focus. We emphasize always keeping the research question in mind and advise users that one should not simply start merging datasets without first examining the research question and the nature of the data, which are more important than the software. We also point out that not all merges are the same and that a merge may not be necessary, depending on the question being asked. A merge may not even be possible if the individual datasets do not contain a variable in common that can be used as the linking variable, and merging should not be considered if the user does not know where one or more of the individual datasets came from. The type of merge that one uses depends on what the final dataset should include, which depends on the research question. Thus, critical thinking skills are woven throughout the workshop. We provide sample research questions—for example, Is there a difference in hospital-acquired infections among New York hospitals?—and then present open data collections where one can find data to help answer them. For this particular sample question, the data can be found in Health Data NY, which is the state's open data portal for hospital and health data for city and state hospitals. We explain the structure of open data portals and the strengths and weaknesses of open data. We want users to understand that finding data that suit their needs is not as simple as it seems with the proliferation of open data collections.

The workshop also discusses best practices for harmonizing individual datasets to prepare them for merging into one dataset. For instance, some open datasets are not updated routinely or consistently (i.e., with all variables updated across years or geographies in the individual datasets to be merged). One policy explanation for this fact is that, in the open data movement, a high priority is given to working with agencies to open up closed data. Once it is open, less priority is given to updating it or adding additional years or variables. For example, datasets that contain data on the same topic but for different years should not be merged if the variables of research interest do not exist in both datasets. In this case, the user should consider restricting the research question to one year of data.

Throughout all instruction and consultations involving open data, we make clear the socially constructed nature of open data. As Best (2001) states,

> Every statistic must be created, and the process of creation always involves choices that affect the resulting number and therefore affect what we understand after the figures summarize and simplify the problem. People who create statistics must choose definitions—they must define what it is they want to count—and they must choose their methods—the ways they will go about their counting. Those choices shape every good statistic, and every bad one. Bad statistics simplify reality in ways that distort our understanding, while good statistics minimize that distortion. Good or bad, every statistic reflects its creators' choices. (161)

Best largely refers to statistics created out of data—sums, estimates, percentages, and rates. With the data underlying statistics being made increasingly open, his critical approach remains important. With any dataset, one should consider which agency issued the data and which data, data definitions, and methods of collection would serve their interests. How was the dataset produced, and is the process transparent to the public? Oftentimes, users are happy to simply find data that are suitable for their research and analysis needs. As part of instruction, librarians can increase users' awareness of the socially constructed nature of open data and encourage a thoughtful approach to identifying their limitations and interpreting their research findings in light of these limitations.

CONCLUSION

This chapter (1) provides an overview of open data in the United States; (2) describes specific trends in data librarianship that apply to open data; (3) identifies critical issues with open data; and (4) provides illustrations of library services in critical data librarianship, including advocacy, preservation, and instruction in open data. Librarians possess expertise in information literacy, government documents, data, and metadata. They have an exciting opportunity to contribute to the open data movement via advocacy and preservation as part of their library services. In addition to consultations and instruction, librarians can engage in collaboration with government officials to elicit background information about open government data to create metadata specific to data. This information would include data-collection procedures, purposes, and instruments, as well as definitions of variables. For open government data to be shared and reused appropriately and preserved over time, this type of metadata is necessary. Yet it is frequently lacking for data that were not created with public reuse in mind. These collaborations do necessitate active and sustained outreach from librarians who can make their case in compelling ways in order to engage government officials who are working to satisfy multiple legal mandates and competing priorities under public scrutiny.

In general, the open data movement provides users with more opportunities to find relevant data for analysis, but it also provides librarians with opportunities to engage in critical data librarianship. The numbers of states and countries developing open data portals is growing, but it is questionable whether all available data can be appropriately used, interpreted, and analyzed. This uncertainty is unfortunate, given that an important objective of open government data is to make government operations more transparent to the public. This objective cannot easily be achieved if the public is not also provided with sufficient information—metadata—to make the data understandable and their analysis meaningful. Numbers are not enough to make data open, and librarians who provide data librarianship services should be well aware of this fact and integrate it into their library services in open data.

REFERENCES

Best, Joel. 2001. *Damned Lies and Statistics: Untangling Numbers from the Media, Politicians, and Activists*. Berkeley: University of California Press.
Brito, Jerry. 2008. "Hack, Mash, & Peer: Crowdsourcing Government Transparency." *Columbia Science and Technology Law Review* 9: 119–22.
Data Documentation Initiative (DDI). 2009. "What Is DDI?" http://www.ddialliance.org/what.
Data.gov. n.d. "Data Catalog." http://catalog.data.gov/dataset.
———. n.d. "Frequently Asked Questions (FAQS)." http://www.data.gov/faq.
———. n.d. "Impact." http://www.data.gov/impact.
———. n.d. "Open Government." http://www.data.gov/open-gov.
Davies, Tim G., and Zainab Ashraf Bawa. 2012. "The Promises and Perils of Open Government Data (OGD)." *Journal of Community Informatics* 8, no. 2.
Dawes, Sharon S. 2010. "Stewardship and Usefulness: Policy Principles for Information-Based Transparency." *Government Information Quarterly* 27, no. 4: 377–83.
Dawes, Sharon S., and Natalie Helbig. 2010. "Information Strategies for Open Government: Challenges and Prospects for Deriving Public Value from Government Transparency." In *Electronic Government*, edited by M. A. Wimmer et al., 50–60. Berlin: Springer.
Dawes, Sharon S., Theresa A. Pardo, and Anthony M. Cresswell. 2004. "Designing Electronic Government Information Access Programs: A Holistic Approach." *Government Information Quarterly* 21, no. 1: 3–23.
Free Government Information. 2013. "When We Depend on Pointing instead of Collecting." http://freegovinfo.info/node/3900.
Gold, Anna. 2007. "Cyberinfrastructure, Data, and Librarians: Part 1." *D-Lib* 13, no. 9. http://www.dlib.org/dlib/september07/gold/09gold-pt1.html.
Gutmann, Myron, Kevin Schürer, Darrell Donakowski, and Hilary Beedham. 2004. "The Selection, Appraisal, and Retention of Social Science Data." *Data Science Journal* 3: 209–21. http://www.digitalpreservation.gov/partners/documents/data-pass_selection_data.pdf.

Hidalgo, Noel. 2014. "BetaNYC's Testimony on Open Data." http://blog.betanyc.org/post/101091748812/betanycs-testimony-to-ny-city-council-oversight.

Hidalgo, Noel, and Jennifer Baek. 2014. "The People's Roadmap to a Digital New York City." http://nycroadmap.us.

Inter-university Consortium for Political and Social Research (ICPSR). 2012. "Phase 3: Best Practice in Creating Research Data; Phase 6: Depositing Data." In *Guide to Social Science Data Preparation and Archiving: Best Practice throughout the Data Life Cycle* (5th ed.), 21–38. Ann Arbor, MI. http://www.icpsr.umich.edu/files/deposit/dataprep.pdf.

Janssen, Marijn, Yannis Charalabidis, and Anneke Zuiderwijk. 2012. "Benefits, Adoption Barriers and Myths of Open Data and Open Government." *Information Systems Management* 29, no. 4: 258–68.

Meijer, Albert. 2009. "Understanding Modern Transparency." *International Review of Administrative Sciences* 75, no. 2: 255–69.

New York City. 2012. *Local Law 11 of 2012—Publishing Open Data.* http://www1.nyc.gov/html/doitt/html/open/local_law_11_2012.shtml.

New York City Department of Information Technology & Telecommunications. 2012. *Open Data Policy and Technical Standards Manual.* http://www.nyc.gov/html/doitt/downloads/pdf/nyc_open_data_tsm.pdf.

NYC Open Data. n.d. "NYC Open Data Tumblr." http://nycopendata.tumblr.com.

———. 2014. "Dashboard." https://nycopendata.socrata.com/dashboard.

Office of Management and Budget. 2009. "Open Government Directive, M10-06." http://www.whitehouse.gov/omb/assets/memoranda_2010/m10-06.pdf.

———. 2013. "Open Data Policy—Managing Information as an Asset, M13-13." https://www.whitehouse.gov/sites/default/files/omb/memoranda/2013/m-13-13.pdf.

Partlo, Kristin. 2009/2010. "The Pedagogical Data Reference Interview." *IASSIST Quarterly* 33–34, nos. 4–1. http://www.iassistdata.org/iq/issue/33/4.

Project Open Data. n.d. "Slash Data Catalog Requirements." https://project-open-data.cio.gov/catalog.

———. 2014. "Project Open Metadata Schema v. 1.1." https://project-open-data.cio.gov/v1.1/schema.

Shields, Milo. 2004. "Information Literacy, Statistical Literacy, Data Literacy." *IASSIST Quarterly* 28, no. 2. http://www.iassistdata.org/iq/issue/28/2.

Sunlight Foundation. 2014. "Open Data Policy Guidelines." http://sunlightfoundation.com/opendataguidelines.

United States Census Bureau. 2015. "American Community Survey." http://www.census.gov/acs/www/data_documentation/documentation_main.

Weinstein, Jeremy, and Joshua Goldstein. 2012. "The Benefits of a Big Tent: Opening up Government in Developing Countries. A Response to Yu & Robinson's *The New Ambiguity of "Open Government."* UCLA Law Review Discourse* 60: 38–48.

White House. 2009. "Memorandum on Transparency and Open Government." http://edocket.access.gpo.gov/2009/pdf/E9-1777.pdf.

Witt, Michael, and Jake R. Carlson. 2007. "Conducting a Data Interview." *Libraries Research Publications.* Paper 81. http://docs.lib.purdue.edu/lib_research/81.

Yu, Harlan, and David G. Robinson. 2012. "The New Ambiguity of 'Open Government.'" *UCLA Law Review Discourse* 59: 178–208.

Chapter Fourteen

Your Metadata's Showing

Open Access and the Future of Bibliographic Control

Laura Krier and Kathryn Stine

Open access to scholarly literature is not a new concept in academic libraries. While the open access movement in publishing will cause sea changes in how libraries operate, open access has a safe home and a strong advocate in libraries. But there is another avenue of openness that has not been explored as thoroughly: open access to library metadata and the products of bibliographic control.

Since 2010, the buzz around open bibliographic metadata has been growing louder. Many libraries and collaborative library projects have tested the open bibliographic metadata waters, providing access to large sets of their catalog records or jumping in to develop policies that facilitate metadata sharing on a large scale. In 2011, OCLC Research and the University of Cambridge collaborated on a JISC-funded study to explore the value of releasing collection metadata openly (OCLC 2011). JISC and the Research Libraries UK (RLUK) announced their open metadata principles in 2011 (Resource Discovery Task Force 2011), the same year that the Open Knowledge Foundation published their "Principles on Open Bibliographic Data" (Coyle et al. 2011). In the past five years, libraries, including Harvard, the British Library, and the University of Michigan, have experimented with releasing their bibliographic metadata on the web. OCLC introduced linked open data in WorldCat, and the Library of Congress (LC) began work on the Bibliographic Framework Transition Initiative, or BIBFRAME, a project aimed at making library metadata open and usable on the web. And in 2014, the LibHub Initiative was established to help all libraries convert their data to BIBFRAME and "build a core set of library data on the Web" (LibHub 2014).

Other library organizations have been exploring new policies specifying how bibliographic metadata can be made available for sharing and reuse. Europeana specifies that all of its metadata are published free of restrictions under a Creative Commons CC0 Universal Public Domain license, though they request that all reuse include attribution. The Digital Public Library of America (DPLA) followed suit by making a strong statement on bibliographic metadata, asserting that metadata contributed to its discovery environment will be made available under a CC0 license. In 2015, the University of California Libraries approved a policy stipulating that metadata managed by its campus libraries be shared with as few restrictions as possible. Library cooperatives and vendors are also joining in, with OCLC clarifying in recent years the terms under which the metadata they make available can be reused. Even EBSCO has announced a policy for metadata sharing and collaboration, which they describe as the "first phase" of a policy designed to give discovery services easier access to EBSCO's abstracting and indexing metadata (EBSCO Information Services 2015).

Not all of these examples facilitate unfettered access to bibliographic metadata or provide unlimited opportunities for metadata reuse, but it is clear that libraries are moving toward more openness when it comes to sharing their metadata. Openly sharing bibliographic metadata seems to fall very much in line with libraries' long-held mission of providing access to information, which has contributed most recently to strong support from many of our professional organizations for open access and fair use. Beyond the seemingly natural alliance between libraries' promotion of open access to resources and their provision of open access to the metadata they have created, libraries should be interested in sharing bibliographic metadata if for no other reason than to remain relevant in an increasingly open web of discovery and access. But what does this move mean for libraries? How does this new work differ from the sharing of bibliographic metadata in which libraries are already engaged? To whom are we opening up this data and why? What are the implications of open bibliographic metadata, both for individual libraries and for the broader library ecosystem?

This chapter explores both the why and the how of open bibliographic metadata. We explore the purpose of library metadata, the history of its sharing, how it can best be used to facilitate resource discovery and access, and how we can encourage new business models and practices around new modes of provisioning and creating library metadata. We uncover some of the barriers to opening library metadata and some of the conflicts in our current practices and mindsets in order to explore solutions and advocate for metadata sharing as a means of supporting the core mission of libraries: making information accessible.

THE HISTORY OF OPEN METADATA IN LIBRARIES

For many people, the current clamor around open bibliographic metadata may seem like unnecessary hype. Libraries have always been advocates of openness, and we have been sharing metadata among ourselves since before the web and popular ideas of openness were even glimmers in the public eye. Our cooperative cataloging models and approaches to standardized authority data provide great evidence that librarians embrace the potential of network-level data sharing.

Libraries have in fact been engaged in sharing bibliographic metadata for more than a century. Charles C. Jewett first proposed the idea of a central cataloging institution in 1852; he suggested that the Smithsonian should create cataloging records to share with libraries around the country (Yee 2009, 68). Over the course of the following fifty years, the idea of a shared cataloging service was further developed. The American Library Association (ALA) was founded in 1876, with one of its purposes being the establishment of a shared cataloging infrastructure. Several shared cataloging experiments were undertaken in the latter half of the nineteenth century, and all of them failed before the Library of Congress instituted the first successful shared cataloging system in 1901. The Library of Congress distributed catalog cards to libraries in the United States for a small fee. The cards were prepared according to established cataloging rules, which were further codified in 1908 and "agreed upon by the American Library Association (ALA) and the British Library" (Yee 2009, 68). This set of catalog rules, the ALA rules, was the "first joint effort between American and British librarians in developing a cataloging code" (Chan 2007, 54), and it set the stage for the consensus-based model still in use today.

From the very beginning, the work of creating Library of Congress catalog records was done cooperatively. The Library of Congress enlisted other government libraries as well as research libraries and depository libraries to create catalog copy for their service. The National Union Catalog, also founded in the early 1900s, was established based on the shared cataloging of four research libraries that all agreed to exchange their printed cards with the Library of Congress (Yee 2009, 72). In order for this cooperative work to be successful, cataloging rules had to be agreed on by all parties involved in creating records. Over the course of the twentieth century, cataloging rules became more solidly established and more widely shared internationally. From the 1941 draft of the ALA catalog rules through the Library of Congress's "Rules for Descriptive Cataloging" to the "Anglo-American Cataloging Rules" and their revisions to the current "Resource Description and Access Rules," the process of establishing cataloging practices has become ever more collaborative and relies on greater consensus across increasingly broad communities.

The advent of computers pushed shared cataloging to new levels. The creation of machine-readable cataloging (MARC) in 1966 was a "watershed moment" for cooperative cataloging (Banush 2010, 247). MARC was designed as a record exchange format, making it easier for the Library of Congress and its partners to share catalog records. These records were still intended for printing and distributing catalog cards, not for displaying records online. Because the focus remained on the catalog card when MARC was being created, many fundamental precepts of cataloging went unquestioned. In 1968, as MARC was being developed and implemented at the Library of Congress, Grose and Line wrote a sharp critique of cataloging practice that was reprinted in the *ALA Bulletin* and cited widely. They raised a number of issues they believed needed to be investigated as this new format was being created, including "whether individual libraries need catalogs of their own stock," what functions catalogs should be serving, and how usable and accessible catalogs are to their intended users (Grose and Line 1968). Many of these same questions remain today, and we would argue that libraries are still asking them because our cataloging technologies were created without rethinking the possibilities offered by computers and networks. Other writers continued to critique the institutions developing and implementing MARC for not questioning and rethinking cataloging practices deeply enough. Philip Bryant in 1980 wrote that the "availability of the new technology did not really result in a radical enough re-evaluation of [the catalog's] role in the future" (Bryant 1980, 136). Geoffrey Allen in 1986 wrote that the "application of automation to cataloging has essentially ossified what had been burgeoning thinking about the function and structure of catalogs" (Allen 1986, 142).

Even while MARC was being developed for easier printing of catalog records, the advent of computer networks was changing the way cataloging was performed and shared. In 1972, the Ohio College Library Center (OCLC) introduced online delivery of MARC records, and other online cataloging utilities quickly followed, including the Research Libraries Information Network (RLIN) and the Washington Library Network (WLN) (Richmond 1981, 24). These networked systems made it easier for individual libraries to receive and contribute Library of Congress bibliographic data using a shared digital repository of catalog records. More and more libraries engaged in cooperative and shared cataloging by joining these bibliographic utilities. The development of the Z39.50 standard for searching and retrieving information across networks and its implementation by the Library of Congress and other libraries further established a culture where catalog records and the labor of cataloging are open and shareable. Using the Z39.50 standard, anyone can search and copy records offered by another library without asking permission or giving credit. These cooperative cataloging endeavors encouraged the expectation that cataloging labor was a public good, at least among libraries.

As cooperative cataloging proliferated, the need for even more standardized cataloging rules grew stronger. Organizations formed to regulate cataloging practices and ensure that records intended for sharing were created according to these standards. Cooperative Online Serials Program (CONSER) was formed in the early 1970s "to convert manual serials cataloging into machine-readable records" (Library of Congress 2015). The Program for Cooperative Cataloging (PCC), formed in 1995, intended to work collaboratively to develop standards, train catalogers, and work toward automation (Wolven 2008, 6). PCC brought other cooperative programs—the Name Authority Cooperative Program (NACO), the Subject Authority Cooperative Program (SACO), and the Bibliographic Record Cooperative Program (BIBCO)—together into a single organization. Eventually, CONSER was merged with PCC (Hirons and Schottlaender 1997, 37). The goal of these programs was to create records that could be shared widely across all bibliographic utilities according to common standards. Being a member of PCC and CONSER meant that you were accepting a level of responsibility to the community to create catalog records that could function like "interchangeable parts" in libraries, no matter the size, purpose, or practices of any individual library (Yee 2009, 74). PCC and CONSER records were expected to meet the high standards of the Library of Congress and the library community as a whole.

Despite these advances in collaborative practice, the growth of consensus-based standards, and the emphasis on participating in work toward a common good, there are significant challenges with cooperative cataloging. There has always been a tension between standardization and localization in cataloging. The standardization introduced by the Library of Congress and its partners in 1901 "made it possible for the smallest library in the country to have the same quality of cataloging as the largest research library" (Yee 2009, 74). However, it also makes maintaining local practices more challenging. In a shared and networked cataloging system, when cataloging rules or access headings change at the national or international level, small libraries may have no choice but to change with them (Allen 1986, 142).

In addition, the consensus-based model libraries have adopted for cataloging rules and standards means that change can take a very long time to implement and can be very political (White 1981, 317). Some have suggested, for example, that the success of the Library of Congress's BIB-FRAME project "will be measured in decades, not years" (Carpenter 2013, 25). The processes for change are "intricate and multi-layered," and they rely on people working in organizations with multiple and varied roles (Boehr et al. 2008, 27). White (1981) also points out that "it is a general management observation that consideration of fundamental change is slow to come when the process is controlled by individuals involved in detailed practice" (317). The detail-oriented nature of the work of cataloging and the consensus-based decision-making process mean that progress toward change can be slow indeed.

In some ways, the card-focused development of MARC and of networked cataloging was inevitable. In 1989, seventeen years after the birth of OCLC and twenty-three years after MARC, 37.7 percent of academic libraries were still using only a card catalog, and another 36.8 percent were using both a card catalog and an online catalog (Harris 1989, 8). Moving away from print catalogs has been a slow process, and online catalogs have not been adopted at a uniform pace. Having limited resources means that libraries are not always able to keep up with the pace of technological change, and in a shared cataloging environment, all must move at the pace of the slowest.

The combination of limited resources, resistance to change, the need for consensus in a political environment, and tension between standardization and localization mean that, almost fifty years after the implementation of MARC, we are still using a record structure that was intended for a print-based world, one that does not integrate well with current nonlibrary technologies or meet the needs of our users or libraries themselves. Because our systems for sharing lag behind the rest of the world's, our data are insulated and inaccessible to anyone outside of libraries.

WHY ARE LIBRARY METADATA DIFFICULT TO SHARE?

If we had no interest in connecting our data to data from outside libraries, it is possible that MARC could continue to work adequately as an exchange format for libraries. MARC has been serving its purpose for fifty years. Libraries have built robust networks for collaboratively creating and sharing bibliographic metadata. We have systems that work with MARC that meet most of our current needs, if we view our needs as largely limited to our own familiar library environments. New library systems with new capabilities are being developed—systems that work with centralized, shared sources of data—and these new systems are still using MARC. After all, library management systems use MARC only for exchanging data, not for storing it; data are most often stored in relational databases and only re-formed into MARC to export and share with other library systems.

We could begin to take advantage of some of the benefits of linking data across libraries simply by changing our content standards, the rules that govern how data are entered into MARC. In an analysis of the state of MARC, Martha Yee (2004) points out that "some commentators have identified problems as being associated with MARC 21 when they are actually associated with cataloging rules" (166) and that the capabilities for library catalogs are limited more by the software than by MARC itself. Her article points out some specific changes that could be made to MARC and to cataloging infrastructure, as well as rules that would enable MARC to achieve some of our goals. Cataloging rules, like Resource Description and Access (RDA), could specify the use of unique identifiers rather than text strings within existing MARC tags, and software could pull information from centralized sources of data, like the Library of Congress Name Authority File, making it easier to keep local data up-to-date with new forms of names, new publication information, and updated subject headings. We could do all of this without moving away from the MARC standard. However, as an exchange format, MARC still poses some challenges and introduces limitations for libraries. There are high costs to using an exclusive and complex data format.

Today, libraries' options for library management software are limited, and they grow narrower every year as companies are merged and acquired. Even as existing companies create new types of software, we must recognize that the market is and will remain a small one because of our unique data standards. Because MARC is such a narrowly used format, few people in the world are knowledgeable about it or interested in working with it. New companies are unlikely to want to build software for libraries because that software would be limited to such a small market; it could not be extended even to other information-related organizations like publishers and booksellers. Because the market is narrow, costs are high. The end result is that libraries are stuck in a limited market where incentives for innovation are small and where developers cannot take advantage of new technologies that are built around more widely adopted data standards.

Our existing systems, bespoke to support library-specific functions, have not necessarily been built with needs for sharing and openness outside of library communities in mind. When these systems were being built, there was little perceived need for data sharing. Once data is imported into library management systems, options for exporting it again may be limited. Data may only be exportable in CSV format, or the specific fields and elements that are exportable may not be flexible. In many cases, libraries are unsure of how to go about exporting data from their systems for sharing with other systems. When working on large-scale projects involving MARC record contributions from many different libraries, we have been surprised by how many systems and metadata experts in these libraries were unsure of how to get MARC records out of their library management systems. Often, librarians were unclear about procedures and uncertain of how to specify export formats. It was not always obvious in which fields various metadata elements would be exported. Although the MARC format is sometimes considered overspecified, library systems do not always create records according to the established MARC standards, and catalogers do not always conform their entries to established rules or local best practices.

That being said, creating MARC records requires extensive training and practice. MARC is a complicated data format. It was created before the birth of relational databases, so the relationships that are a core component of bibliographic data are captured instead in a structure of strings and coded punctuation. In order to create valid MARC records, one must know that the value in one field has an impact on the potential values or even the meaning of another, that strings must be encoded precisely in order to capture the relationships between bibliographic and authority records, and that certain fields require controlled vocabularies or specific types of encoded data. There are so many rules, updates to rules, interpretations of rules, and other details that must be attended to that cataloging is not for the faint of heart. One librarian writes, "The sheer magnitude of text encompassed by codes, rule interpretations, and technical bulletins (not including classification schedules and subject heading lists which also grow and change) can be daunting" (Steinhagen, Hanson, and Moynahan 2007, 276).

As the world of published information has grown more varied, MARC has only grown more complex. New formats, new types of media, and entirely new types of resources mean that the MARC format and its associated content standards are continually being updated. These changes introduce complexity and increase the cost of creating cataloging records. By the late 1980s, there was sufficient concern in libraries about these increasing costs that library administrators were actively searching for solutions. The level of training and the amount of time required for adequate, standards-based original cataloging is expensive. Many libraries have cut costs by creating less-precise cataloging records and eliminating highly trained staff (Harris 1989). The difficulty and expense of cataloging prohibits many libraries from contributing their cataloging labor to shared systems, increasing the burden on organizations like LC and the small number of PCC member libraries. LC has called for greater participation in cooperative cataloging, but this seems doomed to fail as long as our cataloging practices remain complex and challenging (Boehr et al. 2008, 16).

The monetary costs of our complex metadata format should not be our only cause for concern. Sticking with the MARC format also means that our data are not interoperable with data from other sectors. We now live in a world where the possibilities for sharing data are much greater than they were when we started using MARC. The web has opened up possibilities for sharing beyond the library community. Libraries could increase efficiencies by incorporating metadata created by partner organizations, and our metadata could find many potential uses beyond the virtual walls of libraries.

In the first decade of the twenty-first century, the development of web services, service-oriented architecture, and application programming interfaces (APIs) created new opportunities for data exchange and changed the face of the web. These new technologies used distributed systems and open Internet standards "to enable general-purpose interoperability among existing technologies and extensibility to future purposes and architectures" (Papazoglou 2008, 22). This new paradigm of computing shifted the focus of web application development from web pages created for human readers to web data created for machines. In order for web services to work, applications had to be built "in a neutral manner that is independent of the underlying platform, the operating system, and the programming language. . . . This allows services . . . to interact with each other in a uniform and universal manner" (Papazoglou 2008, 11). Open data standards were necessary for these new services to provide value. Early web services relied on XML, but over time, JSON, a simplified format for data exchange, became the more widely used option. JSON is both machine and human readable, and its relatively simple specification makes it easier for developers across the spectrum to share and retrieve data from web services. While these formats and services were being built, library systems were not evolving and adapting to them but were instead continuing to rely on MARC and closed systems. Moving to more modern data exchange technologies would make it easier for libraries to enhance and supplement their cataloging efforts with data from publishers, vendors, and public networks.

In addition to incorporating data into our own systems, new technologies would make it easier for other communities to use our data. Many people outside of libraries are interested in bibliographic data; making our rich data available to them could encourage innovation and creative solutions to common problems in research, discovery, and software development. Enabling our bibliographic data to be used on the open web could allow libraries to connect with new communities. It could spur the development of new tools that enhance the use of libraries by facilitating online searching that connects library resources to other well-established discovery environments, by providing tools to better understand trends made visible through data analysis, and by contributing to existing and unforeseen applications and systems that create and share knowledge beyond library walls. The data we have created over the last century could help researchers to make new connections about knowledge generation and relationships between people, topics, and places. Library metadata can be mined and analyzed in much the same way that OCRed full text has been in order to understand publishing trends and the evolution of domains of study over time. Connecting our data to other data on the web can help users to discover resources of which they might not otherwise have been aware.

More immediately significant for libraries are the potential discovery and access benefits. Moving to a metadata format that is more compatible with web-based technologies could improve discovery of library resources by making them crawlable and discoverable via search engines. Over time, we have seen the use of our catalogs and local search tools shrink. A report published by Ithaka in 2008 reveals that the "library is increasingly dis-intermediated from [faculties'] actual search process" (Housewright and Schonfeld 2008, 30). Researchers and users have many other options for finding information. Libraries have tried many tactics to bring users back to the catalog, but no matter what we do, from building participatory tools to adding fancy discovery layers, we cannot change that trajectory. Rather than trying to coerce users back to our tools, it is time to consider putting our information in places where our users are already searching: on the open web.

    None of these connections and new avenues for discovery will be possible if we continue to create metadata in formats that are only shared among and understood by libraries. Grose and Line (1968) write, "We do not want our catalogs to stand as the largest monuments in an extensive cemetery of dead books" (742). If we do not reconsider how and why we are creating bibliographic metadata, however, that is exactly what our catalogs will become. It is time for bibliographic metadata to be activated as the public good that they were intended to be.

WHAT ARE BIBLIOGRAPHIC METADATA FOR?

One question that must be addressed relates to the purpose of library metadata. Why do we spend so much time, money, and attention on bibliographic metadata? And more important, are the purposes today the same as the purposes that held when our current standards and forms were created? The Library of Congress Working Group on the Future of Bibliographic Control states that bibliographic control, or bibliographic metadata, is used "to facilitate discovery, management, identification, and access." They further point out that "our current approaches to it are direct descendants of the librarianship of the 19th century" (Boehr et al. 2008, 6).

    From the beginnings of modern bibliographic control until the late twentieth century, libraries were crucial discovery conduits for researchers and casual readers alike. There were not many avenues for finding out about new books and articles published in a particular field. The discovery function of library metadata, as well as abstracting and indexing (A&I) services, was crucial. Libraries and A&I services worked in tandem to lay bare the information landscape for users. Researchers used subject access terms to find things they did not know about and might want to access, and they used author access terms to find all the works by a particular author. They turned to libraries to find out about new research, discover what had been published on a particular subject in the past, and learn about new books by their favorite authors. In short, libraries were key links in the information chain. Facilitating discovery was a foundational function of libraries and our metadata.

As the web grew, so did alternate avenues for discovering new ideas, new research, and new resources. One no longer needed to visit the library or a bookstore to find out whether a new book had been published in one's field. Keyword searching began to take the place of subject term access, and websites could easily tell a searcher about every book that an author had written. These days, web search engines are used far more than library databases, and full-text searching of article databases is preferred over the limited access offered by A&I services. Users find themselves on media, publisher, and scholarly society websites more often than library websites when they start their searches on the web. Users can now discover, if not readily access, the information they need almost anywhere online. And as these alternative sources of discovery grow, libraries are no longer the central discovery hubs.

Given these changes in discovery patterns among users, the main purposes of metadata for these users are changing. We must recognize that "most users now conduct their research in multiple discovery environments: search engines, online booksellers, course management systems, specialized databases, library catalogs, and more" (Boehr et al. 2008, 30). Descriptive metadata are created and re-created in all of these information environments, and there is an increasing number of players in this field. The descriptive metadata that libraries have traditionally created may not be as important these days as the metadata we manage that facilitates access. A researcher needs to be able to go from finding out that a particular resource exists, wherever she might find that information, to finding out how she can get it from the library. The descriptive functions of our metadata may therefore be less important in this landscape than the access and holdings functions, which should be our focus.

Descriptive metadata also currently serve an identification purpose. In our current systems, descriptive metadata are necessary to help users know whether the items they found in the library are the same items they discovered online. If we shift our focus away from discovery and toward identification and access, then the types of data we create might be very different. Using common identifiers and links rather than text strings may provide more seamless access in a machine-mediated discovery environment. Holdings metadata will also become crucial, as users need to know whether an item is available to them and how and where they can get access. In a networked information environment, "consistency of description within any single environment, such as the library catalog, is becoming less significant than the ability to make connections between environments" (Boehr et al. 2008, 10). It will become important in a more distributed environment that we use shared vocabularies and identifiers to help users go from discovery to identification to access.

This is not to say that libraries do not need descriptive metadata but rather that this metadata may be put to new purposes and different ends. For example, we will always need to keep some descriptive local data about our collections for management purposes. We need purchasing metadata—how much a resource costs, what funds were spent on it, when it was purchased and received, whether a patron specifically requested it. In order to manage our collections, we need to know how often a particular item is used or accessed, what subject areas it falls into, what its long-term value is within the context of the subject literature. And in order to see our collection as a whole, we need to be able to pull together all the formats and avenues for access to a particular item, whether it is available in print, electronically, or both. We need to be able to see all access points at once, know that they do in fact point to the same intellectual content, and manage our collections across formats in ways that are more seamless. Libraries still need a great deal of descriptive metadata.

The descriptive functions of metadata are also significant for finding and contextualizing rare and unique resources. One benefit to shifting labor away from reproduction of duplicate descriptive metadata for commonly held items is that a greater focus can be placed on unique resources. This focus on unique resources was a key strategic goal highlighted in the Library of Congress's 2008 Working Group on the Future of Bibliographic Control report. Many libraries hold materials that could be of great value to researchers around the world if they were not impossible to find because of cataloging backlogs and the lack of interoperability between library systems, web systems, and special collections systems. Moving to more modern, web-based methods of data formatting and exchange could make it easier to bring special collections materials together with other library materials in searches and make them more discoverable by scholars on the web. The less redundant cataloging work we must do for our regular collections, the more time and energy is freed up to make our special collections accessible.

There are many reasons to move away from the closed MARC format to something more in line with a modern web environment, including improving our own workflows, introducing efficiencies, and enhancing discovery of our resources. The rich, complex, and detailed descriptions that librarians have created may be used in ways we never imagined if we can begin to make them available in more widely used, non-library-specific formats.

METADATA POLICY AND OPENNESS

A crucial area that must be addressed as we move to new data models and means for sharing bibliographic metadata is the question of metadata ownership. Many organizations have already begun to address this problem by issuing statements or establishing policies indicating the conditions under which the metadata shared from their systems can be used; these include OCLC, the Digital Public Library of America, Research Libraries UK, and individual libraries and library consortia, such as Harvard, the University of Michigan, the British Library, the University of California, and many more. Indeed, the extent to which bibliographic metadata can be "owned" can be called into question—because the vast majority of such data is factual information, which is not generally subject to copyright, the concept of ownership may be inappropriate in this context. Additionally, much of the work that has gone into cataloging has arguably been conducted with the goal of establishing access to information as a public good, bringing into further relief questions about whether bibliographic metadata can or should be owned.

Many libraries that have recently released their metadata have done so using what is called a CC0 license, a Creative Commons license stating that the licensed work has been dedicated to the public domain. All rights to metadata released under a CC0 license have been waived, and the data are free and open for all kinds of use and reuse, including commercial reuse. Metadata aggregators like Europeana and the DPLA have data exchange agreements with contributing partners stating that the metadata contributed to them will be released and shared without any copyright restrictions. The DPLA says in its "Policy Statement on Metadata" that it "believes that the vast majority of metadata as defined herein is not subject to copyright protection" and that it asserts no rights over its database of contributed metadata (Digital Public Library of America n.d.).

Other organizations releasing metadata, including OCLC, have released it under an ODC Attribution (ODC-BY) license; this license stipulates that data are free for sharing and reuse, but that they must be attributed to the originator. While tracing metadata provenance may well be valuable in certain situations, attribution requirements for metadata can cause complications when attempting to reuse metadata from a variety of sources. One of the biggest issues is sometimes referred to as attribution stacking; when using data from a variety of sources, which in turn have also used data from a variety of sources, it can be extremely difficult to track attribution across the chain of reuse. Another complication can arise in determining what precisely needs to be attributed—the entire record or its individual data elements. In either case, there are currently limited technical options for formatting and tracking metadata provenance. Ultimately, tracing the origins of bibliographic metadata in a given library system could prove tedious, if not impossible, and metadata originating from organizations requiring attribution may be difficult to release openly.

Ideally, as a community, we might consider bibliographic metadata to be in the public domain already, even without specifying a CC0 license. However, the fact that licenses are being applied and attribution requirements seem to connote ownership (if only to a degree) means that the unimpeded sharing and use of bibliographic metadata is not yet a given. The issue of attribution raises some big questions for libraries. Is it even possible to own bibliographic metadata? If so, who owns the cataloging records we are using? Does the creation of bibliographic metadata by public entities presume that it is a public good? Should bibliographic metadata be considered a public good regardless of its origin? If so, how should we reevaluate our participation in business models that monetize bibliographic metadata?

In some instances, the question of ownership of data has been set aside. For example, on the BIBFRAME mailing list, the developers of BIBFRAME have declared that questions of licensing metadata are out of scope of the BIBFRAME project (Ford 2013). Ignoring the question of data ownership means that some of the key questions about library workflows and business models are not being addressed. Not addressing these questions at the outset of a major rethinking of our data models means we are not taking the opportunity to think through how these new models will work for both libraries and their users; in the end, we may end up losing more than we gain if we do not approach these questions thoughtfully from the start.

There are numerous stakeholders in our current practices of creating and sharing bibliographic metadata: Library of Congress; OCLC; vendors; cooperative cataloging organizations; and, of course, individual libraries and catalogers. Looking at new models for openly sharing bibliographic metadata might threaten some of these organizations and force them to change their business practices. These new models may also affect perceptions of job security and threaten the status quo for cataloging workflows. With major shifts in how bibliographic metadata are created and shared beginning to emerge, it is important for us to revisit cataloging workflows and be aware of where bibliographic metadata originate. Organizations like OCLC have spent decades building services that are largely based on the cooperative labor of their members. What does it mean when an organization releases data created by large numbers of its members and then requires attribution of that data? If attribution is required, then might there also be an expectation that metadata provenance be tracked beyond the collaborative to the institution, if not the cataloger, who contributed it in the first place? And what about companies like book distributors that provide bibliographic records for a fee? Much of their metadata also comes from public organizations like the Library of Congress and the National Library of Medicine. How will business models need to change when increasing amounts of bibliographic metadata are becoming more readily available, accessible, and reusable on the open web?

These are not easy questions, but they must be addressed as libraries begin to move toward open publication of bibliographic metadata. As our data models and the technical infrastructure supporting them change, our policies, concepts of ownership, ideas about what can and should be monetized in the library environment, and our very beliefs about who is qualified to create descriptive bibliographic metadata must change with them.

WHERE ARE WE NOW?

Libraries have begun to recognize that our current practices are preventing us from being part of the modern data ecosystem. We need to meet users where they are and facilitate discovery and traversal of content in ways that are useful and unimpeded by the artificial silos that many of our catalogs have become. Libraries around the world have begun to release bibliographic metadata in a variety of ways, crafting new policies about the use of their bibliographic metadata. However, simply making metadata available or clarifying that they can be reused does not necessarily make them useful.

In 2008, the Library of Congress released the report of the Working Group on the Future of Bibliographic Control. This report emphasizes the need for a "collaborative, decentralized, international in scope, and Web-based" model for bibliographic metadata (Boehr et al. 2008, 1) and discusses the need for metadata that are more machine actionable than our existing MARC format. The Library of Congress's drive toward a new bibliographic future was motivated in part by a lack of resources. Greater collaboration, both within and outside libraries, was perceived as necessary if the library was to continue meeting its charge. But the incentive driving the Working Group's explorations was not just economic. They wanted a "broad definition of bibliographic control that embraces all library materials, a diverse community of users, and a multiplicity of venues where information is sought" (Boehr et al. 2008, 10). The Working Group recognized that the discovery environment was changing. Where libraries had once been the sole location for discovery of information, new venues far beyond the library catalog were coming into existence, and libraries would be better served by getting their information out into those venues.

This 2008 report marked the first stirrings of what would become BIB-FRAME. The Library of Congress announced BIBFRAME in late 2012 and contracted with the firm Zepheira to begin exploring a linked, data-based model for bibliographic metadata. The intention of BIBFRAME is to "provide a foundation for the future of bibliographic description, both on the web, and in the broader networked world" (Library of Congress n.d.). From the start, the model is being designed to be interoperable with other communities rather than focused solely on the needs of libraries.

At around the same time, OCLC announced its own foray into linked data. Working closely with the schema.org vocabulary for structured data on the web, OCLC began to embed Resource Description Framework in Attributes (RDFa, a set of HTML extensions used for describing data) into its

WorldCat database, making this data freely available for indexing by web search engines. The Schema Bib Extend Community Group was formed to introduce key bibliographic concepts into the schema.org vocabulary, a web-based vocabulary that has been implemented by millions of websites and sponsored by several major search engines.

These two endeavors were considered to be "complementary" in a 2013 paper published by OCLC, which speculates that "key concepts for discovery" might best be expressed using the schema.org vocabulary "while the details required for curation and management are expressed in BIBFRAME" (Godby 2013, 9). It remains to be seen what the relationship between these two models might be, but work continues on both projects in parallel.

In late 2012, the National Information Standards Organization (NISO) secured funding from the Andrew W. Mellon Foundation "to bring together as diverse a set of stakeholders as possible to build agreement around a common development path for bibliographic information exchange," acknowledging the multiple approaches being taken in building a new bibliographic infrastructure (Carpenter 2013, 24). The impetus for the Bibliographic Roadmap Initiative, as this project was called, was not just to open pathways for communication among the different library organizations working in this space but also to "address the usability of [bibliographic] data from the perspectives of the broader communities," those other groups who produce, use, and want to use bibliographic metadata (Carpenter 2013, 25).

In addition to these large-scale conceptual projects looking at the overall data model for bibliographic control, libraries around the world are moving ahead and releasing their existing metadata, using different data models and approaches to openness. Harvard released 12 million bibliographic records in 2012, declaring it "one of many steps toward sharing the vital cultural knowledge held by libraries with all" (Duke 2012). The British Library released the British National Bibliography as part of the UK government's principle of opening public data (Deliot 2014). Some larger-scale projects have been undertaken to aggregate and release library metadata across multiple libraries. The DPLA, Europeana, and Open Library are just three examples of organizations committed to providing library data openly. There is an increasing recognition by libraries that our bibliographic metadata is valuable to others outside of libraries. However, all methods of releasing bibliographic data are not created equal when it comes to making that data discoverable and reusable.

Librarians and library organizations have explored three primary models for releasing bibliographic metadata: posting a file of MARC records on a website for free download and reuse; providing access to metadata via an API; and creating an RDF version of metadata and making them available via data dump, content negotiation, or querying. All of these models have their strengths and weaknesses, and all of them have implications for library practices and policies, both individually and collectively.

The easiest and most immediately accessible model for releasing metadata is simply to post a file of MARC records for download. This was the approach taken by Ghent University in Belgium, the Harvard Libraries, the University of Cambridge Libraries, and the University of Michigan. This method has little overhead: no need to decide on a new data model or transform records from their existing formats. A small amount of data cleanup might be necessary, but otherwise, records can simply be exported and posted online as they are.

Unfortunately, this method of data release offers few of the benefits of open metadata. The data are still difficult for those outside the library community to use. A file of MARC records does not make individual items and holdings more discoverable online. The file itself is not searchable until it is downloaded and imported into a system that can read MARC records. As discussed previously, MARC does not work with existing web data-exchange standards and practices, so the benefit of being better connected on the web is lost. A file of MARC records could be usable by other libraries or by library vendors, but it is not useful to communities outside of libraries.

Additionally, this approach raises questions about the ownership of MARC records. Few library catalogs consist entirely of originally cataloged records; most of our MARC repositories contain data from a wide variety of sources, including other libraries, publishers, and vendors. Some significant licensing investigation may need to be done to determine whether a library has the right to share its MARC metadata online. The release of MARC files can place a flag in the sand for an organization regarding many of the metadata policy questions raised earlier. When organizations like Harvard release MARC records, offering no attribution for records that may have originated in other libraries and no explicit authorship information, it reinforces the notion that metadata are not authored and are not necessarily owned by any single library. Individual records within a set may indicate provenance, but as a whole, there is no claim of ownership or copyright and no request that attribution be given if records are repurposed. Other libraries may release MARC records under less-open policies requesting attribution, which would seem to argue for very different standards around ownership and authorship of cataloging labor. Posting MARC records online for reuse makes a claim about ownership, whether one is intended or not.

Another way to make bibliographic data available is via an API. An API specifies the routines, structures, and data formats that are implemented in a particular application, allowing other machines to interact with it. To be made available via API, data must be stored in a database or other accessible system on a web server. If a library management system does not make its data available via API, then data must be extracted, transformed from

MARC, and stored in another database application. Programming and web services expertise is needed, which many libraries do not have. Significantly more overhead may be required, compared to simply posting MARC records online. But APIs provide benefits that MARC dumps do not. Data are made available for access by web developers and other users in ways that are more common in the current web environment. Some organizations providing data via API include the Open Library, LibraryThing, OCLC, and Google Book Search. Library system vendors like Ex Libris and Innovative Interfaces have been developing APIs to make bibliographic and patron data available to other systems on the web, though this development has come along more slowly than expected. There are some drawbacks to releasing data via an API. The data cannot be crawled by search engines or accessed using generic browsers, and there are no standard mechanisms to tie together data retrieved from different APIs. It is not always easy to ascertain the data schema being used in data pulled via API. Data that were originally structured using MARC may be incredibly difficult to access and use in ways that are readily understandable to nonlibrary communities. For example, unless data are transformed before being made available, a third-party user would need to understand cataloging rules in order to know how punctuation is used to separate different data elements. Making data available via an API is a good step forward, but additional steps would need to be taken by both the library and third parties to increase discoverability of the data and make them useable.

The third method that has been explored for releasing bibliographic metadata uses the Resource Description Framework (RDF) data model, a standard model for data interchange on the web. It is specifically intended to represent resources and is a flexible model that ensures interoperability. RDF is not a format; it is a model for describing objects that can be created in a number of different formats, including XML, JSON, and N-Triples. RDF describes things using simple subject-predicate-object statements and enables linking of various entities on the web using Uniform Resource Identifiers, or URIs. The British Library and Europeana employ RDF data models to release their bibliographic metadata, and it is the model being explored by BIBFRAME and by OCLC through the use of schema.org vocabularies.

RDF is all about establishing relationships. The Library of Congress recognizes that "bibliographic control is increasingly a matter of managing relationships," and RDF can serve this function much more easily than MARC (Boehr et al. 2008). Each RDF statement establishes a relationship between the subject and the object of the statement. In the RDF model, the subject is the thing being described—for example, a book. Each thing receives a unique identifier. A variety of vocabularies can then be employed to make statements about the thing. One might say that the book has a creator, using a data element drawn from the Dublin Core vocabulary, and a creation date, using the BIBFRAME vocabulary, and a publication event, using the British Library Terms vocabulary. There is no requirement to use only one vocabulary when describing a subject, and each of these statements establishes a relationship—between the book and the creator, the book and the date, and the book and the publisher.

In RDF, the vocabulary terms themselves also have unique URIs, and representations of the terms can be retrieved via Internet protocols like HTTP. Vocabulary terms drawn from various schemas can be related to each other (using, for example, the Web Ontology Language "sameAs" property) to facilitate better exchange between them. Over the past few years, many commonly used controlled vocabularies, including the Library of Congress Subject Headings, the Library of Congress Name Authority File, the Dublin Core, and the Getty Vocabularies, have been released as RDF, with each term assigned a URI, providing ample opportunities for traversing shared concepts across metadata originating from different sources.

RDF data about bibliographic resources can be released in a variety of ways. Some libraries, including the British Library and the Deutsche Nationalbibliothek, have posted files of RDF data online for download. RDF data can also be made available for querying via the SPARQL query language or as machine-processable data via content negotiation. Content negotiation allows an HTTP client (like a browser or a software application) to specify in which format data should be received, for example as HTML or RDF. A piece of software can request data in an RDF format and process that data in designated ways, while the same data can be viewed by a person via a web browser in a familiar HTML format. OCLC has made WorldCat data available via content negotiation, as well as via data dump. You can see these different formats by viewing the same record in WorldCat in both HTML and RDF. The HTML page for Nicholas Christopher's *A Trip to the Stars* can be viewed at www.worldcat.org/oclc/42863278. At the bottom of the page is a section labeled "Linked Data" that shows an HTML representation of the linked data OCLC has created for this book. Some browsers show a representation of the RDF data in JSON, RDF/XML, or Turtle format. You can see the RDF/XML version at www.worldcat.org/oclc/42863278.rdf and the Turtle version at experiment.worldcat.org/oclc/42863278.ttl. These alternate versions are available for machines to process, as well as for humans to view.

RDF data models require a complete rethinking of how bibliographic metadata are created and used. We are accustomed to thinking about data in terms of records: discrete, self-contained units of information that describe a particular object using a defined set of descriptive elements. RDF breaks apart the idea of the record in favor of an open-world information model where an infinite number of statements can be made about a particular object using an infinite number of vocabularies and data schemas. This open-world model is what makes RDF interoperable; data can be shared across communities without the need to adopt an entire set of rules and practices. Every statement that is made about an object can stand on its own and be disassociated from the remaining statements.

This model can, however, be uncomfortable for librarians. We are used to operating in a closed-world context. The very fact that we refer to our cataloging practices as bibliographic control tells you the degree to which authority, strict management, and codified rules drive our work. Relinquishing that control in favor of an environment where anyone can say anything about anything seems to go against all the principles upon which our cataloging practices have been based.

But moving in this direction does not require us to completely give up the methods of bibliographic control we have employed in the past; in fact, this data model can amplify and enhance these methods. For example, the Library of Congress Subject Headings vocabulary we have used since 1898 to describe the resources in our collections is already being converted into an RDF vocabulary. Subject terms have been given URIs that can be accessed in a variety of formats via HTTP at id.loc.gov. We can continue to use existing subject headings and other controlled vocabularies in an RDF framework, and when designing software to access metadata created by others, we can specify that we only want statements with Library of Congress values as either the subject, predicate, or object of the statement. Opening metadata via RDF does not mean giving up control of how data are created or deemed authoritative.

Releasing data using RDF is one of the best ways to enable reuse and discovery of our bibliographic metadata. RDF data are flexible and can easily be used and understood by other machines that access data on the web. RDF data are interoperable because they do not rely on a single schema for reuse. Releasing data as RDF can, however, require a great deal of up-front work, including deciding on vocabularies for resource description, creating URIs for resources, transforming records, and building web infrastructures to enable data access. The British Library discusses some of the challenges they faced when publishing the British National Bibliography as linked data in a 2014 paper (Deliot 2014). They describe their approach, some of the modeling challenges, problems with moving from MARC, and more, but they also make it clear that, despite the challenges, this is a very doable project. The road to an RDF-based bibliographic future is a long one. Over the past century of creating bibliographic metadata, libraries have built up much of the collaborative infrastructure necessary to make this future feasible. We can rely on this collaborative infrastructure to solve some of the biggest challenges in moving to this environment.

WHAT MIGHT AN OPEN METADATA FUTURE LOOK LIKE?

Linked-data-based metadata systems can have significant implications for libraries and the organizations that support and rely on them. An open metadata ecosystem will potentially debilitate those industries that rely on selling bibliographic metadata to libraries. Organizations like OCLC that rely on the competitive benefit of their vast stores of bibliographic data will have to make drastic changes in the ways they operate. Libraries will need to make significant changes to workflows and technological infrastructures. The ways in which we think about the metadata we create will also need to shift drastically in an open-world information environment.

If it is true that discovery is moving away from library systems and onto the open web, then it is crucial that we get our data on and into the web. But is it useful for every library to publish identical sets of data? Our current infrastructure requires a great deal of duplication of data across libraries: For every copy of *Anna Karenina* in libraries around the world, a nearly identical record is created detailing identical descriptive information. Just moving this duplicative information into web-friendly forms to be crawled by search engines will not necessarily contribute to greater discovery. We already know that the manifestation-level metadata we have been creating cause confusion for our users when they find multiple records for what, on the surface, looks to be the same thing. A new data model would make it easier for patrons to identify resources across formats and editions online and see that a copy of a particular work that interests them can be found in their local libraries. Libraries would be able to focus attention on publishing holdings metadata on the web rather than copying descriptive information into local databases and would be freed up to create descriptive metadata for unique items that could in turn be shared more widely.

We can envision an open, shared metadata ecosystem where libraries are more readily able to tap into available and authoritative core metadata statements about given works, expressions, entities, and subjects but can also make locally relevant statements that lead users to their holdings and provide the unique contextual data they need. To do so, we first have to make a connection between the thing the user has found and the thing we have. This is where linking to metadata already out on the web can be useful. How do search engines work? Search companies like Google keep their relevance ranking algorithms under close wraps, but we do know that they calculate relevance, in part, based on the number of sites linking to a particular site. So, for example, if websites around the world were to create crawlable links to OCLC's WorldCat records for resources, OCLC's WorldCat site would gain prominence in search results. If OCLC WorldCat becomes more prominent in search results, then a user searching for a particular title of a book, for example, might begin to see WorldCat links appearing near the top of search engine results, the same way Amazon results appear now. Even more benefi-cial would be for search engines to take advantage of the semantic markup used to generate links and pull information from library sites into, for example, the Knowledge Graph box that appears in certain search results on Google.

If we were to publish holdings data as links from our systems to a centralized bibliographic database, then location-aware browsers could potentially use those links to find a library close to a searcher, use the RDF data to find out that the item is held, and pull that information forward for a searcher. The set of subject-predicate-object statements in figure 14.1, while not using vocabularies or URIs, demonstrates the potentially short chain of links that would be needed to connect a user to an item in a nearby library.

What is important for providing access is not necessarily providing a lot of descriptive information about a resource. It is identifying that a resource is the same thing—at the work, expression, or manifestation level—that the user wants and that it is available to him.

In this way, our access points still matter—but not perhaps in the way we are used to. In a web environment, access points are not used for human searching but for machine searching, and because of this, they need to be

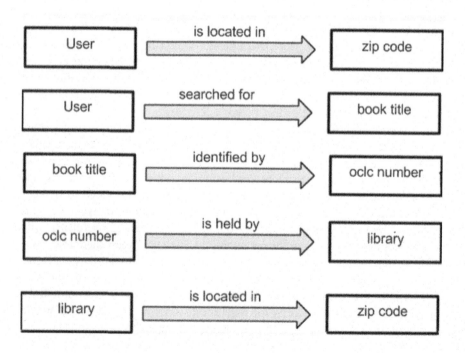

Figure 14.1. Potential links from users to library items.

machine usable. URIs will work better as access points than the text strings we currently use because the web works by linking. Our users do not necessarily need to know the specific subject terms we use, as long as the applications they use can help them traverse the data to find new materials by way of linked identifiers. This new use for access points demonstrates that we need to change how we think about access points, from text strings maintained separately in library catalogs around the world to centralized data maintained in only a few places and linked by libraries in order to facilitate discovery and access.

We need centralized bodies to create canonical identifiers for works, as well as for our existing access points, like subject terms and names. We already have a lot of these organizational bodies; all of the collaborative infrastructure we have built up over the last fifty years has put us ahead of the game. We have an enormous corpus of bibliographic metadata in OCLC and the Library of Congress, including not just bibliographic descriptions but also authority datasets identifying people, places, and things. These metadata already have identifiers and are already, in many ways, used as canonical sources of data. We might no longer need to replicate these data in each individual library but instead be able to contribute our data to centralized stores. Some organizations, including Ex Libris, are already creating systems based on the concept of shared central data stores. Alma's Community Zone of bibliographic records operates using this concept of linking. We already have a system by which authorized users create valid and validated data within these corpora in our Programs from Cooperative Cataloging organizations. Many of our accepted and widely used controlled vocabularies have already been transformed into RDF and given unique URIs. These URIs are maintained by bodies we have long trusted to maintain our collective subject and name authority knowledge. These organizations are well suited to maintain this knowledge in an RDF-based, web-accessible form.

Of course, there remains the question raised by the Library of Congress in 2008: How do we make these institutions sustainable? The Library of Congress does not receive funding for bibliographic services, and there are not enough members contributing cataloging copy to keep up with the amount of work required. The ability to reuse data from outside organizations like publishers and vendors could go a long way toward reducing the cataloging burden, but attention will still need to be paid to our collaborative infrastructure to ensure that it remains viable. In some instances, membership-based organizations may need to rethink their funding models. OCLC maintains its database through membership fees, which allow members to search and download OCLC data into their own systems as well as create new records in the WorldCat database. This kind of funding model would be less feasible in an open cataloging environment. OCLC has already begun shifting to new business models by using its vast database as the foundation for a new type of library management system and selling services based on the database. It is possible—if they can make their services side a reliable source of revenue and if they can build services that rely not on the database as the sole competitive advantage but instead on features, support, and stability—that their database could be offered up as a public good. Other organizations can consider similar models, shifting from providing cataloging records to providing other services libraries need.

We have raised many questions here stemming from the attendant benefits and challenges that libraries face in opening their bibliographic metadata. Opening bibliographic metadata provides libraries an opportunity to make good on the substantial, ongoing work they have put into describing resources for discovery and access. Making bibliographic metadata an open resource fits squarely within libraries' obligation to users, but it will also require thoughtful consideration and resources to ensure that what is shared openly is also useable and useful beyond library walls and systems. Sharing bibliographic metadata as an open resource, even if not outright considering it a public good, ultimately has the potential to provide a return on the investment libraries have long made in establishing shared workflows, reciprocating cataloging expertise, and making use of authority data. Given such potential, libraries can both produce and consume linked open metadata as a means of making bibliographic control more efficient and cost effective and facilitating user discovery of and access to resources. By establishing paths for users to make connections between and across resources, traversing the relationships between them that we seed and encourage when we share RDF-based statements, we can better locate library resources within a broader network of discovery, making them better contextualized and more widely accessible than ever before.

REFERENCES

Allen, Geoffrey G. 1986. "Change in the Catalog in the Context of Library Management." *Journal of Academic Librarianship* 12, no. 3:141–43.

Banush, David. 2010. "Cooperative Cataloging at the Intersection of Tradition and Transformation: Possible Futures for the Program for Cooperative Cataloging." *Cataloging & Classification Quarterly* 48, nos. 2–3: 247–57.

Boehr, Diane, Daniel Clancy, John Latham, Clifford Lynch, and Judith Nadler. 2008. "On the Record: Report of the Library of Congress Working Group on the Future of Bibliographic Control." http://www.loc.gov/bibliographic-future/news/lcwg-ontherecord-jan08-final.pdf.

Bryant, Philip. 1980. "Progress in Documentation: The Catalogue." *Journal of Documentation* 36, no. 2: 133–63.

Carpenter, Todd A. 2013. "Drafting a Road Map for the Bibliographic Future." *Computers in Libraries* 33, no. 3: 23–26.

Chan, Lois Mai. 2007. *Cataloging and Classification: An Introduction.* 3rd ed. Lanham, MD: Scarecrow Press.

Coyle, Karen, Mark MacGillivray, Peter Murray-Rust, Ben O'Steen, Jim Pitman, Adrian Pohl, Rufus Pollock, and William Waites. 2011. "Principles on Open Bibliographic Data." *Open Bibliography and Open Bibliographic Data*. http://openbiblio.net/principles.

Deliot, Corine. 2014. "Publishing the British National Bibliography as Linked Open Data." *Catalogue & Index* 174: 13–18.

Digital Public Library of America. n.d. "Policy Statement on Metadata." http://dp.la/info/about/policies.

Duke, Judy. 2012. "Harvard Releases Library Catalog Records." *Advanced Technology Libraries* 41, no. 5: 1–11.

EBSCO Information Services. 2015. "EBSCO Policy for Metadata Sharing and Collaboration with Discovery Service Vendors." https://www.ebscohost.com/metadata-sharing-policy.

Ford, Kevin. 2013. Communication to the BIBFRAME mailing list.

Godby, Carol Jean. 2013. "The Relationship between BIBFRAME and OCLC's Linked-Data Model of Bibliographic Description: A Working Paper." Dublin, Ohio. http://oclc.org/content/dam/research/publications/library/2013/2013-05.pdf.

Grose, Michael W., and Maurice B. Line. 1968. "On the Construction and Care of White Elephants." *ALA Bulletin* 62, no. 6: 741–47.

Harris, George. 1989. "Cataloging Costs, Issues, and Trends." *Library Quarterly: Information, Community, Policy* 59, no. 1: 1–21.

Hirons, Jean, and Brian Schottlaender. 1997. "The CONSER/PCC Evolution." *Cataloging & Classification Quarterly* 24, nos. 3–4: 37–46.

Housewright, Ross, and Roger Schonfeld. 2008. "Ithaka's 2006 Studies of Key Stakeholders in the Digital Transformation in Higher Education." *Higher Education* 33. doi:10.1080/08841240802100345.

LibHub. 2014. "LibHub FAQ." http://www.libhub.org/faq.

Library of Congress. n.d. "Bibliographic Framework Initiative." http://www.loc.gov/bibframe.

———. 2015. "What Is CONSER?" http://www.loc.gov/aba/pcc/conser/about/aboutcn1.html.

OCLC. 2011. "University of Cambridge and OCLC Research Collaboration on Open Metadata." http://www.oclc.org/research/news/2011/02-25.html#.VeXsHIFpcSg.mendeley.

Papazoglou, Michael. 2008. *Web Services: Principles and Technology*. Harlow, UK: Pearson Prentice Hall.

Resource Discovery Task Force. 2011. "Announcing Our Open Metadata Principles." http://discovery.ac.uk/profiles/principlesprofile.

Richmond, Phyllis A. 1981. "Library Automation in the United States of America." *Program* 15, no. 1: 24–37.

Steinhagen, Elizabeth N., Mary Ellen Hanson, and Sharon A. Moynahan. 2007. "Quo Vadis, Cataloging?" *Cataloging & Classification Quarterly* 44, nos. 3–4: 271–80.

White, Herb. 1981. "We Do, Do, Do, and Don't Know Why: Cataloging Practices Cry Out for Re-Examination." *American Libraries* 12, no. 6: 317–18.

Wolven, Robert. 2008. "In Search of a New Model." *Library Journal* 133: 6–9.

Yee, Martha M. 2004. "New Perspectives on the Shared Cataloging Environment and a MARC 21 Shopping List." *Library Resources & Technical Services* 48, no. 3: 165.

———. 2009. "'Wholly Visionary': The American Library Association, the Library of Congress, and the Card Distribution Program." *Library Resources & Technical Services* 53, no. 2: 68–78.

Chapter Fifteen

DocSouth Data

Open Access Data for Digital Humanities

Stewart Varner

On March 1, 2002, the University of North Carolina Libraries held an event to mark the addition of the one-thousandth item into Documenting the American South, the library's award-winning digital collection of southern history and culture. University librarian Joe Hewitt (2002) notes that the collection had been receiving thousands of hits per day but cautions that he had "personally always been suspicious of the huge numbers you get from counting 'hits'" (para. 5). For this reason, the library had developed software that "measured only interaction with the texts themselves" (Hewitt 2002, para. 6). Based on this method, while the collection had 136,549 page views, it had only 6,465 interactions that Hewitt considers to be the digital equivalent of a book check-out. While this is obviously a much smaller number, it is still an extraordinary usage statistic. For Hewitt (2002), the number confirms that the "*Doc South* reader seems to correlate more closely with our idea of a more reflective traditional library user. I take that as a positive sign—that a carefully selected body of electronic texts will be used as such when made available on the Web" (para. 11).

Today, UNC Library's locally produced digital collections have grown far beyond Documenting the American South. More than 1.2 million items have been scanned, cataloged, and made available online through UNC's digital asset management system. These collections contain high-quality digital representations and descriptive metadata for primary source material, including postcards, correspondence, business records, photographs, and diaries. They have been designed to re-create virtually, as closely as possible, the experience of browsing and researching in the physical archive and are accessed by thousands of researchers from around the world who are able to conduct in-depth research without traveling to Chapel Hill.

Though, as Hewitt notes, these collections have been extremely success-ful at virtualizing certain kinds of research for a "traditional library user," some scholars are beginning to explore tools and techniques that are not so traditional. Text mining in the humanities is emerging as a method of study-ing not just one digitized item but rather the patterns that emerge across entire collections. Unfortunately, the digital collections at UNC were not designed to facilitate this kind of research. UNC is not alone in this situation; most digitization projects, both those led by libraries and those led by com-mercial vendors, have been designed with traditional research rather than text mining in mind.

Working with vendors to find a way to text mine their commercial prod-ucts is currently a complex and often baffling process, but libraries may find that they are in a position to make their own homegrown digitized collections easy to study with emerging tools and techniques. In the summer of 2014, UNC Libraries did just this when it launched DocSouth Data, which provides easy access to the data behind the original Documenting the American South digital collections in formats that are easily processed by common text-min-ing tools. The library was very excited about this project because it presented a way to make open data even more open. Provided with access to these collections in simple and flexible formats, users can remix and reuse the collections more easily than ever before. In order to encourage exactly this type of activity, the library chose to make DocSouth Data available open access and to apply a Creative Commons CC BY license to the project.

This chapter describes the DocSouth Data project, how it fits into the ongoing and evolving story of UNC's digital collections, and how it engages with the library's interests in open access and digital humanities. It explains how the project was designed and provides some examples of both the kind of research that is currently taking advantage of the collections and what kinds of projects may emerge in the future.

A NOTE ON VOCABULARY

This chapter deals with several concepts that are relatively new or in the process of evolving. As a result, the definitions of some terms are not quite settled in the official discourse. For purposes of clarity, the following is a brief explanation of how certain terms are used in this chapter.

Digital Humanities

This label is used to describe the broad range of scholarly activity that results when humanistic inquiry and technology engage with one another. Within this field, one may find humanists—or researchers engaged in humanistic inquiry—who are engaged in online publishing, academic social networking, data visualization, historical GIS projects, classroom technology, and digital pedagogy, as well as humanistic critiques of technology. Using computers to look for meaning by seeking out characteristics, rules, and patterns in digital text is also classified as digital humanities, and it is this flavor of digital humanities with which this chapter is most directly engaged.

Text Mining

Digital humanities projects that use computers to look for meaning by seeking out characteristics, rules, and patterns in digital text can themselves employ a wide range of methods. These methods include but are by no means limited to topic modeling, named entity recognition, sentiment analysis, and word frequency mapping. For some scholars, this work is the original digital humanities, while others use the older term *humanities computing* to describe it.[1] As libraries are increasingly being asked to respond to interest in these kinds of techniques (in the humanities as well as in the sciences), the term *text and data mining*, or simply *TDM*, has begun to emerge in the library and information science literature. This chapter uses the general term *text mining* in order to highlight the fact that all of the items currently available in DocSouth Data are text files and to avoid unnecessary confusion with computational research methods that work with non-text-based data, including numeric data and image data.

Digital Collection

Depending on your role in—and relationship to—the library, the term *digital collection* can mean a variety of things, including:

- collections of digitized and born digital material purchased from vendors,
- locally curated and produced collections of digitized and born digital material based on archival holdings or special collections,
- institutional repositories, and
- the library's collection of e-books.

This chapter only deals with the first two kinds of digital collections and distinguishes between them by referring to *licensed digital collections* and *homegrown digital collections*.

Open Access

Open access, as it is currently understood, was born in Budapest in 2002 and describes a way of making scholarly work available in digital form, online and free of charge and free of most restrictions. The early open access movement focused on journal articles and research data mainly in the sciences, but it has since expanded to include other kinds of scholarship from across the academy. This chapter focuses on digital collections of historical primary source material rather than secondary sources. These library collections are made freely available online with no copyright restrictions and thus conform to the definition of *open access* put forth by Peter Suber (2012), one of the signers of the Budapest Open Access Initiative: "literature that is digital, online, free of charge, and free of most copyright and licensing restrictions" (4).

THE DATA TURN IN THE HUMANITIES

Technology has been integrated (or has encroached) into seemingly every aspect of contemporary life, and humanities research is no different. In the *New Yorker*, Brown University professor of comparative literature Elias Muhanna (2015) writes, "In the past decade, digital scholarship has gone from being a quirky corner of the humanities to a mainstream phenomenon, restructuring funding landscapes and pushing tenure committees to develop new protocols for accrediting digital projects" (para. 12). As digital tools and techniques are adopted by a diversifying group of scholars, it is likely that the use of technology in humanities research will continue to expand for two reasons. First, training opportunities designed to teach humanists how to use text-mining tools are becoming more common. For example, the University of Victoria has hosted the Digital Humanities Summer Institute (DHSI) since 2001, and the University of Maryland (now in partnership with Indiana University–Purdue University Indianapolis) has organized the Humanities Intensive Learning and Teaching (HILT) since 2014. Second, as tools become more powerful and easier to use, more scholars will be encouraged to at least experiment with digital humanities techniques, if not fully embrace them.

The use of computers to conduct humanities research has roots in the 1940s, when Roberto Busa, an Italian Jesuit priest, partnered with IBM to create a digital index of the works of St. Thomas Aquinas (Gold 2012, xiv). More recently, corpus linguistics has used computers to seek out quantitative similarities and differences in large collections of machine-readable texts (corpora). Nevertheless, quantitative techniques are still viewed with skepticism by many humanists, and such fields as literature studies continue to rely heavily on "close reading" methods for careful analysis of texts. Interest in digital techniques among literature scholars took an important step in 2000, when Stanford literary scholar Franco Moretti published an article titled "Conjectures in World Literature" in the *New Left Review*. In this article, Moretti is concerned about how few books literary scholars use to make claims about entire national literatures. Due to the careful attention close reading requires, literary studies often depend on a small canon of texts. Canon formation is a notoriously political process that necessarily leaves out more voices than it can include. Playing off of the concept of "close reading," Moretti calls for "distant reading," a kind of analysis that uses computers to look for distinguishing patterns across a broad digital corpus. Distant reading allows researchers to consider far more texts than they could reasonably master in the course of a career. Moretti (2000) argues that distant reading can be more inclusive and create a more accurate representation of national literatures, "allow[ing] you to focus on units that are much smaller or much larger than the text: devices, themes, tropes—or genres and systems" (para. 10).

A team of researchers at Northeastern University led by Ryan Cordell uses a kind of distant reading to answer an entirely different kind of question. Curious about what stories were frequently reprinted in nineteenth-century American newspapers, the team developed an algorithm that is able to detect duplicate (or near-duplicate) pieces in digitized newspapers from the Library of Congress's Chronicling America collection. The algorithm was developed to look for reprints across 41,829 issues of 132 different newspapers while taking into account the fact that articles were frequently edited for length and enhanced with locally produced content (Smith, Cordell, and Mullen 2015). The algorithm is designed to account for discrepancies arising from the uncorrected OCR output from the digitization process. In an article titled "Reprinting, Circulation, and the Network Author in Antebellum Newspapers" published in *American Literary History*, Cordell (2015) argues that the results produced by the algorithm "can be considered, in essence, a substantial set of enumerative bibliographies of popular newspaper literature" (422). Based on these findings, Cordell (2015) was able to develop a "model of authorship that is communal rather than individual, distributed rather than centralized" (418).

Lauren Klein, assistant professor in the School of Literature, Media, and Communication at Georgia Tech, is engaged in yet another kind of text mining that uses data-visualization techniques to reveal hidden significance in Thomas Jefferson's correspondences. Using the subscription-based *Papers of Thomas Jefferson, Digital Edition*, Klein's research finds that James Hemings, Sally Hemings's brother and Jefferson's enslaved cook, was an extremely important figure in the second president's life, despite the fact that the two men never exchanged letters (a fact that would otherwise render Hemings seemingly absent from the archive). Klein's work did not depend on close readings of individual letters but rather on searching the metadata of the collections for instances where archivists had noted mentions of James Hemings and using that information to create network graphs that "render[ed] visible the archival silences" (Klein 2013, 665). While Klein's work is very different from Moretti's and Cordell's, it provides yet another example of research that is only possible when the digital archive can be approached as a source of data itself and not just a virtual representation of physical items.

As the kinds of text-mining projects, tools, and techniques continue to expand along with the number of scholars who are able and eager to use them, libraries have an opportunity to get involved in this exciting new work. Regardless of technique or tool, most text-mining projects begin by gathering a significant quantity of data in the form machine-readable text. Unfortunately, most digital collections, both homegrown and licensed from vendors, do not make it easy for scholars to build these minable corpora.

TEXT ANALYSIS AND DIGITAL COLLECTIONS

Cordell notes that the team at Northeastern focused on the newspapers in the Chronicling America collection "in large part because its text data is openly available for computational use" (Smith, Cordell, and Mullen 2015, para. 1). The scarcity of data that are ready to use in text-mining projects is a common problem for aspiring text miners. Stephen Robertson (2014), director of the Roy Rosenzweig Center for History and New Media at George Mason University, notes that "part of the explanation for why more historians have not undertaken text mining and topic modeling projects lies in the limited availability of machine readable texts" (para. 7). While some of this scarcity, Robertson explains, is due to the fact that many of the sources preferred by historians are handwritten manuscripts that are difficult to transcribe, it is also the case that the creators of these collections—whether libraries, archives, or commercial vendors—simply have not designed their projects for text mining. This problem is not limited to just a few scholars. Harriet Green and Angela Courtney (2014) surveyed humanities scholars and found that the "ability to mix and reuse digital materials" is one of their primary unmet needs (698).

Many digital collections are not meeting this need because they are built to reproduce traditional archival work as closely as possible by providing researchers access to single-page images. While a digital image is incredibly useful for some researchers, text-mining tools usually depend on corpora of machine-readable texts. Unfortunately, most digital collections do not make it easy for researchers to create such corpora. For one thing, as Robertson suggests, optical character recognition (OCR) software cannot automate the transcription of collections that are based on handwritten documents, and the time involved in hand-transcribing such collections is generally cost prohibitive. Additionally, even if OCR output exists for a collection, it is likely to be uncorrected. While current OCR software is surprisingly effective, with many tools claiming to achieve 99 percent accuracy (Holley 2009), these rates can vary wildly depending on the quality of the source material. A commercial book published in the twentieth century that is in good condition can usually be OCRed with relative ease. Conversely, the OCR transcription of an eighteenth-century newspaper with tiny print, tight columns, and signs of wear and tear will be significantly less accurate.

In addition to problems with content, because most collections are organized around providing access to one page at a time, it is prohibitively inconvenient for most users to create a corpus of machine-readable texts that is large enough to constitute an interesting base dataset. Even if researchers have a way to automate the creation of a minable corpus from a collection of text files or even PDFs, they will still need some way to acquire all of the files in the first place. Due to technical complexity, legal issues, and the sheer size of many digital collections, acquiring all of the requisite files, regardless of format, might be difficult. Bulk downloading can put significant strain on network hardware, and depending on the size of the corpus, the servers where the data live may suffer performance issues from too much activity if the load is not effectively managed. Users may also find that they need to procure additional storage space to cope with massive datasets.

Commercial vendors may have additional concerns as well. One of their major concerns is that allowing bulk downloads could enable users to illegally (or legally, depending on the content) create derivative products that would compete with their own (Smit and van der Graaf 2012, 37). Another problem is that commercial vendors seem to be unsure about how to create a marketable product around data for text mining. Until they have a better sense of how text mining is going to work, they do not want to foreclose possible revenue streams that have not yet even been identified. Furthermore, if a vendor has established a license agreement with a third party to provide access to material they do not own, then that license may prevent them from allowing bulk downloads whether they want to or not.

Despite all the questions and uncertainty, there have been some signs that libraries and vendors are trying to figure out how to answer researcher requests for minable data. For years, it has been common for vendors to suggest that such requests be handled on a case-by-case basis if text mining is not covered by existing licenses. However, this strategy has yielded mixed results. Paul Fyfe at North Carolina State University successfully negotiated a text-mining agreement with Gale in 2014 to do work on their historical databases (Schaffhauser 2014). Conversely, Lawrence Hunter, a professor in the School of Medicine at the University of Colorado, Aurora, reports that, even though he received a text-mining agreement from Wiley, they failed to provide the technical assistance needed to transfer the relevant files (Williams et al. 2014, 10). Max Haeussler, a biologist at the University of California, Santa Cruz, maintains a website to keep track of publisher responses to requests for text-mining rights (http://text.soe.ucsc.edu/progress. html). The records show that receiving permission—or even a reply—is not the norm (Van Noorden 2012, 135). Even in cases where researchers have successfully obtained permission to text-mine and received the files they requested, they are not always convinced that the process is adequate. While she was a postdoctoral fellow in zoology at the University of British Columbia, Heather Piwowar negotiated a trailblazing agreement with Elsevier to mine their subscription content. Despite the fact that Elsevier provided access to most of the data she had requested, Piwowar argues that the process of receiving permission was too time consuming and prioritized the publisher's business interests over the needs of science. In an interview with the Scholarly Publishing and Academic Resources Coalition (SPARC), Piwowar said, "[I]t's just not scalable to have every researcher or every library negotiate the terms of access" (SPARC n.d., para. 25).

In an attempt to be more responsive to user needs while simultaneously guarding against the perceived business threats and technical challenges associated with allowing users to download large swaths of digital text, some vendors have built text-mining tools on top of their collections. JSTOR's Data for Research (DFR) tool is an early example of this strategy. Launched in 2008, DFR gives users access to more than 7 million journal articles, as well as a collection of nineteenth-century British pamphlets. Users can filter search results on a variety of facets and perform some basic text-mining tasks, such as generating word counts and rudimentary topic modeling. In 2014, Gale launched a similar tool that provides access to most of its collections, including its popular newspapers database, for purposes of text mining. Gale provides a term-frequency tool like JSTOR's, as well as a "term cluster" tool that visualizes which words are frequently associated with given search terms. These vendor-supplied text-mining tools solve problems for both vendors and researchers.

By using these tools, vendors are able to maintain control of their collections, and researchers do not need to find a way to collect and store their research data, which can be a significant problem with sizable datasets. However, this solution limits researchers to the collections of a single vendor at a time, making it impossible to create corpora out of a variety of collections. For example, a researcher would find it very difficult, if not impossible, to look for patterns in a corpus of newspapers consisting of individual titles spread across numerous databases controlled by a variety of licenses held by multiple vendors. This situation is unfortunate because, as Ann Okerson (2013) points out, "TDM [text and data mining] can get some of its most exciting results by bringing together very disparate and different bodies of data" (4). Furthermore, vendor-supplied tools tend to be limited to simple techniques, such as word counts, and they allow for few, if any, modifications. Such limitations are likely to frustrate researchers with sophisticated text-mining skills and advanced research questions.

The uncertainty and inefficiency of negotiating text-mining rights on a case-by-case basis and the limitations of vendor-supplied text mining tools have led librarians and researchers to advocate for adding language into license agreements with vendors before signing them, establishing text mining as a potential and legitimate use of the collection. This approach is consistent with the statement on TDM released by the International Federation of Library Associations and Institutions (IFLA 2013), which states, "TDM simply employs computers to 'read' material and extract facts one already has the right as a human to read and extract facts from" (para. 10). The California Digital Library has developed a general agreement that is often used as a model for other libraries that want to insert language about text-mining rights into license agreements. Their agreement simply states that "authorized users may use the licensed material to perform and engage in text mining/data mining activities for legitimate academic research and other educational purposes" (California Digital Library 2011, 3). However, libraries and their researchers must depend on vendors to create a means for accessing the material. As a result, establishing the right to text mine without creating a mechanism to actually get the text leaves a significant question about what researchers will be able to do, regardless of what they are technically allowed to do.

DOCUMENTING THE AMERICAN SOUTH TO DOCSOUTH DATA

While navigating the rapidly and constantly changing landscape of text-mining access to licensed digital collections will likely remain complex for some time, it may be relatively easy for libraries to allow this kind of access to collections they have produced themselves. In response to growing interest in digital humanities generally and text mining specifically, the University of North Carolina at Chapel Hill decided to do exactly that in the summer of 2014 with their long-running and extremely popular Documenting the American South collection. This project raised few of the concerns that can slow down or stop similar projects. Because the vast majority of items that made up the collections are out of copyright, there were few licensing concerns around making these collections available for text mining. Furthermore, unlike commercial vendors, the UNC Library does not view its collections as potential revenue streams. As a result, they were happy apply a CC BY license and allow bulk downloading.

Documenting the American South began as a digitization project in 1996. The first version of the project consisted of just six popular slave narratives held in the Southern Historical Collection at UNC's Wilson Library. The narratives were transcribed by hand, marked up according to the Text Encoding Initiative (TEI), and made freely available online. The following year, the library received a National Digital Library award of $75,000 to expand the collection to include the "voices of women, African-Americans, enlisted men, laborers and Native Americans" (Smith 1997, para. 1). As the project grew, those original items came under the title "First Person Narratives of the American South," and over the next ten years, sixteen other collections joined it under the Documenting the American South umbrella. These collections include "The Church in the Southern Black Community," "The Library of Southern Literature," and "The North American Slave Narratives." The early collections are particularly text heavy, but later collections, such as "Driving through Time: The Digital Blue Ridge Parkway in North Carolina" and "North Carolina Maps," contain multimedia materials as well.

From the beginning, the goal of Documenting the American South was to take advantage of the democratizing potential of emerging information technology, especially the World Wide Web, to create greater access to some of the library's unique and important collections. Commenting on "The North American Slave Narratives" and "The Church in the Southern Black Community" in the essay "Digital Humanities and the Study of Race and Ethnicity," Stephanie Browner (2011) notes that "of the more than 500 texts available, fewer than half would typically be available in print at a major research university library, and as few as 10 or 20 are available to the general reading public via bookstores and public libraries" (213). Natalia Smith, digitization project librarian at UNC and coordinator of the Documenting the American South project, is a publisher-turned-librarian who saw the collections as digital publications. Scholarly introductions written by authoritative scholars were included with each collection, and they were presented as critical digital editions published by the University of North Carolina Library.

The project has been extremely popular. Between 2009 and 2015,[2] the website has received nearly 22 million unique visitors. However, like most digital collections, Documenting the American South was not originally designed to facilitate text mining. DocSouth Data sought to change that by making it easy for researchers to get the machine-readable data behind some of those digital collections. Conceived as an enhancement to the original Documenting the American South and designed with common text-mining tools in mind, DocSouth Data allows users to download four of the library's most popular collections as XML/TEI files and as plain-text files. The four collections chosen to be included in DocSouth Data are

- the Church in the Southern Black Community,
- First-Person Narratives of the American South,
- the Library of Southern Literature, and
- North American Slave Narratives.

These collections were chosen because they are particularly attractive candidates for text mining. All were part of the first wave of digitization projects, and they are almost exclusively text based, which makes them particularly well suited for text mining. Furthermore, because graduate students transcribed each of these collections by hand, the text is extremely reliable, and users do not have to worry about errors as they would with uncorrected, OCR-software-created text. Additionally, each of these collections has a level of internal unity that instantly suggests research questions. This is particularly true of the North American Slave Narrative collection, which is a nearly complete collection of all known narratives of this kind.

Trevor Owens of the Institute of Museum and Library Services reports that researchers who want to use text mining will "try, as quickly as possible, to download data to take it away to use it in their own tools on their own systems." Therefore, unless a dataset is too large to be easily exported, Owens (2015) suggests that a "data dump" is the "best first step for systems to support this kind of scholarly use" (para. 6). Technically, users of the Documenting the American South collections have always been able to download copies of the XML/TEI files through a link at the top of the page for each item. However, in order to get these files, researchers who were interested in performing text mining on the collections would need to open each of the items individually, save the XML or HTML files for each item, combine these files into one corpus file, and strip out any extraneous markup before analysis could begin. While not impossible, this process is certainly tedious. DocSouth Data simply performs these steps for users and organizes all of the files into one zip file that researchers can download with just one click. The zip file contains four documents of technical information and one folder called "data," which contains a "Read Me" file, a table of contents file, and two folders; one folder contains each item in the collection as a plain-text file, and the other folder contains each item in the collection as an XML/TEI file. The plain-text files are for researchers who simply want to look for patterns across entire collections or extract potentially meaningful information. The XML/TEI files were included for researchers who want to use the metadata captured in the TEI header or to exploit some of the structural tags to isolate specific parts of a text.

The process for building the project was relatively straightforward. No new content had to be created because an XML/TEI file for each item already existed. These are the files that sit behind what users see when they look at an item in Documenting the American South. The folders of plain-text files were created by a programmer in the library who wrote a script to strip out all of the XML/TEI tags from the original files. This format is valuable for some distant-reading projects that look for patterns across large corpora using word counts; for these types of projects, XML/TEI tags can be distracting.

Uses

DocSouth Data was designed to be easy to use with a range of common text-analysis tools. Among the tools the developers had in mind was Voyant, a "web-based text reading and analysis environment" (Voyant Tools Documentation n.d.). Created by Stéfan Sinclair of McGill University and Geoffrey Rockwell of the University of Alberta, Voyant creates a variety of visualizations based on word counts. The most basic visualization in Voyant is called Cirrus, which produces word clouds. While these simple visualizations are notoriously problematic, they can be a quick and easy way for users to start to get a sense of word usage. Voyant's word clouds are enhanced to allow users to see exactly how many times a word is used in a text by hovering over that word in the cloud.

To get a more focused look at word usage, researchers can use the Word Trends function. This visualization illustrates how frequently a word is used throughout a text by dividing the text into ten equal parts and plotting the number of time the word appears in each section. The resulting line graph can help researchers get a sense of how important a word might be at different points in the narrative. Users of Voyant can also generate a concordance of a digital text with the Keyword in Context tool. With this tool, a keyword search displays the phrases immediately before and after each occurrence of the search term. This is crucial for understanding what uses of a word is being used at different points in the text.

Voyant allows users to perform very quick, relatively simple functions that are probably best used at the beginning of a research project. Jim Casey, a PhD candidate in English at the University of Delaware, used the data to do some more complex analysis on the North American Slave Narrative Collection. Using the publisher location information in the XML/TEI headers, Casey was able to create a map of where the narratives had been published. Additionally, Casey used the Topic Modeling Tool (https://code.google.com/p/topic-modeling-tool) to help identify clusters of words in the slave narrative collections that often occur together and thus suggest potential topics of interest. Using these "topics," Casey was able to use a second tool called Gephi to create network graphs that illustrate clusters of authors who cover similar ideas. Casey (2014b) argues that this process revealed the "versatile genius" of writer William Wells Brown, whose narrative touches on a much wider variety of themes than any of the others texts in the collection (para. 6).

DocSouth Data and Open Access

An important part of Documenting the American South's story is the evolution of the copyright statements attached to its collections. When the original collection launched in 1996, it simply stated that "all rights [were] reserved" by the library. Part of the explanation for this simple statement is that these were the very early days of the web, and there were still many questions about how copyright should be handled. More substantially, the library at the University of North Carolina saw Documenting the American South as library-based publishing. In an article published in *College and Research Libraries* in 1996, Natalia Smith and UNC associate professor of library and information science Helen Tibbo argue that the then-emerging world wide web was creating an important opportunity for libraries to become publishers. "With today's new digitizing technologies," Smith and Tibbo (1996) write, "libraries . . . may come to the aid of humanistic scholarship by assuming a publishing role as well as their traditional archival function" (536). Smith and the library thus saw this project as analogous to a book, albeit a free and digital book.

In September 2004, the copyright statement on Documenting the American South was revised. In place of a simple "all rights reserved," the site began including a link to an expanded "Copyright/Usage Statement" on the footer of each page. This statement makes it clear that "[m]aterial on this site may be quoted or reproduced for personal and educational purposes without prior permission, provided appropriate credit is given" and reflects a desire to highlight the openness of the collection rather than its status as property of the university. It is important to note that this change came at a time when mass digitization projects were ramping up in many libraries, including at the University of North Carolina.[3] These initiatives were not generally conceived as publishing ventures, as Documenting the American South had been when it began, but rather as access and, to a lesser extent, preservation initiatives.[4] The idea was to create digital surrogates to provide access to unique items without requiring travel or excessive handling. Additionally, the library gained digital surrogates of the items that could be used as back-up copies.

In November 2006, the language in the "Copyright/Usage Statement" was streamlined, though its meaning was not significantly altered; the main difference in language was a more distinct separation between "private and educational" use and "commercial" use. Notably, the statement continued to claim that commercial use was prohibited without the library's permission; because the vast majority of items in Documenting the American South have been in the public domain since the project launched, the library did not have the right to prohibit the use of these texts for commercial purposes.

When DocSouth Data was in development, the library decided that an entirely new "Copyright/Usage Statement" would be needed. The new statement reads:

> Unless otherwise noted, the texts, encoding, and metadata available in DocSouth Data are made available for use under the terms of a Creative Commons

Attribution License (CC BY 4.0: http://creativecommons.org/licenses/by/4.0).
Users are free to copy, share, adapt, and re-publish any of the content in
DocSouth Data as long as they credit the University Library at the University
of North Carolina at Chapel Hill for making this material available.

This statement clarifies that the data are, in the most expansive meaning of
the term, open access. The collections in DocSouth Data are small enough
that they can be distributed via zip file, with no need for the "processing
fees" accompanying reproduction requests from some other collections. The
library decided to adopt a Creative Commons license that merely requests
proper attribution for items in these collections (CC BY) but places no other
real restrictions on use. Closely connected to (though not mandated by) the
open access movement, CC BY licenses free researchers to take the data,
process it however they see fit, and remix it into new kinds of work (Snijder
2015, 1).

It is important that the idea for DocSouth Data came at a time when the
library was heavily involved in campus conversations about open access.
Though open access had been an important issue in academia for several
years, in the summer of 2014, the University of North Carolina at Chapel Hill
began a yearlong process to develop an open access policy for the faculty.
Library staff were extremely active in the task force charged with leading
this conversation on campus, and in May 2015, the faculty council unani-
mously voted to adopt the policy (Library Staff 2015).

UNC's open access policy, like most conversations about open access, is
primarily concerned with scholarly articles; this focus can be traced back to
the Budapest statement of 2002, which called for a "new generation of journals committed to open access" (Chan et al. 2002). However, conversations
about open access need not be limited to articles and journals. Peter Suber,
faculty fellow at the Berkman Center for Internet and Society at Harvard and
signatory to the Budapest statement, argues that, for something to be considered open access, it must meet four criteria:

1. It is digital.
2. It is online.
3. It is free of charge.
4. It is free of most copyright and licensing restrictions.

Though it did not claim the label at the time, Documenting the American
South meets each of Suber's criteria and has been open access since it
launched in 1996. Specifically, it meets the requirements for gratis open
access. In *Open Access and the Humanities*, Martin Eve (2014) describes
gratis open access as "material that is free to read but that comes with no
lowering of permission barriers" (11–12). DocSouth Data goes one step fur-

ther by removing both technical and permission restrictions on the collection, thus meeting the requirements for *libre* Open Access, which Eve (2014) characterizes as the "removal of permission barriers" (12). Describing "Open Access for Machines," Suber (2012) writes, "The ultimate promise of OA is to provide free online data for software acting as the antennae, prosthetic eyeballs, research assistants, and personal librarians of all serious researchers" (122). Though this description sounds futuristic, digital humanists armed with text-mining tools are able to do just that with DocSouth Data.

Next Steps

DocSouth Data was designed to be an experimental first step in determining the needs of researchers, particularly humanities researchers, for text mining digital collections. While the resource itself seems generally useful, there are numerous ways to expand, enhance, and improve the collection. One of the first challenges to address is the problem of discoverability. Currently, users can download the collections from DocSouth Data in one of two ways. First, there is a page within the Documenting the American South site that explains what DocSouth Data is and gives visitors the links for downloading the collections. Second, visitors can download the data directly from the main page of each of the four individual collections that are currently part of DocSouth Data. Unfortunately, finding those links generally requires users to know where to look. Even though the major search engines index the sites, it is not clear exactly how potential users would go about searching for them.

This problem is somewhat mitigated by the fact that Documenting the American South enjoys relatively widespread recognition, and many scholars in related fields already know where to find it. Scholars accustomed to accessing the collections for traditional research may notice DocSouth Data as a recent enhancement and be pleasantly surprised and emboldened to experiment with text mining. However, this group is only a subset of potential users, and it is unclear how others might discover the resource. For example, there may be computer scientists who are primarily interested in text mining as a technique and simply need large amounts of machine-readable text with which to experiment. There may also be humanists who have a research question they want to answer with text mining but who are unsure about where to find appropriate data. DocSouth Data would of course be perfect for such research, but it is unlikely that a researcher who is not already familiar with the collections would stumble upon it.

These obstacles should not be surprising, as discovery is notoriously difficult for digital collections. Add to that the fact that text mining is a relatively new technique for humanists, and it is understandable that finding collections like DocSouth Data would be a challenge. Most of the literature addressing discovery issues with digital collections suggests leveraging social media and popular resources like Flickr and Wikipedia.[5] While the library is actively pursuing such strategies for all of its digital collections, it is geared toward reaching a general audience and not the more specialized audience that would find DocSouth Data useful. One way to address this challenge is to establish repositories of machine-readable data that could serve as "one stop shops" for researchers who are (or want to be) working on text-mining projects. For example, the Internet Archive began a dataset collection designed specifically for large datasets that can be made freely available to the public for reuse and remixing. Another option may be in partnerships with other large digital libraries, such as HathiTrust or the Digital Public Library of America. It is not unreasonable to consider placing open access digital collections in multiple places. Whatever the solution, the goal should be to create a place (or places) where researchers know they can find usable data with reliable metadata for text-mining projects.

One of the key benefits to such an archive of machine-readable data is that it could encourage creative projects that look for patterns across collections created by different content providers. For example, a scholar might want to compare and contrast items in UNC's the Church in the Southern Black Community collection with items from the Sunday School Books in Nineteenth Century America dataset created by the library at Michigan State University. Both collections are currently housed separately at their respective institutions and could likely attract additional usage if they were collocated. This example makes it clear that, in addition to collocation, interoperability is also a challenge, both for those building digital collections and for those using them. In this particular case, both UNC and MSU have made their collections available as TXT files, but there is no real standard practice yet, particularly for digital humanities projects.

With machine-readable, open access, collocated, and interoperable collections available, researchers would find it easy to remix those collections and make them available in the same place. For example, it is easy to imagine that, out of multiple sprawling collections, corpora could be built containing all the available texts published in a particular year or a particular place. Going one step further, using automated part-of-speech tagging, it would be possible to create corpora of just nouns or verbs that could be used to track language shifts geographically or over time. Each of these derivative corpora could then be collocated with their parent collections to facilitate further research.

Actively encouraging this kind of remixing could also help address the persistent and valid critique that libraries and archives—both print and digital—often inadvertently hide some resources by the very process of making others accessible. Decisions about what is illuminated and what is rendered invisible in a collection may be conscious or unconscious, but they are never neutral. For example, the digital edition of the letters of Thomas Jefferson on which Lauren Klein's project depends is thoroughly enmeshed in particular networks of power and domination. In order to find information about James Hemings, Klein had to go to the archive of the man who enslaved him. Versions of this kind of "archival humiliation" happen routinely when information about women is buried in collections named for their husbands, LGBTQ voices are hidden between the lines of "official" narratives, and the records of colonized people must be extracted from the empire's own archives. In a talk given to the Ontario Library Association's Super Conference, Chris Bourg (2015), director of libraries at MIT, noted that "despite the democratizing promise of technology, our digital libraries are no more capable of neutrality than our traditional libraries" (para. 22). Rather than a neutral library, what open access and CC BY enable is a relatively simple way to create counter collections and archives of resistance. Referencing Barbara Smith's *Toward a Black Feminist Criticism*, Bourg (2015) reminded the audience that, when approaching a collection or an archive, it is crucial to ask "Who is missing? Whose experience is being centered?" (paras. 37–38). Truly open collections have the potential to make room for those who are missing and to reframe the narrative with other voices at the center.

CONCLUSION: LIBRARY AS LEADER AND LIBRARY AS PRODUCTIVE PLACE

As cutting edge as digital humanities research can be, DocSouth Data is, in some ways, completely traditional librarianship. At its core, the project has been about providing access to items in the collection in the format researchers need. This approach is clearly in line with the UNC Library's stated mission to provide "collections, expertise, services, and facilities" to support the university's mission "of research, teaching, learning, and public service for the campus community, state, nation, and world" (UNC Libraries n.d., para. 1). Yet, in other ways, DocSouth Data can be seen as part of a different narrative about how academic research libraries are changing. In the article "A Framework for Articulating New Library Roles," Karen Williams (2009) characterizes this evolution as a shift "from a collection-centered model to an engagement-centered one" (3). Williams is primarily concerned in this article with the changing role of librarians, but part of the point is that this shift impacts all levels of the library system, including collections and digital resources.

Of course, the best libraries have never limited themselves to simply building print collections and providing quiet spaces for study. Indeed, if anything qualifies as "traditional librarianship," it is the tradition of rising to the challenge of constantly evolving research needs and positioning the library to be a true collaborator rather than simply a service provider.

Williams's image of the "engagement-centered" model should be taken as a call to libraries and librarians not to "be something else" but rather to embrace their roles as active partners in the entire research life cycle. This means monitoring the academic landscape, being a laboratory for scholarly experimentation, and preparing for the future by maintaining close relationships with their campus communities.

In the case of DocSouth Data, the library did not receive an overwhelming number of requests for text mining the material in Documenting the American South. Rather, librarians had been tracking the growing popularity of digital humanities across campus and the academy and had noted an uptick in interest for text-mining projects involving collections licensed from vendors. Noting that it would be relatively easy for the collections in Documenting the American South to be made available for text mining, the library made a proactive decision to develop and release DocSouth Data. Despite the fact that the project was somewhat speculative, the library felt that the collections were interesting enough to be attractive and that development would be simple enough not to be unbearably disruptive to typical workflows.

Though the library's experience developing DocSouth Data demonstrates the value of opening up digital collections for text mining and remixing, it also highlights the challenges of working with digital collections provided by commercial vendors. Providing free access to information is in the library's DNA, but vendors seem to be stuck trying to figure out how to meet researcher demands for text mining profitably. For libraries, return on investment is measured by how effectively they contribute to the quality of teaching, learning, research, and service at their home institutions. Commercial vendors, on the other hand, have other calculations to consider, and these, along with copyright restrictions, limit researchers to asking only the questions that can be answered by accessible data. Initiatives like DocSouth Data are a way for libraries to enable cutting-edge scholarship today and build toward exciting open access models for the future.

NOTES

1. See Blackwell's *A Companion to Digital Humanities*, edited by Susan Schreibman, Ray Siemens, and John Unsworth (2004), for a lengthy discussion of digital humanities and humanities computing.

2. Though Documenting the American South dates back to 1996, the library only has access to usage statistics going back to 2009.

3. The Preservation Statistics Survey produced by the American Library Association for FY 2014 shows a sharp increase in the early 2000s in materials being prepped for digitization, closely followed by a variety of actual digitization activities.

4. It is out of scope for this chapter to address the complex relationship between digitization and preservation. For more on that issue, see "Recognizing Digitization as a Preservation Reformatting Method" by Kathleen Arthur, Sherry Byrne, Elisabeth Long, Carla Q. Montori, and Judith Nadler (2004), as well as the critique of the report by Andrew Hart (2007).

5. See JISC's "Using Social Media to Promote Your Digital Collections" (Chowcat, Kay, and Stephens 2014).

REFERENCES

Arthur, K., Byrne, S., Long, E., & Nadler, J. 2004, June. "Recognizing Digitization as a Preservation Reformatting Method." *Association of Research Libraries (ARL)*.

Bourg, C. 2015, January 28. "Never Neutral: Libraries, Technology, and Inclusion." *Feral Librarian*. https://chrisbourg.wordpress.com/2015/01/28/never-neutral-libraries-technology-and-inclusion.

Browner, S. 2011. "Digital Humanities and the Study of Race and Ethnicity." In A. Jewell & A. E. Earhart (eds.), *The American Literature Scholar in the Digital Age* (pp. 209–27). Ann Arbor: University of Michigan Press.

California Digital Library. 2011, August. "Standard License Agreement: Publisher and the Regents of the University of California."

Casey, J. 2014a, December 14. "Topic Networks of Slave Narratives, Part 1." http://jim-casey.com/posts/topic-networks-of-slave-narratives.

———. 2014b, December 15. "Topic Network of Slave Narratives, Part 2." http://jim-casey.com/posts/topic-network-of-slave-narratives-part-2.

———. 2015, March 2. "Where Were Slave Narratives Published?" http://jim-casey.com/posts/where-were-slave-narratives-published.

Chan, L., et al. 2002, February 14. "Read the Budapest Open Access Initiative." *Budapest Open Access Initiative*. http://www.budapestopenaccessinitiative.org/read.

Chowcat, I., Kay, D., & Stephens, O. 2014, March 6. "Using Social Media to Promote Your Digital Collections." *JISC*. Accessed August 30, 2015. https://www.jisc.ac.uk/guides/using-social-media-to-promote-your-digital-collections.

Cordell, R. 2015. "Reprinting, Circulation, and the Network Author in Antebellum Newspapers." *American Literary History*, 27(3), 417–45. http://doi.org/10.1093/alh/ajv028.

Eve, M. P. 2014. *Open Access and the Humanities: Contexts, Controversies and the Future.* Cambridge, UK: Cambridge University Press. http://ebooks.cambridge.org/ref/id/CBO9781316161012.

Gold, M. 2012. "The Digital Humanities Moment." In *Debates in the Digital Humanities*. Minneapolis: University of Minnesota Press. http://site.ebrary.com/lib/alltitles/docDetail.action?docID=10551807.

Green, H. E., & Courtney, A. 2014. "Beyond the Scanned Image: A Needs Assessment of Scholarly Users of Digital Collections." *College & Research Libraries*, crl14–612.

Hart, A. 2007. "A Critique of 'Recognizing Digitization as a Preservation Reformatting Method': Microform & Imaging Review." *Microform & Imaging Review*, 33(4), 184–87. http://doi.org/10.1515/MFIR.2004.184.

Hewitt, J. 2002, March 1. "DocSouth 1000th Title Symposium: Remarks by Joe A. Hewitt, University Librarian, UNC-Chapel Hill." *Documenting the American South*. http://docsouth.unc.edu/support/about/jahewitt.html.

Holley, R. 2009. "How Good Can It Get? Analysing and Improving OCR Accuracy in Large Scale Historic Newspaper Digitisation Programs." *D-Lib Magazine*, 15(3/4). http://doi.org/10.1045/march2009-holley.

International Federation of Library Associations (IFLA). 2013, December 19. "IFLA Statement on Text and Data Mining." http://www.ifla.org/publications/ifla-statement-on-text-and-data-mining-2013.

Klein, L. F. 2013. "The Image of Absence: Archival Silence, Data Visualization, and James Hemings." *American Literature*, 85(4), 661–88. http://doi.org/10.1215/00029831-2367310.

Library Staff. 2015, May 6. "UNC Faculty Council Adopts Open Access Policy." *UNC Library News and Events*. http://blogs.lib.unc.edu/news/index.php/2015/05/oa-policy.

Moretti, F. 2000. "Conjectures on World Literature." *New Left Review*, (1), 54–68.

Muhanna, E. 2015, July 7. "Hacking the Humanities." *New Yorker*. Accessed August 29, 2015. http://www.newyorker.com/culture/culture-desk/hacking-the-humanities.

Okerson, A. 2013. "Text and Data Mining: A Librarian Overview." *International Federation of Library Associations: World Library and Information Congress*, 1–6.

Owens, T. 2015, June 19. "Macroscopes & Distant Reading: Implications for Infrastructures to Support Computational Humanities Scholarship." http://www.trevorowens.org/2015/06/macroscopes-distant-reading-implications-for-infrastructures-to-support-computational-humanities-scholarship.

Robertson, S. 2014, May 23. "The Differences between Digital History and Digital Humanities." http://drstephenrobertson.com/blog-post/the-differences-between-digital-history-and-digital-humanities.

Schaffhauser, D. 2014. "NC State Researchers First to Drill into Gale Databases for Data Mining." *Campus Technology*. http://campustechnology.com/articles/2014/11/17/nc-state-researchers-first-to-drill-into-gale-databases-for-data-mining.aspx.

Schreibman, S., Siemens, R., & Unsworth, J. 2004. *Companion to Digital Humanities*. Blackwell Companions to Literature and Culture. Oxford: Blackwell. http://www.digitalhumanities.org/companion.

Smit, E., & van der Graaf, M. 2012. "Journal Article Mining: The Scholarly Publishers' Perspective." *Learned Publishing*, 25(1), 35–46. http://doi.org/10.1087/20120106.

Smith, D., Cordell, R., & Mullen, A. 2015, May 22. "Computational Methods for Uncovering Reprinted Texts in Antebellum Newspapers." *Viral Texts*. http://viraltexts.org/news.

Smith, N. 1997, November. "UNC-CH Library Digitization Project 'Documenting the American South: The Southern Experience in 19th-Century America.'" *D-Lib Magazine*. http://www.dlib.org/dlib/november97/11clips.html.

Smith, N., & Tibbo, H. R. 1996. "Libraries and the Creation of Electronic Texts for the Humanities." *College & Research Libraries*, 57(6), 535–53. http://doi.org/10.5860/crl_57_06_535.

Snijder, R. 2015. "Better Sharing through Licenses? Measuring the Influence of Creative Commons Licenses on the Usage of Open Access Monographs." *Journal of Librarianship and Scholarly Communication*, 3(1). http://doi.org/http://dx.doi.org/10.7710/2162-3309.1187.

SPARC. n.d. "Pushing the Frontier of Access for Text Mining: A Conversation with Heather Piwowar on One Researcher's Attempt to Break New." http://www.sparc.arl.org/news/pushing-frontier-access-text-mining-conversation-heather-piwowar-one-researcher%E2%80%99s-attempt-break.

Suber, P. 2012. *Open Access*. Cambridge, MA: MIT Press.

UNC Libraries. n.d. "Mission Statement: UNC Chapel Hill Libraries." http://library.unc.edu/about/mission.

Van Noorden, R. 2012. "Trouble at the Text Mine." *Nature*, 483(7388), 134–35. http://doi.org/10.1038/483134a.

Voyant Tools Documentation. n.d. "Getting Started." http://docs.voyant-tools.org/start.

Williams, K. 2009. "A Framework for Articulating New Library Roles (Aug. 2009)." *Research Library Issues: A Bimonthly Report from ARL, CNI and SPARC*, 3–8.

Williams, L. A., Fox, L. M., Roeder, C., & Hunter, L. 2014. "Negotiating a Text Mining License for Faculty Researchers." *Information Technology & Libraries*, 33(3), 5–21.

Index

Clement, Gail P., 192, 227
Coalition for Networked Information (CNI), 227
collection role of libraries, 79, 80
colors of open access publishing models, 177
Columbia University Press, 205
commercialization offices for academic creators, 28n3
commercial vendors of digital collections, 297
Committee on Publication Ethics, 65
Common Ground at the Nexus of Information Literacy and Scholarly Communication (Davis-Kahl and Hensley), 162
communication role of libraries/librarians, 193
community practice as source of anxiety, 239–241
compensation, 20
Confederation of Open Access Repositories, 147
Conley, John P., 145, 163
CONSER (Cooperative Online Serials Program), 269
consortium memberships, 66–67
contracts: submission agreements, 161–162; transfer of copyright under, 5. *See also* licenses; rights of authors
conversations, scholarship as, 181–182
cooperative cataloging, 269
Cooperative Online Serials Program (CONSER), 269
copyright: confusion about, 196; DocSouth Data statements, 302–304; fair use, 236, 236–238; fear of violations of, 212–213; gap between author and publisher interests, 9; infringement of, 21; legal resources for, 87–88; librarians' involvement in, 11–12, 37, 38; litigation in, 8; misuse protection, 22–23; publishers *vs.* open access repositories, 217; rights bundled under, 3–4, 5, 6; as threat to dissemination of works, 23–24; transfer of, 5; U.S. Laws, 5, 6, 8. *See also* intellectual property rights; licenses; rhetoric about copyright; rights of authors

Corbett, Hillary, 187–201
Cordell, Ryan, 295, 296
Cormier, Dave, 89
corporate collusion concerns, 218–219
cost of open access. *See* author fees in open access
cost of open education, 83, 85
Cothran, D. Lisa, 163
Council for Undergraduate Research (CUR), 134
Council of Graduate Schools, 242
court cases for copyright enfringement, 8
Courtney, Angela, 296
Courtney, Kyle K., 225–244
Cousin, Glynis, 174, 184
Covey, Denise Troll, 214, 220, 221
Creating a Sustainable Society course, 136, 136–137
Creative Commons: CC BY license, 212, 238, 299, 304, 306; CC0 Universal Public Domain license, 266, 277; contractual requirements of attribution/nonattribution, 25, 27; licensing options, 177–178; open content licenses, 7, 24; restrictions, 82
creative writing as discipline, 222n3
Cronon, William, 205
Cross, William M., 71–96
CUR (Council for Undergraduate Research), 134

Das, Tara, 245–263
DASH (Digital Access to Scholarship at Harvard), 225–226
data. *See* government services and open data; open bibliographic metadata
Data Documentation Initiative (DDI), 250
Data.gov, 246–247, 253
data literacy, 249–250
data-specific metadata, 250–252
Davies, Tim G., 258
Davis, Laura Drake, 143–167
Davis-Kahl, Stephanie, 34, 35, 129–142, 149, 162
Dawes, Sharon S., 254–255
DDA (demand-driven acquisitions), 208
DDI (Data Documentation Initiative), 250
Deliyannides, Timothy, 103
demand-driven acquisitions (DDA), 208

About the Editors

Katherine A. Dickson is a recent graduate of the School of Information and Library Science at the University of North Carolina at Chapel Hill. While in library school, she worked at Duke University's Office of Copyright and Scholarly Communications, where she negotiated issues of fair use and sought permissions in order to facilitate online education classes. Prior to attending library school, she was a practicing attorney for seven years, first in Washington, DC, and then in Chapel Hill, North Carolina. In addition to her MLS and JD, Kate holds a master's degree in American legal history from the University of Virginia.

Kevin L. Smith is the dean of libraries at the University of Kansas and was previously the director of copyright and scholarly communications at Duke University. A lawyer as well as a librarian, Kevin has spent a decade advising university students, faculty, and staff about copyright, licensing, and scholarly publishing. He is a prolific writer on these topics, and his book *Owning and Using Scholarship: An IP Handbook for Teachers and Researchers* was published by the Association of College and Research Libraries in 2014.

About the Contributors

Stephen M. Arougheti is an information specialist lead with Arizona State University (ASU). Mr. Arougheti has been with ASU for three years, prior to which he worked for the Scottsdale Public Library and Arizona Jewish Historical Society. He graduated in 2010 with a master's in library science from the University of Arizona. His research interests include open access, scholarly publishing, copyright, and collection development.

Jill Cirasella is associate librarian for public services and scholarly communication at the Graduate Center of the City University of New York. In this position she oversees reference, instruction, outreach, circulation, interlibrary loan, and thesis/dissertation services and leads the library's scholarly communication initiatives. Jill is a vocal advocate of open access to scholarly literature and seeks to promote understanding and adoption of open access at CUNY and beyond.

Hillary Corbett is the director of scholarly communication and digital publishing at the Northeastern University Library in Boston, Massachusetts. In this role she coordinates the university's electronic theses and dissertations (ETD) program and serves as the university's copyright officer, providing assistance to faculty, staff, and students on issues of intellectual property, copyright, and fair use. She holds an MILS from the University of Michigan and an MA in American studies from the University of Massachusetts at Boston.

Kyle K. Courtney is the copyright advisor for Harvard University, working out of the Office for Scholarly Communication. He works closely with Harvard Library to establish a culture of shared understanding of copyright issues among Harvard staff, faculty, and students. His work at Harvard also includes a role as the copyright and information policy advisor for HarvardX/edX, and founding the Copyright First Responders initiative, which was profiled in *Library Journal* in 2013, for which he was named an Academic Library Mover and Shaker in 2015. Before joining Harvard University, Kyle worked at Harvard Law School as the manager of faculty research and scholarship.

William M. Cross is the director of the Copyright and Digital Scholarship Center at North Carolina State University, where he provides guidance to campus stakeholders on legal issues and open access to scholarship, data, and educational resources. As a student at the University of North Carolina at Chapel Hill, Will earned an MA in technology and communication, a JD, and an MSLS. Before joining the NCSU Libraries, Will worked in academic and law libraries, in constitutional litigation, and at the North Carolina Court of Appeals. Will serves as an instructor in the UNC School of Information and Library Science and lectures nationally on copyright, scholarly communication, and open culture. He has been quoted in such publications as the *Chronicle of Higher Education*, *Library Journal*, and *Techdirt* and publishes regularly on topics ranging from the pedagogy of legal education for librarians to the First Amendment status of video games.

Tara Das is the government information librarian and acting head of the Social Work Library at Columbia University. She has a PhD in anthropology and political science from the University of Pennsylvania and an MLIS from Pratt Institute.

Laura Drake Davis is the digital collections librarian at James Madison University. In this role, Laura leads the establishment and development of the Digital Collections program, including the launch and management of JMU's institutional repository and open access publishing platform, JMU Scholarly Commons. Laura's research interests include campus partnerships to encourage the distribution of student scholarship, the creation and design of digital exhibits, and the intersection of digital scholarship projects and digital collections. She received her MLS from the University of Maryland, College Park, and her BA in music from the University of California, Santa Barbara.

Stephanie Davis-Kahl is the scholarly communications librarian and professor at the Ames Library at Illinois Wesleyan University. She provides leadership for scholarly communication programs, including Digital Commons @ IWU. She is the liaison to the Economics, Educational Studies, and Psychology Departments at IWU and serves as the managing faculty coeditor of the

Undergraduate Economic Review. In 2014, she was named a Mover and Shaker by *Library Journal* and was a recipient of the Education and Behavioral Sciences Section Distinguished Librarian Award.

Anne T. Gilliland is the scholarly communications officer at the University of North Carolina, Chapel Hill. She holds an MS in library and information science from the University of Tennessee and a JD from Capital University. Her legal knowledge supplements more than thirty years' experience working for and on behalf of academic libraries.

Korey Jackson is the Gray Family Chair for Innovative Library Services, working to foster digital publishing initiatives at Oregon State University Libraries and Press. Prior to that role, he was an American Council of Learned Societies public fellow working as the programming coordinator at Anvil Academic, a publisher of digital scholarship in the humanities. He also served as a Council of Library and Information Resources fellow at Michigan Publishing, a press–library collaboration at the University of Michigan designed to rethink (and rewrite) the future of scholarly publishing. While at Michigan Publishing, he worked in the Publishing Services and Outreach division on a range of digital humanities publishing initiatives and programs. Korey earned his PhD in English language and literature from the University of Michigan.

Emily Kilcer is a project coordinator in Harvard University's Office for Scholarly Communication (OSC). There she specializes in working with students, faculty, and staff on such issues as digitization, licensing, copyright, and ETDs. She also serves as a research assistant to Peter Suber's Harvard Open Access Project. Before joining the OSC, Emily gained a decade of experience in the scholarly publishing field.

Laura Krier is a librarian at Sonoma State University, where she manages web services and acts as liaison to the School of Arts and Humanities. She received her MSLIS from Simmons College and her BA from UC Santa Cruz. She might be a little bit obsessed with metadata and creating better, more efficient library systems.

Genya O'Gara is the associate director of the Virtual Library of Virginia (VIVA), a consortium of 72 nonprofit academic libraries within the Commonwealth of Virginia. Genya received her master's in library science from the University of North Carolina at Chapel Hill and her bachelor's degree from Evergreen State College. She has held positions in collection management and special collections at North Carolina State University and served as the director of collections at James Madison University. She has written and presented on emerging models of content development and assessment, with a focus on the roles of academic libraries in scholarly publishing, digital collections, and the management of locally created materials.

Rachel Elizabeth Scott is an assistant professor and integrated library systems librarian at the University of Memphis. Her research focuses on various aspects of information literacy and music bibliography. In addition to teaching an introduction to research methods course, she also enjoys offering instruction to students in social science and humanities. She has recently placed chapters in ACRL, Facet, Rowman & Littlefield, and Theatre Library Association anthologies and articles in *Music Reference Services Quarterly*, the *Reference Librarian*, and *Tennessee Libraries*.

Nancy Sims is fascinated by the pervasiveness of copyright issues in modern life. She enjoys helping individuals and groups understand how copyright may affect their work, both in academia and farther afield in fields such as K–12 teaching, public libraries, arts and crafts, and programming. Her MLIS is from Rutgers University, and her JD is from the University of Michigan.

Emily Symonds Stenberg is the digital publishing and digital preservation librarian at Washington University in St. Louis. She manages content in the university repository Open Scholarship, including graduate theses and dissertations, and works with university groups and units seeking to make their work more broadly available online. She has an MLS from Indiana University and an MFA in creative writing and certificate in museum studies from the University of North Carolina at Greensboro.

Kathryn Stine is metadata product manager at the California Digital Library (CDL), where she leads a team of developers and analysts to maintain and enhance Zephir, a metadata management system designed and implemented by CDL for the HathiTrust. She has a background in managing digital resources and the metadata that describe them in a range of contexts, including digitized print collections, oral history media, visual resources, and archives and special collections. Her interests and expertise are in modeling, designing, and implementing processing and cataloging workflows; coordinating metadata streams; deploying metadata to help researchers uncover relationships between resources; and developing metadata policy to promote access and use.

Polly Thistlethwaite is chief librarian at the Graduate Center, City University of New York, the PhD-granting branch of CUNY. Over many years as a reference librarian, she has assisted the production of a remarkable body of brilliant graduate work. She is an advocate for author choice, open and public scholarship, and applying that scholarship to support social and political change.

Stewart Varner is the digital scholarship librarian at the University of North Carolina at Chapel Hill. As a member of the Research and Instruction team, he works with scholars who want to incorporate technology into their research and teaching by connecting them to library resources. He earned his MLIS from the University of North Texas and his PhD in American studies from the Institute of the Liberal Arts at Emory University.

Micah Zeller is the copyright and digital access librarian at Washington University in St. Louis, where he advises faculty, students, and staff on intellectual property issues that connect to research, teaching, and library services. He is a member of the Missouri Bar, and serves on the Faculty Committee on Intellectual Property and Technology Transfer. He has a JD from Washington University School of Law, where he oversaw creation of its institutional repository, and has worked for University Libraries since 2013.

Hui Zhang is assistant professor, Oregon State University Libraries and Press. As a digital application librarian, Hui is the primary developer of Oregon State University's institutional repository and also a key person in the design and development of library's digital infrastructure. His past projects include embedding altmetrics for journal articles in IR and promoting a wider usage of altmetrics in promotion and tenure. Hui has his PhD of information science from Indiana University and is interested in digital repository, impact metrics, and linked data.

CPSIA information can be obtained
at www.ICGtesting.com
Printed in the USA
BVOW04*1320041216

468671BV00008B/2/P